OUR POLITICAL SYSTEM

India–The Land and the People

OUR POLITICAL SYSTEM

SUBHASH C. KASHYAP

nbt.india
एकः सूते सकलम्
NATIONAL BOOK TRUST, INDIA

ISBN 978-81-237-5251-8

First Edition 2008
Reprints 2009 (twice), 2010, 2011, 2012 (twice), 2013,
2016, 2017, 2020, 2021, 2023, 2025 (*Saka* 1947)

₹ 340.00

Published by the Director, National Book Trust, India
5 Institutional Area, Vasant Kunj, New Delhi-110 070
Website: www.nbtindia.gov.in

Contents

Preface

It is necessary that we, the people of India, know about the political system under which we live and are governed. In a democracy, citizens have to be wide awake and aware of their liberties, rights and responsibilities. Ultimately, the success of our political system will depend largely on our willingness to understand the system and become active participants in the democratic process.

Initially, an infructuous search for a handy book on India's political system propelled me to undertake this project. It was, however, the interest evinced by the National Book Trust, India, that proved decisive and ensured its completion on a high priority basis.

The book endeavours to present an introduction to Indian polity in an easily readable and digestible form. The treatment here is objective, simple and short and yet comprehensive. The effort is to fill a void and a felt need by describing various facets of our political system in a language that is non-technical and free from much of the jargons of the political science. The book is for all citizens and students of all ages and in all disciplines.

Two of my earlier titles, namely *Our Constitution* and *Our Parliament* published by the National Book Trust, India, under their *India – the Land and the People* series were well received and have gone into several editions and many reprints in different languages. This has been very encouraging and satisfying. I hope and trust, this, the third title, being brought out in the same series, would also be welcomed widely and prove successful. It may also soon be available in Hindi and hopefully in other Indian languages.

In preparing the text of this work, I have greatly benefitted from the works of eminent scholars. I remain deeply beholden to them all. Although footnote references have been avoided, a select bibliography and list of references have been given at the end to acknowledge my debt and facilitate further reading. For facts and data, as far as possible, official documents have been relied upon. Also, I must plead guilty of having freely borrowed from my own earlier writings.

I am grateful to my family at home and colleagues at the Centre for Policy Research – Ms. Sonu Trivedi and Ms. Kusum Malik – for their assistance in timely completion of this work. Above all, thanks are due to the National Book Trust, India for taking this work to the people.

I shall feel deeply beholden to the readers for any suggestions for improvement.

SUBHASH C. KASHYAP

1

POLITICAL SYSTEMS
CONCEPTS, FORMS AND TYPES

What is a Political System?

Political system is a social institution dealing with the governance of a state and its relationship with the people. Sometimes loosely referred to as polity, political system of a country generally denotes the structure of institutions that constitute the State and its Government. It delineates the framework and form of inter-relationships between institutions and organs of the State–the Legislature, the Executive and the Judiciary–and the linkage of each with the people. Political system gives shape and form to some fundamental principles round which politics and political institutions have developed or are proposed to be organised to govern the country. Political system also consists of the manner in which the rulers are selected or elected, governments are formed and political decisions taken. Political interactions in society and structures and procedures for decision making are all rooted in a country's political system.

Used in a broader sense, political system also encompasses within its fold international or supra-national organisations like the United Nations, European Union etc. However, despite all the emphasis on globalisation and efforts at nations coming together to form supra-national regional organisations and even governmental institutions, the nation-states and the sentiments of nationalism remain the most dominant. The results of the 2005 referenda over the European Constitution underlined the deep rooted susceptibilities in the matter of eroding national sovereignty in any way. The national political systems remain the most important. These may generally include, non-state institutions like the political parties, as also political behaviour and processes of interaction with other institutions and citizens.

To freely paraphrase and adopt the Hegelian concepts, political system is a result of social evolution through ages. Human beings are by nature social. One cannot live alone. Hence, in order to fulfil elementary needs of food, sex and primitive protection, men and women were naturally inclined to live in a family. But the family was inadequate to satisfy the multifarious needs of the multi-faceted human personality. For better fulfilment, a wider organisation developed, namely –civil society. The diverse human needs were better satisfied in civil society. 'Civil society' evolved laws based on the material needs of human beings. The next higher stage in the process of evolution was the emergence of a 'Political System'. It emerged as a result of the realisation of the "commonality of the interests of the community" as a whole. The civil society, even after the emergence of the State continued "to perform the common place business", but, it came to gradually depend more and more upon the State "for intelligent supervision and moral significance".

Concept of Constitutionalism

The concept of constitutionalism is that of a political system governed by or under a constitution that ordains essentially limited government and rule of law as opposed to arbitrary, despotic, authoritarian or totalitarian rule. Constitution of a country lays down the basic structure of the political system under which its people are to be governed. It establishes the main organs of the state — the legislature, the executive and the judiciary, defines their powers, demarcates their responsibilities and regulates their relationships with each other and with the people. Constitutional government, therefore, should necessarily be democratic government. Also, constitutionalism is a natural concomitant of a written constitution inasmuch as a written constitution is bound to define and delimit the powers and functions of various organs of the state and a government under a written constitution can only be a limited government. But, it is certainly conceivable that some countries — there have been many examples — may have written constitutions which are not really democratic. It can be said that they have constitutions but not constitutionalism. Also, there are instances where there is no written constitution but democracy and constitutionalism prevail. Israel and U.K are obvious examples.

When we talk of constitutionalism, we normally mean that there are rules creating legislative, executive and judicial powers, but also that these rules impose limits on those powers. Often these limits are in the form of individual or group rights against the government, like rights to free expression, association, equality and due process of law. But constitutional limits come in a variety of forms. They can concern such things as the scope of authority (*e.g.*, in a federal system, provincial or state governments may have authority over health care and education while the federal government's jurisdiction extends to national defence and transportation); the mechanisms used in exercising the relevant power (*e.g.*, procedural requirements governing the form and manner of legislation); and civil rights (*e.g.*, in a Charter or Bill of Rights). Constitutionalism in this richer sense of the term is the idea that government can and should be limited in its powers and that the beginning of its authority depends on its observing these limitations.

In discussing the history and nature of constitutionalism, a comparison is often drawn between Thomas Hobbes and John Locke who are thought to have defended, respectively, the notion of constitutionally unlimited sovereignty versus that of sovereignty limited by the terms of a social contract containing substantive limitations. But an equally good focal point is the English legal theorist John Austin who, like Hobbes, thought that the very notion of limited sovereignty is incoherent. For Austin, all law is the command of a sovereign person or body of persons, and so the notion that the sovereign could be limited by law requires a sovereign who is self-binding, who commands himself or herself. But no one can "command" himself or herself, except in some figurative sense. So the notion of limited sovereignty is, for Austin (and Hobbes), as incoherent as the idea of a square circle. Though this feature of Austin's theory has some surface plausibility when applied to the British Parliamentary system, where Parliament is often said to be "supreme" and constitutionally unlimited, it faces obvious difficulty when applied to most other constitutional democracies such as one finds in the United States and Germany, where it is clear that the powers of every organ of the State are legally limited by a constitution.

Another important feature of constitutionalism is that the limits upon the powers of organs must be such as are amendable only by law or by way of "constitutional convention." In other words, those whose powers are constitutionally limited — *i.e.*, the organs of State — must not be legally entitled to change or exceed those limits at their pleasure. Most written constitutions contain amendment procedures which can be triggered by, and require the participation of, the government bodies whose powers they limit. But these procedures invariably require something more than a simple decision on the part of the government of the day to invoke a change. Sometimes constitutional assemblies are required, or super-majority votes, referenda, or the agreement of not only the central government in a federal system but also certain number or percentage of the governments of regional units within the federal system. Amendments to meet the changing societal needs not only facilitate a degree of stability over time (a characteristic aspiration of constitutional regimes), it is arguably a requirement of the very possibility of constitutionally limited government.

Some scholars believe that constitutional rules do not exist unless they are in some way enshrined in a written document. Others argue that constitutions can be unwritten. The latter cite, as an obvious example of this possibility, the Constitution of the United Kingdom. However, it must be noted that alhough the UK has nothing resembling the American Constitution and its Bill of Rights, it nevertheless contains a number of written instruments which arguably form a central element of its Constitution. *Magna Carta* (1215 A.D.) is perhaps the earliest document of the British Constitution, while others include the *Petition of Rights* (1628) and the *Bill of Rights* (1689). Furthermore, constitutional limits are also said to be found in certain principles of the common law, explicitly cited in landmark cases concerning the limits of government power. The fact remains, however, that Britain seems largely to have an unwritten constitution, suggesting strongly that writtenness is not a defining feature of constitutionalism.

The idea of constitutionalism is usually that of putting legal limits on power and authority of State organs. But, there is more to a constitution than constitutional law. It includes constitutional conventions, practices and precedents. Also, it must be undertood in the context of constitutionalism that it is wrong to regard a country's constitution as a mere inert document. For, constitution is not only what is written in the text of the constitution. Constitution is a living organism of functioning institutions. It keeps constantly growing, evolving. Every constitution gets meaning and content only from the manner in which and the people by whom it is operated, the effects it acquires from how it is interpreted by courts of the land and what conventions and practices grow around it in the actual process of its working.

A democratic political system becomes a prerequisite for constitutionalism to flourish. A political system which is in conformity with the principles of constitutionalism must of necessity, *inter alia*, provide restraints and limitations on the exercise of powers by the organs of the State. Sovereignty belongs to the people but constitutionalism forbids the people from attempting political change through violent means. It has got to lay down a system of checks and balances. Separation of powers between the legislature, the executive and the judiciary is one such device and in case of federal systems, distribution of powers between different tiers of government, is another. Arbitrary powers in the hands of any individual or institution-- even if conferred by a constitutional document—are a negation of the concepts of constitutionalism, sovereignty of the people and basic rights of individual citizens.

Rule of Law

It is wrong to interpret the word 'law' in 'Rule of Law' as written law or statute law. It is quite conceivable that a law passed by a legislture may be what Gandhiji called a 'lawless law' – a law that is violative of the principles of 'Rule of Law'. Legislatures while making laws must also adhere to Rule of Law. Rule of Law includes the concepts of natural justice, equity, individual honour and fair play. Nearest equivalent of Rule of Law is the anceint Indian secular concept of *Dharma*.

Rule of Law is to be understood as opposed to arbitrary rule of a person or party. Thus, Rule of Law is an essential prerequisite for democracy.Dicey held that the 'rule of law' embraces four separate features. First, no one should be punished except for breaches of law. Second, there should be equal subjection to the law or 'equality before law.' Third, when law is broken, there must be a certainty of punishment. Finally, the rights and liberties of the individual should be embodied in the 'ordinary law' of the land. This would ensure that when individual rights are violated citizens can seek redressal through the courts.

In its broad sense, the Rule of law is a core western liberal-democratic principle, embodying ideas such as constitutionalism and limited government to which most modern States aspire. According to some scholars, the essential characteristics of Rule of law are:

i. The supremacy of law, which means that all persons (individuals and governments) are subject to law.
ii. A concept of justice which emphasises interpersonal adjudication, law based on standards and the importance of procedures.
iii. Restrictions on the exercise of discretionary power.
iv. The doctrine of judicial precedent.
v. The common law methodology.
vi. Legislation should be prospective and not retrospective.
vii. An independent judiciary.

viii. The exercise by Parliament of the legislative power and restrictions on exercise of legislative power by the executive.

ix. An underlying moral basis for all law.

Sovereignty

In Political Science and Jurisprudential terms, sovereignty is considered to be one of the essential attributes of a State and connotes absolute and supreme power not subject to control by any internal or external authority. Cooley defines a sovereign State as one "where there resides within itself a supreme and absolute power acknowledging no superior". Meanings of sovereignty have varied across history and under different theroritical constructs. But, it does have a core meaning: *'supreme authority within a territory'*. It is a notion of political authority that accepts no superior in internal or external dimensions.

Sovereign authority is exercised within borders, but also, by definition, with respect to outsiders, who are not expected to interfere with the sovereign's governance. The nation-state has been the chief holder of external sovereignty since the Peace of Westphalia in 1648, after which interference in other states' governing prerogatives became illegitimate. State as a holder of sovereignty derives authority from some mutually acknowledged source of legitimacy such as natural law, a divine mandate, hereditary law, a constitution, even international law. Some body of law is ubiquitously the source of sovereignty.

Sovereignty, in purely conceptual terms, can be absolute or non-absolute. But, in fact absolute sovereignty, extending to all matters without any restraints as envisioned by thinkers like Hobbers and Bodin has, in the contemporary context, ceased to be anything more than an abstraction. Ideally and at best, it is possible for an authority to be sovereign over some matters within a territory, but not all. Today, many European Union (EU) member states exhibit non-absoluteness. They are said to be sovereign in governing their defence, but not in governing their currencies, trade policies, and many social welfare policies, which they administer in cooperation with EU authorities as set forth in EU law. Absolute sovereignty has begun to be circumscribed by institutions like the EU, the UN's practices of sanctioning intervention, the international criminal court etc.

The concept of sovereignty has also been used in two contrasting ways—internal and external. In the form of internal sovereignty, it refers to the distribution of power within the state, and leads to questions about the need for supreme power and its location within the political system. In the form of external sovereignty, it is related to the states' role within the international order and to whether or not it is able to operate as an independent and autonomous actor. The concept of sovereignty in international law most often connotes external sovereignty. External sovereignty is often conceived as constitutional independence—a state's immunity from outside interference. It is also external sovereignty that establishes the basic condition of international relations. An assemblage of states, both internally and externally sovereign, makes up an international system, where sovereign entities ally, trade, make war, and peace.

The history of sovereignty can be understood through two broad movements, manifested in both practical institutions and political thought. The first is the development of a system of sovereign nation states, culminating in the Peace of Westphalia in 1648. The second movement is the circumscription of the sovereign state, which began after World War II and has since continued through supranational organisations, the United Nations, regional organisations of States, European integration and the growth and strengthening of laws and practices to protect human rights.

Basis of System-building

Even if we think only in terms of the history of western political thought which we often do, there is a wide variety of models and types under which political systems have been variously classified and categorised from the days of Plato and Aristotle to the present day. The classification of political systems may be based on

(a) the power structure, on what are the chief institutions involved and who wields the levers of political power.

(b) the number of power holders and their use of power.

(c) the manner in which power is acquired, the way succession takes place and transfer of power is effected and how misuse of power is controlled through mechanisms of checks and balances. Transfer of power may be through peaceful constitutional means like free and fair elections as in a modern representative democracy. It may be under hereditary rule as in a monarchy. In a single party or totalitarian situation, it may be through party dictat and strength of armed forces. Also, governments may be overthrown through political or military coup or through revolution.

Categories of States

The form, structure, functions and organs of government are usually related to the type of the political system adopted and the nature of the distribution of powers among the units of Government and organs of the State. The nature and size of the State itself has been a great variable. It must be remembered that nation-states are a relatively recent phenomenon. The concept took shape in Europe and the U.K. and France emerged as the first nation-states followed by Italy and Germany as late as in the nineteenth century only.

Nation-States today may be categorised under (i) Unitary, and (ii) Federal Systems, sometimes also referred to as unitary and federal forms of government according to a constitutional method by which the powers of the government are distributed between the Union or federal government and the governments at State or unit level.

Unitary System: In a unitary nation-state system, all powers are vested in the one Central authority – Central Legislature/ Government – to which authorities in the lower sub-national units are subordinate and function only as its agents. Whatever powers the units exercise are by delegation and subject to being withdrawn at any time.

The classic examples of a unitary system have been U.K., France and New Zealand, even though with regional pressures from Northern Ireland, Scotland and Wales things have of late been changing in the U.K. and there has been considerable devolution of power to local units of governance in France.

Federal System: In a federal polity, usually, there must be a rigid, written constitution, it must be supreme and it must specifically divide legislative and executive powers between the federal government and the governments of the units – the two levels of government both exercising powers in their respective spheres in their own right and independently. In fact, in a classic federation, the federal government enjoys only those powers that are by agreement surrendered to it by the units. Also, there must be an independent supreme court as the arbiter of any disputes between the Union and the units.

The Legislature in a federal system is bicameral with one of the Houses usually representing the States or the constituent units of the federation. Balance of power between the Union and its units varies from federation to federation. There are distinctions on grounds of greater centralisation of power in the federal government with weak units and stronger units with weak or dependent central federal authority. The federal system is believed to bring a sense of unity among the people having diverse cultures, languages and territories. Regional independence of the federating units is so preserved that they do not lose the special characteristics of their community and territory. One of the supreme purposes for the formation of a federation is that all the units can pool their resources to provide maximum benefits to the people. United States, Canada, Australia and Brazil are examples of the federal category.

Multi-tier System: There are multi-tier government models or what may be called multi-tier federal systems where power is decentralised to lower and lower local units and what can be done at the local self government level is left to be done only there under a Gandhian Constitution model or the modern subsidiarity principle followed for example, in Germany and the European Union. Political decentralisation implies the setting up of new levels of government. The creation of autonomous units and establishment of Local Self Government are examples of political decentralisation. Decentralisation brings administration closer to the people and encourages popular participation, thereby, making participatory 'Grassroot Democracy' a reality.

There are also mixed, hybrid or amphibian systems which are neither unitary nor federal but have some features of a classical untiary system and others of a classical federal system.

Forms of Government

Categorising forms of government gives a general idea of the power structure of the governance of a country. There are several systems prevailing in the world – all different from each other. Different forms of Government have different types of political systems. Since, every country's system is unique, categorising forms of government becomes a complex task. Apart from federal and unitary, in a broader sense they have been classified as democratic and authoritarian types; in practice, many represent a hybrid of different forms.

Authoritarian Forms

Citizens are subject to the authority of the state, whatever the form of government. But the term authoritarian is used to describe a state or government which enforces arbitrary or oppressive measures against the people without attempting to consult the people or obtain their consent. The basis of authoritarianism is intolerance of dissent and the presumption that the ruler is always right. There exists a gradation. Also, there are variants of possible authoritarian behaviour.

Absolute Monarchy: Monarchies are usually hereditary. In modern times, several of the hereditary rulers have evolved into constitutional heads of States with real powers transferred to representatives of the people as in U.K., Sweden, Norway, Belgium, Japan, Thailand, Denmark, Netherlands, Spain, Monaco etc. But still there are some States which are governed by absolute monarchs. Absolute monarchies are almost always authoritarian.

Absolute monarchy is that form of government, where the

ruler has full powers to rule over the country without being bound by any laws above his own authority and with no organised opposition allowed. Some examples of absolute monarchy in the modern world are Saudi Arabia, Brunei and Swaziland. In Jordan and Morocco, the monarch (although not absolute) retains considerable power. In Nepal, situation has been oscillating between absolute monarchy and multi-party democracy with a constitutional monarch.

Dictatorship: Dictatorships are always authoritarian. It is a form of government where an absolutist or autocratic ruler assumes sole power. It may be in times of emergency or otherwise. Often dictatorship may result from a seizure of power in a coup through means of arms. But, sometimes a person getting to the top through the ladder of democratic elections may also turn a dictator. Dictatorship erodes all constitutional restraints. It is generally a government where the leader holds an extraordinary amount of personal power, especially the power to make laws without effective check by an elected legislative body.

In modern political parlance, "dictatorship" is associated with brutality and oppression. Association between the dictator and the military is very common, as many dictators assume power through military coups. Some of the modern time dictators have been: Augusto Pinochet of Chile, Fidel Castro of Cuba, Idi Amin of Uganda, Pol Pot of Cambodia.

Totalitarianism: A totalitarian state attempts to control nearly every aspect of personal, economic and political life of the citizens. Benito Mussolini was the first to use the word totalitarian to describe his dictatorship positively. Totalitarian government prohibits all activities which are contrary to regime's goals. It aims at radical restructuring of society to create a new economic order such as communism, or institute racism such as Nazism or reconstitute human nature through fundamentalist extremist religions as by Talibans. Totalitarian rulers enjoy power through secret police, propaganda and suppression of dissent. The main examples of regimes considered totalitarian are Nazi Germany, Fascist Italy, Baathist

Iraq, Communist China under Mao, Cambodia under Khymer Rouge, etc.

Authoritarian is distinguished from totalitarian both in degree and scope. Authoritarian administration is less intrusive and not necessarily backed by the use of force. Typically, the government in an authoritarian regime is run by an elite group that uses repressive means to stay in power. However, unlike totalitarian regimes, there is no desire or ideological justification for the state to control all aspects of a person's life. Totalitarian governments tend to be revolutionary and intend to change the basic structure of society, authoritarian ones tend to be conservative.

Democracy

Literally, the Greek word 'demos' meant 'the people' and 'Kratos' meant 'government' or 'rule'. Democracy, therefore, meant government by the people as against monarchy or dictatorship which were autocratic rule of one person, oligarchy or aristocracy being rule by the few. Basic postulates of democracy are that irrespective of religion, caste, creed, colour or sex and irrespective of the level of economic, educational or professional background, all are equal in the eyes of law and that each individual is capable of governing oneself and of managing ones own affairs the way one deems fit. In a democracy the people are supposed to be their own masters. They have an inalienable right to rule themselves, or to be ruled in the way they like and by the people they choose.

Democracy is a dynamic concept and a popular political ideology that has acquired many different meanings over the course of time and in diverse domains. Much of it comes from changes in society and from the different interpretations and analysis of the consequences of these changes for democracy. In order to make a meaningful assessment of democracy as a system in any country, one must first know and understand the particular country because democratic systems vary greatly in their institutional patterns and other socio-economic, political and cultural dimensions. In addition, it is necessary to be aware of the international settings above and the local conditions below the level of national government.

The greatest merit of successful democracy is that it puts an end to possibilities of overthrow of Government through force of arms. It substitutes methods of debate, discussion and vote for violent strife and use of force in the struggle for power. It enables peaceful change and transfer of power. Ballot substitutes the bullet. Democracy allows legitimate dissent and opposition to grow and prosper and even emerge as an alternative power centre and take over the reins of government constitutionally and peacefully. But, democracy is more than a form of government: it is a way of life, an order of society, a pattern of culture, a model of economic relations, a form of political system and a type of state.

People as Sovereign

In a democracy, by definition, sovereignty vests in the people. But, except in a primordial or revolution situation, sovereignty of the people is merely an abstraction. Also, it may imply a state of anarchy. People in the raw may be nothing more than a mob and absolute power in their hands is like the vast energy in a wild mountainous river running down the hills in its full force and fury, causing extensive damage and devastation. To purposefully utilize that energy, the river has to be tamed and harnessed, dams have to be built and the electricity produced has to be controlled, properly channelised and made useable. Sovereign power cannot be usefully or safely exercised by unorganised people or people without order. Constitutions are the dams that devise political systems to institutionalise and give shape and content to sovereignty. The people need political institutions and instrumentalities for expressing and employing their sovereign power and will.

The people exercise their inalienable right to select the best political system that would meet their needs and enable them to achieve their aspirations. When a nation becomes free from foreign yoke and steps into freedom or when a revolution sweeps the land or when a new sovereign state is otherwise born, the very first and the most fundamental application of their sovereignty by the people is in giving to themselves a polity of their choice. They decide through their constitution the ground rules under which certain powers are devolved or transferred by the people to different organs or functionaries of the state and are to be exercised by them.

Under a democratic system, while the legal sovereign is the supreme law making and law enforcing body, there is behind it the will of the people which is the ultimate and final source of all authority. It is the authority from whose verdict there can be no appeal. According to Dicey, 'Behind the sovereign which the lawyer recognises there is another sovereign to whom the legal sovereign must bow? The legal sovereign cannot last long if it deliberately and continuously opposes the wishes of the people, for the people in the last resort can have recourse to force and establish a new government by means of revolution. The Government can be held directly responsible to the people through means such as periodic elections, local slf-government, referenda, initiative and recall. What is of the utmost importance is that in a democracy, authority has got to be exercised not arbitrarily but in accordance with the laws of the land and with a full sense of accountablity to the people.

Types of Democracy

Democracy is not a single unambiguous phenomenon. In reality, there are a number of theories or models of democracy, each offering its own version of popular rule. There are not merely a number of democratic forms and mechanisms but also, more fundamentally, quite different grounds on which democratic rule is justified. Various terms are used to describe the many variants of democracy – Classical, Protective, Developmental, Deliberative, People's, Guided, Basic and so on. Democratic government has varied considerably over the centuries. Perhaps the most fundamental distinction is between democratic systems that are based upon direct popular participation in Government, and those that operate through some kind of representative mechanism. This highlights two contrasting models of democracy:—Direct democracy and Representative democracy.

Direct democracy comprises a form of democracy wherein all citizens can directly participate in the political decision-making process. Direct democracy in its traditional form is the direct rule by the people over themselves. In the ancient Indian Village Republics and the Greek City States, all the citizens assembled together and decided issues of governance. People, thus, exercised their power directly in deciding matters of State and this kind of polity could be called direct popular or participatory democracy. In this case, both legal and political sovereignty could be said to vest in the people. But with the gradual increase in the size and population of the political units and ultimately with the advent of the modern nation states, it became impossible to arrange for all the people to assemble at a place to discuss matters of State and arrive at decisions smoothly. Also, matters of legislation and State administration grew more and more complex. All forms of direct democracy, therefore, soon became practically extinct from all over the world. By and large, the only issue on which the people at large in different countries vote these days at periodic intervals is selection of their representatives. Modern democracy thus has of necessity to be indirect representative democracy whereunder government is carried on and laws are made by the elected representatives of the people.

In the context of the modern State structures, it is sometimes considered possible to reinvent some characteristics of direct democracy through devices like the following:

- Initiative, the right of the people to make a proposal for legislation;
- Referendum, right of the people to accept or reject the legislative proposal passed by the legislature thereby giving a veto to the people on government legislation.
- Recall, right of the people to call back their representative through petition or referendum; and
- Plebiscite, the right of the people to express their opinion on a particular political issue.

In Switzerland, both at the local and federal levels, there exist provisions both for initiative and referendum. In a few Swiss cantons, even today, issues like closure of schools on a particular day or increase in the price of bread, may be decided by popular vote. There may be a few referenda on very major international issues in some places. Also, there have been provisions in constitutions of some countries (*e.g.* France, Ireland, Japan and Switzerland) whereunder referendum is provided for constitutional amendments.

Representative Democracy came into general favour in post-industrial revolution nation states with large populations. Modern liberal democracies are important examples of representative democracy.

Representative democracy comprises a form of democracy wherein voters choose their representatives to act in their interest. An individual representative may be elected by a particular subset of the total electorate which is called his or her constituency.

A modern representative democracy implies:

(a) periodic, free and fair elections to choose representatives

(b) freedom to form and join political parties of one's choice. It is through political parties that the democratic political system operates and elections are fought to find the representatives of the people and ensure peaceful transfer of power from one to the other. Also, parties function as links between the rulers and the ruled – the government and the people.

(c) universal adult suffrage – right to vote to all adults without any discrimination of race, religion, caste, gender etc., one man (or woman) – one vote

(d) every democratic system recognises the primacy of the will of the majority implying decisions by majority but with adequate protection to religious, linguistic or other such rights of minorities. Every citizen must enjoy full freedom to follow one's religion and to safeguard one's language etc.

(e) equality of all citizens without any discrimination – protection of basic human rights

(f) an independent judiciary – dispute redressal mechanism and justice system

(g) responsible and responsive government – responsible and accountable to the people directly and/or through their representatives and responsive to their urges, aspirations and needs.

(h) existence of a constitution – a basic or foundational law – that ordains the political system, establishes the organs of the State and defines and delimits their roles and relationships with each other and with the people, provides checks and balances and seeks to prevent arbitrary exercise or abuse of power. Every Constitution provides for Legislature, Executive and Judiciary as the main organs of the State. The respective powers of the three organs and the nature of relationship between them – sharing or separation of powers, extent of independence from each other etc. – give rise to different political systems of constitutional representative democracy. The two most outstanding types of representative democracy are (i) Parliamentary and (ii) Presidential.

Parliamentary System

In a parliamentary system, almost by definition, Parliament is supposed to be supreme. There is fusion of the Executive and Legislative powers inasmuch as the Executive comes out of Parliament and remains part of it and responsible to it. The two are not separate centres of power and there is little scope of any dichotomy between the two. All the executive power is really exercised by the Cabinet or the Council of Ministers. The Ministers are Members of Parliament and under the concept of Ministerial responsibility remain accountable to the elected representatives of the people in Parliament. The Parliamentary system lays greater emphasis on the concept of executive answerability to Parliament. The moment, the Council of Ministers/Cabinet loses the support of the majority of the House, (or, to be more exact, when majority in the House comes to be opposed to it), it must go. Any member can bring a vote of no-confidence. The House can also vote out a government on a major Bill or policy issue or by refusing supplies or money appropriations.

In a parliamentary system, the head of the government is different from the head of the State. The constitutional head of the State may be the Crown as in U.K. or the President as in

India while the head of the government is the Prime Minister. U.K. is the classic example of a parliamentary system with a constitutional hereditary monarchy. It is a unitary nation-state. The British have no written Constitution. Parliament lays the laws and in theory at least, British Parliament is still supreme and sovereign. There are no limitations on its powers and the judiciary does not have the same power of judicial review as the U.S. Courts. It is another matter that in practice, the things have considerably changed with the advent of the European Union on the one hand and the assertion of regional identities on the other.

Presidential System

Next to the Parliamentary system, the chief variant of constitutional government and representative democracy is the Presidential system of the U.S. type. There are, of course, many so-called Presidential systems in various parts of the globe which may be neither constitutional nor representative or democratic. Sometimes usurpers of power through coups or other non-democratic, anti-constitutional or violent means may also describe themselves as Presidents. Even military dictators often manage to go about as constitutionally chosen Presidents and heads of State.

As a category of political system within the parameters of representative constitutional democracy, Presidential system is distinguished by the President being elected by the people as the head of the State for a fixed term. He is the centre of power and head of the State as also of the Government. He is almost irremovable during his term of office inasmuch as his tenure is not dependent on retaining the confidence of the Legislature or enjoying majority support for his policies. All the executive power vests in him and he is free to choose the heads of different departments who may be called Secretaries or Ministers. The Presidential system is said to be based on the doctrine of separation of powers and functional differentiation between the Executive, the Legislature and the Judiciary. Unlike the position under the Parliamentary system, the executive or the Ministers are not drawn from or part of or really responsible to the Legislature. Also, judicial review is almost absolute with the Supreme Court deciding from time to time what the U.S. Constitution is. In practice, however, there is more sharing than separation of powers between the three organs of the State, *e.g.* the President having a role in legislation and Congress or its Senate having to approve executive, diplomatic and even judicial appointments and ratifying treaties. It is said that under this scheme, the three organs can be kept on an even keel and conflicts resolved through the system of checks and balances between them.

Presidential-Parliamentary

The Parliamentary system may be said to be laying greater stress on the concept of the responsibility of the Executive while the Presidential system obviously seeks to secure the stability of the executive more. Since both are needed, in some countries of late, mixed systems with features of both Presidential and Parliamentary systems have been experimented with varying degrees of success *e.g.* in France, Sri Lanka, Bangladesh *etc*.

Participatory Democracy

In recent decades, attention in the academia and among political activists has been focussed on making modern representative systems more and more participatory by ensuring direct involvement of citizens in matters of governance and direct people's concerns. This is also sometimes spoken of as empowerment of people through everyday struggles for their rights as well as through harnessing their collective efforts to developing resources for collective well-being. Its main objective is that in matters affecting their lives directly, the ordinary people should come to have a greater say and a decisive voice. It is envisaged that it would enable the transformation of a maximalist state into different and dispersed self-governing entities. It may come close to a bottom up rather than top down approach or the model of grassroots democracy. The total result will be a responsive and accountable government.

Participatory democracy is being considered more and more as not just desirable but necessary. Under conditions of globalization, where the nation level institutions of representation are being subordinated to hegemonic global power with the structures of political and economic decision-making more remote and alienated from people, the politics of participatory democracy has acquired a new relevance.

Several new concepts of variants of democracy that are currently in vogue like Anticipatory, Consensus, Deliberative, Bio-regional or Grassroots democracy may also be broadly subsumed under participatory democracy. But, again, the term which comes closest to the concept of participatory democracy is 'Grass-roots democracy'. Being a variant of participatory democracy, grass-roots democracy is often identified with the struggle for empowerment and various micro-movements brought about at the grass-root levels. It implies participation of the people in defining development goals and devising means to achieve them.

Representation

One of the core concepts of democratic politics is representation. Modern democracies find their concrete manifestation through the idea of representation. Political representation acknowledges a link between two separate entities—government and the governed—and implies that through this link the people's views are articulated or their interests are secured. Elections are the basis of the representative mechanism and representatives are mandated by the people. In practice, however, there is no single, model of representation. It varies from one political system to another, but for a comprehensive understanding of the system of representation, they have been categorised into four broad forms:

1) Territorial Representation
2) Proportional Representation
3) Minority Representation
4) Functional Representation

1) *Territorial Representation* is the system of representation through geographical division of the territory into electoral districts. These are termed as constituencies. These may be either single member or multi-member. When one representative is chosen from each constituency, it is called a single member constituency, on the contrary, when two or more representatives are elected from each of them, it constitutes the model of a 'multi-member' constituency. This system has the virtue of providing direct relationship between the voter and the representatives. However, this system is inequitable. In most cases, the successful candidate gets less than absolute majority of votes.

This system is also known as 'First Past The Post (FPTP) electoral system'. Since the representative is elected on the basis of plurality of the votes, it is also known as the 'Plurality Electoral System'. First-past-the-post ideally should lead to reducing the number of political parties to a greater extent than most other methods, thus making it more likely that a single party will hold a majority of legislative seats. Single-member districts also mean that parties need to appeal to a wide cross-section of the populace rather than a political niche. This should discourage "extremist" parties. First-past-the-post may well be the simplest of all voting systems with specific advantages. It is likely to be quicker, and easier to administer. Elections are less costly to run. Since it is easy to explain and understand, it has a positive impact on voters. Alternative voting systems may alienate some voters who find the systems hard to understand, and who therefore feel detached from the direct effect of their own vote. Some voters see an election primarily as a form of recruitment for an individual representative, a point of contact between the state and themselves. First-past-the-post gives such voters a direct choice of a single candidate, with no extra votes to be shared or balanced between parties. This may be especially important to voters who want to vote for individuals based on particular ethical frameworks that are not party aligned, and who do not want their vote to have a "side effect" of electing others they may not approve of.

The most commonly expressed disadvantage – perhaps

because it is easiest to express and explain – of first-past-the-post is that it frequently produces disproportional results, *i.e.* results in which a party's share of the seats does not match up with its share of the votes. Thus, substantial bodies of opinion can be left out of the final outcome, and a party can obtain a majority of seats without a majority of the vote. The disproportionate nature of this system also means that whole regions may have MPs from only one party. The usual cause for these disproportionate results is that a party has a large number of votes across the entire territory, but they are spread out across the territory rather than being concentrated in particular constituencies. Parties with less overall support, but where that support is concentrated in particular constituencies, will win plurality in those constituencies over a party with widely distributed support. It often seems fundamentally unfair that a party should have a substantially greater or lesser share of seats than their share of the vote.

This presents a problem because it encourages parties to focus narrowly on the needs and well-being of specific electoral districts where they can be sure to win seats, rather than be sensitive to the sentiments of voters everywhere. A further problem is that usually the party in power has the ability to determine where the boundaries of constituencies lie: thus, in order to secure election results, they may use gerrymandering-that is, redistricting or delimitation of constituencies to distort election results by enclosing party voters together in one electoral district.

A further consequence of the system is that many such elections can be considered won before all votes are tallied, once there are no longer enough uncounted votes to override an established plurality count. This can produce a feeling of disenfranchisement among voters

To a greater extent than most other methods, first-past-the-post encourages the tactical voting technique known as "compromising". Voters are pressured to vote for one of the two candidates they predict are most likely to win, even if they ideally do not want to elect either of them, because a vote for any other candidate will be probably wasted and have no impact on the final result.

FPTP also encourages regional parties which can be very popular in one geographical region but have little or no support in other parts of the electorate.

2) *Proportional Representation* is based on the principle of weighing not counting the votes. Representatives are elected to the legislature in proportion to the percentage of votes polled. This means more the people, larger is the representation; smaller the number of people, less is the representation. In such a system there are multi-member constituencies and minority groups are also represented adequately. It is appreciated as the best way to ensure representation to all sections of the people. It gives a sense of security to parties which are in minority.

Proportional Representation can be put to application through following electoral methods:

i) *Single Transferable Vote System:* The major parties may offer as many candidates as there are seats. However, small parties and independents may be able to put up rather fewer candidates. Voters mark their ballot, giving their preferred ranking for some or even all the candidates. Consequently, it is the voters, rather than the party, who have final say over which candidates succeed. A successful candidate must achieve one third of the preferences in a three member constituency, one fourth in a four member and so on. Only in a few cases this is achieved at the first count. For the second count, the least popular candidate is eliminated and his or her votes redistributed according to the second preference shown on them. This process continues for as many counts as are needed until all seats are filled. Although the counting process is complicated, voting is clear and most voters get at least one of their preferences elected.

ii) *List System*: In this system parties list their candidates according to that party's determination of priorities. In a closed list, voters vote for a list, not a candidate. Each party is allocated seats in proportion to the number of votes, using the ranking order on its list. In an open list, voters indicate their order of preference within the list. List system is used in Israel (where the whole country is one closed list constituency), in the Netherlands (open list) and for elections to the European Parliament in the United

Kingdom (closed list) as well as in Finland (using multi-member districts and open lists).

3) *Minority Representation:* If democracy has to be government of all, it has to represent all sections of society. Minorities should be adequately represented as an essential part of democracy. Different methods that are used for minority representation are as follows:

i) Second Ballot System: Under this system, a candidate to be successful must secure fifty percent of the votes polled. If no candidate secures absolute majority, there is a second ballot or run-off polling between two candidates, who secured the highest votes. In the second ballot, the successful candidate wins absolute majority.

ii) Limited Vote System: This system is applicable in a multi-member constituency with at least three seats. The voter is given votes less than the number of seats. But they are not allowed to cast more than one vote for a candidate. In this system, minorities have a chance of capturing one seat, if they are fairly large, united and well organised.

iii) Cumulative Vote System: This system gives as many votes to the voters as there are seats allotted to the constituency. Voter has the power to cast all his votes for one candidate or divide them among different candidates. A well organised minority group can ask its member to cast all his votes in favour of the minority candidate seeking election.

iv) Reservation System: It is a system of representation where the seats in the legislature are reserved for a particular minority community, but the voters may not necessarily belong to that community.

4) *Functional Representation:* This system desires that the basis of representation should be according to the occupational composition of the society. The idea is to give representation to the social, economic and professional groups, having special interests of their own, in the national legislature. This system derived inspiration from the social set-up prevalent in the middle ages when community groups had their autonomous character. However, it took a concrete form in the post-first world war period.

Though the idea of functional representation has an attraction of its own, its demerits far outweigh its merits. It makes the legislature an arena of conflicting functional groups with the result that sectional interests over-ride national interests. It is also a difficult task to make a standard census of all social and economic occupations and then decide in terms of their adequate representation.

Political Party System and Processes

Party is defined as a voluntary association of people united in a cause, opinion etc, in opposition to others who maintain a different one. Political parties mean political organisations engaged in electoral competition with one or more other parties with a goal to capture public office. The term "political parties" emerged in the nineteenth century with the development of representative institutions and the expansion of the suffrage in Europe and the United States.

Political party is not an isolated institution. A study of political party and processes defines its study in the context of all those forces, institutions and agencies that interact with each other and with external environment.

Party system deals with the system of interactions resulting from inter-party activities reflected in how parties relate to each other at the group level, as well as in legislatures and power situations.

Determinants of Party System

Parties which exist in a given community, tend to share common characteristics. The characteristics of a party can be determined by the following three criteria:

1. *General Political System*: Party System is treated as a response to larger aspects of politics. Parties are essentially products of electoral arrangements. Electoral rules govern the forms of party systems under specifiable conditions, the absence of which may lead to different results.

2. *Social Structure and Culture:* Party systems might be treated primarily as structures that politically crystallise socio-

cultural forces. Party systems are susceptible to be conditioned by social structure and culture. Tribally fragmented societies are not likely to produce consolidated or integrated party systems. Various religious groups and divisions of social structure are often mirrored in party systems of particular nations.

3. *Past of Party System*: Histories of the parties play an important role in determining their characteristics. Once formed, they are highly responsive to external factors. But in this process of development, they do not change their basic character. They either retain their essential characteristics or change only very slowly, unless totally destroyed in political upheavals. Their development is largely inherent in their original shape.

All these approaches, however, cannot be viewed as mutually exclusive, they have to be treated as complementary and combined.

Types of Party System

Parties are always the product of a specific historical experience of each society which may not be replicated elsewhere. The activities in which parties engage, their organisational forms and the resources available to them vary considerably. Hence, no uniform characterisation of party system has developed. Depending upon the unique characteristics of each political system, different kinds of party systems have originated. Number of parties is a basic criteria along which party systems vary. On the basis of numerical strength they have been broadly categorised as follows:

1. Single Party System
2. Two-Party System and
3. Multi-Party System

A single party system is characterised by a single party in power either dominating all other groups, trying to absorb the political opposition, or in the extreme cases suppressing all opposition groups which are regarded as counter revolutionary or subversive of the regime. This can be further divided into two sub-categories – totalitarian and democratic. A totalitarian model is opposed to all kinds of opposition while in a democratic case, several groups within the dominant party are allowed to flourish and operate in the political system. Nazi party in Germany and Fascist party in Italy can be placed in the former category and Congress party of India in its earlier years in the latter.

In a two-party system (also called Bi-party system), two parties are sufficiently strong to take part in the struggle for power. One of the significant features of this system is that minor parties also operate along side major ones. American party system consisting of Democratic party and Republican party or British system consisting of Labour party and Conservative party are classic examples of a two-party system.

A Multi-party system is characterised by existence of a number of parties in the political arena. In such a system, due to the existence of number of parties, no party is able to obtain majority in the legislature. Hence, such political systems are characterised by coalition governments. Party systems in Nepal, France and Italy and more recently in India also, can be considered as examples of Multi-party system.

Although party system has been classified as Single-party, Two-party or Multi-party system, in reality we may find the existence of all these categories in the same political system. At some point of time, depending upon the internal conditions of the political processes, a single-party may be dominant, while at others, two parties or even multiple parties may call the shots. The categories have to be studied together for understanding the dynamics of party system and processes in a political system.

Conclusion

An analysis of the various concepts, political systems, and forms and types of Government leads us to the conclusion that each country has to build its own system on the foundations of its historical background, cultural ethos, nature of the population, economic and social infra-structure and available administrative talent and apparatus. Whichever system is best suited to meet its needs is the best.

It is of the utmost importance that information about the system adopted should be widely disseminated. For, the people must know and understand the system under which they live and are governed. Any mismatch between the requirements of the society and the political system is likely to have dire consequences. An edifice built without the firm foundation of people's faith crumbles fast.

2

INDIAN POLITY
FROM THE EARLIEST TIMES TO THE END OF THE COLONIAL RULE

On the attainment of independence from British colonial rule, on the midnight of 14-15 August 1947, India became one of the youngest members of the comity of soverign nations. With the commencement of the Constitution on 26 January 1950, she became a 'Sovereign, Democratic, Republic' with a representative parliamentary system of government. The concepts of nation and representative parliamentary institutions as modern constructs are said to owe their origin and growth in India to our British connection for some two long centuries. It would, however be wrong to premise that the concept of Indian unity was a gift of the British, that democracy and representative institutions were entirely alien to India or that Indian polity was a transplant of the British political system of parliamentary democracy.

Ancient Indian Polity

The consciousness of "We, the people of India" and India's identity and unity belong to the hoary past of the Vedic age in ancient India. The concept of Indian unity in diversity – of the territory of India constituting one country and the people inhabiting it one people – goes back to some five thousand years and more. A unique civilisational bond, naturally bound territory, common social institutions, and shared vision, values and historical and spiritual experience have been responsible for an all-pervading and abiding consciousness of India as a geographical and cultural unit. Similarly, democracy, representative institutions, limitation on the arbitrary powers of rulers and the rule of law were part of the characteristics of ancient Indian polity. In fact, India could well be considered to have been the first cradle of democracy. There is ample historical evidence of republican forms of government, deliberative bodies like the *Sabha* and the *Samiti* and democratic self-governing institutions having existed and thrived in many parts of India from as early as the Vedic age (Circa 3000-1000 B.C.) *i.e.* much before the advent of the Greek city states or the Roman republics. Members of the *Sabha* and *Samiti* – women could also be members – were expected to speak in one voice, they could discuss and argue but in fundamentals they were united and had the same approach, the basis and the aim being national well-being. *Rigveda* enjoined the entire people to get together to set up a strong *Raj Sabha* with distinguished persons from every section of the population – scholars, wisemen and warriors – all devoted to the welfare of the nation.

In ancient Indian polity, the best of the rulers were as much bound by their *Dharma* (code of duties) as the people at large and the different classes thereof were bound by their respective *Dharmas* (codes). If the King violated the laws of *Dharma* (*Rajdharma*) or exceeded his jurisdiction, he was also subject to punishment. The foundational principle was that the government should be conducted not by the will of a solitary person, but jointly with the aid of councillors whose advice was to be respected. Vedic political theory recognised *Dharma* as the true sovereign. And, *Dharma* was not religion but corresponded most closely to the modern concept of the Rule of Law. *Dharma* or the Rule of Law was upheld and enforced by the King. Ideally, the powers of monarch were limited by the will of the people and the customs, usages and injunctions of *Dharmashastra*. The King was required to take an oath of loyalty to the law and the constitution of the realm and to hold in trust the State for achieving the welfare of his people, both material and moral.

The King could not declare war except with the approval

of the *Rashtra Sabha*. Even though King, he could not assume arbitrary powers. The *Sabha*, the *Samiti*, the army and the state treasury supported only a King who functioned according to the will of the people. A person could ascend to the King's thrown only with the approval of the people. He had to specifically seek their agreement to his ruling over them. This also indicated that the concept of sovereignty vesting in the people was recognised. The King almost begged of the people the right to rule. While there can be no denying the fact that ancient polity was predominantly monarchical, there were many instances of elective kingship and in any case, certain democratic institutions and practices were often in-built in the monarchical system. If a King indulged in injustice, lied, made false promises or otherwise defaulted in the discharge of his duties he could be removed by the people. If the King happened to be unjust or tyrannical, Indian polity recognised the people's right to rebel. There are actual references to popular revolts against unjust and tyrannical kings who were sometimes even put to death for their crimes. As Sri Aurobindo puts it:

> ...Indian monarchy previous to the Mahomedan invasion was not, in spite of a certain sanctity and great authority conceded to the regal position and the personality of the King as the representative of the divine power and the guardian of the *Dharma*, in any way a personal despotism or an absolutist autocracy....His power was not personal and it was besides hedged in by safeguards against abuse and encroachment and limited by the liberties and powers of other public authorities and interests who were, so to speak, lesser co-partners with him in the exercise of sovereignty and administrative legislation and control. He was in fact a limited or constitutional monarch....The King was only the guardian, executor and servant of the *Dharma*, charged to see to its observance and to prevent offences, serious irregularities and breaches. He himself was bound to obey it and observe the rigorous rule it laid on his personal life and action and on the province, powers and duties of his regal authority and office.... Inspite of the sanctity and prestige attaching to the sovereign it was laid down that obedience ceased to be binding if the King ceased to be faithful executor of the *Dharma*. Incompetence and violation of the obligation to

> rule to the satisfaction of the people were in theory and effect sufficient causes for his removal. Manu even lays it down that an unjust and oppressive King should be killed by his own subjects like a mad dog, and this justification by the highest authority of the right or even the duty of insurrection and regicide in extreme cases is sufficient to show that absolutism or the unconditional divine right to kings was no part of the intention of the Indian political system.... [*Foundations of Indian Culture*, Pondicherry, 1971 (1995), pp. 329-332].

Side by side monarchies, several republics had also evolved. The Vedic *Gana* was probably in the nature of a tribal democracy looking after military, distributive, religious and social activities. The word *Gana* means 'number' and *Ganarajya* 'the rule of numbers' or 'the rule of the many'. The word *Gana* could, therefore, be equated with the word 'Demos' and the word '*Ganarajya*' with 'democracy' or 'republic'. *Gana* was also the assembly or Parliament and *Ganarajya* consequently denoted 'Government by assembly or Parliament'. The secondary meaning of *Gana* came to be 'Parliament' or 'senate' and republics were governed by such bodies. *Gana* also came to mean 'a republic' itself.

After the great war of *Mahabharata*, large empires began to fade away and the number of republican states grew. As many as sixteen republics including Kashi, Koshal, Magadha, Kuru, Anga, Avanti, Gandhar, Vaishali, Matsya etc. came into being. *Jatakas* make many references to how these republics functioned. The members met in a place called *Santhagar*. People's representatives were elected in open assembly. They selected their *Gopa* who became King and ruled with the help of a Council of Ministers. It is remarkable that both Mahavir and Buddha came from republics. The salient features of these republics have been described by Thompson thus:

> The genius of the people for the corporate action expressed itself in a variety of self-governing institutions with highly developed constitution, rules of procedure and machinery of administration which challenge comparison with modern parliamentary institutions. Reading of the election rules of these bodies, the

> division of villages and districts into electoral units, their rules of debate and standing orders for the conduct of business and maintenance of order in debate, and their committee system, one might wonder whether many standing orders of the House of Commons and of the London County Council are not derived from the regulations of the ancient local bodies, ecclesiastical councils and village assemblies of ancient India. [Giriraj Shah, *Glimpses of Ancient Indian Culture*, NOIDA, 1989, pp. 85-86]

In the fourth century B.C., the republican federation known as the Kshudrak Malla Sangha offered strong resistance to Alexander the Great. Contemporary Greek historians have left descriptions of many republican states in India some of which were described by them as pure democracies while others were said to be 'aristocratic republics'. Near Pataliputra (modern Patna) there was the city of Vaishali. This was the capital city of the Lichchavis. The state is known to have been a republic governed by an assembly of notables with an elected President who was called the *Nayaka*. Pataliputra had an elected municipal council of thirty members with six committees of five members each. There were *Panchayats* for administering justice and courts of appeal. The republican character of Lichchavi polity lasted a thousand years or more. The Greek scholar Megasthenes has also left records of popular assemblies that were preserved in the South and which restrained the power of Kings.

Kautilya's *Arthashastra* is known to be one of the finest treatises on statecraft, political economy and governance in ancient India. The first and foremost duty of a ruler, according to Kautilya is to ensure security and protection of the people. The ruler has to completely identify himself with the people. He has to act on the advice of Minsiters and in the happiness of his people is his own happiness. The dishonest and the corrupt must be dealt with sternly and all ill-gotten wealth should be confiscated. Kautilya emphaises the need for decentralisation of power to the grassroots levels.

Nitisara (Science of Polity or Political Science) of Shukracharya – work of the 10th century – gives us some idea of Indian polity as it was conceived prior to the Turkish and

Afghan invasions. The King was not to act upon his own opinions, but upon the opinion of the majority of the people. 'Public opinion is more powerful than the King as the rope made of many fibres is strong enough to drag a lion'.

An underlying principle of the Indian politico-social system right from the most ancient times was that of a synthesis of autonomies of the village, the town, and the local or regional, territorial or other administrative units. The kingdom or confederated republic was often a means of holding together and synthesising a free and living organic system of autonomies. The chief aim in every case was that of strengthening the system of security against external enemies and ensuring peace and oneness among the participating autonomies. Indian polity even in the most glorious periods of her history had always been (if we must use the modern terminology) a sort of federal or confederal one.

Periods of Absolute Monarchy

After the early centuries of the Christian era, the polity that prevailed in large parts of India was basically absolute monarchy where the word of the King was law; there were no traces of any constitutionalism or rule of law or restraints through elected or otherwise representative, deliberative, law-making or even advisory bodies. There were sometimes very large empires extending almost all over the Indian sub-continent or large parts of it as in the times of the Mauryas, Guptas and the Mughals or the country was divided into a large number of small and big kingdoms. In either case, the rulers were hereditary kings or sub-kings who ruled usually with the assistance of some faithful ministers appointed by them and dependent on royal sweet will for their continuance in office. Thus, we find that Emperor Harsha was a benevolent ruler who depended for his day-to-day administration and vital government policies and programmes on the advice and assistance of his Council of Ministers. The Ministers enjoyed great power. Every minister was allowed to express his opinion freely, frankly and fearlessly and the decisions were generally taken unanimously.

During the medieval period, King-in-Ministry was the usual form of government. The foreign travellers do not speak of any republican States existing during this period; they refer to monarchies with the Ministers being an indispensable wheel of administrative machinery, next in importance only to the King.

Under the Sultanates, the Central Government was modelled on the Persian system with a Consultative Council consisting of four Ministers who existed on the sufferance of the King. Though in actual practice the Sultans had often to give due weight to the views and counsel of responsible Ministers, the monarchy under the Sultanate was a curious anomaly. It neither conformed to the Muslim religious law nor to the earlier Indian traditions or principles. The King was an autocrat and owed his position to no recognised law of succession to the throne. It was only the law of might which entitled him to that office.

During the times of the Mughals, the system of common administrative laws was a great unifying force but ultimately the emperor was the first of the administration. Since no absolute ruler, however diligent, could alone discharge the multifarious duties of the government of an empire, there were the Ministers or Councillors to assist the ruler and to carry out the commands.

It is recorded that there were meetings of Councillors in the *Ghusalkhana* (private Chamber near bathroom) as a practical aid in administration. But nothing required the despot to maintain a fixed number of Ministers, to have a Council in a particular form, to be bound by their advice or even to call its meetings. The Ministers were mere advisers or secretaries of the King. The Council, if any, was not a Cabinet. It was much too formal and vague a body, too subject to royal supervision and too dependent on royal pleasure to be regarded as an effective check on royal power. The Councillors were only to carry out royal policy. They were not responsible to any other constitutional or popular body for their acts.

Panchayats: Grassroots Democracy or Local Self-Government

One of the unique democratic institutions evolved in India by the country's own genius and ethos has been the *Panchayat* system, literally meaning governance by a 'Council of Five.' As an institution of local self-government at the village level, *Panchayat* had its origin in ancient India. A sort of village council or an association of the residents of the village often consisting of the village elders, *Panchayat* or *Gram Sangha* performed administrative and judical functions. Sometimes, the *Gram Sanghas* or *Panchayats* were elected from among the villagers who regulated their own lives through these bodies. We find reference to *Gram Sanghas* in the *Manusmriti* (code of Manu), Kautilya's *Arthashastra* (400 B.C.) and the *Mahabharata*. The *Shanti Parva* of *Mahabharata* refers to a *Sabha* named *Sansad* also. This consisted of the common people and was, therefore, called the *Jan Sansad*. Valmiki's *Ramayana* speaks of the *Ganapada* which was a sort of federation of village republics. Only those persons could become its members who had the general welfare of the people at their hearts. Later, village commonwealths are mentioned in *Sukra Niti* (Sukracharya's *Nitisara*). In fact, the institution of village *Panchayats* in one form or the other, has had an unbroken continuity almost all over India and throughout her long history.

Nehru wrote at length and repeatedly on the democratic traditions and heritage of India. In his *Discovery of India,* he noted that in the olden days "there was a widespread system of self-government in towns and villages and the central government seldom interfered so long as its quota of taxes were paid." It was predominantly an agricultural society and the basic unit was the self-governing or fairly autonomous village. The polity was built up from these village communities grouped in tens and hundreds. The villages were governed by their elected *Panchayats*. In the centre of the village there was the *Panchayat ghar,* where the village elders met. Every year all the free men of the village would meet to elect their *Panchayat*. In times of war or difficulty, "even a *Shudra* or member of the lowest caste could win if he was able enough". According to Nehru:

> A number of villages or small towns were joined together under a *raja* or chief, who was sometimes elected and sometimes hereditary....It appears that the *raja*, although he was the chief man in his State, could not do just what he liked. He was himself subject to Aryan laws and customs, and he could be deposed or fired by his people....Thus, there was a kind of democracy in the Aryan settlements—that is to say, the Aryan inhabitants could to some extent control the government. [*Discovery of India*, pp. 111, 249; *Glimpses of World History*, pp. 24-25]

During the Buddhist period the existence and functioning of regional councils *(Janapadas)*, city councils (*Nagara Sabha*s) or (*Paura Sabha*s) and village assemblies (*Gram Sabha*s) illustrate the operation of democracy at multi-tier grass-roots levels. The *Janapadas* and the *Paura Sabha*s, in fact, could be said to have performed the role of the *Sabha*s and the *Samitis*. The *Paura Sabha* was presided over by a leading citizen, generally a merchant or a banker. Matters of importance were discussed in a joint meeting of the *Paura* and the *Janapada*. It appears from the *Mahabharata* that the members of the *Janapada* as well as the *Paura*, were generally rich people and those who were not rich were not poor either. The *Paura* was divided into several sub-assemblies representing different interests. It was a sort of mother association of different bodies. The twin organism of *Paura* and *Janapada* served as a powerful check on arbitrary authority. Probably there could be no better example than those councils, of the application of local initiative and self-governance.

Nehru also refers to the old inscriptions from South India which tell us how the members of *Panchayats* were elected and what were their qualifications and disqualifications. It is interesting to recall some of the observations on this matter made by Nehru in The *Glimpses of World History*:

> If any member did not render accounts of public funds he was disqualified. Another very interesting rule seems to have been that near relatives of members were disqualified from office. How excellent if this could be enforced now in all our councils

> and assemblies and municipalities. There is mention of a woman's name as a member of a committee. So it appears that women could serve on these *Panchayats* and their committees. Committees were formed out of the elected members of the *Panchayats*, each Committee lasting for a year. If a member misbehaved he could be removed at once. The system of village self-government was the foundation of the Aryan polity. It was this that gave it strength....We find that the Kings and rulers were far from being autocratic rulers. Their power was kept in check by elected *Panchayats*. We find also that there was a fairly advanced system of self-government in the villages and towns, and there was little interference with this by the Central Government. [*Glimpses of World History*, pp. 131-132]

Throughout the periods of monarchical form of Government prevailing all over the country and irrespective of the nature of the Kings or Sultans who ruled, village societal structure remained almost unchanged; village communities in their local affairs continued to be governed by some sort of village councils or *Panchayats*. In Rajasthan, for example, the village council was called *Panchakula* during the medieval times. There was no caste restriction to become members of the village council, though no records appear to be available about the election or selection of the members and their qualifications.

The *Panchayat* system, in fact represented 'an *imperium* in *imperio*, a State within a State, that took care of the people and their culture in the midst of invading armies that swept the length and breadth of the land playing ducks and drakes with its princes and principalities'. Except during periods of anarchy, village society was usually protected by its autonomous institutions which were too deep-rooted to be disturbed by even the chronic instability of Kingdoms of the Middle ages. Though such village communities existed in all parts of India, they seem to have been most systematically organised in South India.

Advent of the British

Almost from the very beginning of recorded history, India had to face a long succession of foreign invasions. Wave after wave of aggressors came and swept her fertile lands. By and large, all the groups of foreign invaders who came to India settled down in this country for good and tried to make it their home. They got 'Indianised' and stuck roots in the soil of this country. The Europeans, however, were an exception. It was in the sixteenth-seventeenth century that they for the first time began taking interest in India on a large scale. The most important among the early entrants were the Portuguese, the Dutch, the French and the British. None of them came to make India their home. They were all attracted by the stories of India's fabulous wealth and affluence and by the excellence of her manufactured goods which had a big market in Europe. They came as trading companies with the avowed aim of increasing trade with India. Till the beginning of the eighteenth century none of these European companies could venture to meddle in this country's politics. The policy of every foreign company was to concentrate on trade and make the maximum profits.

Like other Europeans, the British also came to India as a trading company. The company of the British merchants was incorporated in London on 31 December 1600 under the Charter of Queen Elizabeth. The Company, later on known as the East India Company, set up depots or factories, as they were styled, at Bombay, Madras and Calcutta with a view to 'securing advancement in trade and merchandise'. In course of time, these depots became the three principal settlements to which the others were placed in subordination. So as to be constantly widening their areas of trade and obtaining from the Indian rulers greater concession, the Company soon spread a wide network of military and administrative system. By 1690, they had gained a number of footholds in India by very shrewdly exploiting the internal disunity and discord among the princes of India for their nefarious ends.

The foundation of the British Empire is said to have been laid after the battle of Plassey in 1757, which the Company had 'won by military operations' in Bengal supplemented by Clive's policy of 'trick, bribery and chicanery'.

The 'Revolt' of 1857 – the first phase of India's struggle for freedom – sealed the fate of the East India Company and quickened the pace of events. Under the Government of India Act, 1858, all the Indian territories then in possession of the company became vested in Her Majesty and were to be governed directly 'by and in the name' of the Crown, acting through a Secretary of State.

With the founding of the Indian National Congress in 1885 and its demands for representative institutions began the process of gradual relaxation of imperial control and the beginning of responsible Government in India. From its very inception, the Congress made gradual introduction of representative institutions in the country as the main plank of its platform.

Minto-Morley Reforms

The Morley-Minto reform proposals came in the wake of relentless campaign launched by the Congress for greater and more effective representation in running the affairs of the country. Important changes were made in the constitution and functions of the Indian Legislatures by the Act of 1909. The bodies which were thus far 'councils for the purposes of making laws and regulations' now for the first time, formally got the nomenclature of 'Legislative Councils' under the Act. Both the size and the functions of the Councils were enlarged.

But, the communal system of representation initiated by the 1909 Act poisoned the future public life of India, increased separatist tendencies and ultimately paved the way for demands for the partition of the country. It was the biggest shock to secular Indian nationalism after the suppression of the 1857 revolution and was indeed the greatest victory for the British policy of 'divide and rule'.

The outbreak of World War I (1914-19) brought into sharp focus the principles of self-determination and intensified the spirit of Indian nationalism. India threw herself wholeheartedly on the side of Britain and extended timely assistance 'throughout the progress of the war in man, money and resources'.

The War was said to have induced in India a 'new sense of self-esteem', 'a feeling of profound pride that she had not fallen behind other portions of the British Empire'. Simultaneously, it had aroused political aspirations and expectations. It was hoped that after the conclusion of the War and the victory of Britain and allies, India would be offered appropriate political rewards and that the government would at least announce the grant of some political advancement in the shape of self-government, if not complete emancipation from foreign rule. But, when the War ended with the victory of allies, the government unfortunately failed to show any willingness to respond to Indian opinion.

Montagu-Chelmsford Report

In 1917, when the Home Rule Movement of Mrs. Annie Besant and Lokmanya Tilak was at its climax, the British Prime Minister with a view to assuage popular Indian opinion, appointed Edwin Montagu as Secretary of State for India. Montagu was said to be a supporter of the Indian nationalist feelings. After becoming Secretary of State for India, on 20 August 1917, Montagu made in the House of Commons the historic announcement of the 'Goal of British Policy' being the grant of responsible government to the people of India by stages.

Montagu came to India with a view to considering proposals for constitutional reforms after meeting various national leaders, receiving deputations and examining witnesses from different quarters. When he returned home after the completion of his work, a Report containing the proposed reforms was published in July 1918 over the joint signatures of Secretary of State, Edwin Montagu and Viceroy, Lord Chelmsford. This was later to be known as the 'Montagu-Chelmsford Report' and the 'first comprehensive study that had yet been made of the whole problem of Indian Government'.

The Government of India Act 1919 which followed, introduced many important changes in the Indian constitutional system. The erstwhile Indian Legislative Council was replaced by a bicameral legislature consisting of a Council of State (Upper House) and a Legislative Assembly (Lower House). Even though some power of nominating Members was retained, each House was to have an elected majority. Members were to be elected directly by constituencies delimited by the Rules framed under the Act. The electoral qualifications prescribed varied widely and were based on communal affiliation, residence and property credentials –

(i) ownership or occupancy of a building, or
(ii) assessment to or payment of income-tax, or
(iii) assessment to or payment of municipal or cantonment rates or taxes or local cesses, or
(iv) the holding of land, or
(v) membership of a local body.

The Act of 1919 was not at all favourably received by public opinion in India. Lokmanya tilak termed the 1919 Reforms as 'dissatisfying, disappointing and a sun without morning'.

The Simon Commission

Section 84 of the Government of India Act of 1919 had provided for the appointment of a Royal Commission 'at the expiration of ten years after the passing of the Act...for the purpose of inquiring into the working of the system of government...and the development of representative institutions in British India...' and for reporting 'as to whether and to what extent it is desirable to establish the principle of responsible government, or to extend, modify, or restrict the degree of responsible government...existing therein, including the question whether the establishment of second chambers of the local legislatures is or is not desirable'. Accordingly, a Commission was to be appointed in 1929. In November 1927, two years before it was due, the appointment of a Commission was announced by a Royal Warrant of 26 November 1927. But the Commission's Chairman, Sir John Simon, and all its members were chosen from the British Parliament and it did not include any Indian. The all-white Simon Commission was boycotted by almost all the Indian parties.

Before the Simon Commission could begin its work, the All India Congress Committee at its Bombay session in May

1927 passed a resolution calling upon the Working Committee 'to frame a Swaraj Constitution', based on a declaration of rights for India in consultation with the elected members of the Central and Provincial Legislatures and other leaders of political parties; and place the same before a special meeting of the AICC, with a view to its adoption by the Congress at its next session. The Committee headed by Pt. Motilal Nehru presented a unanimous report within three months, to the All-Parties Conference held at Lucknow on 28 August 1928. This later came to be known as the Nehru Report or the Nehru Committee Report. The Constitution envisaged by the Report in short, was based on the principles of Dominion Status providing for parliamentary system of responsible government both at the Centre and in the Provinces. That is, the executive should be responsible to the respective legislature both at the Central as well as the provincial levels. After the rejection of the Nehru Report and the demand for a Dominion Status, the nationalist opinion in the country was deeply frustrated and the Indian National Congress presided over by Jawaharlal Nehru at its Lahore Session in 1929 declared complete independence or *Purna Swarajya* as its goal.

The period from 1930 to 1934 witnessed a strong nationalist movement under the leadership of the Congress. A series of Round Table Conferences followed in the wake of the Civil Disobedience Movement started by Gandhiji and the severe repression resorted to by the British rulers. The British Government published a White Paper in March 1933 giving a complete outline of a new Constitution. The scheme contained provisions for a federal set-up and of provincial autonomy. There was vehement reaction to the White Paper and it was 'found unacceptable to any nationalist section... Practically all sections of Indian opinion condemned it as waste paper'. The British Parliament constituted a Joint Committee of the two Houses to consider the Government's scheme formulated in the White Paper further. The Joint Committee submitted its report in November 1934. On the basis of the Report, a bill was prepared which was introduced in the British Parliament on 19 December

1934. After its having been passed by the two Houses and Royal assent being given to it on 4 August 1935, it became the Government of India Act, 1935.

Government of India Act, 1935

The Act of 1935 aimed at providing a federal structure. The most remarkable feature of the Act was that it envisaged a 'federation of all India', consisting of the British Provinces and the Indian States willing to join it. The 1935 Act finally broke up the unitary system under which British India had hitherto been administered. The principle of the Constitution of 1919 had been decentralisation rather than federation. Under the new Act, the Provinces were for the first time recognised in law as separate entities, exercising executive and legislative powers in their own field, in their own right, free in normal circumstances from Central control, in that field. The proposed federation could come into being only after Rulers representing not less than half the aggregate population of the Indian States and entitled to one half of the seats allotted to them collectively in the Federal Upper Chamber had acceded to the Federation.

The federal part of the 1935 Act, however, never came into operation as the Princely States could not be persuaded to accede to the Federation. As a result, the Constitution of the Central Government in India remained the same as it was under the Act of 1919 with such modifications as were necessitated by the introduction of autonomy in the Provinces. Thus, no Council of Ministers, responsible to the Legislature, was appointed at the Centre and the powers and functions of the Central Legislature, as provided in the 1919 Act, remained unchanged until the Indian Independence Act, 1947. The Congress felt that the Act had been imposed on India against the declared will of its people. The Indian people, the Congress declared, could only recognise a constitutional structure which had been framed by them. The Congress stood for a genuine democratic State in India where political power has been transferred to the people as a whole and the government is under their effective control. Such a State, the Congress believed, could only come into existence through a Constituent Assembly consisting of the elected representatives of the people of India.

Cripps Mission

The period from 1939 to 1947 is of historic importance in the history of constitutional and political developments in India. The Second World War started in September 1939 and India was made party to it with the declaration of war by British Government. It led to the resignation of Congress Provincial Governments as a protest against the unilateral action of the Imperialist Government in throwing India into war without caring to take the representative governments and political India into confidence. It created an unprecedented constitutional crisis. The provincial autonomy came to an end with the resignation of the Congress Governments. The Central Government assumed all the powers and the Governors became autocratic heads of provincial governments.

It was in 1940 that the League passed the Pakistan resolution demanding division of the country. The British Government made its August 1940 offer to conciliate India. It was rejected and Mahatma Gandhi started individual *Satyagrah*. The war situation became bad and was becoming worse every day. The Japanese entered the War in December 1941 and were knocking at the door of India.

In the meanwhile, a National Government, with the Labour Party as a part of it, was formed in England. The Labour Party had been sympathetic to India. Under these pressures, the British Government sent to India Sir Stafford Cripps as its emissary to discuss the whole question of future of India with the political leaders of India. Under the Cripps Mission proposals, Dominion Status was to be granted soon after the war. A Constituent Assembly elected by the Provincial Legislatures was to frame the new Constitution of India. The obligations of the British Crown towards minorities were to be protected. Provinces were given the right to stay out of the Indian Union. A treaty was to be concluded between the Crown and the Indian Constituent Assembly to transfer power to Indian hands. Indian States were given option to join the Union. A National Government of Indian representatives was to be constituted immediately. But defence was to remain under the control of the Governor-General in Council.

On the failure of the Cripps Mission, the Congress adopted the "Quit India" Resolution in 1942 at its Bombay session. The Congress High Command including Gandhiji was arrested and most of the leading Congressmen all over the country were put behind jail. This was accompanied by a widespread struggle.

With the war nearing its end in 1945, the British Government again took an initiative. The Congress leaders were set free. Lord Wavel made another offer, known as Wavel offer. He invited political leaders for consultation and discussion. This Conference was held at Simla. It however failed.

Cabinet Mission

The year 1946 marked the final phase of constitutional deadlock in India. The Labour Government came to power in England with Attlee as its Prime Minister. Labour Government announced the Cabinet Mission consisting of Secretary of State for India, Lord Pathic Lawrence, Sir Stafford Cripps and A.V. Alexander, to come to India and find a solution for the deadlock. The Mission reached India on 23 March 1946 and immediately started negotiations with the representatives of different parties and groups in India. A joint conference with the representatives of Muslim League and the Congress was held by the Mission on 5 May, but this Conference failed to produce an agreed formula. Thereupon the Cabinet Mission published their own proposals in the state paper on 16 May 1946.

The Mission examined the demand of the League for Pakistan and reached the conclusion that it could not solve the communal minority problem. The Mission felt that the most satisfactory method would be to set up a Constituent Assembly. The Cabinet Mission proposed a three-tier system for the Constitution of India. There was to be a Union of India embracing both British India and Indian States. It was to deal with foreign affairs, defence, and communications, and was to have the powers necessary to raise the finance required for the above subjects. All other subjects and the residuary powers were to be vested in the provinces. The states were to retain all subjects and powers other than those vested in the Union.

The provinces were to form three groups: (a) *Section A* – Madras, Bombay, U.P., Bihar, C.P. and Orissa; (b) *Section B* – Punjab, NWFP., Sindh; (c) *Section C* – Bengal and Assam. Each group was to have its own Executive and Legislature – and was to enjoy such powers as it decided. Below these groups, were to be the provincial administrations which could exercise powers that were left after the allocation of powers to the Union and the groups.

The Muslim League accepted the Mission's scheme of 16 May and also agreed to join the Interim Government on the basis of the Statement of 16 June but it was averse to joining the Constituent Assembly. The Congress, on the other hand, agreed to join the Constituent Assembly with a view to framing India's future Constitution, but rejected the Mission's proposals for the formation of an Interim Government as it could not give up its national character "or accept an artificial and unjust parity, or agree to a veto of a communal group". The Constituent Assembly duly opened on 9 December 1946. It was truly a historic occasion.

Mountbatten Plan

In March 1947, Lord Louis Mountbatten was sent as the new Viceroy to arrange for a smooth transfer of power. He reached India on 22 March 1947. Very soon he came to the firm conclusion that it would not be possible for the Congress and the Muslim League to work together either in the Interim Government or in the Constituent Assembly and the only way, therefore, to prevent the orgy of communal violence from assuming fierce dimensions was to transfer power to Indian hands with the greatest expedition. It was already becoming quite obvious and the Congress had also come to realise that partition of the country was inevitable and was left as the only alternative to utter chaos, anarchy and civil war. Accordingly,

Mountbatten fixed the date of 15 August 1947 for transfer of power.

Mountbatten prepared a plan for partition and after consultations with the leaders of the opposition parties in Britain, a fresh policy statement embodying the Mountbatten Plan was issued on 3 June 1947. The scheme underlying this statement recognised the inevitability of the partition of the country. According to the statement, the constitution framed by the existing Constituent Assembly could not be forced on unwilling parts. As such, it laid down a procedure for ascertaining the wishes of such areas on whether they wanted a separate constituent assembly. The net result and effect of the whole scheme, it was obvious, was to be the partition of India into India and Pakistan.

Indian Independence Act, 1947

Based on the Mountbatten Plan, the British Parliament passed the Indian Independence Bill, 1947. India was made independent by the Act of 1947. It was provided that from 15 August 1947 England would relinquish all control over India. India was divided into two dominions – India and Pakistan. The powers and privileges of the British Government in India were to be transferred to the representatives of the two Dominions of India and Pakistan. Henceforward, the relations of England with India and Pakistan were to be handled by the Commonwealth Secretary of England. India and Pakistan could have their separate Constituent Assemblies. Each of these Assemblies was given unlimited powers to frame a Constitution for its respective country according to its needs. The Indian States were given the option to join either the Indian Dominion or Pakistan. The title of Viceroy was to be dropped and henceforth he was to be called only Governor-General.

The Indian Independence Act, according to Lord Samuel, "was an event unique in history – a treaty of peace without war". Never before had such a large territory and such a vast population achieved its independence through a piece of legislation. On the midnight of 14-15 August, in terms of the

Indian Independence Act, power was transferred to Indian hands. British rule came to an end. India became free. The dream of centuries was fulfilled through not fully. Speaking on the historic occasion in the Constituent Assembly of India, Pandit Jawaharlal Nehru referred to the Pledge of Independence first taken on 26 January 1930, and said:

> Long years ago we made a tryst with destiny, and now the time comes when we shall redeem our pledge, not wholly or in full measure, but very substantially. At the stroke of the midnight hour, when the world sleeps, India will awake to life and freedom. A moment comes, which comes but rarely in history, when we step out from the old to the new, when an age ends, and when the soul of a nation, long suppressed finds utterance.

Freedom brings responsibility. Independent India faced myriads of problems, many of them stupendous. The masses were full of hope in the future and confidence in the leadership. Independence Day on 15 August was naturally celebrated with great enthusiasm all over the country. However, the atmosphere of festivity could not last long. The very next day news of fresh communal riots started pouring in and the nation was submerged in gloom.

The partition did not solve any problems. In fact, it brought in its wake fresh human problems, some of them of staggering dimensions. Unending caravans of refugees poured into India both from Eastern and Western Wings of Pakistan bringing in millions. The Government of India had to shoulder the heavy responsibility of rehabilitating these millions of men and women and children who had been uprooted from their hearths and homes and after losing their all had sought refuge, relief and succour in India. They had to be fed, housed and found some employment and above all, emotionally rehabilitated before freedom could begin to have any meaning for them.

India's independence was still not complete. India was still a dominion with a Governor-General appointed by the British Crown. She continued to be governed by an Act of British Parliament – the Government of India Act, 1935 – as suitably modified and adapted in the context of another Act of the British

Parliament – the Indian Independence Act, 1947. The free people of India had not so far given to themselves a Constitution; the Constituent Assembly was on the job. And, through the Constitution, we had to establish the political system of our choice to govern ourselves.

Framing a new Constitution for India – the first Constitution of the people, by the people and for the people of India – was one of the most formidable and challenging tasks. The Constituent Assembly had to tackle many fundamental issues. On their satisfactory resolution depended the entire future of the new nation. It was no mean achievement that within a period of less than three years, the founding fathers succeeded in evolving a Constitution acceptable throughout the length and breadth of this vast and populous country and one capable of salvaging and strengthening the threads of national unity in the midst of the multiplicity of religions, races and languages and all the regional, social, economic and political diversities. The Constitution was adopted on 26 November 1949. Two months later, on 26 January 1950, it came into force. The pledge of complete independence was fulfilled. The Indian Republic was born. A new democracy began taking shape.

3

POLITICAL SYSTEM
AS ESTABLISHED BY THE CONSTITUTION

Principles of Indian Polity

When the founding fathers sat down in the name of 'We, the People of India' to frame a Constitution and thereby establish a political system suited to our ethos, needs and aspirations, they resolved to constitute India into a Sovereign, Democratic Republic wherein shall be secured to "all its citizen" justice, liberty and equality. Justice was defined as social, economic and political. Liberty included liberty of thought, expression, belief, faith and worship, and equality meant equality of status and of opportunity. Fraternity was important for 'assuring the dignity of the individual and unity of the nation'.

During the Emergency, by the Forty-second amendment of 1976, the words "socialist", "secular" and "integrity of the nation" were added to the Preamble along with a new article on Fundamental Duties. Our supreme constitutional values, therefore, may now be said to be:

- Sovereignty
- Socialism
- Secularism
- Democracy
- Republicanism
- Justice
- Liberty
- Equality
- Fraternity
- Individual dignity, and
- Unity and integrity of the nation

These were the fundamental values which the founding fathers wanted to foster among the people and which they hoped would guide all those who from time to time would be called upon to work the Constitution. These values were further elaborated in the Fundamental Rights, Directive Principles of State Policy and Fundamental Duties of citizens.

Human Rights

Representing the crystallisation of the values and concepts held dear in India's varied and rich cultural heritage and having its roots deep in the motivational forces of the national struggle for independence and coming closely on the heels of the Universal Declaration of Human Rights, inclusion of a bill of rights in the Constitution of India accorded with the contemporary democratic and humanitarian temper and constitutional practice in other nations of the world. Also, it reflected in no small measure the anxiety of the founding fathers to incorporate and implement the basic principles enunciated in the Universal Declaration. In fact, within a year of the adoption of the Universal Declaration of Human Rights, the Assembly incorporated in the Constitution of India the substance of most of these rights. The two parts – the Fundamental Rights and the Directive Principles – of the Constitution of India between them covered almost the entire field of the Universal Declaration of Human Rights.

The rights of all individuals were sought to be protected by an independent judiciary, provision of judicial review of legislation and making the validity of all laws subject to fundamental rights and assigning to the individual the right to move the highest court for the protection of one's constitutional rights contained in the Fundamental Rights chapter. In fact, it is the values enshrined in the Preamble, the Fundamental Rights, the Directive Principles and (subsequently added) Fundamental Duties chapters that permeate the entire Constitution. Parliamentary democracy, adult franchise, independent judiciary, single citizenship, distribution of powers between the Union and the States, all flow from these values.

Adult Franchise

Dr. Ambedkar said in the Constituent Assembly that "by parliamentary democracy we mean `one man, one vote". Almost as an act of faith, the founding fathers decided to opt for universal adult suffrage with every adult Indian without any distinction at once having equal voting rights. This was particularly remarkable in the context of the vast poverty and illiteracy of the Indian populace. Even in the advanced democracies of the West, franchise was extended only gradually.

Our Constitution ensures Universal Adult Franchise to all citizens. Elections to the Lok Sabha, the State Assemblies and to the three-tier gram panchayats are held on the basis of Universal Adult Franchise. Every adult citizen irrespective of caste, religion or sex enjoys equal rights to vote. The age of voting right was changed from 21 years to 18 years as per the 61st amendment of the Constitution in 1988. Only those found guilty of certain election offences and those who are mentally unsound are denied voting rights.

Socialism

In the Preamble as amended, the highest pride of place was accorded to the term 'Socialist' which was mentioned next only to 'Sovereign'. Again, 'Justice, social, economic and political' was put higher than 'Liberty', etc. Also, social and economic justice preceded political justice. The Directive Principles specifically spoke of the state being guided by principles of governance and securing a 'social order' in which 'justice, social, economic and political' informed all institutions of the national life, striving to minimise inequalities in income, ensuring distribution of ownership and control of material resources, preventing concentration of wealth and means of production, providing equal wages for equal work, providing for the right to work and education and such other principles from the book of 'Socialism'. The founding fathers were conscious of the fact that mere political democracy, *i.e.* getting the right to vote once in five years or so was meaningless unless it was accompanied by social and economic democracy. Political equality was not possible unless men were made equal on the social and economic plane as well. Right to vote for a hungry and illiterate man without clothing and shelter meant little. Dr. Ambedkar said:

> We do not want merely to lay down a mechanism to enable people to come and capture power. The Constitution also wishes to lay down an ideal before those who would be forming the government. That ideal is of economic democracy.

Socio-economic justice implied an order under which the basic needs of the common man were fullfilled, where all without any discrimination would enjoy fundamental human freedoms and equality of opportunity. Nehru had told the Constituent Assembly that its first task was 'to free India through a new constitution, to feed the starving people, and to clothe the naked masses, and give to every Indian the fullest opportunity to develop himself according to his capacity'. The Constitution was relevant only as an instrument of social change. A Constitution which was not able to solve the problem of 'the poor and the starving' was merely ' a paper Constitution – useless and purposeless'.

Secularism

The Constitution of India as given to us by the founding fathers did not recognise any state religion. It embodied the principles of non-discrimination on grounds of religion among the fundamental rights *vide* articles 14, 15, 16 and 19. By article 25 it guaranteed that all persons were 'equally entitled to freedom of conscience and the right freely to profess, practice and propagate religion'. Every religious denomination was free to manage its religious affairs (article 26). No one could be compelled to pay for promotion or maintenance of any religion or to take part in any religious instruction; wholly state-funded educational institutions were barred from imparting any religious instruction (articles 27 and 28). The language, script and culture of minorities were protected and no citizen was to be denied admission to any educational institution on the ground only of religion, *etc.* (article 29). Also article 30 ensured the right of minorities to establish and administer their own educational institutions.

Thus, the Constitution could be said to have sought to establish a secular order under which the dominant religion of the majority of the population did not enjoy any special privileges or preferential treatment at the hands of the state and the religious rights of the minorities were protected in different ways. Enunciation of the values of equality, justice and liberty and provision of universal adult franchise for all citizens without any distinction of race, religion, caste, sex or place of birth with special rights and safeguards for minorities was the answer of the founding fathers to all divisive and parochial problems of conflicting religious, linguistic, racial, regional, caste or other ethnic group loyalties.

The partition had taken place on communal lines. However, it was to their great credit that even after agreeing to the partition as the price for freedom, the Indian leaders did not accept the theory that the Hindus and Muslims were two different nations. As Karan Singh puts it, they did not succumb to the temptation of adopting a 'reactive constitution'. On the other hand, they went out of their way, bent over backwards to ensure that every Indian citizen, regardless of his or her religious orientation was treated equally and enjoyed full and equal freedoms and rights. They even went one step further and gave to the religious, ethnic and other minorities certain special rights which were not available to the majority.

The Indian variant of secularism gives equal status to all religions without state patronage to any one religion. The founding fathers had hoped that the Constitution would bring about a social revolution. For them it was, above all, an instrument of social engineering and nation-building.

Building the Nation

The highest aim in the minds of the founding fathers was that of building India as a strong united nation. The concept of a nation as a human aggregate of homogeneous people descending from the same racial ancestry, speaking the same language, following the same religion and living within the same territorial boundaries is both a myth and an abstraction. Nations are made, not born. While strictly speaking, there must be a nation before a nation-state can take shape, in actual practice, many of the present-day nation-states would fail in this test. India was no exception.

In India's traditionally multi-religious, multi-racial, multi-lingual plural society united by a common history, civilisational identity and territory, ethnicity may cut across the dividing lines. In fact, the vast majority of its citizens have multiple identities. The same person may belong to different groups depending upon the distinguishing criterion of religion, language, community, etc. Since society thus gets divided both horizontally and vertically, there are hardly any monoliths left. Every religion has its sects, languages and dialects, and castes and subcastes. Members of almost every religious group would be divided by language, region and caste just as members of every linguistic group may be divided by religion, region, caste, etc. Almost every Indian has identities in terms of his religion, caste, language, state/region etc.

Under the special variant of Indian pluralism, the majority-minority syndrome does not apply to ethnic groups. In states like Nagaland, Arunachal Pradesh, Meghalaya, for instance, the tribal populations are in majority but for that reason, they cannot lose their ethnic group status. Also, the same person may belong both to a majority and a minority, *e.g.* one may be in majority by religion and in minority by language or *vice-versa*. What divides, also unites. Religious affinity would unite co-religionists in various linguistic groups while at the same time dividing each of the linguistic groups, *e.g.*, language may separate a Tamil from a Bengali, but it brings together Tamil-speaking Hindus, Muslims and others under the unifying language umbrella. Similarly, while religion may divide the Hindus and Muslims, it may at the same time unite co-religionists in different linguistic groups.

The national struggle for freedom strengthened the unifying forces and created a strong all-India national consciousness. Some scholars have suggested that India could be called a civilisational national unit right from the most ancient times. We could define India's political identity even today in terms of a 'civilisation state' rather than a 'nation-state'. It is felt that Western scholars who are more used to uni-linear historical models of homogeneity, find it very difficult to appreciate the most characteristic Indian reality which has been that of a special pluralism situation leading to unity and strength – rich variety of hues blending homogeneously into one whole. Through the ages, culture has been the greatest integrating force while politics has tended more to divide. It was so in the past. It is no different today.

Nevertheless, the fact remains that within India, society was always highly stratified. Rich in diversities of various sorts, India was never an ethnic monolith inhabited by people united by a commonality of race, religion and language. It had always been multi-ethnic, multi-racial, multi-lingual and multi-religious. The rich plurality of Indian society was partly due to her openness and tradition of tolerance. India could take pride in being the country where almost all religions of the world were represented and thrived, where the Jews were never persecuted or hounded out and where the Parsees (Zoroastrians) had found refuge and honour. Occasional tensions and strife notwithstanding, different groups had lived here together, cooperating with each other and enriching the cultural mosaic of Indian unity.

India had to pay a very heavy price for independence. Leaders of the Indian revolution failed to prevent the vivisection of the country. Before leaving India, not only had the British divided her between India and Pakistan but they had also left behind the legacy of some 600 and odd princely states. The relationship between these states and the British Government in India was governed by what had come to be known as paramountcy under which the state recognised the suzerainty of the British power over the whole of India. By providing for the lapse of paramountcy, the British had created a situation fraught with many dangerous consequences for the country's future. The 600 odd princely states were free to join any one of the two Dominions or perhaps to even declare their independence. The threatened balkanisation was however prevented as a result of the astute handling of the situation by Sardar Patel. With great tact and superb statesmanship he succeeded in integrating with the rest of India all the princely states which were geographically contiguous with India with the exception of Junagarh, Hyderabad and Jammu & Kashmir. Instruments of accession were signed with them all before 15 August, 1947. Soon after, Indian forces had to be used to defend the freedom and honour of the people inhabiting the princely states of Hyderabad, Junagarh and Jammu & Kashmir. If the integration of states had not been accomplished, not only would India have become divided into over 600 units, but also some one-third of India's territory and some one-fourth of her population in the princely states would have remained deprived of all the benefits of freedom and democracy.

Unity of the nation was further sought to be promoted by the Constitution (including its later amendments) fully protecting its rich diversity. Thus, articles 370 to 371 H laid down special provisions for the States of Jammu and Kashmir, Nagaland, Sikkim, Assam, Manipur, Arunachal Pradesh, *etc.* Under these provisions, *inter alia,* the religious or social practices, tribal customary laws and procedures, rights on ownership and transfer of land, *etc.*, were protected. Special provisions (part XVI of the Constitution) were made for certain classes like the Scheduled Castes, Scheduled Tribes and other backward classes. Also, language and cultural identities of different groups were recognised for promotion and protection by the Constitution.

Citizenship: There existed no concept of Indian citizenship before 26 November 1949. Until then, those of us who lived in British India were under the Crown and as such British subjects governed by the British Nationality Acts and those of us who came from any of the princely States, had the status of British protected persons. Citizenship provisions in the Constitution laid down the law in regard to who would be citizens of India at the time of the commencement of the Constitution. These included provisions for Citizenship (i) by domicile (ii) of migrants from and to Pakistan, and (iii) of Indians residing in foreign countries. The mode of acquisition and termination of citizenship was left by the Constitution for regulation by Parliament by law. Parliament passed the Indian Citizenship Act, 1955 which has been amended from time to time. The latest amendments in 2003 and 2005 have provided for dual citizenship and overseas citizenship. Within certain limitations, persons of Indian origin settled abroad have been allowed benefits of Indian citizenship if the countries of their adoption themselves permit dual citizenship.

It was in keeping with the aim of building an integrated Indian nation and a united fraternity that the Constitution-makers decided to provide for a single Indian citizenship with accompanying rights, benefits and obligations throughout the territory of the Union. All citizens irrespective of the State in which they were born are citizens of India and have the same rights and duties all over the country without any discrimination subject to only a few special protections in case of Jammu & Kashmir, tribal areas etc. and the power of Parliament under article 16 to prescribe residence within a State or Union Territory as a necessary qualification for certain classes of employment under the State or Union Territory. Also, all Indian citizens travelling abroad do so on Indian passport and represent Indian identity and loyalty to one entity that is the Republic of India.

Emergency Provisions

Again, to protect the unity and security of India, Part XVIII of the Constitution permits the state to suspend some of the civil liberties and the application of certain federal principles during states of emergency. The Constitution provides for three categories of emergencies: a threat by "war or external aggression" or by " armed rebellion" (National Emergency); a "failure of constitutional machinery" in a state (President's Rule); and a threat to the financial security or credit of the nation or a part of it (Financial Emergency).

National emergency proclamations have been issued three

times since the commencement of the Constitution. The first was in 1962 during the border war with China. Another was in 1971 when India went to war against Pakistan following Pakistani aggression. The result was the independence of East Pakistan, which became Bangladesh. In 1975 the third Emergency was imposed in response to an alleged threat by "internal disturbances" stemming from the political opposition to Indira Gandhi. President's Rule in the States has been imposed frequently – over 100 times – and it is often criticised as being politically motivated. Financial Emergency has never been imposed so far.

Choice of Model

The adoption of a democratic polity, parliamentary government and representative legislative institutions after independence from colonial rule did not mean that the British institutions as such were being transplanted in India. They were actually institutions of the colonial model as it had developed in India. Parliamentary institutions as we know them today, had had an organic growth on the Indian soil. They grew through many relentless struggles for freedom from foreign rule and successive doses of constitutional reforms grudgingly and haltingly conceded by the British rulers.

Even during the early days of the freedom struggle, one of the nationalists' chief demands used to be that the British should concede to their Indian subjects the same institutions and freedoms that they themselves enjoyed back home. The seeds of the colonial model of the parliamentary system in India can be traced back to this demand. Founding fathers of the Indian Constitution were fascinated by British parliamentary institutions and aspired to have the same for themselves in India. They said goodbye to British rule, but embraced the colonial model of governance. It is not surprising, therefore, that the Constitution of free India reproduced large parts of the Government of India Act, 1935, which was the British Parliament's blueprint and charter for dividing India. As K.M Munshi put it:

> We must not forget a very important fact that during the last hundred years, Indian public life has largely drawn upon the traditions of British Constitutional Law. Most of us have looked up to the British model as the best. For the last thirty or forty years, some kind of responsibility has been introduced in the governance of this country. Our constitutional traditions have become Parliamentary. After this experience, why should we go back upon the tradition that has been built for over a hundred years and buy a novel experience? [*C.A. Deb.*, Vol. VII, p. 984]

Replying to criticism in the Constituent Assembly, Dr. Ambedkar similarly said:

> As to the accusation that the Draft Constitution has produced a good part of the provisions of the Government of India Act, 1935, I make no apologies. There is nothing to be ashamed of in borrowing. It involves no plagiarism. Nobody holds any patent rights in the fundamental ideas of a Constitution. [*C.A. Deb.*, Vol. VII, p. 37]

The founding fathers thought that for a country of India's size, diversity, background and needs, a system of representative parliamentary democracy with universal adult franchise would be the most suited.

Structure of Indian Polity

Presidential-Parliamentary

India is a Republic and the head is the President in whom all the executive power vests and in whose name it is to be exercised. He is also the Supreme Commander of the armed forces. It has been held, however, that unlike the U.S. President, our President is only a nominal or constitutional head of the executive; he acts only with the aid and advice of the real political executive which is the Council of Ministers. The Ministers are collectively responsible to the popular House of Parliament *i.e.* the Lok Sabha. Thus, following the British pattern, the Constitution of India has basically adopted, both at the Union and State levels, the parliamentary system of government with ministerial responsibility to the popular House as against the U.S. system of Presidential Government with separation of powers and a nearly irremovable President as the Chief Executive for a fixed term. In the U.S. system, the President chooses his team of ministers from among the citizens at large and the ministers are not members of the legislature while in the Parliamentary System, the Ministers are from Parliament and remain part of it and responsible to its House of the People. The Parliamentary System may be said to be laying greater stress on the concept of the responsibility of the executive while the Presidential system obviously promotes more the stability of the executive.

However, there are several fundamental differences and departures. To name a few: the U.K. Constitution is unitary,

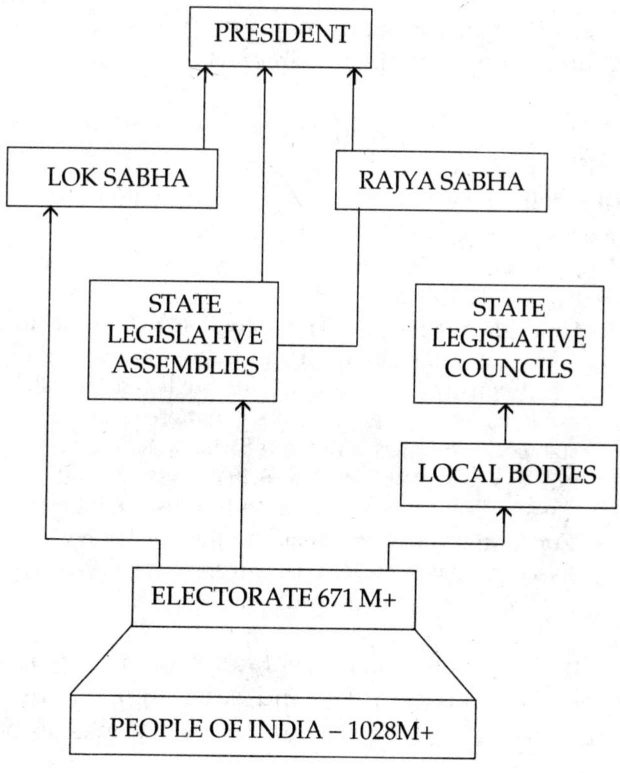

while ours is largely federal. They are a monarchy with a hereditary King while we are a republic with an elected President, unlike the British we have a written constitution and our Parliament, therefore, is not sovereign and legislation passed by it is subject to judicial review. Our Constitution includes a charter of justiciable fundamental rights which are enforceable by the Courts not only against the executive but also against the legislature.

The founding fathers preferred the parliamentary form because they had some experience of operating it and there were advantages in continuing established institutions. After a long struggle for responsible government and against arbitrary executive authority, they were naturally allergic to a fixed term irremovable executive. In a highly pluralistic society with India's size and diversity and with many pulls of various kinds, they believed that the parliamentary form was the most suited for accommodating a variety of interests and building a united India.

Discussing the problem of making a choice between the U.S. Presidential model and the British parliamentary model, both of which were democratic, Dr. Ambedkar had said in the Constituent Assembly:

> A democratic executive must satisfy two conditions: 1) it must be a stable executive and 2) it must be a responsible executive. Unfortunately, it has not been possible so far to devise a system which can ensure both in equal degree. You can have a system which can give you more stability but less responsibility or you can have a system which gives you more responsibility but less stability. The American and the Swiss systems give more stability but less responsibility. The British System on the other hand gives you more responsibility but less stability....The Draft Constitution in recommending the Parliamentary system of Executive has preferred more responsibility to more stability. [*C.A. Deb.*, Vol. VII, p. 32]

In the British parliamentary system, Parliament was supposed to be supreme and sovereign. There were no limitations on its powers, at least in theory, inasmuch as there was no written constitution and the Judiciary had no power of judicial review of legislation. In the U.S. system, the Supreme Court with its power of judicial review and of interpreting the Constitution had assumed supremacy.

In India, the Constitution had arrived at a middle course and a compromise between the British sovereignty of Parliament and American judicial supremacy. We are governed by the rule of law and judicial review of administrative action is an essential part of rule of law. Thus, courts can determine not only the constitutionality of the law but also the procedural part of administrative action [*State of Bihar v. Subhash Singh*, AIR 1997 SC 1390]. But, since we have a written constitution and the powers and functions of every organ are defined and delimited by the Constitution, there is no question of any organ, not even Parliament, being sovereign. Both Parliament and the Supreme Court are supreme in their respective spheres. While the Supreme Court may declare a law passed by Parliament *ultra vires* as being violative of the Constitution, Parliament may within certain restrictions amend most parts of the Constitution.

Centralised or Decentralised

Generally power is exercised in two ways—centralised and decentralised. Democratic societies give preference to decentralised way of exercising power. It is giving strength and priority to the local administrative system. The Panchayati Raj system in India has this objective in view.

India is a nation with a large population, wide geographical areas and a lot of varieties. It is not possible for such a nation to meet the requirements of the people effectively, merely with a centralised system of administration. There has been an attempt to give more powers and responsibilities to the local self-government institutions through the 73rd and 74th amendments of the Constitution. With some 3.2 million elected rulers from Panchayats to Parliament, it becomes possible to make the democratic governance more effective. [See Chapter 8. 'Decentralisation and Local Government]

Federal-Unitary

It is difficult to put our political system in any strict mould of a federal or unitary type; it has features of both. Reasons for this unique unitary federal mix are to be found in the constitutional history of India, the sheer size of the country and the nature of her complex diversities based on religion, language, region, culture etc. [See Chapter 7. 'Indian Federalism']

Respective Powers and Functions of the Three Organs of the State

The most cardinal function of the political system is to establish the three organs of the State – the Executive, the Legislature and the Judiciary, to demarcate their responsibilities and spheres of jurisdiction and authority, and to regulate their relationship with each other and with the people. In a traditional simplistic manner, it may be said that the job of the Legislature is to make laws, the executive executes and administers the laws, and the judiciary interprets laws and adjudicates disputes in accordance with the laws. The Union government is divided into three distinct but interrelated branches: legislative, executive, and judicial. As in the British parliamentary model, the leadership of the executive is drawn from and remains responsible to the legislative body.

Executive

Under the British system, the head of the State is the hereditary monarch. But, as the relationship between the King and the Parliament has evolved over the centuries, real political and executive power has come to be vested in the Cabinet while the King has become a constitutional, nominal or ceremonial head only. The doctrine of ministerial responsibility means that for every act of State it is the ministers who are responsible to the people through their elected representatives in Parliament. We, in India, do not have a monarchy. Also, we are not a small unitary State like the United Kingdom (U.K.). We are a large republic and a Union of States like the United States with an elected President at the head of the Republic in whom all executive power of the Union vests. We are thus in the unique position of being at once a parliamentary polity and a Republic with a President. [See Chapter 4. 'The Executive']

Legislature

The supreme legislature of the Union of India is called the Parliament. The Parliament consists of the President and the two Houses: the Rajya Sabha (Council of States) and the Lok Sabha (House of the People). Article 79 begins by saying that there shall be a Parliament for the Union which means that there must always be a Parliament for the Union. Of the three constituents of Parliament, only the Lok Sabha is subject to dissolution. The Rajya Sabha is a permanent or continuing House and one-third of its members retire at the expiration of every second year, thus, making the term of an individual member as six years.

The President has a specific authority with respect to the function of the legislative branch. The President is authorised to convene Parliament and give his assent to all parliamentary bills before they become law. The President is empowered to address either house or both houses together, and to require attendance of all of its members. The President also may send messages to either house with respect to a pending bill or any other matter. The President addresses the first session of Parliament each year. [See Chapter 5. 'Parliament and State Legislatures']

Parliament and the Executive

After a new Lok Sabha is duly elected and constituted, the President invites the leader of the party or parties commanding the support of more than half of the members of the Lok Sabha, to form the government. While the Prime Minister – not necessarily always – usually is a member of the Lok Sabha, the Ministers are drawn from both Houses of Parliament. A person other than a Member of Parliament may also be appointed as Minister, but he has to vacate the office after six months unless, in the meanwhile, he manages to get himself elected to either of the two Houses. Since the Council of Ministers is collectively responsible to Lok Sabha (article 75), Ministers are under a constitutional obligation to resign collectively as soon as they lose the confidence of Lok Sabha.

The scheme of the Constitution thus represents a real fusion of the highest executive and legislative authorities. The relationship between the Executive and Legislature is one that is most intimate and ideally does not admit of any antagonism or dichotomy. The two are not visualised as competing centres of power but as inseparable partners or coparceners in the business of government. Strictly speaking, Parliamentary system of government should mean Government by Parliament. But, the Parliament is a large body. It does not and cannot itself govern. The Council of Ministers may in a sense be described as the grand executive committee of Parliament charged with the responsibility of governance on behalf of the parent body. In other words, the Executive is not a separate or outside body. Inasmuch as the Council of Ministers is drawn from and remains part of Parliament and responsible to Lok Sabha, the relationship may be said to be that of a part to the whole and one of interdependence. There is, however, a clear distinction between the functions of the Executive and the functions of Parliament (article 75). The Parliament is to deliberate, discuss, legislate, advise, criticize and ventilate public grievances. Also, it has a legitimatizational role.The Executive is to govern, albeit on behalf of Parliament and the People.

While the Executive has almost unlimited right to initiate and formulate legislative and financial proposals before Parliament and to give effect to approved policies unfettered and unhindered by Parliament; the latter has the unlimited power to call for information, to discuss, to scrutinize and to put the seal of popular approval on proposals made by the Executive. The Executive remains responsible and the administration accountable to Parliament. The function of Parliament is to exercise political and financial control over the Executive and to ensure parliamentary surveillance of administration.

Judiciary

The Constitution of India establishes an independent judiciary with powers of judicial review. The High Courts and the Supreme Court form a single integrated judicial structure with jurisdiction over all laws—Union, State, Civil, Criminal or Constitutional. The judiciary not only adjudicates disputes and acts as the custodian of individual rights and freedoms but may from time to time need to interpret the Constitution and review legislation to determine its *vires* vis a vis the Constitution. The word of the Supreme Court is the final law of the land. The Supreme Court also functions as the arbiter of any disputes in regard to jurisdiction and distribution of powers between the States or between the Union and the States. Provisions in regard to the judiciary are contained in Part V, Chapter IV titled 'The Union Judiciary' and Part VI, Chapters V and VI titled 'The High Courts in the States' and 'Subordinate Courts' respectively. It is, however important to emphasize that unlike other federal systems, for example, that of the United States, we do not have separate hierarchies of federal and State Courts. For the entire republic of India, there is one unified judicial system one hierarchy of courts with the Supreme Court as the highest or the apex court and as the only arbiter in matters of relations between the Union and the States and the States *inter se.*

Parliament and the Judiciary

Parliament has the power to make laws regulating the constitution, organisation, jurisdiction and powers of the Courts. It was laid down in the Constitution that the number of Judges other than the Chief Justice would not be more than seven. The Parliament was, however, empowered to prescribe a larger number of Judges by law (article 124). Under our Constitution, the Parliament may by law:

i. extend the jurisdiction of a High Court to, or exclude the jurisdiction of a High Court from, any Union territory;
ii. establish a common High Court for two or more States or for two or more States and a Union territory; and
iii. constitute a High Court for a Union territory or declare any

Court in any such territory to be a High Court for all or any of the purposes of the Constitution (Art.241).

A judge of the Supreme Court or any High Court can be removed from his Office by the President, only on a joint address passed by both Houses of Parliament with a special majority. Parliament is not empowered to discuss the conduct of any Judge of the Supreme Court or of a High Court in the discharge of his duties except in the case of such a motion.

Parliament may by law provide for the establishment of an administrative tribunal for the Union and a separate administrative tribunal for each State or for two or more States. The law made under the provision may specify the jurisdiction and powers of the tribunals. Such law may exclude the jurisdiction of all Courts, except the jurisdiction of the Supreme Court under article 136, with respect to certain specified matters (articles 323A and 323B). Further, the Constitution empowers Parliament to create an all India judicial service which shall not include any post inferior to that of a district judge [articles 312(1) and (3)].

The validity of any proceedings in either House of Parliament cannot be questioned before a court of law on the ground of any alleged irregularity of procedure [articles 122(1) and 212(1)] [*Kihoto v. Zachilhu,* AIR 1993 SC 412]. The presiding officer of each House or any other officer or Member of Parliament who is for the time being vested with the powers to regulate procedure, or to enforce or carry out the decision of either House of Parliament, is not subject to the jurisdiction of the courts in exercise of those powers [articles 122(2) and 105(3)].

No member of Parliament is liable to any proceedings in any court in respect of anything said or any vote given by him in Parliament or any committee thereof. Also, publication of any report, paper, votes or proceedings of Parliament by or under authority of a House of Parliament is protected against any court proceedings [articles 105(2) and 194(2)]. [See Chapter 6. 'The Judicial System']

Conclusion

The Indian political system is unique in many ways. It cannot be fitted in any particular mould or model. It is a blend of the federal and unitary and presidential and parliamentary. It attempts a balance between the fundamental rights of the individual on the one hand and the socio economic interests of the people and security of the State on the other. Also, it presents a *via media* between the principles of parliamentary sovereignty and judicial supremacy. It represents a real fusion of the highest executive and legislative authorities. The relationship between the executive and the legislature is one that is most intimate and ideally does not admit any antagonism or dichotomy. The two are not visualised as competing centres of power but as inseparable partners or co-parcners in the business of government.

The judiciary in India is also an authority co-ordinate with the Legislature and the Executive. Parliament has the power to make laws regulating the constitution, organisation, jurisdiction and powers of the Courts. According to the Constitution, Chief Justice and Judges of the Supreme Court and High Courts are to be appointed by the President. They cannot be removed from the office except through a process prescribed in the Constitution. The Parliament may by law provide for the establishment of an administrative tribunal for each State or for two or more States.

The Parliament is not empowered to discuss the conduct of any judge of the Supreme Court or a High Court in the discharge of his duties except in the case of a motion for presenting address to the President praying for the removal of a judge. The validity of any proceedings in either House of Parliament cannot be questioned before a court of law on the ground of any alleged irregularity of procedure.

Judiciary plays a very important role under its power of judicial review. The courts may declare a law made by Parliament *ultra vires* the Constitution and as such, null and void and unenforceable. Article 13 of the Constitution clearly prohibits the making of any law by Parliament or State

Legislature or by any other authority, which may be inconsistent with or in derogation of any of the Fundamental Rights contained in Part III of the Constitution.

The basic function of the courts is to adjudicate disputes between individuals, between individuals and the State, between the States and between the Union and the States and while so adjudicating, the courts may be required to interpret the provisions of the Constitution and the laws. And, the interpretation given by the Supreme Court becomes the law honoured by all courts of the land.

Parliament in India is not as supreme as the British Parliament where in principle Parliament is supreme and until recently, no judicial review of legislation was permitted. At the same time judiciary in India is not as supreme as in the United States of America which recognises virtually no limit on the scope of judicial review.

4

THE EXECUTIVE

GOVERNMENT AND ADMINISTRATION

The Executive is that branch of the government or that organ of the State which executes, implements and administers the laws enacted by the Legislature. In a narrower sense, it is also the body that rules or governs and is often equated with government itself.

THE UNION EXECUTIVE

Under article 73 of the Constitution, the executive power of the Union extends to all matters with respect to which Parliament may make laws and to the exercise of all powers that accrue to the Government of India from any international treaty or agreement. It is important to remember that all executive power has to be exercised in accordance with the Constitution.

THE PRESIDENT

Position and Functions

Article 52 of the Constitution says that there shall be a President of India. The position of the President in our polity is one of the highest honour, dignity and prestige. As Nehru said in the Constituent Assembly, it was not intended to make the President of India a mere figurehead. All executive power of the Union is vested in him and is to be exercised by him either directly or through officers subordinate to him in accordance with the Constitution on the aid and advice of the Council of Ministers. 'Officers subordinate' are supposed to include Ministers (*Emperor v. Srinath*, AIR 1945 PC 163). All executive action of the Government of India is taken in his name. The Supreme Command of the Defence Forces is vested in him and is to be exercised in accordance with law (articles 53 and 77). The President appoints the Prime Minister and on his advice other Ministers. All the Ministers hold office during the pleasure of the President (article 75).

Along with the two Houses of Parliament, the President is an integral part of Parliament. This is in keeping with the principle that in a parliamentary system of government, the executive is part of Parliament. The President summons the two Houses to meet, prorogues their sittings, and may dissolve the Lok Sabha (article 85). He addresses the members of the two Houses assembled together at the beginning of the first session each year and after each General Election. The President may also, otherwise, send messages to Houses of Parliament or address either or both of them. All Bills after being passed by the two Houses of Parliament must receive the assent of the President in order to become laws. Bills belonging to certain categories (*e.g.* money bills) can be introduced and proceeded with only with the President's recommendation (articles 79, 85 87, 111 and 117). When during the Ninth Lok Sabha an amendment proposing pension to members of Parliament after only a year's service was allowed to be introduced and passed without President's recommendation, President Venkataraman did not give his assent to the Bill.

When both Houses of Parliament are not in session and the President is satisfied about the need for immediate action, he can promulgate ordinances which have the same force and effect as laws passed by Parliament (article 123). These are in the nature of interim or temporary legislation. For, their continuance is subject to parliamentary approval and enactment of laws to replace the ordinances. The President's power to issue ordinances extends to only those matters on which Parliament can make laws. The Supreme Court has upheld the legitimacy and validity of the President's power to issue ordinances. [*A.K. Roy v. Union of India*, AIR 1982 SC 710; *R.K. Garg v. Union of India*, AIR 1981 SC 2139].

There are certain other functions which the President is required to perform under the Constitution in relation to Parliament. He appoints the Speaker *pro tem* of Lok Sabha and an acting Chairman of Rajya Sabha as and when the need arises. He summons the joint sitting of both Houses in case of final disagreement between them on a Bill. The President causes to be laid, every year, before Parliament, the Budget of the government, referred to in the Constitution as the "annual financial statement" and certain other reports of constitutional functionaries like the Comptroller and Auditor General of India, Finance Commission, Union Public Service Commission, and the Commissions for Scheduled Castes and Scheduled Tribes and Backward Classes. He may nominate not more than two members of the Anglo Indian Community to Lok Sabha, if he is of the opinion that the community is not adequately represented in the House. The President also nominates 12 members to the Rajya Sabha from amongst persons having special knowledge or practical experience in respect of such matters as literature, science, art and social service. Besides, he is empowered to decide, after obtaining the opinion of the Election Commission, whether any member duly elected attracts the disqualifications laid down in article 108 of the Constitution. His decision in the matter is final.

All the high functionaries of the State including the judges of the Supreme Court and of the High Courts, the Attorney General of India, the Comptroller and Auditor General of India, the Governors etc. are appointed by the President (articles 76, 124, 148, 155 and 217).

Under article 72, the President has the power to grant pardons, reprieves, respites or remissions of punishment or to suspend, remit or commute the sentence of any person in all cases where the punishment has been awarded by a Court Martial, is for an offence against a Union law, or is a sentence of death. The power of the President under article 72 is independent of the judiciary. He does not function as a court of appeal. The idea is to enable correction of any judicial error. Also, the President may decide to give relief from what may appear to him to be too harsh a punishment. The President, however, cannot be compelled to give a hearing to a petitioner. The courts cannot interfere with the decisions of the President on merits, but they can look into whether the President has considered all relevant materials. [*Hukam Singh v. State of Punjab*, AIR 1975 P&H 902; *Harbans v. State of U.P.*, AIR 1982 S.C. 849; *Kuljit v. Lt. Governor*, AIR 1982 S.C. 774; *Maru v. Union of India*, AIR 1980 S.C. 2147; *Godse v. State of Maharastra*, AIR 1961 SC 600; *Nanavati v. State of Bombay*, AIR 1961 S.C. 122; *State of Punjab v. Joginder Singh*, (1990) GLJ 1464 (SC)].

In the exercise of all his functions, the President has to act in accordance with the advice of the Council of Ministers (article 74). In the exercise of the function of granting pardons *etc.* also, the President is taken to be acting only on the advice of the Council of Ministers.

Under article 352, the President may proclaim a state of emergency in the whole or any part of India if he is satisfied that a grave situation exists whereby the security of India or part of its territory is threatened by war or external aggression or armed rebellion. Under article 354, the President may restrict or prohibit the distribution of revenues. When a proclamation of emergency is in operation, the President may suspend the enforcement of fundamental rights (article 359). Under article 356, in case of failure of constitutional machinery in any State, the President may impose by proclamation President's rule in that State. Article 360 empowers the President to declare financial emergency. Thus, the emergency powers of the President are drastic and far reaching.

To sum up, the President has (1) executive powers to be exercised by him directly or through officers; (2) powers to appoint high functionaries of the State including judges of the Supreme Court and High Courts; (3) military powers as the Supreme Commander of the armed forces with the authority to declare war and peace; (4) power to grant pardon, reprieve *etc.*; (5) diplomatic powers including appointment of ambassadors and receiving the credentials of foreign diplomatic representatives; (6) legislative powers including powers to summon and prorogue Houses and dissolve Lok Sabha, assent to Bills *etc.* and issue ordinances having the force of law; (7) Emergency powers.

Despite all this array of impressive powers, our President's position is conceived as that of a constitutional head of State. It has to be remembered that article 53 itself makes it clear that the executive power of the Union has to be exercised by the President "in accordance with the Constitution" and the exercise of the powers of the President as the Supreme Commander of the armed forces has to be "regulated by law". (*U.N. Rao v. Indira Gandhi*, AIR 1971 S.C. 1002; *Sanjeev v. State of Madras*, AIR 1970 S.C. 1102). Also, under article 60, the President takes an oath "to preserve, protect and defend the Constitution and the law". Article 74(1) requires the President to act only with the aid and advice of the Council of Ministers in the discharge of all his functions. This follows also from our adoption of the parliamentary form of Government with ministerial responsibility. The Supreme Court through various decisions has upheld the position that the President is a constitutional head who must act on the advice of the Council of Ministers and that the real executive power in our system vests in the Council of Ministers. [*Samsher Singh v. State of Punjab*, AIR 1974 SC 2192; *U.N. Rao v. Indira Gandhi*, AIR 1971 SC 1002; *M/s Bishamber Dayal Chandra Mohan v. State of U.P.* AIR 1982 S.C. 33; *Ram Jawaya v. State of Punjab*, AIR 1955 S.C. 544] Also, the Constitution does not make any distinction between normal times and Emergency in the matter of the exercise of President's powers. There is no special provision for any discretionary exercise of powers during the Emergency. Article 74 governs exercise of all powers by the President and as such the President is as much bound by the advice of Council of Ministers during Emergency as during normal times. By the 44th constitutional amendment, the position was finally put beyond all doubt and it was made clear that Emergency can be declared by the President only after receiving in writing a communication regarding the Union Cabinet having decided to advise him to do so.

Even though the Constitution makes it obligatory for the President to act on advice of the Council of Ministers, there are some grey areas where the President may still have to use his own judgement and wisdom. These are:

1. Appointment of the Prime Minister [article 75(1)] in a situation where no single party or alliance commands the clear support of the majority of the Lok Sabha members. Obviously, the President cannot appoint the new Prime Minister on the advice of the outgoing Prime Minister who may have lost the election or the support of the House.
2. Appointment of a Prime Minister in case of sudden death (for example, by assasination as in the case of Indira Gandhi) of the incumbent, where the ruling legislature party is unable to meet immediately to elect a leader, there is no settled seniority among Cabinet ministers and a name from outside the Cabinet is suggested.
3. Dissolution of Lok Sabha [article 85(2)(b)] on the advice of a Council of Ministers that may have lost the majority support in Lok Sabha or against whom a vote of no confidence may have been passed.
4. Dismissal of Ministers [article 75(2)] in case the Council of Ministers loses the confidence of the House but refuses to resign.

The acceptance of the advice of the Council of Ministers by the President is not automatic or mechanical. Before entering upon his office, every President has to take an oath to preserve, protect and defend the Constitution and the law. No President can be said to be bound to accept an advice which he finds to be unconstitutional or *mala fide*. The President is entitled to consider it by applying his mind and holding necessary consultations with the Attorney-General and other independent experts. The 44th Amendment allows to the President an opportunity to advise and caution the Council of Ministers and seek reconsideration of any matter before the President puts his seal of approval and accepts the proposed course of action.

In some situations, the role of the President may become most crucial and decisive. This happened, for instance, when Charan Singh, Rajiv Gandhi and Chandra Shekhar came to be appointed to the office of Prime Minister.

A question was raised whether a person who was not a member of either house of Parliament could be appointed Prime Minister. It was held that under article 75(5), such a person could be a Minister for six months and since the Prime Minister was also a Minister he could be appointed from among non members if he had the confidence of the House [*S.P. Anand v. H.D. Deve Gowda,* AIR 1997 SC 272].

Under the Proviso to article 74 inserted in 1978 by the 44th Amendment, the President may require the Council of Ministers to reconsider their advice. He shall, of course, act on the reconsidered advice. But according to article 74 (2), " the question whether any, and if so what advice was tendered by the Ministers to the President shall not be inquired into in any court". Of course, the Government itself is not barred from producing on its own any papers relating to the cabinet decisions and advice to the President and the Court can then look into them. [*State of M.P. v. Nandlal,* AIR 1987 SC 251; *S.P. Gupta v. Union of India,* AIR 1982 SC 149; *State of Rajasthan v. Union of India,* AIR 1977 SC 1361] It is true that in *Kartar Singh's case,* the Supreme Court held that the Court was within its rights to look into the basis of the advice tendered by the Council of Ministers to the President. But, in view of the very clear words of article 74(2), the view in *Kartar Singh v. State of Punjab* (JT (1994) 2 SC 423) may not be fully correct and may need review.

When a Bill is presented to the President for his assent under article 111, he may declare that he assents to the Bill or withholds assent. There is no time limit prescribed for the President giving his assent or declaring his decision to withhold it. But the President may, as soon as possible, also return the Bill, if it is not a money Bill, for reconsideration to the Houses of Parliament. When after reconsideration, the Bill is passed with or without amendments, and is presented to the President again, he shall not withhold his assent.

Inasmuch as giving assent to Bills is one of the functions of the President to be discharged on the advice of the Council of Ministers, it is open to him to seek clarificatory information from the Prime Minister under article 78(b) or to send a Bill back to the Government for reconsideration under Proviso to article 74(1). Presumably this is what was done by the President in cases of the controversial Postal Bill and the Bill seeking *inter alia* to provide to Members of Parliament pension after merely one year's service.

Twice during his tenure, President Narayanan was reported to have returned for reconsideration to his Council of Ministers its advice regarding imposition of President's rule in U.P. and Bihar. The 'satisfaction' stipulated under article 356 is of one single authority, that of the President acting on the advice of the Council of Ministers or, in other words, that of the Union Government. It may be debatable whether in view of article 74(2), what transpires between the President and his Ministers should become matters of public debate and controversy.

Election of the President

When the question of the method of the election of the President came up for consideration before the Constituent Assembly, one of the suggestions made was that he should be elected directly by the people under universal adult franchise. On the other extreme was a suggestion that members of the two houses of Parliament alone may elect the President. The Constituent Assembly devised a unique mechanism, which represented a middle course.

Since the membership in the two houses of Parliament was likely to be dominated by one party, election of the President merely by a majority of members of the Union Parliament could make him a nominee of the ruling party like the Prime Minister and such a President could not represent the constituent States of the Union. On the other hand, if the President was elected directly by the people, he could become a rival centre of power to the Council of Ministers which would have been against the parliamentary system with ministerial responsibility. As Nehru said in the Constituent Assembly, we could not have a directly elected President and not give him "real powers".

Like the President of the United States, our President is also elected by an electoral college. But, here the electoral college consists of the elected members of the two Houses of Parliament and Legislative Assemblies of the States (article 54). The thinking in the Constituent Assembly was that such an electoral college would make the President the elected representative of the whole nation with a clear voice given to the States as well.

Article 58 of the Constitution lays down that no person shall be eligible for election as President unless he (a) is a citizen of India; (b) has completed the age of thirty five years; and (c) is qualified for election as a member of the House of the People. A person shall not be eligible for election as President if he holds any office of profit under the Government of India or the Government of any State or under any local or other authority subject to the control of any of the said Governments. But a person shall not be deemed to hold any office of profit by reason only that he is President or Vice President of the Union or the Governor of any State. Dr. S. Radhakrishnan and Dr. Zakir Husain contested the election to the office of the President of India in 1962 and 1967, respectively, without resigning from the office of Vice President of India. However, notwithstanding the constitutional provisions, Shri V.V. Giri, who was then the Vice President and Dr. N. Sanjiva Reddy, who was the Speaker of Lok Sabha, resigned their respective offices before filing their nomination papers for election to the office of President in 1969. Dr. N. Sanjiva Reddy again resigned from the office of Speaker in 1977 before a nomination proposing him as a candidate for the office of President was filed. Vice President, Shri R. Venkataraman and Vice President, Dr. S.D. Sharma, who contested and won the Presidential Election in 1987 and 1992 respectively did not resign from the office of Vice President till they assumed the office of President of India.

The Presidential and Vice Presidential Elections Act, 1952 and the Rules framed thereunder regulate all matters relating to or connected with the election to the offices of the President and the Vice President of India. The Act of 1952 was amended in 1974 and 1997 to make certain changes therein in the light of the experience gained during the elections held earlier. Similarly, the Presidential and Vice Presidential Election Rules 1952, were also revised. The main requirements of the Act are:

i. A nomination paper for election to the office of President of India should be completed in the prescribed form, subscribed by the candidate as assenting to the nomination and also by at least fifty electors as proposers and at least fifty electors as seconders. Before 1997, the number of proposers and seconders required was only ten each. The requirement was held to be in order because article 58 provided only the qualifications for eligibility and not the requirements for a valid nomination; [*Charan Lal Sahu v. Neelam Sanjeeva Reddy*, AIR 1978 SC 499]
ii. Each nomination paper should be accompanied by a certified copy of the entry relating to the candidate in the electoral roll for the Parliamentary constituency in which the candidate is registered as an elector.

Article 55 provides that, as far as practicable, there shall be uniformity in the scale of representation of the different States at the election of the President; the election shall be held in accordance with the system of proportional representation by means of the single transferable vote and the voting shall be by secret ballot. The article also provides that for the purpose of securing uniformity among the States *inter se* as well as parity between the States as a whole and the Union, the number of votes which each elected member of Parliament and of the Legislative Assembly of each State is entitled to cast at such election shall be determined in the following manner:

a. Every elected member of the Legislative Assembly of a State shall have as many votes as there are multiples of one thousand in the quotient obtained by dividing the population of the State by the total number of elected members of the Assembly;
b. If, after taking the said multiples of one thousand, the remainder is not less than five hundred, then the vote of each member referred to in (a) above shall be further increased by one.

Table 4.1

Total population of the State (Andhra)	:	43,502,708
Total No. of elected Members in the Assembly	:	294
No. of votes for each	:	43,502,708
		1000 x 294
	=	147.96 or
		148

c. Each elected member of either House of Parliament shall have such number of votes as may be obtained by dividing the total number of votes assigned to the members of the Legislative Assemblies of the States under (a) and (b) above by the total number of elected members of both Houses of Parliament, fractions exceeding one half being counted as one and other fractions being disregarded.

The total number of members in the electoral college for the 1997 Presidential election, for example, was 4,848 as detailed below:

a.	Rajya Sabha	:	233
b.	Lok Sabha	:	543
c.	State Assemblies	:	4,072
	Total	:	4,848

The value of the vote of each Member of Parliament (both Rajya Sabha and Lok Sabha) was arrived at by dividing the total value of all the votes assigned to elected members of Legislative Assemblies (5,49,511) by the total number of the elected members of the two houses of Parliament (776). The value of the vote of each member of Parliament thus came to 708. The value of the vote of each member of the State Legislative Assembly differed from State to State depending on the strength of the Assembly and the population of the State as per the 1971 census. The lowest value was in respect of Sikkim (7) and the highest in respect of Uttar Pradesh (208).

The method of providing parity between the States as a

whole on the one hand and the Union on the other meant that the whole process was weighted in favour of the representatives of the States. They got double representation first as members of the Council of States and secondly as members of the State Assemblies. This was done deliberately to make the office of President command unquestioning support from the entire country and the constituent States. The idea of providing uniformity in the scale of representation of different States *inter se* was broadly to provide representation on the basis of population and to respect the 'one man one vote' principle and the concepts of one Indian Citizenship and equality among all citizens.

The system of proportional representation by single transferable vote for the Presidential election was adopted presumably and simply because it was believed to give representation to minorities. There was hardly any discussion on the point in the Constituent Assembly. The proposal was just accepted. The system is hardly very relevant in a single member constituency situation. The system is useful only when there are more than one seat to be filled by the same electorate at the same poll. In fact to call the present system proportional representation by single transferable vote is a misnomer. It could better be called a system of alternate vote because it does in practice operate as such.

There have been thirteen Presidential Elections so far. The only person to be elected without a contest was Dr. Sanjiva Reddy in 1977. The most hotly contested election was that of Shri V.V. Giri when second preference votes had to be counted. The only person to be elected to the office of President for two terms was Dr. Rajendra Prasad. The election, which was, politically most interesting and caused the greatest anxiety in political circles was that of 1987 when besides Shri R. Venkataraman and Justice Krishna Iyer, there was a third valid candidate.

Since the commencement of the Constitution, the following persons have adorned the office of the President of India.

Table 4.2

Presidents of India

Name	*Took Office*	*Left Office*
Dr. Rajendra Prasad	26 January 1950	13 May 1962
Dr. Sarvepalli Radhakrishnan	13 May 1962	13 May 1967
Dr. Zakir Hussain	13 May 1967	3 May 1969
Varahagiri Venkata Giri [Acting]	3 May 1969	20 July 1969
Muhammad Hidayat Ullah [Acting]	20 July 1969	24 Aug. 1969
Varahagiri Venkata Giri	24 Aug. 1969	24 Aug. 1974
Fakhruddin Ali Ahmed	24 Aug. 1974	11 Feb. 1977
Basappa Danappa Jatti [Acting]	11 Feb. 1977	25 July 1977
Neelam Sanjiva Reddy	25 July 1977	25 July 1982
Giani Zail Singh	25 July 1982	25 July 1987
Ramaswamy Venkataraman	25 July 1987	25 July 1992
Dr. Shankar Dayal Sharma	25 July 1992	25 July 1997
Kocheril Raman Narayanan	25 July 1997	25 July 2002
Dr. A. P. J. Abdul Kalam	25 July 2002	25 July 2007
Smt. Pratibha D. Patil	25 July 2007	*In Office*

One of the most noteworthy things during Presidential Elections till recently was that most often many nominations were filed. Although most of these were non serious candidates and their nominations on scrutiny were found to be invalid, this did make the point very loudly that in our democracy any citizen without any distinction could aspire to occupy the highest office. Before the 1997 Presidential election, an effort was made to curb the number of non-serious candidates by increasing the required number of proposers and seconders from ten each to fifty each and the amount of security deposit from Rs.2500 to Rs.15,000.

Election Disputes

Article 71 of the Constitution lays down that all doubts and disputes relating to or connected with the Presidential and Vice

Presidential elections shall be enquired into and decided by the Supreme Court whose decision shall be final. A person who is neither a candidate nor an elector cannot file a suit challenging the validity of the election of the President. [*N.B. Khare v. Election Commissioner of India,* AIR 1958 SC 139]

Article 62(1) provides that an election to fill a vacancy caused by the expiration of the term of office of President shall be completed before the expiration of that term. Article 56(1) provides that the President shall hold office for a term of five years from the date on which he enters upon his office. He can resign his office by writing under his hand addressed to the Vice President. The President shall, notwithstanding the expiration of his term, continue to hold office until his successor enters upon his office.

In the Presidential Election case, on a reference made by the President under article 143(1) [A.I.R. 1974 SC 1682] the Supreme Court held that election to the office of the President cannot be postponed or invalidated on the ground that the electoral college was incomplete or not fully constituted because of some State Assembly having been dissolved. The election of the President or the Vice President cannot be called in question simply on the ground of there being any vacancy among the members of the electoral college.

Procedure for Impeachment

Article 61 lays down that the President may be removed from his office by impeachment on grounds of violation of the Constitution. The charge for impeachment may be preferred in either House of Parliament by a resolution signed by at least one fourth of the total number of members of the House and passed by a majority of not less than two thirds of the total membership of the House. When a charge is so preferred by one House, it shall be investigated or got investigated by the other House and if a resolution is passed by this other House by a majority of 2/3rd of its total membership, the President shall stand removed from his office from the date of the passing of the resolution.

Vice President

Next to the President of India, the highest position in the Official Warrant of Precedence is accorded to the Vice President. His office, therefore, is highly prestigious. Article 63 of the Constitution says that there shall be a Vice President of India. The Vice President shall be the *ex officio* Chairman of Rajya Sabha (article 64). This follows the U.S. practice. As the Chairman of Rajya Sabha, he presides over the proceedings of the House and functions with reference to all its members as the counterpart of the Speaker in Lok Sabha. But, as the Vice President as such, no functions have been assigned to him in the Constitution. By practice, he has come to have several ceremonial functions like meeting ambassadors, visiting foreign dignitaries *etc*. Article 65 lays down that he shall act as the President in the event of a vacancy in the office of President by reason of his death, resignation or removal or otherwise. In case the President is unable to discharge his functions owing to absence, illness or any other cause, the Vice President shall discharge his functions. While acting as President or discharging the functions of President, the Vice President shall not perform the duties of the office of the Chairman of Rajya Sabha (article 64).

It has been proved on many occasions, *e.g.* when two of our Presidents Dr. Zakir Hussain and Fakhruddin Ali Ahmed died in office and Vice Presidents V.V. Giri and B.D. Jatti acted as President, that the contingency functions of the Vice President are of crucial importance to the nation.

The Vice President is elected by an electoral college consisting of the members of the two houses of Parliament in accordance with the system of proportional representation with single transferable vote (article 66). This is intended to ensure that he enjoys the confidence of both the houses of Parliament.

The term of the office of the Vice President is five years and election to the office has to be completed before the expiration of the term. All doubts and disputes regarding this election shall be enquired into and decided by the Supreme Court. The Vice President may resign from his office by writing under his hand to the President. He may also be removed from his office by a resolution passed by a majority of all then members of Rajya Sabha and agreed to by Lok Sabha (articles 67, 68 and 71). The Vice President shall not be a member of either house of Parliament or of a State Legislature (article 66).

The eligibility conditions for election of a person as Vice President are the same as those for election as President except that for the former, the candidate must be qualified for election as a member of the Rajya Sabha (article 66).

Since the Constitution of the two Houses of Parliament in 1952, the following persons have occupied the office of the Vice-President:

Table 4.3
Vice-Presidents of India

Name	*Tenure*
Dr. Sarvepalli Radhakrishnan	1952-1962
Dr. Zakir Hussain	1962-1967
Varahagiri Venkatagiri	1967-1969
Gopal Swaroop Pathak	1969-1974
B.D. Jatti	1974-1979
Justice Mohammad Hidayatullah	1979-1984
R. Venkataraman	1984-1987
Dr. Shankar Dayal Sharma	1987-1992
K.R.Narayanan	1992-1997
Krishan Kant	1992-2002
Bhairon Singh Shekhawat	2002-2007
Hamid Ansari	2007-in office

Council of Ministers

Article 74 of the Constitution lays down that there shall be a Council of Ministers with the Prime Minister at the head to aid and advise the President who shall, in the exercise of his functions, act in accordance with such advice. The President may, however, require the Council of Ministers to reconsider such advice. The President shall act on the advice tendered after such reconsideration.

That there shall be a Council of Ministers has to be

understood to mean that it shall always be there. The Constitution does not envisage a situation where there will be no Prime Minister or no Council of Ministers. There is no provision for failure of constitutional machinery (as under article 356) and direct President's rule at the Union level.

Acceptance by the President of the advice tendered by the Council of Ministers has become obligatory particularly after the 42nd and 44th Constitutional Amendments. Before the amendments also the Supreme Court had taken the view that the advice was binding in all cases. (*Samsher v. State of Punjab,* AIR 1974 SC 2192)

Even after the dissolution of Lok Sabha, the President, in the exercise of his powers, was bound by the aid and advice of the Council of Ministers. It was held by the Supreme Court in *U.N. Rao v. Indira Gandhi* (A.I.R. 1971 SC 1002) that any exercise of powers by the President without the advice of the Council of Ministers shall be unconstitutional as being violative of article 74(1).

The decisions of the Cabinet are taken confidentially and the advice tendered to the President is also protected by confidentiality between the President and the Council of Ministers. As such, these cannot be questioned in a court of law. Of course, there is no bar to the court looking at them if these are produced by the Government. [*S.P. Gupta v. Union of India,* AIR 1982 SC 149; *State of Rajasthan v. Union of India,* AIR 1977 SC 1361; *State of M.P. v. Nandlal,* AIR 1987, SC 251; *Choudhary v. Government of Bihar,* AIR 1980 SC 383]

Under article 75, the Prime Minister is appointed by the President and other Ministers are appointed by him on the advice of the Prime Minister. The Ministers hold office during the pleasure of the President. But, the Council of Ministers is collectively responsible to Lok Sabha.

The Constitution (Ninety-first Amendment) Act, 2003 inserted the following new clauses to article 75:

> (1A) The total number of Ministers, including the Prime Minister, in the Council of Ministers shall not exceed fifteen per cent, of the total number of members of the House of the People.

> (1B) A member of either House of Parliament belonging to any political party who is disqualified for being a member of that House under paragraph 2 of the Tenth Schedule shall also be disqualified to be appointed as a Minister under clause (1) for duration of the period commencing from the date of his disqualification till the date on which the term of his office as such member would expire or where he contests any election to either House of Parliament before the expiry of such period, till the date on which he is declared elected, whichever is earlier.

While the President is to be fully guided in the discharge of all his functions by the advice of the Council of Ministers with the Prime Minister at its head, it is not clear as to on whose advice he performs the most crucial function of appointing the Prime Minister. So far as the letter of the Constitution goes, the President can appoint almost anyone as the Prime Minister but he has to remember that under the Constitution the Council of Ministers headed by the Prime Minister has to be responsible to the House and would have to go if it does not command or loses the confidence of the Lok Sabha. The President, therefore would appoint only a person who, in his best judgement would be acceptable to the House. If a party or a pre-election alliance commands absolute majority support in the Lok Sabha, there is no difficulty. For, the President in such cases, following well established parliamentary practices and conventions, has to invite the Leader of the majority party, front or alliance to take over as the Prime Minister and form a Government. But, where no single party or coalition is in a position to form a Government on its own, the role of the President in choosing the Prime Minister becomes most delicate and difficult. He may have to use all his abilities to decide on the leader most likely to command the confidence of Lok Sabha. He may call the leader of the single largest party or alliance first or seek to be satisfied in advance about a leader having the support of more than half of the members of the Lok Sabha. Since in any case, ultimately it is necessary for the Prime Minister to have the confidence of the Lok Sabha and it is the responsibility of the President to find out who can command such confidence, the most logical and above board solution would be that instead of getting involved in political controversies, appointing someone and then asking him to seek a confidence vote in the House, the President can ask the House itself to elect its leader who can then be appointed by the President as the Prime Minister.

While the Ministers are also appointed by the President and said to hold office during the pleasure of the President, in actual effect, it means they are selected by the Prime Minister (the President cannot appoint anyone not recommended by the Prime Minister) and hold office at his pleasure. If the Prime Minister is unhappy or dissatisfied with any Minister, he can advise him to resign, advise the President to dismiss him or tender the resignation of his Council of Ministers and then reconstitute it after deleting the name of the Minister in question.

In the U.K. the concept is that of individual and collective responsibility of Ministers. Our Constitution, however, provides only for collective responsibility which means that there can be no no-confidence in a single Minister. The entire Council of Ministers is jointly responsible to Lok Sabha for all acts of Government. Therefore, it stands or falls together. If it loses the confidence of the House, the entire Council of Ministers must resign. Also, collective responsibility would mean that the Ministers must not speak in public in different voices. If any Minister disagrees with a decision taken or a policy adopted by the Cabinet, he must either resign or own equal and joint responsibility.

Again, in the U.K., historically, the concept of ministerial responsibility was a by product or corollary of the doctrine that the King can do no wrong. Since the King could not be held responsible for any wrong acts of the State, ministers came handy as a peg to hang responsibility on. For every act of the State, there was a Minister responsible. Every order of the Crown or any public act had, therefore, to be countersigned by a Minister.

In India, on the other hand, ministerial responsibility was conceived and evolved on the basis of the highest principles of representative democracy, as the responsiblity of the Government to the directly elected representatives of the people in the Lok Sabha. Actually, in India acts of the State are done in the name of the President and required to be countersigned by way of authentication not by a Minister but by a Secretary (or other authorised officer) to the Government in accordance with the rules made by the President (article 77).

Cabinet

The Constitution speaks only of Ministers. It does not indicate any classification or categories of Ministers into Cabinet Ministers, Ministers of State, Deputy Ministers etc. While Prime Minister is mentioned as one heading the Council of Ministers, there is no reference made to any Deputy Prime Minister. In *K.M. Sharma v. Devilal*, [AIR 1990 SC 528], oath by Devi Lal as Deputy Prime Minister was questioned as being *ultra vires* the Constitution as the Constitution provided only for the 'Prime Minister' and 'Ministers'. The Court upheld the oath as valid but said that 'Deputy Prime Minister' was only a descriptive term and did not confer on him any powers of the Prime Minister. Also, the Constitution mentions only the Council of Ministers and makes no reference to the Cabinet except in article 352 (as amended in 1979) where Cabinet is defined as the Council consisting of Ministers of Cabinet rank. For all practical purposes, it is the Cabinet which takes policy decisions and advises the President. The whole Council of Ministers including all categories of Ministers almost never meets to transact any business.

Cabinet Secretariat

The Cabinet Secretariat is headed by the Cabinet Secretary and works under the direct charge of the Prime Minister. The subjects assigned to the Cabinet Secretariat are (i) to provide secretarial assistance to the Cabinet and its Committees, (ii) to be responsible for the administration of the Government of India (Transaction of Business) Rules, 1961 and the Government of India (Allocation of Business) Rules 1961, facilitating smooth transaction of business in Ministries/Departments of the Government by ensuring adherence to these rules. The Cabinet

Secretariat is a useful mechanism for promoting inter-Ministerial coordination.

Rules of Government Business

Under article 77, the Government of India (Allocation of Business) Rules, 1961 are made by the President. The Rules allocate items of Government business to different Ministries/ Departments. Each Ministry or Department is usually headed by a Secretary and is assigned to a Minister in charge. [For the organisational structure of Government of Indis see Annexure].

Prime Minister

The Prime Minister of India is the Head of the Union Government, as distinct from the President of India, who is the Head of State. Since India has adopted the Westminster model of parliamentary democracy, it is the Prime Minister who oversees the day-to-day functioning of the Government of India. The Prime Minister is assisted in this task by his Council of Ministers, comprising Cabinet Ministers, Ministers of State with Independent Charge, Ministers of State who work with Cabinet Ministers, and Deputy Ministers.

Although it is considered most desirable for the Prime Minister to be a member of Lok Sabha, he can be a member of either House – the Rajya Sabha or the Lok Sabha. As Prime Minister, he is usually but not necessarily the Leader of the House to which he belongs. The Prime Minister is also the Chairman of the Planning Commission of India.

As head of the Council of Ministers, the Prime Minister oversees the work of all the Ministries. He presides over Cabinet meetings, which are normally held in the Cabinet Room of the Prime Minister's Office. The Union Cabinet functions on the principle of "collective responsibility".

The Prime Minister's Office, popularly known as the 'PMO', is located at South Block. The South Block is one of the two secretariat blocks (the other is known as North Block) that flank Rashtrapati Bhavan – the residence of the President of India.

The PMO provides secretarial assistance to the Prime Minister. It is headed by the Principal Secretary to Prime Minister. Often a Minister of State is assigned to PMO to assist the Prime Minister. The PMO includes the anti-corruption unit and the public wing dealing with grievances.

The subject-matter of files required to be submitted to the Prime Minister depends on whether he is holding direct charge of the Ministry or whether there is a Cabinet Minister or Minister of State (Independent Charge) in charge of the Ministry. In the case of the latter, most matters are dealt with by the Cabinet Minister / Minister of State-in-charge. Only important policy issues, which the Minister concerned feels should be submitted to the Prime Minister for orders or information, are received in the PMO. In cases where the Prime Minister is the Minister-in-charge, all matters requiring Ministerial approval not delegated to the Minister of State / Deputy Minister, if any, are submitted for orders. The Prime Minister has traditionally been the Minister-in-charge of the Departments of Space, Atomic Energy, and Ministry of Personnel, Public Grievances and Pensions.

Since the Prime Minister is Chairman of the Planning Commission, relevant files are forwarded to the PMO for his comments and clearance. Some of the important matters that require the Prime Minister's personal attention include the following:

(a) Important defence-related issues;
(b) Decorations, both civilian and defence, where Presidential approval is required;
(c) All important policy issues;
(d) Proposals for appointment of Indian Heads of Missions abroad and requests for grant of agreement for foreign Heads of Missions posted to India;
(e) All important decisions relating to the Cabinet Secretariat;
(f) Appointments to State Administrative Tribunals and the Central administrative Tribunal, UPSC, Election Commission, statutory/ constitutional Committees, Commissions attached to various Ministries;
(g) All policy matters relating to the administration of the Civil Services and administrative reforms;

(h) Special Packages announced by the Prime Minister for States are monitored in the PMO and periodical reports submitted to Prime Minister; and
(i) All judicial appointments for which Presidential approval is required.

Duty has been specifically cast on the Prime Minister to keep the President informed of all decisions relating to administration and legislation, to furnish such information in these matters as the President may call for and to place before the Council of Ministers, if so desired by the President, any matter on which a decision might have been taken by a Minister (article 78).

In a parliamentary system of Government, the Prime Minister occupies a unique position as the most powerful functionary who controls both the Parliament and the Executive. Increasingly parliamentary Government has come to be regarded as Prime ministerial Government. As the head of the Council of Ministers, the Prime Minister is the head of the Government. Also, he is the leader of his party or/and of a coalition of parties in Parliament and usually the Leader of the popular House. In the ultimate analysis, however, much depends on the personality of the Prime Minister and the level of acceptance and support he commands from the nation, his party or alliance and Parliament. The Prime Minister enjoys large powers of patronage. All the Ministers are appointed at his recommendation and stand dismissed at his demand. The Prime Minister allots work among the Ministers. Also, he can change their portfolios at will. The Prime Minister is the channel of communication between the Council of Ministers and the President.

Questions relating to the relationship between the Prime Minister and the President and between the Prime Minister and other Ministers have been subject matters of controversy right from the commencement of the Constitution. The perceptions of Sardar Patel as Home Minister and Nehru as the Prime Minister varied widely. Similarly, there were fundamental differences between the first President Dr. Rajendra Prasad and the first Prime Minister Jawaharlal Nehru. Despite all the amendments and judicial clarifications about the President being only a constitutional head, differences were reported between President Zail Singh and Prime Minister Rajiv Gandhi. More recently, relations between the holders of the two offices have been mature and cordial.

Occupants of the office of the Prime Minister of India since Independence have been as follows:

Table 4.4

Name	*Tenure*	*Party*
Shri Jawaharlal Nehru	15 Aug. 1947 – 27 May 1964	Congress
Shri Gulzari Lal Nanda [Acting]	27 May 1964 – 9 June 1964	Congress
Shri Lal Bahadur Shastri	9 June 1964 – 11 Jan. 1966	Congress
Shri Gulzari Lal Nanda [Acting]	11 Jan. 1966 – 24 Jan. 1966	Congress
Smt. Indira Gandhi	24 Jan. 1966 – 24 March 1977	Congress
Shri Morarji Desai	24 March 1977 – 28 July 1979	Janata Party
Shri Charan Singh	28 July 1979 – 14 Jan.y 1980	Janata Party
Smt. Indira Gandhi	14 Jan.y 1980 – 31 Oct. 1984	Congress (I)
Shri Rajiv Gandhi	31Oct. 1984 – 2 Dec. 1989	Congress (I)
Shri V. P. Singh	2 Dec. 1989 – 10 Nov. 1990	Janata Dal
Shri Chandra Shekhar	10 Nov. 1990 – 21 June 1991	Janata Dal (S)
Shri P. V. Narasimha Rao	21 June 1991 – 16 May 1996	Congress (I)
Shri Atal Bihari Vajpayee	16 May 1996 – 1 June 1996	Bharatiya Janata Party
Shri H. D. Deve Gowda	1 June 1996 – 21 April 1997	Janata Dal
Shri Inder Kumar Gujral	21 April 1997 – 19 March 1998	Janata Dal
Shri Atal Bihari Vajpayee	19 March 1998 – 22 May 2004	Bharatiya Janata Party
Dr. Manmohan Singh	22 May 2004 – in office	Congress (I)

THE STATE EXECUTIVE

The Constitution of India contains not only the Constitution of the Union but also constitutions for the States. With special provisions for some of the individual States, it may be said that there are several State Constitutions within the Constitution of India. Generally speaking, provisions for the States follow the Union pattern. The parliamentary system of Government with a constitutional Head and with ministerial responsibility to the popular House of the Legislature holds equally good at the State level. The real executive power is exercised by the Ministers. 'Satisfaction' of the Governor means the satisfaction of the Council of Ministers. [*Ram Jawaya Kapur v. State of Punjab,* AIR 1955 SC 549; *Shamsher Singh v. State of Punjab,* AIR 1974 SC 2193]

The State of Jammu & Kashmir, which is an integral part of India, is the only one to have a separate State Constitution of its own. However, several other States enjoy special status and have certain special provisions applicable to only each one of them separately, *e.g.* States of Maharashtra and Gujarat (article 371), Nagaland (371A), Assam (371B), Manipur (371C), Andhra Pradesh (371D & 371E), Sikkim (371F), Mizoram (371G), Arunachal Pradesh (371H) and Goa (371I).

Office of the Governor

According to article 153, there shall be a Governor for each State. The same person may sometimes be appointed as Governor of two or more States. The Governor is appointed by the President (article 155). The prescribed term of office for a Governor is five years but he holds office at the pleasure of the President (article 156). The pleasure of the President is not justiciable. The Governor has no security of tenure. He may be removed by the President at any time. [*Surya Narain v. Union of India,* AIR 1982 Raj. 1]

No person can be appointed a Governor unless he is a citizen of India and has completed the age of 35 years (article

157). Also, the Governor cannot be a member of Parliament or of any of the State Legislatures. If any member is appointed as Governor, his seat in the legislature shall be deemed to have been vacated on the date of assuming the charge of Governor's office. The Governor cannot hold any office of profit.

Every Governor is entitled to free official residence and other emoluments, *etc.* as may be determined by Parliament by law or as under the Second Schedule of the Constitution. In *Hargovind v. Raghukul* (AIR 1979 SC 1109), the Supreme Court held that the office of the Governor was not an office of profit under the Government.

Every Governor and every person discharging the functions of Governor has to take an oath to faithfully execute the office and to preserve, protect and defend the Constitution and the law (article 159).

The Constitution Commission (NCRWC) and the Supreme Court have repeatedly iterated the recommendations of the Sarkaria Commission in the matter of appointment of Governors and said that only an eminent, detached figure from outside the State should be appointed Governor after consultation with the Chief Minister.

In the discharge of all his functions, with a few exceptions in certain cases, the Governor is to be guided by the aid and advice of the Council of Ministers (article 163).

While both the President of the Republic and the Governor of a State are constitutional heads, there are some fundamental differences between the position of the President and the Governor, *viz.* (i) while the President is elected, the Governor is nominated; (ii) while the President can be removed only by the difficult process of impeachment, the Governor holds office during the pleasure of the President; (iii) while the President is bound by the advice of the Council of Ministers in the discharge of all his functions, in the case of Governors the aid and advice provision applies "except in so far as" the Governor is required to function "in his discretion" (article 163). The 42nd Amendment had amended article 74 to provide that the President "shall" act in accordance with the advice. Such an amendment, however, was not made in the corresponding article 163 applicable to Governors. It has been held that generally the Governor cannot act "except in accordance with the advice of his ministers". [*Sanjeevi v. State of Madras,* AIR 1970 SC 1102; *U.P. Service Commission v. Suresh,* AIR 1987 SC 1953; *Sunit Kumar v. Government of West Bengal,* AIR 1950 Cal. 274]

There are certain areas where the Governor may have to use his own wisdom and discretion, *e.g.* in (a) appointing a new Chief Minister in a situation where no single party or leader commands majority support; (b) dismissing a Ministry where it refuses to resign even after losing majority support in the House or after being defeated on a no confidence motion; (c) dissolution of the Assembly on the advice of a Chief Minister who has lost majority support; (d) determining the royalty for mineral licenses to District Councils in case of tribal areas of Assam, under the Sixth Schedule; (e) advising the President of the failure of the constitutional machinery and to impose President's rule; and (f) giving or withholding assent to Bills, returning a Bill for reconsideration of the House/s or reserving it for the consideration of the President.

When a Chief Minister of U.P. was dismissed by the Governor after a group of members withdrew their support and the Governor appointed another person as the Chief Minister without a majority test on the floor of the House and the High Court ordered the reinstatement of the former Chief Minister, the Supreme Court ordered a special session of the State Assembly to have a composite floor test between the two contending claimants of Chief Ministership. [*Jagdambika Pal v. Union of India,* AIR 1998 SC 998]

The executive power of the State is vested in the Governor and is to be exercised by him either directly or through officers subordinate to him in accordance with the Constitution (article 154). The executive power of the State is coextensive with its legislative power. Where an item happens to be in the Concurrent List, the executive power of the State will be subject to the powers conferred on the Union by the Constitution or the laws. [articles 246 and 162; *State of M.P. v. Jain*, AIR 1981 SC 2045]

The Governor appoints the Advocate-General of the State, the Chairman and members of the State Public Service Commission and the judges of Subordinate Courts (articles 165, 316, 283 and 284).

The Governor appoints the Chief Minister and other ministers on the advice of the Chief Minister. All the Ministers hold office during the pleasure of the Governor but the Council of Ministers is collectively responsible to the Legislative Assembly of the State. This in practice means that only the person likely to be most acceptable to the House is to be appointed as the Chief Minister, and that the Council of Ministers holds office so long as it does not lose the confidence of the House and that each Minister continues only so long as the Chief Minister wants. (article 164).

All executive action is to be taken in the name of the Governor. The Governor may make rules for the more convenient transaction of business of the State and for allocation of work among the Ministers. A decision of the Council of Ministers does not become operative as a Government order unless expressed in the Governor's name and duly authenticated in accordance with the rules made by the Governor. [article 166; *State of Kerala v. Lakshmikutty*, AIR 1987 SC 331; *B.L. Cotton Mills v. State of West Bengal*, AIR 1967 SC 1145]

The Constitution (Ninety-first Amendment) Act, 2003 inserted the following new clauses to article 164:

> (1A) The total number of Ministers, including the Chief Minister, in the Council of Ministers in a State shall not exceed fifteen per cent of the total number of members of the Legislative Assembly of that State.
>
> Provided that the number of Ministers, including the Chief Minister, in a State shall not be less than twelve.
>
> Provided further that where the total number of Ministers, including the Chief Minister, in the Council of Ministers in any State at the commencement of the Constitution (Ninety-first Amendment) Act, 2003 exceeds the said fifteen per cent, of the number specified in the first proviso, as the case

may be, then, the total number of Ministers in that State shall be brought in conformity with the provisions of this clause within six months from such date as the President may by public notification appoint.

(1B) A member of the Legislative Assembly of a State or either House of the Legislature of a State having Legislative Council belonging to any political party who is disqualified for being a member of that House under paragraph 2 of the Tenth Schedule shall also be disqualified to be appointed as a Minister under clause (1) for duration of the period commencing from the date of his disqualification till the date on which the term of his office as such member would expire or where he contests any election to the Legislative Assembly of a State or either House of the Legislature of a State having Legislative Council, as the case may be, before the expiry of such period, till the date on which he is declared elected, whichever is earlier.]

Under article 171(3)(e) and (5), the Governor may nominate to the Legislative Council of the State where it exists one sixth members from among persons having special knowledge or practical experience in respect of literature, science, art, cooperative movement and social service. He may also nominate to the Legislative Assembly a person from the Anglo Indian community if he feels the community needs representation and is not adequately represented in the Assembly (article 333).

Under article 168, the Governor is a part of the Legislature of the State. He summons and prorogues the two Houses of the Legislature (in case of bicameral Legislatures) and can dissolve the Legislative Assembly of the State (article 174). He addresses the members of the Legislature and may send messages (articles 175, 176). Without the Governor's assent, no Bill can become law even after its being passed by the two Houses (article 200).

After a Bill is passed by the Legislative Assembly and the Legislative Council, if any, it is presented to the Governor, presumably with the advice of the Council of Ministers, for his assent to the Bill as passed. The Governor may (i) give his assent to the Bill; (ii) withhold his assent; (iii) reserve the Bill for the consideration of the President or; (iv) except in case of a Money Bill, return the Bill for reconsideration with his message as soon as possible (article 200). There is a fifth possibility which is often not mentioned, *viz.* that of returning the Bill to the Government seeking certain clarifications or information in regard to the Bill and in effect suggesting reconsideration of the advice earlier given by the Council of Ministers for assenting to the Bill (article 167).

If a Bill is returned by the Governor to the Legislature with a message, it will be considered accordingly and if passed again with or without amendments, it will be assented to. Except when the Bill is returned to the Government or reserved for consideration of the President, the Governor may be said to be acting only on the advice of the Council of Ministers in either of the four options. In any case, the exercise of Governor's power in this regard cannot be questioned in a court of law (see, for example, *Bharat Seva Ashram v. State of Gujarat*, AIR 1987 SC 494).

Under article 213, the Governor may promulgate ordinances during the period when the House or both the Houses where there are two Houses of State Legislature are not in session. This power corresponds to the power of the President under article 123. The ordinances have the same force and effect as laws passed by the Legislature and assented to by the Governor. Also, they are subject to the same restrictions as laws passed by the Legislature. Thus, the Governor is barred from promulgating an ordinance without instructions from the President (i) if a Bill containing the same provisions would have required President's prior sanction for introduction; (ii) if a Bill containing the same provisions would have been reserved by the Governor for the consideration of the President; or (iii) if a State Act containing the same provisions would have been invalid without the President's assent.

Every ordinance promulgated by the Governor has to be laid before the State Legislative Assembly (before both the Houses in case of a bicameral State Legislature) and shall cease to operate at the expiry of six weeks from the reassembly of the Legislature or even earlier if a resolution disapproving it is passed. The ordinance may be withdrawn by the Governor at any time (article 213). The notorious misuse of ordinance making powers of the Governor was highlighted in *D.C. Wadhava v. State of Bihar* [(1987) 1 SCC 378]. The Bihar Governor promulgated 256 ordinances during 1967-1981. All these were kept going by being repromulgated again and again. The court held that it was "a subversion of the democratic process" and a "fraud on the Constitution". This power is to be most sparingly used only to meet extraordinary situations. It cannot be allowed to be "perverted to serve political ends".

Under article 202, the Governor is required to cause to be laid before the House or Houses of the Legislature the budget or the Annual Financial Statement. A Money Bill cannot be introduced and a Demand for Grant cannot be moved without the recommendation of the Governor. Even amendments would require recommendation.

The Governor has been given the power to grant pardons, *etc.* and to suspend, remit or commute the sentence of any person convicted of an offence against any law relating to a matter to which the executive power of the State extends (article 161). The power, of course, has to be exercised on the advice of the Council of Ministers. In *K. M. Nanavati v. State of Bombay* (AIR 1961 SC 99), the Supreme Court held that it is open to the Governor to grant a full pardon at any time even during the pendency of the case in the Supreme Court, but the Governor cannot so exercise his power of suspension of the sentence for the period when the Supreme Court is seized of the case. The Governor's power of suspension was held to be subject to the rules framed by the Supreme Court.

Union Territories

The seven Union Territories are administered by the President generally acting through an administrator (article 239). In case of Delhi, Andaman & Nicobar and Pondicherry, the administrator is called the Lt. Governor. Governor of Punjab is concurrently the Administrator of Chandigarh. Dadra & Nagar Haveli and Daman and Diu have one administrator and Lakshadweep has one for itself.

Coalition Governments

During 1989-1999, there were five general elections for Lok Sabha – 3 in 4 years (1996-1999). In all these elections, no single party emerged with a majority of seats in the House. This aroused considerable concern about political stability, especially in the context of the needs of national development efforts and the far-reaching changes in international economic and security paradigms. During ten years, there were seven governments. In the situation of a hung house where no single party commanded majority support, India got either minority governments or governments formed by a workable multi-party alliance.

The Constitution has no provision in regard to single party or coalition governments. It only speaks of the Prime Minister/ Chief Minister being appointed by the President/Governor and the Council of Ministers being responsible to Lok Sabha/State Assembly.

Coalition is the *ad hoc* coming together or entering into an alliance of two or more separate parties, persons or interests, for a temporary period and with a specific objective of taking combined action like formation of government and carrying on the activities of the State. Coalition arrangements presume that the parties coming together retain their distinct identities but they usually agree on a common minimum programme or an agenda to be followed by their government. Some sacrifice of party principles and freedom to pursue its own manifesto or party agenda is naturally involved.

For the major part of the last 60 years of independence, single party (Congress) governments have been in power at the Union level. Until 1967, the same party dominated the scene and formed governments in most of the States also. Only after the 1967 general elections, in many States, non-Congress coalition governments were formed by parties and groups coming together on anti-Congress platforms of Samyukta Vidhayak Dals (S.V.D.)

At the Union level, one-party monopoly of power of the Congress was first broken in 1977 when in the wake of emergency excesses, Congress was badly mauled. Under the J.P. movement, the Janata Party achieved spectacular victories. Shri Morarji Desai became the Prime Minister at the head of a Janata Government. Confronted by a no-confidence motion, Morarji resigned on 15 July 1979. Another non-Congress Council of Ministers, this time headed by Charan Singh, was installed. Lok Sabha was summoned to meet on 20 August 1979 to enable Charan Singh Ministry to seek a vote of confidence. But, Charan Singh never faced the House and resigned. The Janata experiment had failed badly. Non-Congressism did not prove strong enough as a cementing force between disparate groups.

The 1980-89 decade was again of Congress monopoly of power at the Union level. The second break-through for anti-Congress parties came towards the end of 1989 when the common platform of Janata Dal was forged. Congress (I) performance at the general election was dismal. For the first time in India's parliamentary history, no party had secured a clear majority to be called upon to form the government. A minority government of the Janata Dal was formed in December 1989 by V.P. Singh with the support of the BJP and the left parties from outside. It was the first time that a minority government was formed at the Union level in India. It secured a vote of confidence on 21 December 1989. It was for the first time that such a motion was moved and passed to test the legitimacy of the government on the floor of the House. But, V.P.Singh Government could not complete even a year in office. Following the withdrawal of support by BJP and its allies, V.P.Singh lost majority support in the House. His government was defeated on a confidence motion on the floor of the House. In November 1990, leader of a breakway group from Janata Dal, Chandra Shekhar formed another minority government with the outside support of the Congress (I) Party.

Later, when in March 1991, Congress (I) members staged a walk-out and announced boycott of proceedings of the House, Chandra Shekhar resigned. The second Janata experiment of a non-Congress front had failed. Also, the experiment of minority governments run by outside support had flopped. At the tenth

General Election, a clear majority to form a stable government again eluded every party. Congress (I) was returned as the single largest party but short of an absolute majority. It formed a minority government with Narsimha Rao at the head. This was the third minority government and continued as such for nearly two-and-a-half years but Rao succeeded in gaining majority by generating splits in other parties and securing group defections to his side by offering money, ministerships etc. The Rao government lasted nearly its full five-year term.

During 1996-1998, there were two general elections both returning fractured mandates. In both these elections, Congress (I) for the first time, was relegated to the second position having secured only 140 seats each time. The BJP rose and continued to be in the first position as the single largest party even though without a clear majority. Atal Bihari Vajpayee who was appointed the Prime Minister in 1996, failed to prove majority support on the floor of the House and resigned after being in office merely for 13 days. This was followed by two successive Janata Dal-led United Front minority coalition governments headed by Deve Gowda and Inder Kumar Gujral and supported by the Congress from outside. Thus, these could be said to be the first two coalition governments at the Union level and the coalition era could be said to have begun in 1996 and has continued since.

Following withdrawal of support by one of the alliance partners – AIADMK – Vajpayee Government lost on the floor of the House by a single vote after a life of thirteen months in office. The adverse vote turned out to be a blessing in disguise for the Vajpayee Government inasmuch as the thirteenth General Election held in September-October 1999 returned the BJP led National Democratic Alliance (NDA) with a convincing majority. The Congress Party which became the main opposition under the leadership of Sonia Gandhi was further decimated to the lowest ever position in Lok Sabha. The NDA formed its government.

NDA was a pre-poll alliance of some 24 parties. This was the third Vajpayee Government and the fourth coalition government in four years. A few months before completing its full five-year term successfully, the Vajpayee Government called for fresh elections. The 14th general election to Lok Sabha returned another coalition government in May 2004. This was formed by the United Progressive Alliance (UPA) headed by the Congress and supported from outside by the Left Parties. [Also see under Chapter 10. 'Elections and Political Parties']

Caretaker Government

At the level of States, if the government cannot be carried on in accordance with the Constitution, there is provision for President's rule. But, at the Union level, the Constitution envisages that there shall always be a Council of Ministers to aid and advise the President who shall act in accordance with the advice tendered. There is no provision in the Constitution for anything like a caretaker government. The term has come to be used in common parlance to describe the status of a Council of Ministers that has resigned on having lost the confidence of the Lok Sabha or otherwise but is asked by the President to continue till alternative arrangements are made. If an alternative government cannot be formed immediately and general elections have to be held, the outgoing Council of Ministers may have to hold charge till the conclusion of elections and formation of new government. In any case, the presumption is that such an arrangement is for as short a period as absolutely necessary, that elections, if necessary, are held at the earliest possible and that during the interregnum no new schemes are launched or major policy decisions taken by the Government unless dictated by demands of national security and the like.

Permanent Services

In a modern democratic polity, civil services are an inevitable ingredient of the governmental apparatus. It is, in fact, the non political and non elected functionaries who are responsible for carrying on the administration under the direction and control of the elected representatives of the people and in accordance with rules and laws.

The bureaucracy in India is the product of two different sets of influences: the old colonial British traditions and the demands of the post-independence democratic welfare State system. Indian bureaucracy or the civil service has been one of the most well known in the world. In fact, the term 'civil service' was first used for the employees of the East India Company who served in departments other than military. One of the earliest demands of Indian nationalist opinion was to rationalise the structure and functions of the civil service to provide a greater share to Indians in the administration of their country. As a result of increasing pressure and resentment in India, in 1922 the British Government finally bowed to the demand for holding simultaneous Civil Service examinations in India and England. Also, from then on, the Imperial Civil Services (ICS) were to be called the Indian Civil Service (ICS).

At the time of independence, we inherited a well-organised framework of All India Services. In addition, there was a network of central, provincial and subordinate services. The two All India Services, the Indian Administrative Service and the Indian Police Service, were created in 1946 on the British pattern. The attainment of independence and the introduction of the system of parliamentary democracy made the civil services fully accountable to the political executive and the Parliament.

Article 309 provided for the regulation of recruitment and conditions of service of Union and State Government services by appropriate Legislatures subject to the provisions of the Constitution. Until any such laws were enacted, the services were to be regulated by rules made by the President or the Governor as the case may be.

Article 310 laid down the principle that every Government employee in a defence service or a civil service held his office during the pleasure of the President or the Governor. It was, however, possible to provide in special cases by contract to pay compensation for early termination of service. Besides, there were special constitutional safeguards in case of certain high functionaries like the judges of the Supreme Court and High Courts, the Chief Election Commissioner, Comptroller and

Auditor General, members of the Public Service Commissions, *etc.* who could not be removed from their offices except in the manner laid down in relevant articles (124, 217, 317, 324 etc.). Also, separate provisions were made for regulating the recruitment and conditions of service of certain categories of public servants, *e.g.* officers and staff of Legislature Secretariats (articles 98 and 187), employees of the Supreme Court and the High Courts (articles 146 and 299) and persons serving the Indian Audit and Accounts Department (article 148). Article 309 did not apply to them.

Article 311 sought to place certain limitations on the exercise of the pleasure principle in respect of civil servants. Thus, no civil servant could be dismissed or removed by an authority subordinate to the appointing authority and no civil servant could be dismissed or removed or reduced in rank except after an inquiry informing him of the charges against him and giving him a reasonable opportunity of being heard in respect of those charges. The protection was not available to defence employees and even in case of civil employees it did not apply if the penalty was any other than dismissal, removal or reduction in rank. The article, however, made no distinction between a person holding a temporary post and one holding a permanent post.

All India services are distinguished from Central and State services inasmuch as members of Central services are concerned with only the affairs of the Union and those of State services with State matters while members of the All India services are common to the Union and the States and serve by turns both the Union and State Governments. Two All India services—the Indian Administrative Service and Indian Police Service—are mentioned in the Constitution itself. Article 312 lays down that if Rajya Sabha passes a resolution by two thirds majority to the effect that it is necessary or expedient in national interest to create one or more all India services, including All India Judicial Service, Parliament may by law provide for such services. Parliament has under this article enacted the All India Services Act, 1951 creating certain all India Services in addition to the

IAS and the IPS which had been already created in 1948. Article 312 also empowers Parliament to regulate the recruitment and conditions of service of persons appointed to All India services.

Article 312A inserted by the Constitution (28th Amendment) Act, 1972 empowers Parliament to vary or revoke conditions of service of persons appointed to the Civil Service of the Crown in India before the commencement of the Constitution. Article 313 contains a transitional provision saying that until otherwise provided, all the laws in force applicable to any public service would continue. Article 314 which sought to provide protection to existing officers of certain services was repealed by the 28th Amendment.

Public Service Commissions

Article 315 lays down that there shall be a Public Service Commission for the Union and a Public Service Commission for each State. Two or more States may opt for a Joint Commission. On request, the Union Service Commission may also agree to serve some needs of a State.

The Public Service Commissions are envisaged as independent constitutional institutions not subject to governmental or political interference or control and charged with the responsibility of recruitment and management of public services. All expenses of the Union and State Service Commissions are charged on the Consolidated Fund of the Union or the State concerned (Article 322).

The Supreme Court has held that the function of the Commission is purely advisory and if the Government fails to consult it in any matter specified for consultation, a public servant affected thereby cannot expect a remedy in a court of law under article 320. But where consultation is provided for by law or regulation, it will constitute a legal obligation. [articles 320 321 and 323; *State of U.P. v. Srivastava,* AIR 1957 SC 912; *State of U.P. v. Rajasthan,* AIR 1988 SC 162; *Keshav v. U.P. HESC,* (1985) ISCC 671; *Neelima v. State of Haryana,* AIR 1987 SC 169] [See Chapter 10. 'Independent Offices']

Administrative Tribunals

The Constitution (Forty Second Amendment) Act, 1976 inserted a new part Part XIVA and articles 323A and 323B to empower Parliament and State Legislatures to set up by law administrative tribunals for the adjudication of disputes and complaints in all service matters relating to recruitment and conditions of service of public employees. Tribunals may also be set up for certain other matters like taxation, labour and industry, land reforms, elections, rent laws etc. Several such tribunals have since been set up, excluding the jurisdiction of certain level of Courts. Thus the Administrative Tribunals Act 1985 setting up tribunals for resolving service disputes takes away the jurisdication of High Courts while appeal lies to the Supreme Court under article 136 only (*Sampath v. Union of India*, AIR 1987 SC 386; *Tamilmani v. Union of India*, AIR 1992 SC 1120). In *L. Chandra Kumar v. Union of India* (AIR 1997 SC 1125). It was held that clause 2 (d) of article 323A and clause 3(d) of article 323B are unconstitutional to the extent that they exclude the jurisdiction of the High Courts and the Supreme Court.

Administrative Reforms

In the field of public administration and role of civil services, some of the controversies that need urgent attention are:

i. *The GeneralistAdministrators vs. Specialist Professional*: Both are needed and must learn to work together in national developmental interests.

ii. *The Ministers vs. Civil Servants:* While public policy has to be laid down by the Ministers, interference in day to day administration is bound to demoralise the civil servants. Rules and norms should be respected.

iii. *Official Secrets Act vs. Right to Information Act:* If the new RTI is implemented properly, it has the potential of making a dent in levels of corruption. But the danger of civil servants becoming unduly circumspect in their notings has to be guarded against.

iv. *Committed vs. Neutral Services:* The highest traditions of civil service neutrality have to be married to commitment to development goals and people's welfare above political party or other vested interests. The civil servant must be able to give correct, non-partisan advice without fear or favour.

v. *Responsibility to the People:* Each level of authority in administration has to be accountable to the next upto the Council of Ministers which is responsible to the people through their representatives in Parliament. [See Chapter 5. "The Legislature"]

The Constitution Commission (NCRWC-2002) considered all those matters in depth and made recommendations of far-reaching importance. These included:

i. The questions of personnel policy including placements, promotions, transfers and fast-track advancements on the basis of forward-looking career management policies and techniques should be managed by autonomous Personnel Boards for assisting the high level political authorities in making key decisions.
ii. Above a certain level—say the Joint Secretary level—all posts should be open for recruitment from a wide variety of sources including the open market.
iii. Officials, before starting their career, in addition to the taking of an oath of loyalty to the Constitution, should swear to abide by the basic principles of good governance.
iv. The constitutional safeguards have in practice acted to shield the guilty against swift and certain punishment for abuse of public office for private gain. A major corollary has been erosion of accountability. It has accordingly become necessary to re-visit the issue of constitutional safeguards under article 311 to ensure that the honest and efficient officials are given the requisite protection but the dishonest are not allowed to prosper in office. A comprehensive examination of the entire concept of administrative jurisprudence has to be undertaken to rationalize and simplify the procedure of administrative and legal action and to bring the theory and practice of security of tenure in line with the experience of the last more than 50 years.
v. The civil service regulations need to be changed radically in the light of contemporary administrative theory to introduce modern evaluation methodology

The Government of India is seized of the problems of public administration reforms and the Second Administrative Reforms Commission has been at work.

Conclusion

'Stability' and 'responsibility' are the twin pillars of democracy and in order to achieve these twin pillars, Government must provide 'good governance'. Good governance has to be necessarily democratic, participatory, transparent, accountable and citizen-friendly. It must be responsible to the people and responsive to their aspirations and needs. It must be able to concentrate on development and people's welfare.

To make the administration citizen-friendly, mechanisms have to be developed for citizens' grievance ventilation and redressal. Politicisation of bureaucracy and interference of administration in the lives of citizens will need to be ended. Questions of appointment, promotion, transfer of civil servants and their interface with Ministers, *etc.* have to be looked into; and healthy norms of accountability to the people established through necessary administrative reforms.

5

PARLIAMENT AND STATE LEGISLATURES
STRUCTURE AND FUNCTIONS

In the system of parliamentary democracy, that we adopted for our country, it is natural that Parliament should occupy a place of primacy and pre-eminence in the structure of governance. Parliament of India is the supreme law making body of the Union. Also, it is the highest representative institution of the people. The bicameral Union Legislature called 'Parliament' is the pivot on which the political system of the country revolves. Under the provision of universal adult franchise, the people exercise their sovereign power while casting their votes to elect representatives to the popular House of the Union Parliament. And, the Parliament becomes the people's institution *par excellence* through which the sovereign will of the people finds expression. In parliamentary system, we use the terms 'first reading', 'second reading' and 'third reading' of Bills. The Bills have to be read to Members of 'Parliament'. When a Bill is read to Members the first time, it is called the first reading and so on. The whole idea is that in Parliament we talk and discuss, try to persuade and take decisions through discussion and persuasion.

Article 79 of the Constitution begins by saying that there shall be a Parliament for the Union which means that Parliament must always be there. At the level of States, their legislatures occupy similar position. It is important to remember that in a parliamentary polity, just as government is responsible to the legislature, the legislature is also responsible to the people who are the ultimate sovereign.

Composition of Parliament

The Parliament consists of the President and the two Houses – the Rajya Sabha (Council of States) and the Lok Sabha (House of the People). Of the three constituents of Parliament, only the Lok Sabha is subject to dissolution. The Rajya Sabha is a permanent or continuing House and there must always be a President or a person performing the functions of the President.

The President

The principle that in a parliamentary system of government, executive is part of Parliament is also symbolised by the President of the Union who is the Head of the State and in whom all the executive power of the Union vests being a constituent functionary of Parliament. Even though, the President does not sit or participate in the discussions in either of the two houses, he exercises several powers and performs important functions in respect of Parliament. The President is elected by an Electoral College consisting of the elected members of the two Houses of Parliament and Legislative Assemblies of the States. [See Chapter 4. 'The Executive']

Rajya Sabha

Under the Constitution, the Rajya Sabha or the Council of States, as its name indicates, is the House of the representatives of the States. It consists of a maximum of 250 members – 238 elected by the elected members of the State Legislative Assemblies and 12 nominated by the President. Elections to the Rajya Sabha are indirect and based on proportional representation and single transferable vote system (article 80(4)). The different States of the Union have not been given equal representation in Rajya Sabha. The number of representatives from each State in India depends largely on its population. There are at present 245 members in Rajya Sabha, distributed among different States and Union Territories as follows:

Table 5.1

	States	No. of Members
(1)	Andhra Pradesh	18
(2)	Arunachal Pradesh	1
(3)	Assam	7
(4)	Bihar	16
(5)	Chhattisgarh	5
(6)	Goa	1
(7)	Gujarat	11
(8)	Haryana	5
(9)	Himachal Pradesh	3
(10)	Jammu & Kashmir	4
(11)	Jharkhand	6
(12)	Karnataka	12
(13)	Kerala	9
(14)	Madhya Pradesh	11
(15)	Maharashtra	19
(16)	Manipur	1
(17)	Meghalaya	1
(18)	Mizoram	1
(19)	Nagaland	1
(20)	Orissa	10
(21)	Punjab	7
(22)	Rajasthan	10
(23)	Sikkim	1
(24)	Tamil Nadu	18
(25)	Tripura	1
(26)	Uttaranchal	3
(27)	Uttar Pradesh	31
(28)	West Bengal	16
(29)	NCT of Delhi	3
(30)	Pondicherry	1

And twelve nominated members according to article 80(1)(a) of the Constitution.

Unlike Lok Sabha, Rajya Sabha is a permanent body and it is not subject to dissolution. One-third of its members retire on the expiry of every second year. The term of an individual member of the Rajya Sabha is six years (article 83).

Rajya Sabha was duly constituted for the first time on 3 April 1952 and it held its first sitting on 13 May the same year.

Lok Sabha

The Lok Sabha or House of the People is composed of representatives of the people chosen by direct election. Every citizen of India who is not less than 18 years of age is entitled to vote in the elections to the Lok Sabha unless he is otherwise disqualified under law (article 326). The maximum strength of the House envisaged by the Constitution is 552. The Constitution provides that the Lok Sabha shall consist of not more than 530 members chosen by direct election from territorial constituencies in the States, and not more than 20 members to represent the Union Territories (article 81). In addition, President may nominate not more than two members to represent the Anglo Indian Community (article 331). At present Lok Sabha consists of 545 members. The elective seats in Lok Sabha are divided among the 28 States and the 7 Union Territories as given in Table 5.2.

Besides, two members have been nominated to represent the Anglo-Indian community.

The elective membership is distributed in such a manner that the ratio between the number of seats alloted to each State and the population of the State is, as far as possible, the same for all States [article 81(2)]. Seats in the Lok Sabha are reserved for the Scheduled Castes and Scheduled Tribes on the basis of their population ratios in respective States. Originally it was only for ten years but is being extended everytime for the next ten years. Under the latest amendment, it is now for 60 years, *i.e.* until the year 2010 (articles 330 & 334).

The term of the Lok Sabha, unless dissolved earlier, is five years from the date appointed for its first meeting. However, while a proclamation of emergency is in operation, this period can be extended by the Parliament by law for a period not exceeding one year at a time and not exceeding in any case a period of six months after the proclamation has ceased to operate (article 83).

Table 5.2

	States	No. of Members
(1)	Andhra Pradesh	42
(2)	Arunachal Pradesh	2
(3)	Assam	14
(4)	Bihar	40
(5)	Chhattisgarh	11
(6)	Goa	2
(7)	Gujarat	26
(8)	Haryana	10
(9)	Himachal Pradesh	4
(10)	Jammu & Kashmir	6
(11)	Jharkhand	14
(12)	Karnataka	28
(13)	Kerala	20
(14)	Madhya Pradesh	29
(15)	Maharashtra	48
(16)	Manipur	2
(17)	Meghalaya	2
(18)	Mizoram	1
(19)	Nagaland	1
(20)	Orissa	21
(21)	Punjab	13
(22)	Rajasthan	25
(23)	Sikkim	1
(24)	Tamil Nadu	39
(25)	Tripura	2
(26)	Uttar Pradesh	85
(27)	Uttaranchal	5
(28)	West Bengal	42
Union Territories		
(1)	Andaman & Nicobar Islands	1
(2)	Chandigarh	1
(3)	Dadra & Nagar Haveli	1
(4)	Daman & Diu	1
(5)	Delhi	7
(6)	Lakshadweep	1
(7)	Pondicherry	1

The Constitution of India came into force on 26 January 1950. The first general elections under the new Constitution were held during the year 1951-52 and the first Parliament with the two Houses – the Rajya Sabha and the Lok Sabha – came into being in April 1952. Given below are the dates of constitution and dissolution of the first to the fourteenth Lok Sabhas.

Table 5.3

	Date of Constitution of the House	Date of Dissolution of the House
First Lok Sabha	17.4.1952	4.4.1957
Second Lok Sabha	5.4.1957	31.3.1962
Third Lok Sabha	2.4.1962	3.3.1967
Fourth Lok Sabha	4.3.1967	27.12.1970
Fifth Lok Sabha	15.3.1971	18.1.1977
Sixth Lok Sabha	23.3.1977	22.8.1979
Seventh Lok Sabha	10.1.1980	31.12.1984
Eighth Lok Sabha	31.12.1984	27.11.1989
Ninth Lok Sabha	2.12.1989	13.3.1991
Tenth Lok Sabha	20.6.1991	10.5.1996
Eleventh Lok Sabha	15.5.1996	4.12.1997
Twelfth Lok Sabha	10.3.1998	26.4.1999
Thirteenth Lok Sabha	10.10.1999	6.2.2004
Fourteenth Lok Sabha	17.05.2004	–

It would be seen that none of the Lok Sabhas has so far stood dissolved on the expiry of its term. Whether days, months or years before the date of expiry, every Lok Sabha has been dissolved. The term of the Fifth Lok Sabha during internal emergency, was extended by two years but that House did not complete the extended term and was dissolved.

Membership

Qualification for Membership: Article 83 of the Constitution lays down the qualifications for membership of the two Houses of Parliament. In order to be eligible to be chosen as a member, a person must be a citizen of India and not less than 30 years of age in case of Rajya Sabha membership and not less than 25 years of age in case of Lok Sabha membership. Additional qualifications may be prescribed by law.

Disqualifications for Membership: Under article 102, a person shall be disqualified for being chosen as and for being a member of either House (i) if he is not a citizen of India or otherwise owes allegiance to a foreign State, (ii) if he is an undischarged insolvent or one declared by a competent court to be of unsound mind, (iii) if he holds any office of profit under the Union or a State Government other than the office of Minister or any office exempted by Parliament by law, and (iv) if he is otherwise disqualified under any law made by Parliament. Also, a person may be disqualified on grounds of defection under the Tenth Schedule which was added to the Constitution by the 52nd Amendment.

If any question arises whether a member of either House has become subject to any disqualification, it shall be decided by the President after obtaining the opinion of the Election Commission and in accordance with that opinion except in case of disqualification on grounds of defection where the matter will be decided by the Speaker Lok Sabha or Chairman Rajya Sabha as the case may be (articles 102(2) and 103).

The job of Parliament and its Members is to represent the people, to lay down policies, to make laws and to exercise surveillance over executive action. With the exception of Members who become Ministers, other Members are not expected to exercise any executive powers by accepting any office of profit under the Government. If those charged with the responsibility of overseeing the executive, themselves become part of the executive establishment or become beholden to the executive for an office of profit under the Government, obviously they cannot be expected to faithfully perform any worthwhile oversight functions. That is why, article 102 of the Constitution provides that apart from certain other things, holding an office of profit under the Government would constitute a disqualification for membership of Parliament. Giving a somewhat arbitrary power to the Parliament/State

Legislatures, it is provided that any offices can be exempted from disqualification.

Constitutional provisions for State Legislatures corresponding to articles 102 and 103 are articles 191 and 192.

A Member was recently (March 2006) divested of her Rajya Sabha Membership by the President on the advice of the Election Commission as per article 103 of the Constitution. Several other cases were pending decision. However, before a decision could be taken Parliament passed an amendment to the Parliament (Prevention of Disqualification) Act, 1959 to exempt from disqualification holders of offices of profit retrospectively *w.e.f.* 1959.

Office Of Profit

The Parliament (Prevention of Disqualification) Act, 1959 (amended from time to time) declares the offices of profit under the Government which do not disqualify the holders thereof for being chosen as, or for being, members of Parliament.

The term 'office of profit under the Government' has not been defined in the Constitution or the Representation of the People Act, 1951 or the Parliament (Prevention of Disqualification) Act, 1959. The Courts or other authorities have, however, stated in this connection certain broad criteria:

(i) The essential characteristics of an office of profit are (1) it involves an appointment by the State in one form or the other, (2) it carries emoluments payable mostly periodically, (3) it is for a limited period, (4) it is terminable, (5) it is not assignable, (6) it is not heritable, (7) the holder of the office must be *sui juris*.

(ii) Profit in article 191 (article 102 for Parliament) of the Constitution of India does not necessarily mean any remuneration in cash but it certainly means some kind of advantage or gain which can be perceived. But, the mere influence which one gains by virtue of his position as member of a Committee which has no remuneration attached to it is not an office of profit within the meaning of article 191 of the Constitution, and the member of such a Committee would suffer no disqualification by being a member thereof.

(iii) Profit connoted the idea of pecuniary gain. If there is really a gain its quantum or amount would not be material but the amount of money receivable by a person in connection with the office he holds may be material in deciding whether the office really carries any profit.

(iv) The emoluments attached to office may be in the nature of pay, salary, honorarium, fees, daily allowance, travelling allowance etc. Where salary is attached to an office, it immediately and indisputably makes the office an office of profit.

(v) If consideration is paid in the shape of remuneration *i.e.,* sitting fee, or attendance fee, it becomes a profit inasmuch as it does not even purport to cover any actual expenses. Such consideration or remuneration should be deemed to constitute 'profit' even though on detailed accounting it may be found that no financial advantage has in fact been gained by the member in question.

(vi) Travelling and halting allowances received by a member of an Area Committee are not remuneration but represent reimbursement of out of pocket expenses and a member of an Area Committee does not, thereofore, hold an office of Profit within the meaning of article 191 of the Constitution and is not disqualified for membership.

(vii) According to the Parliament (Prevention of Disqualification) Act, 1959, if a person is not entitled to any remuneration other than compensatory allowance as defined in section 2(a) of the Act, he will not incur disqualification for receiving that remuneration.

(viii) In order that an office may be an office of profit, it is not necessary that there must be some sort of regularity of income. Neither is it necessary that there should be actual making of profit by the incumbent; it is enough if the holder of the office may reasonably be expected to make a profit out of it.

(ix) For the purpose of deciding the question of disqualification, so long as any profit was attached to an office, it did not matter whether the profit had in fact been appropriated or not. Therefore, there was no distinction for the purpose between the members who drew the allowances and those who did not. Some offices may be considered offices of profit even if the actual payment of emoluments attached might have fallen into disuse.

Under the Government

(i) The source from which a person receives profit is not the sole test as to whether he holds an office of profit under the Government within the meaning of article 102(1)(a) of the

Constitution. The power to appoint and remove is also one of the tests and if a person is appointed by the Government to an office of profit and is removable by the Government from the office, he would be a person holding an office of profit under the Government even though he is not paid out of the Government funds.

(ii) The power conferred on the State Government to exercise control and supervision over the working of the University will not make the University, or its officers, subordinate to the State Government in the sense that they would be disqualified to be chosen as and for being members of the State Legislature. The Vice-Chancellor is appointed by the Governor in his capacity as Chancellor of the University, distinct from his office as the head of the Executive, and the appointment cannot be deemed to have been made by, nor can the office of the Vice-Chancellor be said to be under the State Government by virtue of the appointment having been made by the Governor in another capacity.

(iii) The power of the Government to appoint a person to an office of profit or to continue him in that office or revoke his appointment at their discretion and payment from out of Government revenues are important factors in determining whether that person is holding an office of profit under the Government, though payment from a source other than Government revenue is not always a decisive factor.

(iv) A person serving as a teacher in a school receiving grant-in-aid from Government does not hold an office of profit under the Government merely because the school receives grant from the Government for payment of a portion of the dearness allowance and the pay. The real test would be whether the Government of the State had the power to remove a person from office. If so, it must be held that the person holds that office under the Government of the State and this is irrespective of whether the salary attached to the office is paid by the State or paid out of some other funds.

(v) To determine whether an office is under the Government, it is not necessary to see whether the Government have some disciplinary or supervisory powers over the incumbent of the office.

(vi) For holding an office of profit under the Government, one need not be in the service of Government and there need be no relationship of master and servant between them. Several factors enter into the determination of this question – the appointing authority, the authority vested with power to terminate the appointment, the authority which determines the remuneration, the source from which the remuneration is paid, the authority vested with power to control the manner in which the duties of the office are discharged must all co-exist and each must show subordination to Government and it must necessarily follow that if one of the elements is absent, the test of a person holding an office under the Government, Central or State is not satisfied. The source from which the remuneration is paid is not decisive. Whether stress will be laid on one factor or the other will depend on the facts of each case.

(vii) The disqualification of a person who holds an office of profit does not cease on his submitting an unqualified resignation of his office but only when his resignation is accepted by the proper authority.[1]

Vacation of Seats

Article 101 lays down that a member shall be required to vacate his seat in a House if he is elected to both Houses of Parliament or to a House of State Legislature. In the latter case, if the member does not resign his seat in the State Legislature, his seat in the House of Parliament may be declared vacant. A seat may also stand vacated if a member becomes subject to any disqualification or voluntarily resigns his seat. The House may declare a seat vacant if the concerned member fails to attend the House for more than 60 days without permission.

Anti-Defection Law

Defection may be defined as abandonment of loyalty, duty or principle, or of one's leader or cause. In parliamentary political life, the term has come to mean change of party affiliation or allegiance by the member of a legislature. The traditional term for the latter was, however, floor-crossing which had its origins in the British House of Commons where a legislator moved from

---

1. For further details regarding office of profit as disqualifiction for membership, see Subhash C. Kashyap, *Parliamentary Procedure*, Universal, New Delhi, 2000, Vol.2, pp. 2132-37.

the Government to the Opposition side or *vice versa*. The phenomenon of defection was not something altogether unknown to the older democracies like Great Britain. Political stalwarts like William Gladstone, Joseph Chamberlain, Winston Churchill and Ramsay McDonald were known to have changed their party allegiance at one time or another – some of them even more than once. Likewise in Australia, Canada and the USA, there had been instances of politicians defecting from one party to another. It is, however interesting that the need or the desirability of banning defections by law or through a constitutional provision was not considered in any of the western democracies. The only countries to pass anti-defection laws have been four countries in South Asia *viz.* India (1985), Pakistan (1997), Sri Lanka (1978) and Nepal (1997). In all the four countries, the Anti-defection laws proved ineffective. In India, the result was a larger number of defections, with groups instead of individuals defecting. In Nepal also, group defections and toppling of governments could not be prevented. In Pakistan, the operation of the law was stayed by the court and subsequently democracy itself was toppled by military dictatorship.

Indian politics had seen defections right from the pre-independence Central Legislative Assembly and Provincial autonomy days. The year 1967 however ushered in an unprecedented era of political instability and horse-trading preceding and following the formation of coalition governments in several States. The formation of such coalition governments was most often a marriage of convenience. They were constituted of heterogeneous elements – political parties coming together to share power often having no ideological similarity. Several State Governments fell like the proverbial nine pins in quick succession. The fall was usually brought about by dissatisfied and disgruntled legislators who, it was widely believed, could not be accommodated as Ministers and the like or otherwise lucratively recompensed. They changed their party affiliations and were welcomed with open arms by other political parties which, though in minority, cherished the dream of forming a Government on the strength of such synthetic majority. This gave rise to a very unhealthy trend whereby legislators were lured away from their political parties with a view to toppling the existing Governments and forming new ones with different permutations and combinations.

Between the fourth and the fifth general elections in 1967 and 1972 from among the 4,000 odd members of the Lok Sabha and the Legislative Assemblies in the States and the Union Territories, there were nearly 2,000 cases of defection and counter-defection. By the end of March 1971 approximately 50 per cent of the legislators had changed their party affiliations and several of them did so more than once – some of them as many as five times. One MLA was found to have defected five times to be a Minister for only five days. For sometime, on an average more than one legislator was defecting each day and almost one State Government falling each month due to these changes in party affiliations by members. In the case of State Assemblies alone, as much as 50.5 per cent of the total number of legislators changed their political affiliations at least once. The percentage would be even more alarming if such States were left out where Governments happened to be more stable and changes of political affiliations or defections from parties remained very infrequent. That the lure of office played a dominant part in this "political horsetrading" was obvious from the fact that out of 210 defecting legislators of the various States during the first year of "defection politics", 116 were included in the Council of Ministers in the Governments which they helped to form.[2]

Immediately after the general elections held in December 1984, the President of India said in his Address to both Houses of Parliament assembled together on 17 January, 1985 that the Government intended to introduce in that session a Bill to outlaw defections. In fulfillment of that assurance, the Government introduced the Constitution (Fifty-second Amendment) Bill in the Lok Sabha on 24 January, 1985.

2. See Subhash C. Kashyap, *The Politics of Power*, New Delhi, 1974.

In order to bring about a national consensus on the Bill, the Prime Minister held prolonged consultations with the leaders of Opposition groups. The Government acceded to the demand of dropping a controversial clause from the Bill relating to disqualification of a member on his expulsion from his political party for his conduct outside the House.

The Bill was passed by Lok Sabha and Rajya Sabha on 30 and 31 January, 1985, respectively. It received the President's assent on 15 February, 1985. The Act came into force with effect from 1 March, 1985 after issue of the necessary notification in the Official Gazette.

The Constitution (Fifty second Amendment) Act, 1985 amended articles 101, 102, 190 and 191 of the Constitution regarding vacation of seats and disqualification from membership of Parliament and the State Legislatures and added a new schedule (Tenth Schedule) to the Constitution setting out certain provisions as to disqualification on grounds of defection. The Tenth Schedule *inter alia* provided that:

i. an elected member of Parliament or a State Legislature, who has been elected as a candidate set up by a political party, and a nominated member of Parliament or a State Legislature who is a member of a political party at the time he takes his seat would be disqualified on the ground of defection if he voluntarily relinquishes his membership of such political party or votes or abstains from voting in the House contrary to any direction of such party;

ii. an independent member of Parliament or a State Legislature will be disqualified if he joins any political party after his election;

iii. a nominated member of Parliament or a State Legislature who is not a member of a political party at the time of his nomination and who has not become a member of any political party before the expiry of six months from the date on which he takes his seat shall be disqualified if he joins any political party after the expiry of the said period of six months;

iv. no disqualification would be incurred where a member claims that he belongs to a group representing a faction arising from a split in a party or merger of a party in another provided that in the event of a split the group consists of not less than one third of the members of the legislature party and in case of a merger of not less than two thirds of the members of the legislature party concerned;

v. no disqualification is incurred by a person who has been elected to the office of the Speaker or the Deputy Speaker of the House of the People or of the Legislative Assembly of a State or to the office of the Deputy Chairman of the Council of States or the Chairman or the Deputy Chairman of the Legislative Council of a State, if he severs his connection with his political party;

vi. the question as to whether a member of a House of Parliament or State Legislature has become subject to disqualification will be determined by the Chairman or the Speaker of the respective House; where the question is with reference to the Chairman or the Speaker himself it will be decided by a member of the concerned House elected by it in that behalf;

vii. the Chairman or the Speaker of a House has been empowered to make rules for giving effect to the provisions of the Schedule. The rules are required to be laid before the House and are subject to modifications/disapproval by the House;

viii. all proceedings in relation to any question as to disqualification of a member of a House under the Schedule will be deemed to be proceedings in Parliament within the meaning of article 122 or, as the case may be, proceedings in the Legislature of a State within the meaning of article 212; and

ix. notwithstanding anything in the Constitution, no court will have any jurisdiction in respect of any matter connected with the disqualification of a member of a House.

The Constitution (Fifty second Amendment) Act, 1985, which has since popularly come to be known as the Anti Defection Law, has been the subject matter of a controversy from the very beginning. It has been questioned on several grounds *viz.*, that it is violative of the basic structure of the Constitution, that it is beyond the competence of Parliament, and that it gives preference to expediency over principles. Several writ petitions challenging the validity and constitutionality of the 1985 enactment were also filed in the Supreme Court and various High Courts. The paragraph which barred the jurisdiction of the courts was struck down as being *ultra vires* the Constitution by the High Court of Punjab and Haryana. In *Kihoto v. Zachillhu* (AIR 1993 SC 412), the Supreme Court found that there were legal infirmities in the passage of the Anti-Defection Law inasmuch as the Constitution Amendment Bill had not been ratified by the requisite number of State Assemblies before being presented for the President's assent. Also, the Speaker's functions under the 10th Schedule called for a judicial determination of issues under the law and the process of determining the question of disqualification could not be considered part of the proceedings of the House and as such not amenable to judicial review. The Supreme Court struck down Para 7 of the Schedule barring the jurisdiction of Courts and declared that while operating under the Anti-Defection Law, the Speaker was in the position of a tribunal and therefore his decisions like those of all tribunals were subject to judicial review.

The fact that certain provisions of the Tenth Schedule were found to be amenable to entirely different interpretations by different presiding officers created terrible uncertainty and fluidity in the application of the law and brought to limelight a number of defects. It was agreed on all sides that the Tenth Schedule of the Constitution which embodied the Anti Defection Law had several serious lacunae which had caused tremendous damage to our body politic and that amendments were called for urgently.[3]

At the Union level, two Governments of V.P. Singh and Chandra Shekhar fell in quick succession. Even though Chandra Shekhar formed the Janata Dal(S) Government and won the confidence of the House on a substantive motion, all the members of the ruling Janata Dal(S) were either those who had been expelled by V.P. Singh and declared "unattached" by Speaker Ray or those against whom show cause notices for disqualification under the Anti Defection Law had been issued.

3 For a commentary on the subject see Subhash C. Kashyap, *Anti-Defection Law and Parliamentary Privileges*, Tripathi, Bombay, 1995; revised edition, Universal, New Delhi, 2003.

Speaker Ray recognised the split as a one time process. Janata Dal(S) was recognised as a political party with 54 members. The seven members who joined after the date of split were disqualified.

In another case of Janata split, on 7 August, 1992, 20 of the 59 members of the Janata Dal appeared before Speaker Patil physically in one group, at the same time and claimed that they belonged to a group and should be seated separately from the Janata Dal members headed by V.P. Singh. Even though eight of these members had been expelled earlier by the Janata Dal leadership in two separate spells, the Speaker allotted them separate seats in the House. In his final decision on 1 June 1993. Speaker Patil held that political parties had no right under the Constitution to expel members from the legislature party so as to take away their constitutional status as members elected on a particular party ticket and (ii) that the 20 members did not suffer from any disability as on 7 August 1992 and since they had the requisite strength of one third on that day, they constituted a valid faction of the Janata Dal Parliamentary Party. Most significantly, the Speaker agreed that the Anti Defection Law was defective and needed review and reform.

The Constitution Commission (NCRWC) recommended that all defectors—whether individual or in groups of one-third *etc.*—should be disqualified for continuing as members. They must resign and seek fresh election and until reelection, they should stand debarred from holding any public office of a minister or any other remunerative public post. Following the recommendation, the Constitution (91st Amendment) Act 2003 amended the Tenth Schedule of the Constitution and inserted a new article 361B. It omitted the provision of party split being a protection against disqualification on grounds of defection. Also, it disqualified for appointment on remunerative political posts all those disqualified for membership on grounds of defection. However, the protection of 'merger' still stays.

Functions of Parliament

Parliament of India, like all Westminster-style parliamentary democracies, is a multi-functional institution performing a variety of roles that are inter-related and often meshing into one another. Some of the cardinal roles and functions of the Parliament may be described as follows:

- To form or end the Government
- To represent the Electorate
- To legislate
- To hold the government accountable for its actions
- To monitor the expenditure of public funds
- To be a forum for debate
- To be a forum for the expression of grievances
- To call for information

To form or to end the Government

The Parliament of India, like all parliamentary democracies, forms the government. This is particularly due to the fusion of powers between the legislative and the executive branches of the Government. Members of Parliament, from the largest party in the Lok Sabha or of late from the largest coalition, form the Government at the centre.

When the Parliament is sitting, the continuance of the government in office depends from moment to moment on its retaining the confidence of the House of the People. The House may at any time decide to throw out the government by a majority vote, *i.e.* if the ruling party loses the support of the majority of the members of the House, its Government goes. No grounds, arguments, proofs or justifications are necessary. When the House clearly and conclusively pronounces that the government of the day does not command its support, it must resign.

Representation of the Electorate

The primary function of the Parliament is to represent the people. It is the supreme forum through which people seek to realise their aspirations, urges and expectations. The Parliament like a barometre represents the changing moods and the needs of the people. The Members of Parliament are the elected representatives of the people and they act as the chief communication channel between the people, Parliament and the Government. Multiplicity of political parties in Parliament represents the multi-cultural and plural society of India. In recent years, the emergence of coalition governments, Common Minimum Programmes and agreements to disagree are some of the mechanisms which reflect the multifarious needs of the Indian people and the multilinearity of Indian culture.

Legislation

The process of legislating, making laws, is the most basic day-to-day function of parliament. Under articles 245 and 246 Parliament can make laws for the whole or any part of India within its area of competence as defined and delimited under the distribution of legislative powers between the Union and the States *vide* the Seventh Schedule. In regard to the Union List, the Parliament's jurisdiction is exclusive. Both the Union and the States have concurrent power to legislate in respect of entries in the concurrent list. In case of conflict between the Union and the State laws, the former prevails (article 254). Also, the residuary powers vest in the Union Parliament (article 248 and entry 97 of the Union List). A large number of articles empower the Parliament to make laws in various matters by saying things like 'save as otherwise provided by Parliament by law', 'Parliament may by law.....' or 'until Parliament by law prescribes' *etc.* Parliament may by law change the name, the boundaries, area etc. of the States or establish new States (articles 2,3 and 4), increase the number of judges of the Supreme Court or establish additional courts (articles 124, 247). Under article 249, Parliament may legislate even on matters in the State List. Under article 253, it may legislate for implementing a treaty or agreement with a foreign country even though the matter falls in the State List. Also, in circumstances of President's rule (article 356) or proclamation of Emergency (article 352), Parliament can legislate in the State field.

Governmental Accountability

Under our system, after a policy is laid down, a law is passed or money is sanctioned, it is the administration which is required to execute and implement. Since Parliament embodies the will of the people, it must be able to oversee the way in which public policy is carried out so as to ensure that it keeps in step with the objectives of socio-economic progress, efficient administration and aspirations of the people as a whole.

The various procedural devices like the system of Parliamentary Committees, Questions, Calling Attention Notices, Half-an-Hour discussions, *etc.* through which the Parliament gets informed, also constitute very potent instruments for effecting parliamentary surveillance over administrative action. Significant occasions for the review of administration are provided by the discussions on the Motion of Thanks on the President's Address, the Budget demands, and particular aspects of governmental policy or situations. These apart, specific matters may be discussed through motions on matters of urgent public importance, private members' resolutions and other substantive motions.

Monitoring the Expenditure of Public Funds

Parliamentary control over public finance – the power to levy or modify taxes and the voting of supplies and grants – is one of the most important checks against the Executive assuming arbitrary powers. No taxes can be legally levied and no expenditure incurred from the public exchequer without specific parliamentary authorization by law (articles 114 116 and 265). The Constitution also provides for an annual statement of the estimated receipts and expenditure—budget—to be placed before Parliament. Other means by which Parliament exercises control over the public exchequer is through Public Accounts Committee, Committee on Public Undertakings, Estimates Committee and the Report of the Comptroller and Auditor General.

The Comptroller and Auditor General: [See Chapter 10. 'Independent Offices']

A Forum for Debate

During debate and discussion on legislative proposals or Finance Bills, motion to consider and approve government policies, motion of thanks on the President's Address, Budget, *etc.* members are free to express themselves and to say what is good for the country and what modifications in the existing policy are required. The government is sensitive to parliamentary opinion; in most cases they anticipate it; in some cases they bow to it and in some others they may feel that they cannot make any change consistent with their commitments and obligations and political philosophy. Nevertheless during discussions members have full liberty to criticise the administration for their past performance and suggest how they should behave in the future or how a particular measure should be carried out or implemented. The discussions are important for they indicate parliamentary mood and bring the impact of public thinking on the administrative apparatus which may otherwise remain immune to public sentiments and feelings. It is as well that the parliamentary debates should serve to remind the administration of their duties and obligations. Parliamentary debates affect the administrative thinking and action in a variety of ways and the subtle influence which cannot be measured in terms of any visible units pervades through all the ranks of administration – high and low.

A Forum for the Expression of Grievances

Parliament acts as a forum for ventilation of the grievances of the people, their difficulties and their passions, anxieties and frustrations. Various grievances, needs and aspirations of the people are discussed in the Parliament and necessary legislation is taken up in this regard. In recent decades, emphasis has shifted more and more to representational and grievance ventilation role of the Parliament. It is the peoples' institution *par excellence*.

Informational Role

Information is vital to Parliament. It is the first essential requisite for effective discharge of any of its functions. To call for information is perhaps the greatest power of the Parliament. Parliament's right to be informed is unlimited except that if divulging of certain information is likely to prejudice vital national interest or the security of the State, it may not be insisted upon. So far as the activities of the Government are concerned, it is the duty of the Government itself to feed the Parliament with information which is full, truthful, precise and supplied in time. This is done by the ministers making statements on the floor of the House, laying reports and papers on the Table of the House or placing documents in the Parliament Library. All these constitute a wealth of information which becomes immediately public and can be used to raise discussions in the House.

The most well-known and effective mechanism through which members on their own elicit information is that of asking questions in the Houses of Parliament. The minister may be put to a gruelling test by means of searching supplementaries which may be so framed as to expose the weakness of the administration. Through the members' questions sometimes, the ministers concerned themselves get better informed about the departments under their charge and the weak spots therein requiring priority attention. As follow up of what may be an incomplete answer to a question, a member may demand a half-an-hour discussion. Members may ask on matters of urgent public importance Short Notice Questions for oral answers. Still another procedural device is that of the Calling Attention Notices. A member may, with the previous permission of the Speaker, call the attention of a minister to any matter of urgent public importance and request the Minister to make a statement on the subject. Members can also write to the concerned ministers and ask for the information they may need and the information is usually supplied.

Another method for the Parliament to inform itself and receive necessary feedback is through the reports of various parliamentary committees. In the process of their scrutiny, the committees ask searching questions and collect extensive and valuable information from the government ministries and departments, public undertakings, *etc*. under examination. This procedural device has also become an important tool for eliciting information on matters of urgent public importance and has been very popular with members from both sides of the House.

Other sources of information include the mass media, political parties, interest groups and so on. Parliament has also its own institutionalised sources of information, called the Parliament Library and its Research, Reference, Documentation and Information Services. These remain at the disposal of members and supply non-partisan, objective and strictly relevant information on demand, promptly and often at short notice, as also in anticipation of the members' needs in discharge of their parliamentary duties.

Other Functions

Besides, Parliament exercises multifarious functions, for example, in matters like the amendment of the Constitution, the impeachment of the President, removal of Supreme Court and High Court judges, Comptroller and Auditor General, Chief Election Commissioner, Presiding Officers of the two Houses etc. (articles 61, 124, 217, 148, 324 and 90;).

Presiding Officers of the Houses

The Constitution provides for a Speaker and a Deputy Speaker for the Lok Sabha and a Chairman and a Deputy Chairman for the Rajya Sabha. The Vice President of India is the *ex officio* Chairman of Rajya Sabha. A Deputy Chairman is chosen by the House from among its own members. The Speaker and the Deputy Speaker are chosen by the Lok Sabha from among its members. In the absence of the Speaker in the House, the Deputy Speaker discharges the functions of the Speaker. Similarly, in the absence of the Chairman, the Deputy Chairman presides over the Rajya Sabha. While so presiding, the Deputy Presiding Officer in either case exercises all the powers of the Presiding Officer in the House. (articles 64, 89, 91 and 93 95).

Generally speaking, the position of the Speaker in India more or less corresponds to that of the Speaker of the House of

Commons. His office is one of prestige, splendour and authority. He is the head of Lok Sabha. The smooth and orderly conduct of the business of the House is primarily his responsibility. Within the House and in all matters connected with the House, his word is final. His salary and allowances are charged on the Consolidated Fund of India that is, they do not have to be voted by Parliament. His conduct cannot be discussed except on a substantive motion. He does not vote in the House except when there is an equality of votes. [articles 94, 96, 100(1) and 112(3)(b)].

The Constitution gives the Speaker a special position in so far as relations between the two Houses in certain matters are concerned. He determines what matters are financial matters which fall within the exclusive jurisdiction of Lok Sabha. If he certifies a Bill to be a 'Money Bill', his decision is final (article 110). Whenever, in the event of final disagreement between the Houses on a legislative measure a joint sitting is called, he presides over such a joint sitting and all the Rules of Procedure in such a sitting operate under his directions and orders [articles 108 and 118(4)].

The Speaker or Deputy Speaker of Lok Sabha vacates his office if he ceases to be a member of the House, he can resign by writing to the Deputy Speaker/Speaker and he can be removed by a resolution of the House, with 14 days' notice, passed by a majority of all the then members of the House (article 94). A similar provision exists for the Deputy Chairman Rajya Sabha in article 90. Irrespective of the dissolution of the House, the Speaker, however, continues in office until immediately before the first sitting of the new House (article 94, proviso 2).

Fourteen persons have occupied the high office of the Speaker of Lok Sabha thus far, as given in Table 5.4.

Sessions of Parliament

It is for the President to summon each House of Parliament from time to time. But article 85(1) provides that six months must not intervene between two sessions. Normally there are three sessions of Parliament each year *viz.* the Budget Session

Table 5.4

	Name	From	To
1.	G.V. Mavalankar	15 May 1952	27 Feb. 1956
2.	M.A. Ayyangar	8 March 1956	10 May 1957
3.	M.A. Ayyangar	11 May 1957	16 April 1962
4.	Sardar Hukam Singh	17 April 1962	16 March 1967
5.	N. Sanjeeva Reddy	17 March 1967	19 July 1969
6.	G.S. Dhillon	8 Aug. 1969	19 March 1971
7.	G.S. Dhillon	22 March 1971	1 Dec. 1975
8.	Bali Ram Bhagat	5 Jan. 1976	25 March 1977
9.	N. Sanjeeva Reddy	26 March 1977	13 July 1977
10.	K.S.Hegde	21 July 1977	21 Jan. 1980
11.	Bal Ram Jakhar	22 Jan. 1980	15 Jan. 1985
12.	Bal Ram Jakhar	16 Jan. 1985	18 Dec. 1989
13.	Rabi Ray	19 Dec. 1989	9 July 1991
14.	Shivraj V. Patil	10 July 1991	22 May 1996
15.	P.A. Sangma	23 May 1996	23 March 1998
16.	G.M.C. Balayogi	24 March 1998	20 October 1999
17.	G.M.C. Balayogi	22 October 1999	3 March 2002
18.	Manohar G. Joshi	10 May 2002	2 June 2004
19.	Somnath Chatterjee	4 June 2004	In office

(Feb. May), the Monsoon Session (July Sept.) and Winter Session (Nov. Dec.). In the case of the Rajya Sabha, however, the Budget Session is split up into two sessions with a three to four week break in between so that it has four sessions in a year. The schedule of sessions may get varied during an election year or under other special circumstances.

Leaders of Opposition

Leaders of opposition in the Rajya Sabha and the Lok Sabha are both accorded recognition by law since 1977. They are entitled to salary, allowances, staff and other facilities comparable to a Cabinet Minister.

Conduct of Business and Legislative Procedure

Each House is the master of its procedure and may make rules for regulating its procedure and conduct of business subject to the provisions of the Constitution (article 118). The validity of any proceedings in Parliament cannot be questioned in a court of law on grounds of any alleged irregularity of procedure and no officer or member of Parliament is subject to jurisdiction of courts in respect of exercise of any powers in the matter of regulating procedure or conduct of business in Parliament (article 122).

Some of the basic rules of procedure and conduct of business have been laid down in the Constitution itself. Thus, article 100 provides (1) that except where otherwise provided in the Constitution (*e.g.* in the case of Constitutional Amendments, impeachment of the President, removal of the Presiding Officers, judges *etc.*), all questions at any sitting of either House or joint sitting of the Houses shall be determined by a majority of votes of the members present and voting other than the presiding officer who shall exercise a casting vote only in case of an equality of votes; (2) that all proceedings of either House shall be valid irrespective of any vacancies in membership or any unauthorised participation in debate or voting; and (3) that the quorum to constitute a meeting of either House shall be one tenth of the total number of members.

Except Money Bills and other Financial Bills, a Bill may originate in either House. Such a Bill, before being presented to the President for his assent, must be passed by both the Houses either without any amendment or with such amendments as may be agreed to by both Houses. In case of final disagreement between the two Houses on any Bill other than a Money Bill, the President may summon a joint sitting of the two Houses to resolve the differences (articles 107 and 108).

Financial Bills

The Constitution makes a distinction between Money Bills and Financial Bills. Generally speaking, a Financial Bill may be any Bill which relates to revenue or expenditure. Besides providing for any of the matters specified in the Constitution for a Money Bill, a Financial Bill may also provide for other matters. For the sake of convenience, the Financial Bills may be divided into two categories: Category A: those Bills which make provisions for any of the matters specified in article 110 for the Money Bills but do not contain solely those matters, *e.g.* a Bill which contains a taxation clause, but does not deal solely with taxation. Category B: those Bills containing provisions involving expenditure from the Consolidated Fund (articles 110 and 117).

Special Procedure for Money Bills

Article 110 defines a Money Bill as a Bill which contains only provisions regarding taxes, borrowings, custody of the Consolidated and Contingency Funds, appropriations, declaring of any expenditure as charged on the Consolidated Fund, receipt and custody of money in the Consolidated Fund, audit of the accounts of the Union (or of a State) or any other incidental matters. A Bill shall not become a Money Bill simply because it provides for imposition of fines or other pecuniary penalties, or for payment of fees for licenses, or for fees for services rendered or by reason that it provides for imposition, regulation etc. of any tax by any local authority or body for local purposes. In case of any question arising whether a Bill is a Money Bill, the decision of the Speaker shall be final. While being presented to the President for his assent, every Money Bill has to be certified by the Speaker as such a Bill (article 110). A Money Bill can be introduced only in the Lok Sabha and only on the recommendation of the President. After it is passed by the Lok Sabha and transmitted to Rajya Sabha, the latter may make its recommendations, if any, within a period of 14 days and the Lok Sabha may accept or reject all or any of the recommendations. The Bill is deemed to be passed by both the Houses with the amendments accepted by Lok Sabha. If no amendment recommended by Rajya Sabha is acceptable to Lok Sabha or if the Bill is not returned by Rajya Sabha within 14 days, it is deemed to have been passed by both the Houses in the form in which it was passed by Lok Sabha (article 109).

Assent to Bills

Article 111 says that when a Bill passed by the two Houses of Parliament is presented to the President, the President shall either assent to the Bill or withhold assent therefrom. He may return a Bill, if it is not a Money Bill, to the Houses for reconsideration. If the Bill is passed again with or without any amendments and presented to President for assent, he shall not withhold assent (article 111). Another option available to the President is to seek some information or clarifications or to return the Bill to the Government *i.e.*, the Council of Ministers, for reconsidering their advice for according assent to the Bill (articles 74(1) and 78(b)). This is presumably what President Zail Singh did in case of the Postal Bill and President Venkataraman did in case of the Bill seeking to give pension to Members of Parliament after just one year's service.

Procedure in Financial Matters

The Budget: The President is required to cause to be laid before both Houses of Parliament in respect of each financial year a statement of the estimated receipts and expenditure of the Government. This is termed the annual financial statement or the budget. The estimates of expenditure embodied in the annual financial statement show separately:

(a) the sums required to meet expenditure described by the Constitution as expenditure charged upon the Consolidated Fund of India; and

(b) the sums required to meet other expenditure proposed to be made from the Consolidated Fund of India and shall distinguish expenditure on revenue account from other expenditure.

The expenditure charged on the Consolidated Fund of India shall include:

(a) the emoluments and allowances of the President and other expenditure relating to his office;

(b) the salaries and allowances of the Chairman and the Deputy Chairman of the Council of States and the Speaker and the Deputy Speaker of the House of the People;

(c) debt charges for which the Government of India is liable including interest, sinking fund charges and redemption charges, and other expenditure relating to the raising of loans and the service and redemption of debt;

(d) (i) the salaries, allowances and pensions payable to or in respect of judges of the Supreme Court; (ii) the pensions payable to or in respect of judges of the Federal Court; (iii) the pensions payable to or in respect of judges of any High Court which exercises jurisdiction in relation to any area included in the territory of India or which at any time before the commencement of this Constitution exercised jurisdiction in relation to any area included in a Governor's Province of the Dominion of India;

(e) the salary, allowances and pension payable to or in respect of the Comptroller and Auditor General of India;

(f) any sums required to satisfy any judgment, decree or award of any court or arbitral tribunal;

(g) any other expenditure declared by the Constitution or by Parliament by law to be so charged (article 112).

Estimates and Demands for Grants

Estimates relating to expenditure charged on the Consolidated Fund are not submitted to the vote of Parliament but discussion thereon is not barred. Other estimates are presented to Lok Sabha in the form of demands for grants and the Lok Sabha may either assent to or refuse any demand. It may also assent to a demand subject to a reduction in the amount asked for. Every demand for grant must receive the prior recommendation of the President (article 113).

Appropriation Bills

After the Demands for grants are voted by the Lok Sabha, a Bill is introduced for appropriation out of the Consolidated Fund of India, moneys required to meet the grants are voted by the House and the expenditure is charged on the Consolidated Fund. No amendment is permitted which seeks to vary the amount or alter the allocation of any grant head or vary the amount of any charged expenditure. Appropriation Bill is necessary because no money can be drawn from the Consolidated Fund without parliamentary sanction through an Appropriation Act. Additional, supplementary or excess grants may be voted separately but the same procedure shall apply to them as well (articles 114, 115).

Article 116 provides for (i) a vote on account, *i.e.* grants being made in advance of the budget approval and completion of the whole procedure, (ii) an exceptional grant which does not form part of the current service of any financial year, and (iii) a grant to meet an unexpected demand of large magnitude or of an indefinite character (article 116). Parliament may by law regulate the procedure for the purpose of timely completion of the financial business. (article 119).

Language in Parliament

Hindi and English have been declared by the Constitution to be the languages for conducting business in Parliament. The Presiding Officers may, however, allow any member not proficient in either to address the House in his mother tongue (article 120). Simultaneous interpretation facilities exist in the two Houses for rendering speeches made in other languages into Hindi and English.

Parliamentary Committees

Parliamentary Committees assist the Houses of Parliament in the efficient discharge of their functions and in giving close consideration to legislative and other matters that come up before them. A good deal of parliamentary business is transacted in the Committees as the time at the disposal of the Houses is limited and insufficient to make a thorough and detailed examination of the varied and voluminous legislative and other work to be transacted in Parliament. Through the various parliamentary devices like questions and debates, it is not able to exercise more than a sporadic supervision of administration. In order to make parliamentary surveillance more effective and meaningful and ensure accountability of the Executive to Parliament, the role of Parliamentary Committees is vital. The review of administrative action and the examination of numerous and complicated legislative and budgetary proposals and subordinate legislation require expertise and close scrutiny which is not possible in the Houses of Parliament with the Lok Sabha consisting as it does of 545 members and Rajya Sabha of 245 members.

A Parliamentary Committee in Lok Sabha, by formal definition, means a Committee which is appointed or elected by the House in pursuance of a motion, or nominated by the Speaker and which works under the direction of the Speaker and presents its report to the House or to the Speaker and the Secretariat for which is provided by the Lok Sabha/Rajya Sabha Secretariat. But not every Committee consisting of members of Parliament is a Parliamentary Committee. There are other Committees consisting entirely of members of Parliament, *e.g.* Consultative Committees attached to various ministries and departments, but they are not Parliamentary Committees.

The origin of Committee system in India can be traced back to the first Legislatures after the advent of British rule in India under the Charter Act of 1853 and the Government of India Act, 1919.

After the Constitution came into force, the Committee system underwent transformation. Taking advantage of the past experience, an organised system of Committees was adopted by Lok Sabha right from its beginning in 1952. Not only did the number of Committees increase but their functions and powers were also enlarged. A full fledged Committee system in our Parliament got established with the setting up of 17 subject based/departmentally related Standing Committees to cover the entire gamut of Government activities. The initiative for setting up such Committees was taken during the eighth Lok Sabha period when three Committees on Science and Technology, Agriculture and Food, and Environment and Forests were set up. The seventeen new Committees were set up during the period of the Tenth Lok Sabha. [By the Fourteenth Lok Sabha the number of these Committees has risen to 24]. Also, among the more recent parliamentary committees are (i) the committee of the two houses called the Committee on the Empowerment of Women and (ii) the Lok Sabha Committee on Members of Parliament Local Area Development Scheme.

The composition of the Committees represents all sections of the House and shades of opinion. The different Parties and Groups are represented on the Committees in proportion to their respective strength in the House. As such, a Committee is a microcosm of the whole House. The proceedings in the Committees are less formal and the procedure is more flexible than in the House. Unlike in the House, a member can speak more than once in a Committee. This leads to more comprehensive and judicious consideration of the issues under consideration of the Committees. Moreover, the Committee system saves the time of the House for the discussion of important matters and prevents Parliament from getting lost in details and thereby losing hold on matters of policy and broad principles.

There are two types of Parliamentary Committees in India *viz.* (i) Standing Committees and (ii) *Ad-hoc* Committees.

Standing Committees are those which are constituted by the House or the Speaker every year or from time to time, as the case may be and are permanent in nature in the sense that they examine different issues and present their reports to the House or the Speaker from time to time during their term. *Ad hoc* Committees are appointed for a specific purpose and they become *functus officio* as soon as they have completed the task assigned to them and presented their report.

Standing Committees may be categorised in terms of the nature of their functions as follows:

i. Financial Committees, *e.g.* Committee on Estimates, Committee on Public Accounts and Committee on Public Undertakings
ii. Subject Committees or Departmentally Related Standing Joint Committees of the two Houses
iii. House Committees, that is, Committees relating to the day to day business of the House, *e.g.* Committee on Absence of Members from the Sittings of the House, Business Advisory Committee, Committee on Private Members' Bills and Resolutions and Rules Committee
iv. Enquiry Committees, *e.g.* Committee on Government Assurances, Committee on Subordinate Legislation, Committee on Papers Laid on the Table and Committee on the Welfare of

Scheduled Castes and Scheduled Tribes.

v. Service Committee, *e.g.* General Purposes Committee, House Committees, Library Committee and Joint Committee on Salaries and Allowances of Members of Parliament.

Ad hoc Committees may be broadly put into two categories:

i. Select or Joint Committees on Bills which are appointed to consider and report on particular Bills.
ii. Committees which are constituted from time to time to inquire into and report on specific matters. Thus Railway Convention Committee is an *Ad hoc* Committee which is appointed from time to time to examine the finances of the Railways and to review the rate of dividend which is payable by the Railway undertaking to the general revenues.

Members of Rajya Sabha are also associated with the Committee on Public Accounts, Committee on Public Undertakings, Committee on the Welfare of Scheduled Castes and Scheduled Tribes and the departmentally related Committees.

In the case of Committee on Public Accounts, as per established convention, a member belonging to one of the major Opposition Parties/Groups is appointed Chairman of the Committee.

Sittings of Parliamentary Committees are held in private. It is not permissible for a member of the Committee or any one else who has access to the proceedings of the Committee, to communicate, directly or indirectly to the press any information regarding its proceedings etc. before its report has been presented to the House. There are no public hearings before the Committees and the press is not permitted.

The three Financial Committees play a crucial role in the task of a detailed scrutiny of governmental spending and performance, thereby securing the accountability of the administration to Parliament in financial matters. They are the watch dogs of Parliament. The accountability of the administration to the Parliament is not direct and is exercised through Ministers, but in the Committees, the civil servants come face to face with Committees when they are called for oral evidence and are subjected to extensive examination. The relentless crusade of the Financial Committees to this end keeps the administration on its toes. The elaborate procedure for follow-up of the recommendations of these Committees by way of 'Action Taken Reports' is essentially an Indian innovation.

In addition to the three Financial Committees, the subject-based, departmentally- related Committees embrace the entire spectrum of administration for in in-depth and continuous scrutiny of administrative performance and have strengthened the process of accountability and parliamentary surveillance.

Table 5.5

Ministries/Departments under the jurisdiction of the Standing Committees

Sl. No.	Name of the Committees	Ministries/Departments
	PART I	
1.	Committee on Commerce	(1) Commerce and Industry (2) Textiles
2.	Committee on Home Affairs	(1) Home Affairs (2) Law and Justice (3) Personnel, Public Grievances & Pensions (4) Development of North-Eastern Region
3.	Committee on Human Resource Development	(1) Human Resource Development (2) Youth Affairs and Sports (3) Health and Family Welfare
4.	Committee on Industry	(1) Heavy Industries and Public Enterprises (2) Steel (3) Small Scale Industires (4) Agro and Rural Industries
5.	Committee on Science & Technology & Forests	(1) Science & Technology (2) Space (3) Ocean Development

contd...

Table 5.5 contd.

	(4) Environment & Forests
6. Committee on Transport, Tourism and Culture	(1) Civil Aviation (2) Road Transport and Highways (3) Shipping (4) Tourism and Culture
PART II	
7. Committee on Agriculture	(1) Agriculture (2) Water Resources (3) Food Processing Industries
8. Committee on Information Technology	(1) Communications and Information Technology (2) Information and Broadcasting
9. Committee on Defence	Defence
10. Committee on Energy	(1) Coal and Mines (2) Non-conventional Energy Sources (3) Power (4) Atomic Energy
11. Committee on External Affairs	External Affairs
12. Committee on Finance	(1) Finance (2) Planning (3) Statistics and Programme Implementation (4) Disinvestment
13. Committee on Food, Civil Supplies and Public Distribution	Consumer Affairs, Food and Public Distribution
14. Committee on Labour and Welfare	(1) Labour (2) Social Justice and Empowerment (3) Tribal Affairs
15. Committee on Petroleum & Chemicals	(1) Petroleum and Natural Gas (2) Chemicals and Fertilisers
16. Committee on Railways	Railways
17. Committee on Urban and Rural Development	(1) Urban Development and Poverty Alleviation (2) Rural Development

The number of Departmentally Related Standing Committees has since gone up to 24. The changes have been as follows:

i. Committee on 'Food, Civil Supplies and Public Distribution' is renamed as the Committee on 'Food, Consumer Affairs and Public Distribution'.
ii. Committee on 'Labour and Welfare' is renamed as Committee on 'Labour' only.
iii. Committee on 'Petroleum & Chemicals' is renamed as Committee on 'Petroleum and Natural Gas'.
iv. Committee on 'Urban and Rural Development' becomes a Committee on 'Rural Development' only.
v. Committee on 'Transport and Tourism' becomes a Committee on 'Transport, Tourism and Culture'.

The seven new Committees created are: (a) Committee on Chemicals and Fertilisers; (b) Committee on Coal & Steel; (c) Committee on Water Resources ; (d) Committee on Health and Family Welfare; (e) Committee on Personnel, public grievances, Law and Justice; (f) Committee on Social Justice and Empowerment; (g) Committee on Urban Development.

Parliamentary Privileges

Article 105 of the Constitution provides for the powers, privileges etc. of the Houses of Parliament and of the members and committees thereof. 'Privilege' means a special or exceptional right or freedom or an immunity enjoyed by a particular class of persons or some individuals. In its legal sense it means an exemption from some duty, burden, attendance or liability to which others are subject. Privilege can also be defined as a right which others do not have. Parliamentary privileges are those special rights belonging to each House of Parliament, its members and committees, without which they cannot perform their functions in the manner they are expected to. The privileges are granted with a view to maintaining the independence of action and the dignity of the position of the Houses of Parliament, their committees and members and to enable them to function without any let or hindrance. The privileges, in practice, give rise to certain powers, immunities and exemptions. It does not, however, imply that the privileges belonging to members place them on a footing different from that of an ordinary citizen in the eyes of law unless there are good reasons in the interest of Parliament itself to do so. The basic law is that all citizens including members of Parliament should be treated equally before the law. They have the same rights and liberties as ordinary citizens except when they perform their duties in Parliament. The privileges are available to the members only when and to the extent that they are functioning as representatives of the people in Parliament and discharging their parliamentary responsibilities. The privileges do not, in any way, exempt the members from their normal obligations to society which apply to them as much and perhaps more closely in that capacity, as they apply to others.

Also, the purpose of the people, through the Constitution, granting to Members certain privileges is only to enable the latter to serve the people without any hindrance. Ideally, these should never be allowed to degenerate into a conflict between the privileges of Members against the rights of the citizens.

It has been held by the Supreme Court in the *Searchlight* case that the freedom of speech conferred on members under article 105 is subject only to those provisions of the Constitution which regulate the procedure of Parliament and to the Rules and Standing Orders of the House, but is free from any restrictions which may be imposed by any law made under article 19(2) upon the freedom of speech of an ordinary citixzen. Any investigation outside Parliament in respect of anything said or done by members in the discharge of their parliamentary duties would amount to a serious interference with the members' right. Even though a speech delivered by a member in the House may amount to contempt of court, no action can be taken against him in any court. A court, being an outside authority, does not have the power to investigate the matter. Article 122 forbids any inquiry by courts into proceedings of Parliament.

The courts of law in India have recognised that a House

of Parliament or a State Legislature is the sole authority to judge as to whether or not there has been a breach of privilege in a particular case. It has also been held that the power of the House to commit for contempt is identical with that of the House of Commons and that a court of law would be incompetent to scrutinise the exercise of that power. The immunity from external influence or interference, however, does not mean an unrestricted licence of speech within the walls of Parliament. It is important to remember that the privileges of the Houses and members and committees thereof are subject to other provisions of the Constitution being construed harmoniously. Thus, for example, the privilege of freedom of speech in Parliament will be subject to rules of procedure framed by Houses of Parliament under article 118 and article 121 forbids discussion in Parliament on the conduct of judges except on a motion for their removal. [*M.S. Sharma v. Sri Krishna Sinha*, AIR 1959 SC 395].

In 1965, the Supreme Court in its advisory opinion in *Special Reference* Case of 1964, (*Keshav Singh's* case), observed as follows:

> In dealing with the effect of the provisions contained in clause (3) of article 194, whenever it appears that there is a conflict between the said provisions and the provisions pertaining to Fundamental Rights, an attempt will have to be made to resolve the said conflict by the adoption of the rule of harmonious construction.

The Allahabad High Court, in their judgement in *Keshav Singh's* case dated 10 March 1965 (*i.e.* delivered after the advisory opinion of the Supreme Court), observed as follows:

i. In our opinion, both upon authority and upon a consideration of the relevant provisions of the Constitution, it must be held that the Legislative Assembly has, by virtue of article 194(3) the same power to commit for its contempt as the House of Commons has.

ii. In our opinion, the provisions of article 22(2) of the Constitution cannot apply to a detention in pursuance of a conviction and imposition of a sentence of imprisonment by competent authority

iii. Since we have already held that the Legislative Assembly has the power to commit the petitioner for its contempt and since the Legislative Assembly has framed rules for the procedure and conduct of its business under article 208(1), the commitment and deprivation of the personal liberty of the petititoner cannot but be held to be according to the procedure laid down by law within the meaning of article 21 of the Constitution.

iv. Once we come to the conclusion that the Legislative Assembly has the power and jurisdiction to commit for its contempt and to impose the sentence passed on the petitioner, we cannot go into the question of the correctness, propriety or legality of the commitment. This Court cannot, in a petition under article 226 of the Constitution, sit in appeal over the decision of the Legislative Assembly committing the petitioner for its contempt. The Legislative Assembly is the master of its own procedure and is the sole judge of the question whether its contempt has been committed or not.

The Government, therefore, decided that an amendment of the Constitution was not necessary. It was of the opinion that the Legislatures and the Judiciary would develop their own conventions in the light of the opinion given by the Supreme Court and the judgement pronounced by the Allahabad High Court. It may, therefore, be seen that the judgement of the Supreme Court in the *Searchlight* case is final till today insofar as matters of privilege are concerned.

The more important of the privileges, namely freedom of speech in Parliament and immunity of members from any proceedings in courts in respect of anything said or any vote given by them in Parliament, are specified in article 105 of the Constitution.

1. There shall be freedom of speech in Parliament subject to the provisions of the Constitution and to the rules and standing orders regulating the procedure of Parliament.
2. No member of Parliament shall be liable to any proceedings in any court in respect of anything said or any vote given by him in Parliament or any committee thereof, and no person shall be so liable in respect of the publication by or under the authority of either House of Parliament of any report, paper, votes or proceedings. [*Tej Kiron v. Sanjiva,* AIR 1970 SC 1573; *Gatish v. Harisadhan* (1956) 60 CWN 971, A.I.R. 1961 SC 613]

3. In other respects, the powers, privileges and immunities of each House of Parliament, and of the members and the committees of each House, shall be such as may from time to time be defined by Parliament by law, and, until, so defined, shall be those of that House and of its members and committees immediately before the coming into force of section 15 of the Constitution (Forty Fourth Amendment) Act, 1978.
4. The provisions of clauses (1), (2) and (3) shall apply in relation to persons who by virtue of this Constitution have the right to speak in, and otherwise to take part in the proceedings of a House of Parliament or any committee thereof as they apply in relation to members of Parliament.

In other words, each House, its Committees and members in actual practice, shall enjoy the powers and privileges (other than those specified in the Constitution) that were available to the British House of Commons as on 26 January 1950.

The most important of parliamentary privileges is that of freedom of speech while performing parliamentary duties. Article 19 also gives a citizen the right of free speech but articles 105 and 194 lay special emphasis on the right of free speech of members of the legislatures. Under article 19, the right of free speech is subject to reasonable restrictions, for instance, the law of libel. An ordinary person who speaks something libellous is liable to be proceeded against but a member of Parliament speaking in the House or in one of its committees is immune from any attack on the ground that his speech was libellous or defamatory.

Members have to give expression to public grievances and raise various matters of public importance. In doing this, members should not suffer any inhibition and they should be able to speak out their mind and express their views freely. Inside the House or Committees of Parliament, a member is absolutely free to say whatever he likes subject only to the Constitution and internal discipline of the House or the Committee concerned; no outside authority has any right to interfere. Freedom of speech is absolutely necessary for a member to function freely without any fear or favour in the Committees and in the Houses of Parliament. Unless whatever a member says enjoys immunity from legal action, he cannot be expected to speak freely and frankly. The Constitution provides, therefore, that no action can be taken against a member of Parliament in any court or before any authority other than Parliament in respect of anything said or a vote given by him in Houses of Parliament or any Committee thereof.

In a highly controversial decision in the JMM Bribery case, the Supreme Court had held that M.P.s taking bribe for voting could not be proceeded against in any court because it was covered by privilege law of article 105 of the Constitution. In the more recent cases of expulsion of 11 members of Parliament for accepting cash for asking questions in Parliament, the Constitution Bench of the Supreme Court has held that the Houses of Parliament have the power to expel their members. Since the Lok Sabha had asserted its rights and decided not to accept court notices in this regard, the Judiciary and the Legislature were said to be in for a confrontation. But, while upholding the principle that exercise of power by the legislature was amenable to judicial review and scrutiny to see that constitutional provisions were not breached, the Supreme Court recognised the power of Parliament to expel its members under article 105(3). [*Raja Ram Pal v. Speaker Lok Sabha*, 10 January 2007, *Manupatra*]

The power of the House to punish for its own breach of privilege and contempt is "akin in nature to the power of the Supreme Court to commit for its own contempt from which there is no appeal". In the case of its own members, punishment may include "suspension...and expulsion from the House".

It is important to remember that there is a clear distinction between disqualification for being a Member under articles 102 and 103 and expulsion from the House under the powers given by article 105. The most relevant constitutional provision apart from article 105 is article 122, which categorically bars the courts from enquiring into the validity of any proceedings in Parliament on the ground of any alleged irregularity of procedure. Those with constitutional powers for regulating the conduct of business and procedure or maintaining order in Parliament are not "subject to the jurisdiction of any court in respect of exercise" of those powers unless "gross illegality or violation of costitutional provisions" is involved.

In *Tej Kiran v. Sanjeeva Reddy* (1969), when notices were issued to the Speaker and four members to appear before the Delhi High Court, the House decided to ignore the notices. Subsequently, the case was dismissed by the court. In 1975 also, a court notice was ignored and the relevant papers were passed on to Minister of Law for taking such action as he deemed fit to apprise the court of correct constitutional position. Again, the case was dismissed. In July 1988 when two court notices were received, the Speaker observed that as per well established practice and convention of Lok Sabha, he had decided not to respond to the notices and that he had passed on the relevant papers to Minister of Law and Justice for taking such action as he might deem fit to apprise the court of correct constitutional position and well established conventions of Lok Sabha in that regard. There were similar instances in the years 1990 and 1991 and the same stand was taken by the Speaker.

It was thus far held that the control of the House over its proceedings was "absolute" and could not be interfered with by the courts. In the U.K., the House has unquestioned disciplinary powers over the conduct of its members both inside and outside the House and includes the power of expulsion. Our Parliament has always claimed that it has *inter alia* the power to expel its members for breach of its privileges, contempt or lowering the dignity of the House or conduct unbecoming a Member. This power was actually resorted to in the Mudgal case in 1951 (even though he escaped expulsion by resigning) and in Mrs. Gandhi's expulsion from Lok Sabha in 1978 (although later the expulsion was retrospectively rescinded by the House itself in 1981). The Judgements of the High Courts were conflicting and the Supreme Court had no occasion to pronounce on the power of the House to expel a Member. It was, therefore, very wise and appropriate for the Court to refer the matter to a Constitution Bench to clear the constitutional points. Apart from conceding to Houses of Legislatures the power to discipline and even expel its members, the law now declared by the Supreme Court in *Raja Ram Pal* case is that "the Court has the jurisdiction to examine the procedure adopted" to see that "there is no abuse or misuse of power by the Legislature" and no "illegality or violation of constitutional provisions."

Codification of Privileges: Article 105(3) of the Constitution stipulates that, apart from the privileges mentioned in the Constitution itself, Parliament may, from time to time, define its privileges by law. No law, however, has so far been enacted by Parliament in pursuance of this provision to define the powers, privileges and immunities of each House and its members and the Committees thereof. As far as the constitutional stipulation "until defined by Parliament by law" and the question of defining or codifying the parliamentary privileges are concerned, opinions are divided. It is however clear that the Constitution makers did envisage codification.

Role of the two Houses

The two Houses of Parliament have equal powers and status in all spheres except in financial mattes and in regard to the responsibility of the Council of Ministers which are the exclusive domain of the Lok Sabha. Thus, a Money Bill cannot be introduced in the Rajya Sabha and whether a particular Bill is a Money Bill is decided by the Speaker of the Lok Sabha [article 110(3)]. Rajya Sabha has no power either to amend or reject a Money Bill. It can only make recommendations on the Money Bill. If such a Bill is not returned to Lok Sabha within a period of 14 days, the Bill is deemed to have been passed by both the Houses at the expiration of the said period of 14 days in the form in which it was passed by Lok Sabha. Rajya Sabha may discuss the Budget but it has no power to vote on Demands for Grants (article 113). Finally, Rajya Sabha has no power to pass a vote of no-confidence in the Council of Ministers which is exclusively responsible to the Lok Sabha [article 75(3)].

It should not, however, be taken to mean that the Rajya

Sabha is less important or has been given a secondary position in relation to the Lok Sabha. The powers of the Rajya Sabha are at par with those of the Lok Sabha in case of other Bills. Every non-financial measure must be passed by both Houses individually before it can become an Act. Rajya Sabha has equal powers with the Lok Sabha in important matters like the impeachment of the President, removal of the Vice-President, constitutional amendments and removal of the judges of the Supreme Court and the High Courts (articles 56, 61, 67, 124 and 217). President's ordinances, proclamations of emergency and the proclamations of the failure of constitutional machinery in a State must be placed before both Houses of Parliament (articles 123, 352 and 356). Disagreement between the two Houses on a Bill, other than a Money Bill and a Constitutional Amendment Bill is resolved by both the Houses in a joint-sitting where matters are decided by majority vote. Such a joint sitting of the two Houses is presided over by the Speaker of the Lok Sabha (articles 108 and 118).

Further, the Constitution has assigned some special powers to the Rajya Sabha. It alone has the power to declare that it would be in national interest for the Parliament to legislate in respect of a matter in the State List. If by a two-thirds majority, Rajya Sabha passes a resolution to this effect, the Union Parliament can make laws for the whole or any part of the country even with respect to a matter enumerated in the State List (article 249). Also, Parliament is empowered to make laws providing for the creation of one or more All India Services common to the Union and the States, if the Rajya Sabha declares by a resolution supported by not less than two thirds of the members present and voting that it is necessary or expedient in the national interest to do so (article 312). [See Chapter 7. 'Parliament-Executive-Judiciary']

The State Legislature

The Legislature of a State consists of the Governor and the Legislative Assembly except that in some States there are two Houses—the Legislative Assembly and the Legislative Council.

At present only, Andhra, Bihar, U.P., Maharashtra, Tamil Nadu and Karnataka States have a Legislative Council (article 168). The Legislative Council in Andhra has been revived most recently, during 2007 only. Jammu and Kashmir also has a Legislative Council but that is under the separate constitution of the State.

It is left to the Legislative Assembly of each State to decide whether to recommend to Parliament abolition of the Council where one exists or to seek establishment of one if none exists (article 169).

Under the Constitution, the Legislative Assembly of a State shall consist of not more than 500 and not less than 60 members chosen by direct election from territorial constituencies. The Legislative Council shall not exceed one third of the total membership of the Legislative Assembly of that State subject to a minimum of 40. One third of the members shall be elected by municipalities, district boards and other local authorities as specified by Parliament by law, one twelfth shall be elected by graduates' constituency, one twelfth by the teachers' constituency, one third by members of the Legislative Assembly and the remainder, *i.e.* one sixth, shall be nominated by the Governor. Elections to the Council are to be held by the system of proportional representation by single transferable vote (articles 170, 171).

The term of the Legislative Assembly shall be five years. The Council shall be a continuing House not subject to dissolution but one third of its members shall retire every two years (article 172).

In order to be eligible for membership a person must be a citizen of India, must take an oath to the Constitution, must be not less than 25 years of age in case of the Assembly and not less than 30 years in case of the Council (article 173) as on the date of nomination *(Hussain v. Nijalingappa,* AIR 1969 SC 1034).

The house or each house of the State Legislature is from time to time summoned to meet by the Governor who may also prorogue the house or either house and dissolve the Legislative Assembly. The period for which the house/s should meet or the required duration of the sessions is not laid down in the Constitution but the gap between two sessions must be less than six months (article 174).

Article 175 provides for the right of the Governor to address or send messages to the House or Houses of the State Legislature. Under article 176, the Governor is obliged to address the House or the Houses assembled together at the beginning of the first session each year and at the commencement of the first session after each general election to the Legislative Assembly of the State (article 176). All the Ministers and the Advocate General have a right to speak and take part in the proceedings of the house/s (article 177).

The State Legislature has exclusive jurisdiction to legislate on items in the State List and concurrent jurisdiction in respect of items in List III (articles 245 and 246).

The position of the Legislative Council in a State is similar to that of the Rajya Sabha at the Union level. This applies *inter alia* to the privileges and immunities of legislatures, disqualification of members, relation between the two Houses, legislative procedure, origin of money bills, etc.

The assembly has a Speaker and a Deputy Speaker elected by the House and having the same position and functions as their Lok Sabha counterparts. The Council, however, also has a Chairman and Deputy Chairman elected by the Council (articles 178 and187).

General rules for conduct of business in the Legislative Assembly/Council (articles 188 and 189), provisions regarding disqualification of members, vacation of seats, penalty for unauthorisedly sitting in the house (articles 190 193), powers, privileges and immunities for houses of legislatures and members and committees (article 194), salaries and allowances of members (article 195), Legislative procedure including that for passing Money Bills and other Bills (articles 196-200 and 208 212), procedure in financial matters (articles 202-207) are all very similar to corresponding provisions in regard to the Union Parliament. Articles 200 and 201 however, *inter alia* provide for the Governor reserving some Bills for the consideration of the President and then the President assenting to the Bills or withholding assent. Corresponding to the President's power under article 123, the Governor also enjoys power to issue ordinances (article 213).

Legislature in Union Territories

Parliament may by law create for any territory a legislature and a Council of Ministers. Such a legislature and Council of Ministers exist for the Union Territory of Pondicherry and for the National Capital Territory of Delhi. The Legislative Assembly in Pondicherry may make laws in respect of matters in List II or III of the 7th Schedule in so far as these mattes are applicable to the Union Territory. This applies to the Delhi Assembly also with some exceptions. The legislative and executive powers in respect of public order, police and land and all matters related to these three areas have been retained by the Union to be handled through the Lt. Governor of Delhi. Certain categories of Bills require prior approval of the Union Government for introduction in the Assembly. Some Bills, both in Delhi and Pondicherry, may also be reserved by the Lt. Governor for the assent of the President.

The administrator of a Union Territory enjoys powers of promulgating ordinances like the Governors of States (article 239B). The President has been empowered to make regulations for peace, progress and good government of all the Union Territories except where a legislature is functioning (article 239A and 240).

Conclusion

The extent of its legislative jurisdiction, the constituent powers it possesses, its role in emergencies are all indicative of the sweep and scope of the power and jurisdiction of the Parliament. Parliament under our political system has proved its relevance potential during the last half-a-century and more. In the institutions of the State, it remains pre-eminent and effective despite all the debate about its decline and erosion in esteem during recent years. However, Parliament of India cannot be described as a sovereign body in the sense that the British Parliament was understood to be. It has vast but not unlimited powers. The authority and jurisdiction of our Parliament are limited by the powers of the other organs, the distribution of legislative powers between the Union and the States, the incorporation of a code of justiciable fundamental rights, the general provision for judicial review and an independent judiciary. Also, under the rulings of the Supreme Court, there are limits to the constituent powers of Parliament inasmuch as it cannot alter what have come to be called 'the basic features of the Constitution'. Despite these limitation on its authority, such powers, as it possesses under the Constitution are adequate for it to fulfil the role that is assigned to it.

6

THE JUDICIAL SYSTEM
SUPREME COURT, HIGH COURTS AND SUBORDINATE COURTS

Among the foundational objectives of our polity, the founding fathers accorded the highest place to justice. The Preamble to the Constitution spoke of the resolve to secure "Justice, social, economic and political" to "all its citizens". It was natural that the people turned to judiciary as the bastion of hope for getting protection against injustice.

One of the unique features of the Indian Constitution is that, notwithstanding the adoption of a federal system and existence of Central Acts and State Acts in their respective spheres, it has generally provided for a single integrated system of Courts to administer both Union and State laws. At the apex of the entire judicial system, exists the Supreme Court of India below which are the High Courts in each State or group of States. Below the High Courts lies a hierarchy of Subordinate Courts. Panchayat Courts also function in some States under various names like Nyaya Panchayat, Panchayat Adalat, Gram Kachheri, etc. to decide civil and criminal disputes of petty and local nature. Different State laws provide for different kinds of jurisdiction of courts.

A new era in the legal and judicial history of this country, dawned in 1950, when the law of the Constitution assumed vital importance, because a legally sovereign Constitution, embodying the Rule of Law, regulating various functions of governmental organs and rights of citizens under a democratic order, began to operate. Supreme Court together with the High Courts under the Constitution, became an extremely important factor in determining the pace of social transformation towards the goals visualised in the Preamble to the Constitution. The Constitution held the promise and prospects of JUSTICE, LIBERTY, EQUALITY and FRATERNITY: assuring dignity to the individual and the unity of the nation. It guaranteed fundamental rights to citizens against the State itself.

THE SUPREME COURT

Constitution of the Supreme Court

On 28 January 1950, the Supreme Court came into being. The inauguration took place in the Chamber of Princes in the Parliament building which also housed India's Parliament. It was here, in this Chamber of Princes, that the Federal Court of India had sat for 12 years between 1937 and 1950. This was to be the home of the Supreme Court for years that were to follow until the Supreme Court acquired its own present premises in 1958.

The original Constitution of 1950 under article 124 envisaged a Supreme Court with a Chief Justice and 7 puisne Judges—leaving it to Parliament to increase this number. In the early years, all the Judges of the Supreme Court sat together to hear the cases presented before them. As the work of the Court increased and arrears of cases began to accumulate, Parliament increased the number of Judges from 8 in 1950 to 11 in 1956, 14 in 1960, 18 in 1978 and 26 in 1986 including the Chief Justice. As the number of the Judges has increased, they sit in smaller Benches of two and three—coming together in larger Benches of 5 and more only when required to do so or to settle a difference of opinion or controversy. [Also see under 'Appointment of Judges' below]

Appointment of Judges

In order to be appointed as a Judge of the Supreme Court, a person must be a citizen of India and must have been, for atleast five years, a Judge of a High Court or of two or more such Courts in succession, or an Advocate of a High Court or of two or more such Courts in succession for at least 10 years or he must be, in the opinion of the President, a distinguished jurist [article 124(3)].

Supreme Court Judges retire upon attaining the age of 65 years. A judge may be removed from his office only by an order of the President passed after an address by each House of Parliament for his removal "on the ground of misbehaviour or incapacity" supported by a majority of the total membership of that House and by a majority of not less than two thirds of the members present and voting is presented to him in the same session. The procedure may be regulated by Parliament by law [articles 124(2), (4) & (5)].

Every person appointed as a judge of the Supreme Court, before he enters upon his office, takes an oath before the President or some person appointed in that behalf by him in the form prescribed in the Constitution. The Constitution prohibits a person who has held office as a judge of the Supreme Court from practising law before any court in the territory of India [articles 124(6) & (7)].

When the office of the Chief Justice of India is vacant or when the Chief Justice is unable to perform the duties of his office due to absence, the President shall appoint an Acting Chief Justice from among the judges of the Court to perform the duties of the Chief Justice (article 126).

If at any time there is no quorum of judges of the Supreme Court available to hold or continue any session of the Court, the Chief Justice of India is empowered to appoint *ad hoc* judges in the Supreme Court from among judges of the High Courts, having qualifications to be appointed judges of the Supreme Court, for such period as he deems necessary. He can do so only with previous consent of the President and after consultation with the Chief Justice of the High Court concerned.

The judge so appointed is duty bound to give priority to the Supreme Court duties. The Chief Justice of India may also invite a retired judge of the Supreme Court or a retired judge of the High Court having the qualification to be a judge of the Supreme Court, to sit and act as a judge of the Supreme Court for such period as he deems necessary. This too can be done with the previous consent of the President and also of the person to be so appointed (articles 127 and 128).

Jurisdiction of the Supreme Court

One of the significant features of the Constitution of India is the area, extent and nature of the jurisdiction of the Supreme Court. The founding fathers and the elected representatives of the people vested this Court with vast jurisdiction and pervasive powers. Almost every area of legislative or executive activity was put within the scrutiny of this Court, barring matters of policy, fiscal matters, and political questions for which there were no judicially manageable standards. Under article 142 of the Constitution "The Supreme Court in the exercise of its jurisdiction may pass such decree or make such order as is necessary for doing complete justice in any cause or matter pending before it."

Original, Appellate and Advisory Jurisdiction: The exclusive original jurisdiction of the Supreme Court extends to any dispute between the Government of India and one or more States or between the Government of India and any State or States on one side and one or more States on the other or between two or more States, if and insofar as the dispute involves any question (whether of law or of fact) on which the existence or extent of a legal right depends (article 131).

The original jurisdiction of the Supreme Court also extends to cases of violation of the fundamental rights of individuals and the Court can issue several writs for the enforcement of these rights (article 32). It is empowered to issue directions, orders or writs, including writs in the nature of *habeas corpus, mandamus, prohibition, quo warranto* and *certiorari* to enforce them. It is a unique feature of our Constitution that in principle, any individual can straightaway approach the highest court in case of violation of his fundamental rights.

Under the new article 139A inserted by the 44th Amendment in 1978, the Supreme Court may transfer to itself cases from one or more High Courts if these involve questions of law or of great importance. Also, the Supreme Court may transfer cases from one High Court to another in the interests of justice. The Supreme Court, if satisfied that cases involving the same or substantially the same questions of law are pending before it and one or more High Courts or before two or more High Courts and that such questions are substantial questions of general importance, may withdraw a case or cases pending before the High Court or High Courts and dispose of all such cases itself. Under the Arbitration and Conciliation Act, 1996, International Commercial Arbitration can also be initiated in the Supreme Court.

The appellate jurisdiction of the Supreme Court can be invoked by a certificate granted by the High Court concerned under articles 132(1), 133(1) or 134 of the Constitution in respect of any judgement, decree or final order of a High Court in both civil and criminal cases, involving substantial questions of law as to the interpretation of the Constitution. Appeals also lie to the Supreme Court in civil matters if the High Court concerned certifies : (a) that the case involves a substantial question of law of general importance, and (b) that, in the opinion of the High Court, the said question needs to be decided by the Supreme Court. In criminal cases, an appeal lies to the Supreme Court if the High Court (a) has on appeal reversed an order of acquittal of an accused person and sentenced him to death or to imprisonment for life or for a period of not less than 10 years, or (b) has withdrawn for trial before itself any case from any Court subordinate to its authority and has in such trial convicted the accused and sentenced him to death or to imprisonment for life or for a period of not less than 10 years, or (c) certified that the case is a fit one for appeal to the Supreme Court. Parliament is authorised to confer on the Supreme Court any further powers to entertain and hear appeals from any judgement, final order or sentence in a criminal proceeding of a High Court.

The Supreme Court has a very wide appellate jurisdiction over all Courts and Tribunals in India. Under article 136, the Supreme Court, at its discretion, may grant special leave to appeal from any judgement, decree, determination, sentence or order, in any cause or matter passed or made by any court or tribunal in the territory of India. The powers of the Supreme Court to grant special leave to appeal are far wider than the High Courts' power to grant certificates to appeal to the Supreme Court under article 134. The Supreme Court can grant special leave against judgements of any court or tribunal in the territory, except the military courts, and in any type of cases, civil, criminal or revenue. But, the Supreme Court has itself said that it will grant special leave to appeal only in cases where there has been gross miscarriage of justice or where the High Court or Tribunal is found to have been wrong in law. If the judgement of the court below shakes the conscience and shocks the sense of justice, Supreme Court shall interfere. [*Haripada Dey v. State of West Bengal*, AIR 1965 SC 757; *Martu v. State of U.P.*, AIR 1971 SC 1050; *Ram Saran v. C.T.O.*, AIR 1962 SC 1326; *Muniswamy v. Ranganathan*, (1991) 2SCC 139; *Mahesh v. State of Delhi*, (1991) Cr LJ 1703 (SC)]

There are provisions for reference or appeal to the Supreme Court under article 317(1) of the Constitution, Section 257 of the Income Tax Act, 1961, Section 7(2) of the Monopolies and Restrictive Trade Practices Act, 1969, Section 130-A of the Customs Act, 1962, Section 35-H of the Central Excise and Salt Act, 1944 and Section 82C of the Gold (Control) Act, 1968. Appeals also lay to the Supreme Court under the Representation of the People Act, 1951, Advocates Act, 1961, Contempt of Courts Act, 1971, Enlargement of Criminal Appellate Jurisdiction Act, 1970, Trial of Offences Relating to Transactions in Securities Act, 1992, Terrorist and Disruptive Activities (Prevention) Act, 1987 and Consumer Protection Act, 1986. Election Petitions under Part III of the Presidential and Vice Presidential Elections Act, 1952 are also filed directly in the Supreme Court.

The Supreme Court has special advisory jurisdiction in matters which may specifically be referred to it by the President of India under article 143 of the Constitution. The President may seek the opinion of the Supreme Court on any question of law or fact of public importance on which he thinks it expedient to obtain such an opinion. On such reference from the President, the Supreme Court, after giving it such hearing as it deems fit, may report to the President its opinion thereon. The opinion is only advisory, which the President is free to follow or not to follow. The first such reference was made in the *Delhi Laws case*, (1951) SCR 747.

A recent instance was of the present President Abdul Kalam seeking (in August 2002) the advice of the Supreme Court under article 143 in connection with the controversy between the Election Commission and the Government on elections in Gujarat. The issues related to the limits on the powers of the Election Commission under article 324, the impact of article 174 on the jurisdiction and powers of the Commission and whether the Commission could recommend promulgation of President's rule in a State. The President may also seek the opinion of the Supreme Court, through a similar reference on any treaty, agreement, covenant, engagement, sanad or other similar instrument which had been entered into or executed before the commencement of the Constitution, and has continued in operation thereafter.

Under articles 129 and 142 of the Constitutions the Supreme Court has been vested with power to punish for contempt of Court including the power to punish for contempt of itself. In case of contempt other than the contempt referred to in Rule 2, Part-I of the Rules to Regulate Proceedings for Contempt of the Supreme Court, 1975, the Court may take action (a) *Suo motu*, or (b) on a petition made by Attorney-General, or Solicitor General, or (c) on a petition made by any person, and in the case of a criminal contempt with the consent in writing of the Attorney-General or the Solicitor-General.

Under Order XL of the Supreme Court Rules the Supreme Court may review its judgment or order but no application for review is to be entertained in a civil proceeding except on the grounds mentioned in Order XLVII, Rule 1 of the Code of Civil Procedure and in a criminal proceeding except on the ground of an error apparent on the face of the record.

Article 129 provides that the Supreme Court shall be a court of record and shall have all the powers of such a court. Being the highest court of the land, its proceedings, acts and decisions are kept in record for perpetual memory and for presentation as evidence, when need be, in support of what the law is. Being a court of record implies that its records can be used as evidence and cannot be questioned for their authenticity in any court. [*Daphtary v. Gupta*, AIR 1971 SC 1132; *Namboodripad v. Nambiar*, AIR 1970 SC 2015]

The Judiciary not only adjudicates disputes and acts as the custodian of individual rights and freedoms but may from time to time need to interpret the Constitution and review legislation to determine its vires *vis-a-vis* the Constitution. The Supreme Court has the power to review its own judgements and orders subject to laws made by Parliament and rules of the Supreme Court itself (article 137).

Under article 138, the Supreme Court shall have such further jurisdiction and powers with respect to any of the matters in the Union List as Parliament may by law confer. It shall have such jurisdiction and powers with respect to any matter as the Government of India and the Government of any State may by special agreement confer, if the Parliament by law provides for the exercise of such jurisdiction and powers by the Supreme Court. This enlarges the jurisdiction of the Supreme Court and provides it with very special jurisdiction to hear cases of most urgent nature directly and in its original jurisdiction for speedy disposal.

Article 139 lays down that Parliament may by law confer on the Supreme Court power to issue directions, orders or writs in matters not already covered under article 32. Under article 140, Parliament may by law supplement the powers of the Supreme Court. Law declared by the Supreme Court is binding on all courts in India *vide* article 141. [*Vineet Narain v. Union of*

India, AIR 1998 SC 889; *Dwarikesh Sugar Industries Ltd. v. Prem Heavy Engineering Works (P) Ltd.*, AIR 1997 SC 2477] But no law can be taken to have been declared where no reasons are given. Also, what is binding is the principle or the ratio of the decision and not findings on facts, opinions or arguments. [*Supreme Court Employees v. Union of India*, AIR 1991 SC 334; *Ramesh v. Union of India*, AIR 1990 SC 560; *C.I.T. v. S.E.W.*, AIR 1993 SC 43; *Krishan v. Union of India*, (1990) 4 SCC 207 (CB)] Decrees and orders of the Supreme Court shall be enforceable throughout India and civil and judicial authorities shall act in aid of the Supreme Court (articles 142 & 144).

For purposes of giving effect to the directions and decisions of the Supreme Court, all authorities, civil and judicial, in the territory of India, have been made subordinate to the authority of the Supreme Court inasmuch as all these are required to "act in aid of the Supreme Court" (article 144). The Supreme Court may from time to time, and with the approval of the President, make rules for regulating generally the practice and procedure of the Court.

The officers and staff of the Supreme Court are appointed by the Chief Justice of India or such other judge or officer of the court as he may direct (articles 145 & 146).

Attorney-General

The Attorney-General for India is appointed by the President of India under article 76 of the Constitution and holds office during the pleasure of the President. He must be a person qualified to be appointed as a Judge of the Supreme Court. It is the duty of the Attorney-General for India to give advice to the Government of India upon such legal matters and to perform such other duties of legal character as may be referred or assigned to him by the President. In the performance of his duties, he has the right of audience in all Courts in India as well as the right to take part in the proceedings of Parliament without the right to vote. In discharge of his functions, in courts, the Attorney-General is assisted by a Solicitor-General and four Additional Solicitors General.

Advocates

There are three categories of Advocates who are entitled to practise law before the Supreme Court of India:

(i) ***Senior Advocates:*** These are Advocates who are designated as Senior Advocates by the Supreme Court of India or by any High Court. The Court can designate any Advocate, with his consent, as Senior Advocate if in its opinion by virtue of his ability, standing at the Bar or special knowledge or experience in law the said Advocate is deserving of such distinction. A Senior Advocate is not entitled to appear without an Advocate-on-Record in the Supreme Court or without a junior in any other court or tribunal in India. He is also not entitled to accept instructions to draw pleadings or affidavits, advise on evidence or do any drafting work of an analogous kind in any court or tribunal in India or undertake conveyancing work of any kind whatsoever but this prohibition shall not extend to settling any such matter as aforesaid in consultation with a junior.

(ii) ***Advocates-on-Record:*** Only Advocates-on-Record are entitled to file any matter or document before the Supreme Court. They can also file an appearance or act for a party in the Supreme Court.

(iii) ***Other Advocates:*** Advocates whose names are entered on the roll of any State Bar Council maintained under the Advocates Act, 1961 can appear and argue any matter on behalf of a party in the Supreme Court but they are not entitled to file any document or matter before the Court.

THE HIGH COURTS

The High Court stands at the head of a State's judicial administration. The Constitution provides for a High Court for each State. Parliament may, however establish by law a common High Court for two or more States or for two or more States and a Union territory (articles 214 and 231). There are 18 High Courts in the country, three having jurisdiction over more than one State. Among the Union Territories, Delhi alone has a High Court of its own. Other six Union Territories come under the jurisdiction of different State High Courts. [See Table]

Table 6.1

Jurisdiction and Seats of High Courts

Name	Year	Territorial Jurisdiction	Seat
Allahabad	1866	Uttar Pradesh	Allahabad (Bench at Lucknow)
Andhra Pradesh	1954	Andhra Pradesh	Hyderabad
		Bombay	
	1862	Maharashtra, Goa, Dadra and Nagar Haveli and Daman and Diu	Mumbai (Benches at Nagpur, Panaji and Aurangabad)
Calcutta	1862	West Bengal	Kolkata (Circuit Bench at Port Blair)
Chhattisgarh	2000	Bilaspur	Bilaspur
Delhi	1966	Delhi	Delhi
Guwahati	1948	Assam, Manipur, Meghalaya, Nagaland, Tripura, Mizoram and Arunachal Pradesh	Guwahati (Benches at Kohima, Aizwal & Imphal, Shillong, Agartala and Itanangar)
Gujarat	1960	Gujarat	Ahmedabad
Himachal Pradesh	1971	Himachal Pradesh	Shimla
Jammu & Kashmir	1928	Jammu & Kashmir	Srinagar & Jammu
Jharkhand	2000	Jharkhand	Ranchi
Karnataka	1884	Karnataka	Bangalore
Kerala	1958	Kerala & Lakshadweep	Ernakulam
Madhya Pradesh	1956	Madhya Pradesh	Jabalpur (Benches at Gwalior and Indore)
Madras	1862	Tamil Nadu & Pondicherry	Chennai
Orissa	1948	Orissa	Cuttack
Patna	1916	Bihar	Patna
Punjab & Haryana	1966	Punjab, Haryana & Chandigarh	Chandigarh
Rajasthan	1949	Rajasthan	Jodhpur (Bench at Jaipur)
Sikkim	1975	Sikkim	Gangtok
Uttaranchal	2000	Uttaranchal	Nainital

[*Source*: *India 2006*, Pub. Div., I&B, GOI]

Each High Court comprises of a Chief Justice and such other Judges as the President may, from time to time, appoint (article 216). Judges of the High Court are appointed by the President after consultation with the Chief Justice of India, the Governor of the State and in case of appointment of all judges other than the Chief Justice, the Chief Justice of the High Court.

To be appointed a High Court judge, a person must be a citizen of India with ten years' service in a judicial office or ten years' experience as a High Court advocate. On appointment, every High Court judge must take an oath of office. Every High Court judge shall hold office until he attains the age of 62. He cannot be removed from his office except in the manner provided for removal of a judge of the Supreme Court. Further, to ensure the independence of the office of a High Court judge, it is laid down that after being a permanent judge of a High Court, a person shall not plead in any court in India except the Supreme Court or other High Courts. Every High Court judge is entitled to a salary and allowances as may be settled by Parliament by law or as specified in the Second Schedule to the Constitution.

Judges may be transferred from one High Court to another by the President after consulting the Chief Justice of India (article 222). However, the Supreme Court has held that judicial review is necessary to check arbitrariness and that a High Court judge cannot be transferred without his consent but that only the judge affected can question it. [*Union of India v. Sankal Chand*, AIR 1977 SC 2328; *K. Ashok Reddy v. Govt of India*, JT (1994) I S C 40] The President may appoint an acting Chief Justice for a High Court. Also, in case of need, the President may appoint additional and acting judges of the High Court for a period not exceeding two years. The Chief Justice of a High Court may, with the consent of the President, appoint a retired judge to sit and act as a judge (articles 215, 217 and 224A).

Every High Court has full control over its staff. The salaries and allowances of the judges and of the High Court staff are all charged on the Consolidated Fund of the State. Appointments of officers and staff of a High Court are made by the Chief Justice of the Court or by such other judge or officer of the Court as he may decide. The terms and conditions of service of the staff and officers of the Court should appropriately be settled by rules made by the Chief Justice and approved by the President (article 229). The jurisdiction of a High Court may be extended to or excluded from a Union territory (article 230).

Article 226 lays down that every High Court shall have power throughout the territory under its jurisdiction to issue to any person or authority directions, orders or writs including writs of *habeas corpus*, prohibition, *quo warranto* and *certiorari* or any of them for the enforcement of the fundamental rights or for any other purpose. Thus, while the Supreme Court's writ jurisdiction extends only to cases of violation of fundamental rights, the High Courts under article 226 enjoy much wider powers and can issue writs in all cases of breach of any right. This becomes obvious from the use of the term "for any other purpose". The High Court may set aside an illegal order, may declare the law or the right, may order relief by way of, for example, refund of illegal tax etc. Just as the law declared by the Supreme Court is binding on all courts in India, that declared by the High Court is binding on all subordinate courts within the State or within the territory covered by the jurisdiction of the High Court. [*State of Orissa v. Madan Gopal* (1952) SCR 28; *Rambhadraiah v. Secretary*, AIR 1981 SC 1653; *Desai v. Roshan*, AIR 1976 SC 578; *State of M.P. v. Bhailal*, AIR 1964 SC 1006]

In appeals by special leave against the Patna High Court orders in writ petitions alleging large scale misappropriation of public funds to the extent of several hundred crores of rupees in the Animal Husbandry Department (Fodder Scam), the Supreme Court directed the High Court to ensure that a fair, honest and complete investigation was completed by the CBI and all persons against whom a *prima facie* case for trial was made out were identified and put on trial in accordance with law. The High Court's jurisdiction extended to examining the manner of investigations and considering the question of extension of time. [*Union of India v. Sushil Kumar Modi*, AIR 1997 SC 314]

It needs to be remembered that the remedy through a writ in cases other than those of violation of fundamental rights is not a normal one and is not expected to be granted as a matter of routine. It is an extraordinary remedy which can be expected in special circumstances and only under the discretion of the Court. Judiciary is not supposed to lay down policy and no court or tribunal can compel the government to change its policy involving expenditure. [*Himmat Lal Shah v. State of U.P.*, AIR 1954 SC 403; *Abraham v. ITO*, AIR 1961 SC 609; *Bhopal Sugar Industry v. ITO*, AIR 1967 SC 549; *State of Rajasthan v. Karam Chand*, AIR 1965 SC 913; *Union of India v. Tejram*, (1991) 3 SCC 11; *Kartar Singh v. State of Punjab*, JT (1994) 2 SC 423]

Where any High Court is satisfied that a case pending in the lower courts involves a substantial question of law as to the interpretation of the Constitution, it may withdraw the case and either itself decide it or determine the said question of law and return the case to the lower Court for determination (article 228).

Like the Supreme Court, each High Court is also to be a Court of record and of original and appellate jurisdiction with all the powers of such a court including the power to punish for its contempt (article 215).

Advocate-General

There is an Advocate-General for each State, appointed by the Governor, who holds office during the pleasure of the Governor. He must be a person qualified to be appointed as a Judge of High Court. His duty is to give advice to the State Governments upon legal matters and to perform such other duties of legal character, as may be referred or assigned to him by the Governor. The Advocate General has the right to speak and take part in the proceedings of the State Legislature without the right to vote.

Writs

The power to issue writs has been vested in the High Courts with a view to ensure quicker justice and early relief to persons whose rights are violated with impunity and who would suffer irreparably if a ready and speedy remedy is not made available without going into avoidable technicalities. There are five well known writs.

Habeas Corpus literally means a demand to produce the body. It applies in a case where a person is alleged to have been illegally detained. The issuance of the writ means an order to the detaining authority or person to physically present before the Court the detained person and show the cause of detention so that the Court can determine its legality or otherwise. If the detention is found to be illegal, the detained person is set free forthwith. Since now, after the 44th Amendment, article 21 cannot be suspended even during the proclamation of Emergency, this becomes a very valuable writ for safeguarding the personal liberty of the individual.

While the Supreme Court can issue the writ of *habeas corpus* only against the State in cases of violation of fundamental rights, the High Court can issue it also against private individuals illegally or arbitrarily detaining any other person.

Mandamus is a command to act lawfully and to desist from perpetrating an unlawful act. Where A has a legal right which casts certain legal obligations on B, A can seek a writ of *mandamus* directing B to perform its legal duty. *Mandamus* may lie against any authority, officers, government or even judicial bodies that fail to or refuse to perform a public duty and discharge a legal obligation. The Supreme Court may issue a *mandamus* to enforce the fundamental right of a person when its violation by some governmental order or act is alleged. The High Courts may issue this writ to direct an officer to exercise his constitutional and legal powers, to compel any person to discharge duties cast on him by the Constitution or the statute, to compel a judicial authority to exercise its jurisdiction and to order the Government not to enforce any unconstitutional law.

Prohibition is issued by a higher Court to a lower Court or tribunal and is intended to prohibit it from exceeding its jurisdiction. Writ of *prohibition* is not issued against administrative agencies. It is available only against judicial and quasi judicial bodies.

Certiorari also lies against judicial and quasi judicial authorities courts and tribunals and means 'to be informed'. When, for example, a tribunal acts without jurisdiction or in excess of it and issues an illegal order, that order can be quashed by a writ of *certiorari.* Such a writ may lie even against an administrative body affecting individual rights. [*Union of India v. Nambudri* (1991) 2 JSC 302]

Quo Warranto is a question asking 'with what authority or warrant'. The writ may be sought to clarify in public interest the legal position in regard to claim of a person to hold a public office. An application seeking such a writ may be made by any person provided the office in question is a substantive public office of a permanent nature created by the Constitution or law and a person has been appointed to it without a legal title and in contravention of the Constitution or the laws.

Besides writs, the High Courts under article 226 may also issue other directions and orders in the interests of justice to the people. [*T.C. Basappa v. Nagappa,* AIR 1954 SC 440]

THE SUBORDINATE COURTS

The subordinate courts, at the level of districts and lower, have almost similar structure all over the country. They deal with civil and criminal cases in accordance with their respective jurisdictions and administer the Code of Civil Procedure and the Code of Criminal Procedure. Each State is divided into judicial districts. The subordinate judiciary in each district is headed by a District and Sessions Judge. The usual designations on the civil side are District Judge, Additional District Judge, Civil Judge. On the criminal side, we have Sessions Judge, Additional Sessions Judge, Chief Judicial Magistrate, Judicial Magistrate etc. The Governor in consultation with the High Court appoints the district judges. A person who is not already in Government Service should have at least seven years' experience at the bar to become eligible for the position of a district judge (article 233).

Appointment of persons other than district judges to the judicial service of a State shall be made by the Governor in accordance with rules made thereunder. Besides the State Public Service Commission, the High Court has to be consulted in the matter of such appointments (article 234).

The administrative control of the High Court over the district courts and other lower courts is full inasmuch as postings, promotions and grant of leave etc. to any person belonging to the judicial service of a State and holding any post inferior to the post of a judge is vested in the High Court. [(article 235); (*Tej Pal v. State of U.P.* (1985) 3 SCC 604; *State of Assam v. Ranga Mohammed*, AIR 1967 SC 903)]

Independence of the Judiciary

Independence of the judiciary is the cornerstone of our judicial system. In a representative democracy, administration of justice assumes special significance in view of the rights of individuals that need protection against executive or legislative interference. This protection is given by making the judiciary independent of the other two organs of the government and supreme in its own sphere. An independent and supreme judiciary is also an essential requisite of a federal polity, wherein there is a constitutional division of powers between the federal government and governments of the constituent units and a functional division of powers between the executive, legislature and judiciary. Also, an independent and impartial judiciary is an essential requisite for ensuring human rights and protecting democracy. Only an independent judiciary can act effectively as the guardian of the rights of the individual and that of the Constitution.

There are many devices in the Indian Constitution which ensure the independence of the Courts. Independence is ensured by the judges

i. subscribing to an oath or affirmation,
ii. having security of tenure, 65 years of age for the Supreme Court and 62 years for the High Courts,
iii. not being removable except through a special procedure,

iv. having their privileges, allowances and perks protected and charged on the Consolidated Fund,
v. being given the power to punish for their contempt,
vi. not being subject to discussion on the floor of a legislature for their conduct,
vii. functioning in open courts,
viii. recruitment, appointment and control of their own staff by the Supreme Court and the High Courts, and
ix. debarring the judges of the Supreme Court from practicing in India after retirement and allowing High Court judges post retirement practice only at the Supreme Court or other High Courts.

But, even judiciary has to act within its constitutionally ordained domain and within the limits of its jurisdiction. Judges also are not above the law. Rule of law and laws of the land apply to them as to any other citizen. If anything, they have added responsibilities because of the position they occupy. They are also fully accountable to the people for what they do or do not do.

The independence of judiciary implies that judicial proceedings are conducted fairly and that the rights of the parties are respected and matters before the courts are decided impartially, on the basis of facts and in accordance with the law, without any improper influences, inducements, pressures, threats or interference, direct or indirect, from any quarter or for any reason. Everyone shall have the right to be tried by ordinary courts or tribunals using established legal procedures.

Due Process of Law Vs. According to the Procedure Established by Law: The U.S. Constitution (Constitutional Amendments) provides that a man may not be deprived of his right to liberty and property except according to due process of law. The Indian Constitution, however, lays down that a man may not be deprived of his rights to liberty except according to the procedure established by law. The due process of law gives wide scope to the Supreme Court to grant protection to the rights of its citizens. It can declare laws violative of these rights void not only on substantive grounds of being unlawful, but also on procedural grounds of being unreasonable. Our Supreme Court, while determining the constitutionality of a law, however is expected to examine only the substantive question, *i.e.*, whether the law is within the powers of the authority concerned or not. It is not expected to go into the question of its reasonableness, suitability or policy implications.

The Supreme Court pronounces its judgement on a specific case through a specific petition. It does not give its opinion or advice on a general reference. There should be an aggrieved person who petitions the Court to challenge the constitutionality of the statute which has adversely affected his rights. He has to show that he has sustained or is in immediate danger of sustaining some direct injury as a result of the enforcement of the statute, and that the injury complained of is justiciable.

Judicial Review

Judicial review means the power of the highest court of the land to finally pronounce upon the legality or otherwise of a legislative act in so far as it conforms, or does not conform, to the provisions of the Constitution of India. The Constitution being the fundamental law of the land, every legislative enactment, whether of the Union or of the States must conform to it. The higher courts in India are endowed with powers of judicial review of legislation. But, if an Act of Parliament is set aside by the judiciary as *ultra vires* or violative of the Constitution, Parliament can reenact it after removing the defects for which it was set aside. Also, Parliament may, within the limits of its constituent powers, amend the Constitution in such a manner that the law no longer remains unconstitutional. Thus, the Parliament in India is not as sovereign as the British Parliament where no judicial review of legislation is permitted. At the same time, the judiciary in India is not as supreme as in the United States of America which recognises virtually no limit on the scope of judicial review and the pronouncement of the Supreme Court in regard to the legality of a legislative measure is final. India has adopted a middle course and a compromise between the British sovereignty of Parliament and American

Judicial Supremacy. Since we have a written Constitution and the powers and functions of every organ are defined and delimited by the Constitution, there is no question of any organ – not even Parliament – being sovereign. Both Parliament and the Supreme Court are supreme in their respective spheres.

Article 32 in the Chapter on Fundamental Rights specifically confers the power of judicial review on the Supreme Court. Under this article every citizen has a right to move the Supreme Court by appropriate proceedings for the enforcement of the rights conferred in Chapter III. The Supreme Court can hear the petition in its original jurisdiction and for the enforcement of any of the rights conferred. Under article 226, State High Courts have been given similar power, *i.e.*, the power to issue to any person or authority, within its territorial jurisdiction, directions, orders, or writs.

Fundamental Rights in the Constitution make judicial review specially relevant. Article 12 guarantees fundamental rights against all State action. And 'State' under this article has been defined to include the Government and Parliament of India and the Government and the Legislature of each of the States and all local or other authorities within the territory of India or under the control of the Government.

Article 13 declares all laws inconsistent with or in derogation of the fundamental rights to be void to the extent of inconsistency. Up to 1967, the Supreme Court accepted the view that an Act amending the Constitution was not 'Law' in the definition of article 13(2). But, in the *Golaknath case*, the Supreme Court ruled by a majority judgement that an Act amending the Constitution was also 'law' under this definition and therefore subject to judicial review. The Constitution (Twenty fourth Amendment) Act, 1971 inserted clause 13(4) in the Constitution, laying down that an Amendment to the Constitution is not 'law' under the definition of article 13(2). In the *Keshvanand Bharti case*, the Supreme Court upheld this position.

Cases may also be filed before the Supreme Court by a State Government, or by an affected private individual or a party, claiming that in enacting a particular law, the concerned government exceeded its jurisdiction with regard to the division of powers under the Seventh Schedule. While reviewing such enactment, the Supreme Court will examine whether jurisdictional limits have been transgressed and if on that ground the law deserves to be struck down as *ultra vires* the Constitution.

JUDICIAL ACTIVISM AND PUBLIC INTEREST LITIGATION

Judicial Activism

Certain eventualities may be conceived where the judiciary may sometimes overstep its normal jurisdiction and intervene in areas otherwise in the realm of the legislature: (i) when the legislature fails to discharge its responsibilities; (ii) in case of hung legislature, when the Government it throws up is weak, insecure and busy in the struggle for self-survival and therefore unable to take any decision which displeases any caste, community or other group; (iii) those in power may be afraid of taking honest hard decisions for fear of losing power and for that reason may have political issues referred to courts as issues of law in order to mark time and delay decisions or to pass on the odium of strong decision making to the courts; (iv) where the legislature and the executive fail to protect the basic rights of the citizens like the right to live a decent life in healthy surroundings or to provide an honest, efficient and just system of laws and administration; (v) where the courts of law are misused by a strong authoritarian parliamentary party government for ulterior motives as was sought to be done during the emergency aberration; (vi) Lastly, sometimes the courts may themselves knowingly or unknowingly, become victims of human, all too human weaknesses of craze for populism, publicity, playing to the media and hogging the headlines. Also, the courts may try to expand their areas of jurisdiction and arrogate to themselves more functions and powers than legitimately belong to them.

Judges, like the legislators, come from the same social milieu. No institution has monopoly rights to weaknesses or to making mistakes. Courts may also go wrong and make mistakes. Even the Supreme Court recognises that it is not infallible and therefore there have been so many instances of revising and changing its views in the matter of interpretation of laws and the provisions of the Constitution.

What has come to be called "Judicial Activism" was born as a corrective to inaction or failure of the executive and the legislature to provide clean, competent and citizen-friendly governance. "Judicial Activism" may also be looked at as a facet of Judicial review. According to the former Chief Justice of India, Justice J.S.Verma, if implementation of rule of law which is the bedrock of democracy, is the basic responsibility of the judiciary, then it is the obligation of judiciary to see that every aspect which is essential for proper implementation of rule of law is taken care of. The obligation of the judiciary is to ensure that not only judiciary does its work, but also that every agency or instrumentality which is involved in the interpretation of law, functions effectively. Judicial activism must necessarily mean the active process of implementation of the rule of law, essential for the preservation of a functional democracy.

The essence of Judicial activism is an active justice delivery system. Judicial activism in India very largely had its source in the introduction of Public Interest Litigation (PIL). Traditionally, the general practice was that, before the court took up a matter for adjudication, it had to be satisfied that the petitioner had a *locus standi* in it and that no one except the affected person approached the court for redress. Public Interest Litigation introduced a new dimension. In the beginning, the application of PIL was confined only to improving the lot of the disadvantaged sections of the society who by reason of their poverty and ignorance were not in a position to seek justice from the courts and, therefore, any member of the public was permitted to maintain an application for appropriate directions.

In the Judges' Transfer case, the seven judge Constitution Bench of the Supreme Court held that any member of the public even if not directly involved but having "sufficient interest" can approach the High Court under article 226, or in case of breach of fundamental rights the Supreme Court, for redressal of the grievances of the persons who cannot move the Court because of "poverty, helplessness or disability or socially or economically disadvantaged position". The Court can be approached even through a letter in such a case (*S.P. Gupta v. President of India*, AIR 1982 SC 149). After this judgement, it has been open to public minded individual citizens or social organisations to seek judicial relief in the interest of the general public.

The High Courts and the Supreme Court may now entertain matters in which interest of the public at large is involved. The Court can be moved by any individual or group of persons either by filing a Writ Petition at the Filing Counter of the Court or even by addressing a letter to Hon'ble the Chief Justice highlighting the question of public importance for invoking this jurisdiction. Several matters of public importance have become landmark cases. A Writ Petition filed at the Filing Counter is dealt with like any other Writ Petition and processed as such. In case of a letter addressed to Hon'ble the Chief Justice the same is dealt with in accordance with the guidelines framed for the purpose.

PIL has come to stay in the Indian judicial system. Courts have been judiciously active in giving relief in social action litigation—ranging from labour to victims of custodial violence, to the excesses committed by the Executive. Several issues ranging far and wide over the spectrum of daily living are being covered by such litigation.

In *Bandhua Mukti Morcha v. Union of India* (AIR 1984 SC 803), an organisation dedicated to the cause of release of bonded labourers informed the Supreme Court through a letter that they conducted a survey of the stone quarries situated in Faridabad District of Haryana and found that there were a large number of labourers working in such quarries under "inhuman and intolerable conditions" and many of them were bonded labourers. The petitioners prayed that a writ be issued for proper implementation of the various provisions of the Constitution and Statutes with a view to ending the misery, suffering and helplessness of those labourers. The court treated the letter as a writ petition and appointed a Commission consisting of two advocates to visit these stone quarries, make an enquiry and report to the court on the matter.

In *Lakshmi Kant Pandey v. Union of India*, a writ petition was filed on the basis of a letter complaining malpractices indulged in by social organisations and voluntary agencies engaged in the work of offering Indian children to foreign parents. It was alleged that in the guise of adoption, children of tender age were not only being exposed to a long dreadful journey to distant countries at great risk to their lives but also to uncertainty as to their shelter and future. Chief Justice P.N. Bhagwati laid down certain principles and norms to ensure the welfare of the children and directed the Government and various agencies dealing with the matter to follow them ((1987) 1 SCC 667).

In recent years, the Supreme Court has issued directions to control pollution, to check the evil of child prostitution, to revive a sick company to protect the livelihood of 10,000 employees, to look into the danger to safety in building a dam, to segregate the children of prostitutes from their mothers, to provide insurance to workers in match factories, to protect the Taj Mahal from environmental pollution etc. [*Subhash v. State of Bihar*, AIR 1991 SC 420; *Vishal v. Union of India*, (1990) 3 SCC 318; *Workers of Rohtas Industries Ltd. v. Rohtas Industries Ltd.*, AIR 1990 SC 491; *Tehri Bandh v. State of U.P; Gaurav Jain v. Union of India*, AIR 1990 SC 292; *Mehta v. State of T.N.*, AIR 1991 SC 417; *M.C. Mehta v. Union of India*, AIR 1997 SC 734] However, it has been held that non justiciable political matters cannot be brought before the court under the guise of public interest litigation. [*Maharshi v. the State*, AIR 1990 All. 52] *Locus standi* to file a petition depends on the facts as they exist. Even a journalist may file a writ petition if the case falls in the categoty of public interest litigation. On the other hand, if personal interest litigation is sought to be fought as public interest litigation,person instituting such litigation may be made to pay the costs. The Court should not allow an unscrupulous person to vindicate his personal grudge in the garb of public interest. [*Rugmani v. Achutha*, AIR 1991 SC 983; *Bholanath v. State of U.P.* (1990) Supp SCC 151; *Subhash v. State of Bihar*, AIR 1991 SC 420; *Chhetriya Pradushan v. State of T.N.*, AIR 1991 SC 417; *Chetriya Samiti v. State of U.P.* (1991) I SCJ 130]

The innovative judicial approach to "Public Interest Litigation" came handy in case of acute social injustice, economic exploitation, denial of human rights, corruption and other offences against public interest. Even hyper-activism of judiciary was justified under the powers of judicial review. It drew its strength, relevance and legitimacy from the support it elicited from the people because of their total disenchantment with the other organs of the State run by the politicians and the bureaucrats. But, the scenario has since changed. People are beginning to lose faith in the Judiciary as well. Judiciary also can no more be said to be entirely free from maladies of corruption, inefficiency and misuse of authority that afflict other organs of the State. Some time back, a retiring Chief Justice of India himself publicly stated that upto 20 per cent of the judges in the country were corrupt and they brought the entire judiciary into disrepute.

It has come to be believed widely that in the name of public interest, judiciary has begun to invade the exclusive legislative and executive domains, to exceed its legitimate jurisdictional limits and arrogate to itself more powers than what the founding fathers gave it. Courts have been taking substantial governmental functions even in areas like mosquito eradication, Dengue fever and fumigation, garbage clearance etc. Questions are sometimes raised about the practical viability, feasibility and implementability of some of the court verdicts. Fears are expressed of the courts being misused for vested political group interests and of the courts overstepping the limits of judicial discretion, not exercising the essential judicial restraint and causing judicial excesses.

Reading into the Constitution what is *non est* and in effect legislating or even making the Constitution *e.g.* in the matter of the appointment of judges, misinterpreting parliamentary privileges and immunities in the JMM bribery case and allowing protection to M.P.s taking bribe of crores for casting their vote, holding even truth not to be a defence in contempt of court cases, laying down public policy or issuing executive orders to public bodies and State authorities in different areas. In any case, judicial activism cannot be a solution to our problems. At best it can act as a temporary measure or as an emergency medication inasmuch as the Judiciary cannot take over the functions of either the executive or the legislature.

In the ultimate analysis orders of the courts have also to be given effect to only by the administration which functions under the political Executive. Judiciary has to be very cautious and must ensure that a situation is not reached where its orders or directives are no more fully respected or obeyed or are found to be just unimplementable. The courts have begun to see that in the name of public interest litigation, false, frivolous, fraudulent or private interest motivated issues are not entertained.

MAJOR ISSUES IN INDIAN JUDICIAL SYSTEM

Appointment of Judges

Under article 124(2), Supreme Court Judges are to be appointed by the President "after consultation with such of the judges of the Supreme Court and of the High Courts as the President may deem necessary". The proviso to the article says that "in the case of appointment of a judge other than the Chief Justice, the Chief Justice of India shall always be consulted. The only obligation for the Government thus was to consult the Chief Justice and other judges. Significantly, the appointment was not required to be made `in consultation' but only `after consultation'. In actual practice, after receiving the opinion of the Chief Justice, the Cabinet deliberated on the matter and advised the President in regard to persons to be appointed. The President acted on the advice. In case of the Chief Justice, the seniormost judge was usually appointed. The convention, however, was ignored when in the '70s, a couple of Chief Justices were appointed superseding their more senior colleagues.

Requirement to consult and making an appointment "after" consultation cannot have the effect of converting the judiciary – the consultee – into the appointing authority. Speaking in the Constituent Assembly on 24 May 1949, Dr. Ambedkar had refused to accept the suggestion of making "concurrence" of the Chief Justice necessary in the matter of appointment of a judge. He said:

> ...after all, the Chief Justice is a man with all the failings, all the sentiments and all the prejudices which we as common people have; and I think, to allow the Chief Justice practically a veto upon the appointment of judges is really to transfer the authority to the Chief Justice which we are not prepared to vest in the President or the Government of the day... This is a dangerous proposition.

In the *S.P. Gupta vs. Union of India* case (1982), the court held that the consultation must be effective and involve exchange of views and examination of merits but it did not mean concurrence and ultimately the executive had the last word in the matter.

It is known that when the executive enjoyed a decisive voice in the matter of appointment of judges, the system worked most satisfactorily for several decades. It could be no body's case that the judges appointed when the Executive had a decisive voice were not the best or that they did not maintain judicial independence. In fact, we had some of the greatest judges during the period. However, later some appointments were made on considerations other than merit and seniority. Political, partisan and other extraneous factors were said to have determined some selections. The question was considered by a nine-judge Bench in the second judges' case [*Supreme Court Advocates-on-Record Association v. Union of India*, (1993)]. Gupta's case was overruled somewhat unceremoniously particularly with a strong and critical comment *viz.* "The majority view in S.P. Gupta – is an easily exploded myth, a bubble which vanishes on a mere touch". Mr. Justice Verma, delivering the majority judgement, stressed the constitutional purpose of selecting the best available persons as judges. The result of the landmark judgement was that the wings of the political executive were clipped and its powers curbed. While according to the Constitution (article 124) for appointment of judges the authority was with the President *i.e.* with the Executive, the second judges' case, in effect, made the Judiciary the appointing authority and converted the Executive (the President) into a consultee or a rubber stamp. The appointments had still to be made by the President on the advice of the Council of Ministers. But the Chief Justice, in consultation with other senior judges was supposed to be in the best position to decide upon the best persons to don the Bench. While the executive could exercise the necessary check before forwarding the advice to the President, it was not expected to substitute its own judgement for that of the CJ in regard to the suitability of those to be appointed. Thus, the Supreme Court practically took over the power of appointment of judges in its own hands, notwithstanding the clear words in article 124(2) of the Constitution. As a safeguard, it mandated the Chief Justice associating two of his seniormost colleagues in the selection process. The procedure for appointment was revised in the light of this judgement in 1994 to the effect that the decisive view in the matter of the appointment of judges shall be that of the Chief Justice of India and in case of a vacancy in the office of the Chief Justice of India, the seniormost judge shall be appointed unless the retiring Chief Justice reported that he was unfit.

But then, the pendulum of misuse of discretionary powers could swing to the other extreme. The Chief Justice could recommend names without consulting his senior brother judges. When there was intense lobbying on who were the most deserving to be appointed and certain names were suggested which seemed to violate the norms set by the Supreme Court itself in regard to seniority and merit of the recommendees and the need to consult senior brother judges, the executive had to step in again. Instead of clearing the names of persons recommended for appointment, the President (as advised by the Council of Ministers) made a reference to the Supreme Court under article 143 to seek its opinion. The reference did not question the Verma judgement. The nine-judge advisory opinion of 28 October, 1998 only reaffirmed the basic guidelines given there. Only some clarifications and safeguards were provided. The Chief Justice had to consult four senior most judges of the Supreme Court and if two of the four disagreed on some name, it could not be recommended. In effect, decisions were to be taken by consensus whereunder the Chief Justice and at least three of the other four must agree. In the meantime, one Chief Justice retired and another took over. Fresh recommendations were made and accepted.

Controversies in matters connected with the appointment of judges are fraught with grave consequences for the health of a polity that prides itself in being founded on constitutionalism, the rule of law and the independence of the judiciary. Also, institutions like the Presidency and the Supreme Court and high functionaries such as the President and the Chief Justice of the Supreme Court ideally should always remain above conflictual and confrontational discourses and disputes. That independence of the judiciary and people's faith therein are not allowed to be eroded in any way is as much the responsibility of the President and the Council of Ministers as of the Chief Justice of the Supreme Court and other judges. Also, it is in the self-interest of both the executive and the judiciary to zealously guard and preserve the established norms.

To resolve problems in the area of appointment of judges the device of a National Judicial Commission has been suggested.

Removal of Judges

Every judge of the Supreme Court holds office until the age of 65 years. A judge may be removed from his office only by an order of the President, passed after an address by each House of Parliament for his removal "on the ground of misbehaviour or incapacity" supported by a majority of the total membership of that House and by a majority of not less than two thirds of the members present and voting, is presented to him in the same session. The procedure may be regulated by Parliament by law (article 124). There has been only one case – that of Justice Ramaswamy – when proceedings for the removal of a judge were undertaken. But, the motion for presenting an address to the President for his removal failed to get the required majority in Lok Sabha.

Contrary to the common belief, there is no provision in our Constitution for the impeachment of a judge. The impeachment is provided for the President and none else. Also, there is a fundamental difference between removal procedure and impeachment procedure and between the impact of the adoption of a motion for impeachment and the passing of a motion for presenting an address to the President seeking orders for the removal of a judge. The grounds for the impeachment of the President have to concern 'violation of the Constitution' while an address for removal of a judge has to be on the ground of "misbehavior or incapacity". In case of impeachment, the moment the motion is passed by the two Houses, the President forthwith ceases to be the President. But in case of the motion for removal, it is for the President to consider issuing necessary orders or advise reconsideration *etc.*

Contempt of Court

A sensitive and controversial issue is that of the power of the courts to punish for their contempt. Articles 129 and 215 of the Constitution provide for the Supreme Court and the High Courts being courts of record and having all the powers of such courts including the power to punish for their own contempt. The Contempt of Courts Act, 1971 has codified the law in the matter. Contempt may be defined to mean wilful disobedience of the court, in any manner lowering the authority of the court or interfering with or obstructing the administration of jusitce. It does not inhibit genuine and well-intentioned criticism of courts or their functioning. Also, fair and reasonable criticism of a judicial act in the interest of public good cannot constitute contempt.

However, the law as it has emerged from judicial decisions does not allow even truth to be a valid defence against charge of contempt of court. Also, the courts have sought to make a distinction between criticism made by a former judge and law minister which may be permissible and criticism by other citizens which must be "checked". This is anti-democratic and violative of the freedom of expression, right to equality and non-discrimination clauses. It is necessary that the contempt law and more particularly the exercise of powers under it are reviewed objectively and in an ordinary citizen-friendly perspective.

The Constitution Commission (NCRWC) suggested that it may be laid down by constitutional amendment that "it shall open to the court on satisfaction of the *bona fides* of the plea and of the requirements of public interest to permit a defence of justification by truth." The Commission had also suggested that no court other than the Supreme Court and the High Courts should be allowed to exercise any power to punish for contempt of itself.

The Contempt of Courts (Amendment) Bill 2004 passed by Lok Sabha on 22 February 2006 seeks to amend the original 1971 Act to provide that the court may permit, in any proceeding for contempt of court, justification by truth as a valid defence if it is sastisfied that it is in public interest and the request for invoking it is *bona fide*. This is in acceptance of the NCRWC recommendation.

Procedural Delays

The most pressing problem facing the judiciary is its inability to deliver speedy justice. Millions of cases remain pending for years in courts at various levels. Many times the accused persons spend longer years in jail than the maximum jail sentence prescribed for the offence they are alleged to have committed. Sometimes delays are deliberately engineered. The VIP accused are protected by the 'state security apparatus' at public expense. Criminal cases against them keep getting adjourned repeatedly and remain pending for years. Such cases create adverse public opinion and general public tend to lose faith in the judicial system of the country.

Expensive Justice

Costs of seeking justice are extremely high and ordinary citizens can hardly afford it. Justice is no longer a natural right. In fact, it is a very high-priced privilege. High rates of legal fees imply that the person seeking justice has to dig into his pocket for his case to move. If the fees are not paid, the complaint does not get processed. The expense involved in the search for justice does not even end with the court fees. Added to it is the cost of the bonds, lawyers' professional fees, the price of transcript of court proceedings and, so on...

Amending of the Constitution and Basic Features Doctrine

During the period 1950-1972, the question of the amendability of fundamental rights came before the Supreme Court in three different cases, namely, *Shankari Prasad Vs. Union of India* (AIR 1951 SC 458); *Sajjan Singh Vs. State of Rajasthan* (AIR 1965 SC 845) and *Golak Nath Vs. State of Punjab* (AIR 1967 SC 1643). Until the Supreme Court decision in the *Golak Nath case*, the law was as follows:

i. Constitution Amendment Acts are not ordinary laws and are passed by Parliament in exercise of its constituent powers as contradistinct from ordinary legislative powers. There is no separate constituent body for the purposes of amendment of the Constitution, constituent power also being vested in 'Parliament'.

   (Later as late as in 1981 the Supreme Court confirmed that the amending power under article 368 is a constituent power independent of the scheme of the distribution of legislative powers under the Seventh Schedule. [*Sasanka v. Union of India,* AIR, 1981 SC 522)]

ii. There is no limitation placed upon the amending power, that is to say, there is no provision of the Constitution which cannot be amended. The terms of article 368 are perfectly general and empower Parliament to amend the Constitution without any exception whatever.

iii. Fundamental Rights guaranteed under the Constitution (Part III) are subject to Parliament's power to amend the Constitution.

In the *Golak Nath case*, the Supreme Court by a 6:5 majority reversed its earlier decisions and held that the fundamental rights enshrined in the Constitution were transcendental and immutable, that article 368 of the Constitution laid down only the procedure for amendment and did not give to Parliament any substantive power to amend the Constitution or any constituent power distinct or separate from its ordinary legislative power, that a Constitution Amendment Act was also law within the meaning of article 13 and as such Parliament could not take away or abridge the Fundamental Rights even through a Constitution Amendment Act passed under article 368.

In 1973, in *Kesavananda Bharati Vs. State of Kerala* (AIR 1973 SC 1461) the Supreme Court reviewed the decision in the *Golak Nath case*. Ten of the 13 Judges held that article 368 itself contained the power to amend the Constitution and that 'law' in article 13 (2) did not take in a constitutional amendment under article 368. The law declared in *Golak Nath case* was accordingly overruled. On the question whether the amending power under article 368 is absolute and unlimited, seven Judges, constituting a majority, held that the amending power under article 368 was subject to an implied limitation; a limitation which arose by necessary implication from its being a power to "amend the Constitution". By a majority of 7:6 the Court ruled that "Article 368 does not enable Parliament to alter the 'basic structure' or framework of the Constitution". What constituted the basic structure was, however, not clearly made out by the majority and remained an open question.

Following this decision in the *Kesavananda case*, clauses (4) and (5) were inserted in article 368 by the Constitution (42nd Amendment) Act, 1976, to dilute the limitation of 'basic features' to the amending powers of Parliament. These clauses say that (a) there are no limitations, express or implied, upon the amending power of Parliament under article 368(1), which is a 'constituent power', and that (b) a Constitution Amendment Act would not, therefore, be subject to judicial review on any ground. But the applicability of the doctrine of basic structure was reaffirmed by the Supreme Court in *Indira Gandhi vs. Raj Narain* (AIR 1975 SC 2299) and *Minerva Mills Vs. Union of India* (AIR 1980 SC 1789). In the latter case, the Court held clauses (4) and (5) as void, on the ground that this amendment sought to totally exclude judicial review, which was a 'basic feature' of the Constitution. The court further said:

> "Since the Constitution had conferred a limited amending power on the Parliament, the Parliament cannot under the exercise of that limited power enlarge that very power into an absolute power. Indeed, a limited amending power is one of the basic features of the Constitution and, therefore, the limitations on that power cannot be destroyed. In other words, Parliament cannot, under article 368, expand its amending power so as to acquire for itself the right to repeal or abrogate the Constitution or to destroy its basic and essential features. The donee of a limited power cannot by the exercise of that power convert the limited power into an unlimited one."

The court, however, did not show where in the Constitution, the power of amendment had been said to be a qualified or limited power except for the procedural requirements laid down in article 368. Be it as it may, the present state of the doctrine of 'basic features' is that so long as the decision in the *Kesavananda case* is not overturned by another full Bench of the Supreme Court, any amendment to the Constitution is liable to be interfered with by the Court on the ground of affecting one or other of the basic features of the Constitution.

In the *Kesavananda case,* Justice Sikri (para 302) had tried to tabulate the basic features of the Constitution as follows:

i. Supremacy of the Constitution
ii. Republican and democratic form of government
iii. Secular character of the Constitution
iv. Separation of powers
v. Federal character of the Constitution.

In the same case, Justice Hegde and Justice Mukherjee included the sovereignty and unity of India, the democratic character of our polity and individual freedom in the elements of the basic structure of the Constitution. They believed that Parliament had no power to revoke the mandate to build a Welfare State and an egalitarian society. Justice Khanna also said that Parliament could not change our democratic government into a dictatorship or hereditary monarchy nor would it be permissible to abolish the Lok Sabha and the Rajya Sabha. The secular character of the State could not, likewise, be done away with.

In *Indira Nehru Gandhi Vs. Raj Narain* (AIR 1975 SC 2299) Justice Chandrachud found the following to be the fundamental elements of the basic structure of the Constitution:

i. India as a sovereign democratic republic
ii. Equality of status and opportunity
iii. Secularism and the freedom of conscience
iv. Rule of law

The same Judge in the *Minerva Mills case* added the 'amending powers of Parliament', 'Judicial review' and 'balance between the Fundamental Rights and the Directive Principles' to the list of elements basic to the Constitution.

The concept of basic structure was further developed by the Supreme Court and the position that the basic features cannot be altered even by constitutional amendments was further confirmed and more essential features of the basic structure were added in *Waman Rao case.* [AIR 1981 SC 271); *Bhim Singhji case* (AIR 1981 SC 234); *S.P. Gupta vs. Union of India* (Transfer of Judges case, AIR 1982 SC 149); *Sampath Kumar's case* (AIR 1987 SC 663); *Kihoto Hollohon v. Zachilhu,* AIR 1993 SC 412; *L. Chandrakumar v. Union of India,* (AIR 1997 SC 1125)]. In *P.V. Narasimha Rao v. State* (AIR 1998 SC 2120), Justice S.C. Agarwal held that "Parliamentary Democracy" was part of the basic structure of the Constitution.

In the *S.R. Bommai case* regarding the dismissal of BJP Governments in Madhya Pradesh, Himachal Pradesh and

Rajasthan, Justice Jeevan Reddy and Justice Ramaswamy reiterated that federalism *inter alia* was a basic feature of the Constitution. Justice Ramaswamy held that a democratic form of Government, federal structure, unity and integrity of the nation, secularism, socialism, social justice and judicial review were among the basic features of the Constitution.

In some cases, there was a difference of opinion among the Judges as regards a particular element forming an element of the basic features. For example, Chief Justice Ray did not find it possible to hold the concept of free and fair elections as a basic feature whereas Justice Khanna, in the same case, found this principle to be an element of the fundamental features of the Constitution (*Indira Nehru Gandhi case*). Justice Chandrachud did not subscribe to the view that the Preamble to the Constitution holds the key to its basic structure. Justice Beg, on the other hand, found that the Court can find the test (of constitutional validity) primarily in the Preamble to the Constitution. The Preamble, he believed, furnished the yardstick to be applied even to constitutional amendments.

It is thus evident that so far there has been no consensus in this regard among the Judges and no majority judgment is available laying down the features of the Constitution that may be considered 'basic'. The Court has not foreclosed the list of the basic features as suggested by different Judges in different cases. In the *Indira Nehru Gandhi* case, Justice Chandrachud observed that "the theory of basic structure has to be considered in each individual case, not in the abstract, but in the context of the concrete problem."

The Basic Features Doctrine of the Supreme Court, besides its vagueness and lack of clarity is open to more fundamental objections. Every word of the Constitution should be understood in its normal, natural meaning. In the *Kesvananda Bharti case* itself, the Supreme Court has said that unless otherwise indicated, every word is supposed to have been used in the Constitution in its normal or ordinary connotation and should be given the plain common sense meaning. Unfortunately while interpreting the Constitution and the laws, the Supreme Court itself does not always do that. The purpose of interpretation is to ascertain the intent of the framers from the words used. We must go-by what the Constitution says and not by what judges say it says. We have to first try to read and understand the Constitution and then to critically evaluate what others, including judges, have to say about it. Unfortunately, too little attention is paid to the text of the Constitution and too much emphasis is laid on the case law and the past verdicts of the courts.

Constitution of a country is its foundational law and lays down the basic features of its polity. Every provision of the Constitution is the basic law of the land. Its provisions can hardly be so divided as to make some parts of the Constitution basic and others peripheral. The Constitution determines the basic structure of the political system, establishes the organs of the state and defines and delimits their jurisdictional realms and responsibilities and regulates their relationships with each other and with the people. All the three organs – *i.e.* including the judiciary – are responsible to the people who are the ultimate sovereigns. Every act of the Executive, Legislature and the Judiciary has to be tested on the alter of the Constitution and the weal of the people for its validity and legitimacy. None of the three organs is outside the state and none above the people.

The Constitution of India does not contain any provision in regard to basic features. There is nothing to suggest that the Constitution makers wanted any provisions of the Constitution to be absolutely unamendable. It was certainly not beyond the ingenuity of the founders to provide for it if they wanted it to be so. In fact, all the evidence is to the contrary. It was repeatedly declared in the Constituent Assembly and elsewhere by Nehru, Ambedkar and others that they did not wish to bind the succeeding generations, that, to use Nehru's words, "if you make anything rigid and permanent you stop a nation's growth, the growth of a living, vital, organic people".

If the sovereign people through their representatives cannot bring about desired change, who will? What the Supreme Court has done is to assume to itself a power of veto on all constitutional amendments. Instead of interpreting the amendment clause of the Constitution and declaring the law, the court, in effect, says that it will decide in each case whether to permit Parliament to amend the Constitution. In other words, the constituent power gets transferred from the elected representatives of the people to the judges of the Supreme Court. The Supreme Court is not above the Constitution and laws. It is also accountable to the ultimate sovereigns, the people of India and that just as the power to amend is said to be a limited power only to amend, the Supreme Court's own power to interpret and declare the law cannot be extended to making or rewriting the provisions of the Constitution. To paraphrase differently Supreme Court's own observations about Parliament's amending powers, one is tempted to say:

> Since "the Constitution had conferred a limited" power of judicial review and of interpreting the Constitution only for "doing complete justice" within its "jurisdiction", the Supreme Court cannot "under the exercise of that limited power enlarge that very power into an absolute power". Indeed, limited judicial review "is one of the basic features of our Constitution and, therefore, the limitations on that power cannot be destroyed". In other words, the Supreme Court, under article 32, 141 and 142 cannot expand its power of interpretation so as to acquire for itself the right to amend or prevent amendment to the Constitution on the ground of a self-invented 'basic features' doctrine and thereby in effect destroy the most basic feature of Indian polity, namely the primacy of the people and democracy as a Government of the people, by the people and for the people. It is the people and the Constitution framed by their representatives that have given certain limited powers to the Supreme Court as to other organs. "The donee of a limited power cannot by exercise of that power convert the limited power into an unlimited one.

Conclusion

There is every need to review the working of the judiciary during the last half-a-century and more, to assess how far our justice delivery system has been able to provide equal justice to all the people as ordained by the basic scheme of the Constitution. And, if we have failed or there are shortcomings in the system, we have to see what can be done to remedy the situation. How far the judiciary has been able to fulfil the role expectations and how can we prevent the fault lines from bringing down the entire edifice can best be examined by focusing on the problems that have arisen in the course of interplay of the judiciary with the executive, the legislature and the people at large. An alternative or supplementary approach may be to look at systemic problems of the judiciary and its constraints in relating to the other organs of the State, becoming more citizen-friendly and providing speedy justice at affordable costs. Possibly, a distortion in the mechanism of checks and balances or overstepping the jurisdictional limits could have resulted in aberrations.

Unfortunately, in the entire intellectual discourse on constitutional and political reforms, judiciary has been generally treated as a 'holy cow', there is tremendous reluctance to judge the judges and consider reforming the system of judicial administration. On an objective analysis, however, the case for some far-reaching judicial reforms may be found to be unassailable and at least deserving of as much importance and urgency as reforms in any other area.

The fundamental problem with the entire system of administration of justice is that it is not citizen-friendly with concerns of ordinary citizens, having the lowest priority, if any. The net result is erosion of public faith in the judicial system and subversion of the rule of law.

Growing awareness of their rights among the people; the trend of judicial scrutiny of every significant governmental action and the readiness even of the executive to seek judicial determination of debatable or controversial issues, at times, may be, to avoid its accountability for the decision, have all resulted in the increasing significance of the role of the judiciary in general and of Supreme Court in particular.

The judiciary has commanded considerable respect from the people of this country. The societal perception of judges is the judiciary's greatest strength. The judiciary in India, inspite of its quite visible drawbacks continues to enjoy some faith and confidence amongst the public.

Without the Judiciary, there can be no rule of law. Unless its house is in order, it cannot exercise effective control over the Executive and the Legislature. The people of India have a tremendous stake in the judiciary which has been their sheet anchor and last hope. More than power, it is only the moral authority that can sustain the judiciary. A few corrective measures are absolutely necessary to restore its health and make the institution more effective and accountable.

The recent decisions in regard to making truth as an admissible defence in Contempt of Court Cases and setting up a National Judicial Commission to ensure the accountability of judges are welcome steps in the right direction.

7

INDIAN FEDERALISM

UNION-STATE RELATIONS

Indian polity has been variously described as quasi federal, federal with a strong unitary or pro centre bias, federal in structure but unitary in spirit, federal in normal times but with possibilities of being converted into a purely unitary one during Emergency, *etc*. Some scholars have viewed it as a kind of polity covered by some variant of federalism. Today, one hears of all kinds of 'innovative' federalisms – cooperative, asymmetric, executive, emergent, responsible, parliamentary, populist, legislative, competitive, fiscal, restructured, reluctant, quasi or even non-federal federalism.

Generally speaking. federalism is a system of government in which power is constitutionally divided between a central authority and constituent political units (like states or provinces). The two levels of government are interdependent, and share sovereignty. Under a federal system, the Constitution is the supreme power from which authority of every organ is derived. An independent judiciary is necessary to treat as void every act which is inconsistent with the Constitution. The Constitution must necessarily be "rigid" *i.e.* not easily amendable. It must be either legally immutable, or else capable of being changed only by some authority above and beyond the ordinary legislative process.

Actually, federalism is a device for sharing power in a situation of territorially-based pluralism. As a political system, it can be a meaningful performer only for a society faced with territorially identifiable ethnic or other diversities. It is an arrangement between separate territorial entities to share power through free democratic will. Our pluralism is not territory-based. Our diversities are within and cut across territorial units and in a sense, they are our greatest strength and a great cementing force for national unity. Diversity is not division and unity does not mean uniformity or conformity. Also, the unity of India and integrity of the nation as concepts are very different from national or political integration.

Our polity cannot be considered only unitary because it provides, for example, for distribution of executive and legislative powers between the Union and the States and provisions affecting the powers of the States or Union State relations cannot be amended without ratification by the States. It cannot be considered strictly federal either, because the residuary powers vest in the Union. Under article 249, the Union Parliament can invade the State List. Under articles 356 and 357, on the ground of failure of constitutional machinery in any State, all its executive and legislative powers may be taken over by the Union and under articles 352 to 354, the Constitution can be converted into an entirely unitary one inasmuch as during Proclamation of Emergency, the executive and legislative powers of the Union extend to matters even in the State List. Finally, under articles 2, 3 and 4, new States may be formed and areas, boundaries or names of existing States altered by the Union Parliament by ordinary law passed by simple majority votes.

As Dr. Ambedkar said, rigidity and legalism were the two serious weaknesses of federalism. The Indian system was unique in that it created a dual polity with a single Indian citizenship which could be both unitary and federal according to requirements of time and circumstances. When the British power was established in India it was highly centralised and unitary. To hold India under its imperial authority, the British had to control it from the Centre and ensure that power remained centralised in their hands. A strong central authority was for the British both an imperial and an administrative necessity. The Charter Act of 1833 carried the process of centralisation in India to an extreme degree by depriving the Governments of Madras and Bombay of all legislative powers and concentrating them in the Governor General-in-Council at Calcutta. This act also expressly vested in the Governor General in Council the superintendence, direction and control of the whole civil and military Government of India. The Government of India Act 1919, provided for a considerable measure of devolution of authority to the provinces. The Joint Committee on Constitutional Reforms in 1934 observed:

> Notwithstanding the measure of devolution on the provincial authorities which was the outcome of the Act of 1919, the Government of India is and remains in essence a unitary and centralised Government, with the Governor General in Council as the keystone of the whole constitutional edifice.

When the Commonwealth of India Bill came up for discussion in the British House of Commons, the Government spokesman Malcolm Hailey, among other things, significantly said that some kind of federation was inevitable as the ultimate objective to be kept in view. The problems of princely states and of British commercial interests were also raised as grounds for the continuation of a strong central authority under the direct control of the British masters. Both the Simon Commission (1927-29) and the Butler Committee (1927-30) visualised, even though as a distant ideal, a federal Union for the whole of India.

The Government of India Act of 1935 proposed to set up a federal polity in India, with a central government and the Provinces deriving their jurisdiction and powers by direct devolution from the Crown. The Federation envisaged by the 1935 Act never came into being. The Provincial autonomy part of the 1935 Act was put into operation. Since a limited responsible Government was established only at the provincial level, the nationalists naturally asked for more powers for provincial legislatures. The experiment was, however shortlived.

In any case, the country as a whole continued to be ruled under the 1919 Act by a central authority only until 1947. And, since under the 1919 Act, there was a central government, a central legislature, a system of central laws *etc.*, even after the new Constitution, the bureaucracy could not discard the colonial hangover and the use of these terms continued.

When the Constituent Assembly first met in 1946 and early 1947, the idea was to have a federation with a Centre having limited powers. Before the Union Constitution Committee could transact any worthwhile business, the Mountbatten Plan of 3 June 1947 was announced. All hopes of preserving the unity of India vanished and the partition of the country on communal lines became a firm decision. As was expected, a decisive swing followed in favour of a strong Centre. The Union Constitution Committee and the Provincial Constitution Committee decided, at a joint meeting on 5 June, that in view of the 3 June announcement, the limitations imposed by the Cabinet Mission's plan on the form of the constitution no longer existed. Once partition had become a reality, there was no need to appease the Muslim League and restrict the powers of the Union Government. The Union Constitution Committee meeting of 6 June 1947 tentatively decided that the Constitution should be a federal structure with a strong Centre, and that there should be three exhaustive lists with residuary powers vesting in the Centre.

On 5 July 1947, the Union Powers Committee had presented a second report to the President of the Constituent Assembly emphasising that the "soundest framework for the Constitution was a federation with a strong Centre". The report said that the severe limitation on the scope of central authority in the Cabinet Mission's Plan was a compromise accepted by the Assembly much against its judgement of the administrative needs of the country in order to accommodate the Muslim League. The Union Powers Committee was unanimous in its view that it would be injurious to the interests of the country to provide for a weak central authority which would be incapable of ensuring peace, of coordinating vital matters of common concern, and of speaking effectively for the whole country in the international sphere. Meanwhile, 600 and odd princely states were integrated with the emerging Indian Union. As a result, the number of State units in the Indian Union was brought down to manageable proportions.

In the context of these developments, the Drafting Committee decided in favour of describing India as a "Union of States", although its Constitution might be federal in structure. The emphasis on India being a Union was to convey the fact that it was not the result of a compact or agreement between the constituent units but a declaration by the Constituent Assembly deriving its authority from the one people of India. Further, the conceptualisation was clearly intended to convey the federal nature of the polity but with a subordinate position to the States and structural functional balance in favour of the supremacy of the Union. The point was upheld by the Supreme Court in *West Bengal v. Union of India* (AIR 1963 SC 1241).

Asserting that the use of the term 'Union' instead of 'federation' was deliberate, Dr. B.R. Ambedkar, the Chairman of the Constitution Drafting Committee, said:

> The use of the word "Union" is deliberate... "Though the country and the people may be divided into different States for convenience of administration, the country is one integral whole, its people a single people living under a single imperium derived from a single source.

Dr.Ambedkar tried to explain the significance of using the term "Union of States" instead of "Federation of States" in the following words:

> The Drafting Committee wanted to make it clear that though India was to be a federation, the federation was not the result of an agreement by the States to join in a federation and that the federation not being the result of an agreement, no state has the right to secede from it. The federation is a Union because it is indestructible.

The text of the Constitution does not use the term 'federal' or 'federation'. The Supreme Court has spoken of the Indian Union as 'federal', 'quasi federal' or 'ambhibian' meaning sometimes 'federal' and sometimes 'unitary' (*State of Rajasthan v. Union of India*, AIR 1977 SC 1361). The predominant concern of the founding fathers as also of the various Commissions and Committees appointed since Independence to consider reorganisation of States or Union State relations—the JVP Committee, the Dar Commission, the States Reorganisation Commission, the Rajamannar Committee, the Sarkaria Commission, *etc.* has been that of the unity and integrity of India. The SRC report concluded:

> It is the Union of India which is the basis of our nationality....States are but limbs of the Union, and while we recognise that the limbs must be healthy and strong...it is the strength and stability of the Union and its capacity to develop and evolve that should be the governing consideration of all changes in the country.

Since our independence in 1947, India's unique experiment in federal democracy has served us well to unify the country and to provide vitality to the people to live with all our glorious diversity. Over the last 59 years, Indian democracy has achieved a certain degree of maturity in successfully managing and containing the inevitable socio- political conflicts to a large extent through checks and balances provided in our Constitution. The working of the Constitution for 56 years has demonstrated the inherent strength and resilience of the federal structure in withstanding the stresses and strains of diverse aspirations of the people.

Union-State Relations

Distribution of powers – legislative, administrative and financial – constitutes the pivot of federalism.

Legislative Relations

Articles 245 to 255 contain a charter of the distribution of legislative powers between the Union and the States. Parliament may make laws for the whole or any part of India. The Legislature of a State may make laws for the whole or any part of the State. Any State law would be void if it has extra territorial operation (*Kochuni v. State of Madras*, AIR 1960 SC 1080) unless sufficient nexus can be shown to exist between the object and the State (*State of Bombay v. RMDC*, AIR 1957 SC 699; *Tata Iron & Steel Co. v. State of Bihar*, AIR 1958 SC 452). Laws made by Parliament, however, cannot be questioned on grounds of extra territorial operation (article 245). The Seventh Schedule to the Constitution embodies three lists, *viz.* the Union List, the State List and the Concurrent List consisting of 97, 66 and 47 items respectively. Even after the changes in the Schedule brought about by Constitution Amendment Acts, the numbers of entries in the three lists have remained the same. Where some entry in full or in part is omitted (*e.g.* entry 33 in the Union List), the omission has been indicated by putting stars (***) and indicating in the footnote the name and number of the relevant Amendment Act. Similarly, where a new entry is added, it is given a supplementary number by alphabets A, B, C, *etc.* Amendments in the three lists have been effected by the third, sixth, seventh, fifteenth, thirty-second, forty-second and forty-sixth amendments. But, the largest number of changes were made by the seventh and the forty-second amendments. Article 246 lays down that the Union Parliament would have exclusive jurisdiction to make laws in regard to items in the Union List, the State Legislature would have exclusive power to make laws in respect of items in the State List and both the Union and State Legislatures could legislate in the area of items included in the Concurrent List. In the three fold distribution of legislative powers, residuary powers of legislation have been left with the Union (article 248). Also, Parliament has been given the power to make any law for the whole or any part of the country to give effect to any international treaty, agreement, convention or decision (article 253).

The Union List, the longest of the three lists, consists of important subjects like Defence, Foreign Affairs, Railways, Communication, Banking and Currency *etc.*, subjects which are of common interest to the Union and with respect to which uniformity of legislation throughout the Union is essential. Subjects which allow for diversity of interest and treatment are included in the State List and matters in which uniformity of legislation throughout the Union is desirable but not essential are included in the Concurrent List. Although the States are given exclusive powers over the subjects in the State List, there are two exceptions to this general rule. Under article 249, if the Rajya Sabha declares by a Resolution supported by two thirds of the members present and voting that it is necessary or expedient in the national interest that Parliament should make laws with respect to any matter enumerated in the State List, Parliament is competent to make laws on that matter for the whole or any part of India. Such a resolution remains valid for a year; it can be extended by another year by a subsequent resolution. Any law passed under this provision would cease to be in force within six months after the end of the year.

Again under article 250, Parliament is empowered to make laws on any item included in the State List for the whole or any part of India while a Proclamation of Emergency is in operation. The maximum duration of validity of such laws will be six months after the expiry of the Emergency.

In case of inconsistency between laws made by Parliament under articles 249 and 250 and laws made by State Legislatures, the law made by Parliament shall prevail and the State law shall be inoperative to the extent of repugnancy while the law made by Parliament remains in effect (article 251). Under the Doctrine of Pith and Substance, any jurisdictional conflict between the Union and the State/s in regard to their legislative competence can be settled by the court ascertaining the substance of the matter relating to an item in one list or the other.

The Parliament may enter the State List by invitation also. If two or more State Legislatures consider it desirable that any of the matters within their exclusive legislative competence should be regulated by parliamentary legislation and pass resolutions to that effect, the Parliament can undertake necessary legislation. However, the legislation so passed has effect only in the States which had requested and those others which may adopt it afterwards by resolutions passed in that behalf (article 252). Some of the entries in the Union List themselves empower Parliament to take over to itself, by making the requisite declaration by law, certain spheres and subjects from the State field (Seventh Schedule, *e.g.* entries 7, 23, 24, 27, 52, 54, 56, 62, 63, 64 & 67).

These alterations are not to be treated as amendments to the Constitution and can be effected if the Parliament passes a Bill by a simple majority on the recommendation of the President. Such a Bill is required to be referred to the legislatures of the States concerned for expressing their views thereon within the time allowed for the purpose. However, this reference in practice, does not fetter the hands of the Parliament. Parliament has been empowered to abolish or create a Legislative Council in a State by a simple procedure not involving an amendment of the Constitution. It can be done by an Act of Parliament, if the Legislative Assembly of the State passes a resolution to that effect by a special majority (article 169).

All this, however, does not imply that the States in India have been intended to be made merely administrative agents of the Union. Within the limits laid down in the Constitution, the Union and the States are independent of each other. One is not subordinate to the other in its own field. In the words of Dr. Ambedkar, "the States are as sovereign in the field which is left to them by the Constitution as the Centre is in the field which is assigned to it". The authority of one is to coordinate with the other. In fact, the relationship between the Union and the States in India represents a compromise between normal division of powers under which States enjoy autonomy within their own spheres and need for national integrity and a strong Union under exceptional circumstances. The arrangement has come to be subsumed under what is sometimes called a system of cooperative federalism.

Administrative Relations

Articles 256 to 265 seek to regulate administrative relations between the Union and the States. It is common in federal systems that the administrative relations between the Union and the States are fraught with difficulties. The Constitution of India seeks to achieve a smooth working relationship between the two levels. It provides that the executive powers of the State Government are to be exercised in such a way as to ensure compliance with the laws made by parliament. The Union Executive is also empowered to give such directions to a State as may appear to the Government of India to be necessary for the purpose.

Article 257 similarly provides that the executive power of every State shall be so exercised as not to impede the exercise of the executive power of the Union and the Union may issue necessary directions in that regard and for protection of railways and maintenance of means of communication of national or military importance. Any extra expenditure incurred by the State for the purpose of fulfilling Central directives is to be reimbursed by the Centre to the State. The provision in Article 261, directing that full faith and credit shall be given to public acts, records and judicial proceedings of the Union and the States in all parts of the Indian territory, adds a lot to the smooth working of Union State relations. Parliamentary control over Inter State rivers and provisions for adjudication of any Inter State water disputes were designed to take away a whole host of possibilities of friction between Union and States and between States themselves (article 262). In fact the Constitution makers did not want anything to be left to chance; hence the arrangements for Inter State Councils. Article 263 empowers the President to establish an Inter State Council to enquire into and advise upon Inter State disputes and matters of common interest between States or between the Union and the States and make recommendations for better coordination of policy and action.

Under article 258, the President may with the consent of a State Government entrust to that Government or its officers functions in relation to any matter to which the executive power of the Union extends. Similarly, under article 258A the Governor of a State may with the consent of the Union Government entrust to that Government or to its officers functions in relation to any matter to which the executive power of the State extends.

Financial Relations

In regard to the financial relations between the Union and the States too, one can find the general tendency of Indian federalism for centralisation. The Union may be said to be financially more powerful but given the nature of the country's needs for growth through planned economy this may be not only very desirable but entirely necessary. The States, however, have their own resources; the Union provides substantial amounts to the States by way of grants-in-aid, share proceeds of certain taxes, etc. The provision for the appointment of a Finance Commission every five years to examine the distribution of tax proceeds between the Union and States and to determine the principles which should govern the grants in aid has contributed to the generally smooth financial relationship between the Union and the States.

Article 265 upholds the salutary democratic principle of 'No taxation without representation' and categorically declares that no taxes can be imposed without the authority of law. Also, it adds, no taxes can be 'collected' except as under the authority of law.

A scheme for the distribution of revenues between the Union and the States is laid down in articles 268 to 273. The proceeds of all the taxes levied by the State are fully retained by the concerned States themselves while taxes in the Union List may be in part allotted to the States.

Thus, taxes that belong exclusively to the Union include Customs, Corporation Tax, taxes on capital value of assets, surcharge on income tax, etc. and taxes in respect of matters in the Union List.

Taxes belonging exclusively to the States include land revenue, Stamp Duty on items included in the State List, taxes on passengers and goods carried on inland waterways, lands and buildings, mineral rights, animals and boats, road vehicles, advertisements, consumption of electricity, luxuries, amusements etc., taxes on entry of goods into a local area, State tax tolls, fees in respect of matters in the State List and taxes on professions, trades, etc. not exceeding Rupees 2500 per annum.

Stamp duties on Bills of exchange *etc.* and duties of excise on medicinal and toilet preparations mentioned in the Union List shall be levied by the Union but collected and appropriated by the States and form part of their revenues except in the case of Union Territories.

Duties in respect of succession to property other than agricultural land, estate duty in respect of property other than agricultural land, terminal taxes on goods or passengers carried by railways, sea or air, taxes on railway fares and freights, taxes on transactions in stock exchanges, taxes on sale or purchase of newspapers and on advertisements therein, taxes on inter State sale or purchase of goods other than newspapers, taxes on inter State consignment of goods, shall all be assigned to the States concerned and distributed among the States as may be decided by Parliament by law. The proceeds attributable to Union Territories, however, shall form part of the Consolidated Fund of India (article 269).

There are some taxes like income tax and excise duties in the Union List which are levied and collected by the Union but their proceeds are distributed between the Union and the States. After a Finance Commission has been constituted, Presidential Order in regard to distribution of proceeds from income tax shall issue after considering the Commission's recommendations. In case of excise duties, the distribution of proceeds shall be determined by Parliament by law (articles 270 272).

Articles 273, 275 and 282 provide for three kinds of grants-in-aid and the circumstances in which these may be extended to the States by the Union. Thus, grants may be given by the Union to the States of Assam, Bihar, Orrisa and West Bengal in lieu of export duty on jute and jute products (article 273). Grants may be given to any State in need as may be deemed essential (article 275). Under article 282 the Union or a State may make a grant for any public purpose irrespective of that purpose being outside the legislative jurisdiction of the Union or State concerned.

Article 274 requires that in case of Bills affecting taxation in which States are interested, in effect, prior recommendation of the President would be necessary.

The State Legislatures may by law levy taxes on professions, trades, callings or employment. The total amount of these taxes payable by an individual shall not exceed Rs. 2500 per annum. The provision would not affect the power of Parliament to make laws in respect of income from professions etc. (article 276)

Inter-governmental Agencies

Union-State relations in India have enlarged into an extended network of organisations and agencies. The forums and agencies that really make the Indian federation tick can be broadly classified into three categories: (1) Inter-governmental agencies, *e.g.* National Development Council (NDC), Inter State Council (ISC), and ministerial and secretaries level meetings; (2) federal agencies having implications for the States as well. For example the Planning Commission, the Finance Commission, a number of independent regulatory authorities in sectors such as electricity, telecommunications, Central Vigilance Commission (CVC), Central Bureau of Investigation (CBI), Central Reserve Police Force (CRPF), etc.; (3) inter-State conferences of Chief Ministers/ Governors/ Vice Chancellors etc. [Also *see* Chapter 10. 'Independent Offices']

National Development Council

It is a unique forum, which brings together the executive heads of the Union and the States – the two orders of government in the country of sub-continental plural and federal diversities. It is an extra constitutional body set-up by a Cabinet resolution in 1952. The National Development Council is consulted in the formulation of the plans. Its main function is to review the working of the national plan from time to time. In practice, the Council makes recommendations pertaining to the overall size and structure of the plan. The Plan in draft is placed before it for its general approval. The Council also meets periodically to undertake review of the plan, thus, securing its coordinated implementation.

Inter State Council

The Inter-State Council was set up on 28 May 1990 through a Presidential order. In pursuance of the decision taken by the Council, a Standing Committee of the Council was constituted in December, 1996 under the Chairmanship of the Home Minister to function as a core group to go in depth into various issues that would come up for consideration before the Council.

The Inter-State Council was reconstituted on 11 November 1999. The Prime Minister has nominated the Union Minister for Home Affairs, Minister for Defence, Minister for Finance, Minister of Commerce and Industry, Minister for Chemicals and Fertilizers, and the Minister for External Affairs as members of the Council. In addition, the Prime Minister has approved that the Minister for Human Resource Development, the Minister for Mines and Minerals and the Minister for Railways will be permanent invitees to the Council. A surrogate Inter-State Council was, however, set up by the Nehru Government in 1952 in the National Development Council (NDC) for Union-State clearance of Five Year Plans and to look into related issues of economic development in the country.

The Inter-State Council has held five meetings so far and the following main decisions have been taken in these meetings:-

i) The Council has taken decisions on 125 of the 247 recommendations of the Sarkaria Commission Report in different meetings.

ii) The Council approved the alternative scheme of devolution of share in Central taxes to States as recommended by the Standing Committee.

iii) As there was no consensus on article 356 of the Constitution, the Council decided to refer the matter back to the Sub-Committee, constituted by the Standing Committee in its Sixth meeting, to evolve consensus formats for consideration in the Standing Committee.

iv) The Council has taken decision that the Ministry of Law with the assistance of other Ministries concerned should take up an exercise to fine tune laws to Centre-State interface.

v) The Council decided that on the subject of delay in State Bills referred for President's consideration there should be time bound clearance of Bills referred. The Bills should not be reserved for President's consideration in a routine manner and should be reserved when constitutionally they are required to be so referred for the purposes listed in the Sarkaria Commission.

Finance Commission

Article 280 of the Indian Constitution enjoins upon the President of India to constitute a Finance Commission (FC) "within two years from the commencement of the Constitution and thereafter at the expiration of every fifth year or at such earlier time as the President considers necessary". The use of the words 'thereafter' and 'at the expiration of every fifth year or at such earlier time' are *prima facie* suggestive of the periodic, and therefore temporary, nature of the Finance Commissions.

Apart from its constitutional status, the sanctity and importance of a Finance Commission is greatly enhanced by the fact that its recommendations form the fulcrum balancing inter-governmental financial relations in our federation. It is precisely in aid of this purpose – developing and maintaining healthy federal financial relationship – that the President is empowered to set up a Finance Commission even earlier than at the expiration of five years.

The First Finance Commission was constituted under article. 280 by a Presidential Order dated 22 November 1951, under the chairmanship of KC Neogy. The XII *i.e.* the latest Commission was set up by a Presidential order *vide* Min. of Finance notification dated, 1 November, 2002.

Very broadly, the Finance Commission performs two kinds of functions:

(a) Preparatory functions *viz.*, collection /collation of data, its analysis; discussions/studies leading to preparation of background notes/papers etc., and,

(b) Deliberative / Recommendatory functions.

---

4 *Report of the Member-Secretary XII Finance Commission,* vide his D.O. no. TFC/11019/3 dated 11 August 2003, http://fincomindia.nic.in/fincomnet/rpt_intra/func_tfc.doc

The temporary set up of Finance Commissions has decided disadvantages. Each time a Finance Commission is set up it requires altogether fresh time consuming exercise of assembling/recruiting staff on temporary basis, finding suitable accommodation, making it serviceable, organising work methods and work schedules, activating some corresponding arrangements at State levels, and racing to meet its deadline; overcoming all administrative, financial roadblocks. What is worse, the benefit of information collected, details and results of studies organised by one Finance Commission are usually not available to its successor. The Finance Commission Division of the Union Ministry of Finance, which was intended to tide over some of these problems, has not delivered the intended benefits.

The inter and intra governmental fiscal relations in a fast changing economic scenario requires the attention of an independent, permanent, expert body like the Finance Commission. As the Finance Commission is by our Constitution obliged to recommend to the President, at least at the intervals of five years if not before, how the inter-governmental transfer of financial resources should take place, it is desirable and necessary that it should be a continuing Commission. The continuity is needed to ensure constant and consistent upgradation of requisite data, monitoring of fiscal performance of both, the Centre and States, studied exploration of available options as course correcting mechanism, and generally to ensure that when the President calls for its recommendations under article 280 of the Constitution, it is able to give off its best.[4]

Growth of relations: Incidentally, in the field of Union-State relations, it needs to be specially stressed that a great deal of damage has been caused as a result of the wrong use of the terms 'Centre-State'. 'Central legislature', 'Central laws', etc. These are an unfortunate hangover from the days of the centralised government during the colonial rule. 'Centre' and 'Union' create very different images and connote very different concepts. 'Centre' is a point in the middle of the circle while 'Union' is the whole circle. The relationship between the Union and the States is between the whole and its parts and not between the centre of authority and its peripheries. The Constitution of India conceived of the division of the country into States, to repeat Ambedkar's words, only "for convenience of administration." It sought to achieve a smooth working relationship between the two levels of the Union and the States by tilting heavily in favour of the Union in all the fields of legislative, administrative and financial relations. That is not to deny, contradictory as it may seem, that the Constitution has many features of a federal structure.

During the colonial period, the Congress talked of linguistic units as a device to contain and counter the communal divide. After independence, linguistic states were accepted under pressure and against the Congress perception, and because the process became irreversible and necessary in the struggle for political power. The uniqueness of India's political architecture allowed India to emerge from the colonial past to be the world's largest functioning democracy and federal polity. In the first phase after Independence, there were several strong unifying factors:

1. the memories of the recent struggle for freedom and the sacrifices made for national unity;
2. the trauma of Partition, the riots, the unprecedented migrations and the gigantic problems of rehabilitation, integration of States, tackling the food crises, etc.;
3. strong charismatic leadership both at the Union and the State levels with excellent rapport among them and with the people;
4. one-party dominance practically all over the country; and
5. the needs of social engineering, the central Planning Commission, grants-in-aid to the States and so on.

In the second phase, however, cracks in the system began to appear and many divisive, fissiparous, regional or sub-national loyalties and tendencies came to the fore to weaken the Indian Union concept, but at the same time as a reaction reinforcing centrist urges. Some of these can be enumerated:

1. the linguistic States changed the entire political paradigm;
2. with the departure of charismatic leaders from the scene, the

leadership both at the Union and the State levels became mediocre and weak;
3. the end of one-party dominance saw several new regional parties born in different parts, some even came to power and national parties became weaker;
4. widespread craving for a more federal structure implying need for greater sharing of power and patronage;
5. rise of a larger and more powerful middle class with political ambitions and conflicts of employment opportunities;
6. craving for regional or sub-national identities as the means to political power; and
7. rise of a rich farmer class with trading interest conflicts with the other states, lobbying for pricing policies for farm products, royalties for natural resources and so on.

A special feature of the Indian scheme is that the geographic boundaries of the States have often been reorganised. In 1956, they were organised on linguistic basis. Several States were then created as needed. Later, more States were formed, *e.g.* Haryana, Himachal Pradesh, Nagaland, Manipur, Mizoram, Arunachal Pradesh and Goa. The ease with which the map of India has been redrawn and reorganisation of States effected during the last more than fifty years bears eloquent testimony to the unique resilience and flexibility of the political system and efficacy of its conflict resolution mechanisms. In 2001, 3 large States were bifurcated to create three new States of Jharkhand, Uttaranchal and Chhattisgarh to respect and encourage the local aspirations of the people and the process goes on. It is this dynamic process that is the source of the greatest strength to the system.

In the present scenario both integrational and disintegrational -centripetal and centrifugal—forces are at work at the same time at various levels—political, economic, administrative and emotional. Thus, some of the factors standing for national unity are:

i) history of a common ancient civilisation and culture, and record of political organisation as a single state, attempted repeatedly and often achieved, for example, by Ashoka and Akbar and later, by the British colonial masters;

ii) development of communications, modern technology and economic development factors with an indivisible and interdependent economy;

iii) the new economic policy of liberalisation, market economy and globalisation;

iv) administrative and legal unity through all-India services, common laws and unified judiciary; despite erosion in judicial credibility, continuing faith in the higher judiciary as a fair arbiter;

v) despite a multi-party coalition UPA partners – lie the NDA partners earlier – under the leadership of the Congress, fortunately, are broadly agreed on a common programme, succeed in somehow managing sharp differences that arise among them and are conscious of the need to stay together in their own interest and to swear by a common vision of national unity;

vi) dynamics of GOI-aided projects implemented locally through the State machinery; and

vii) fragmented nature of diversities constituting strength for unifying forces

On the other hand, the divisive factors are language, caste, community and vote bank politics of parties. It is said that throughout history, strong centralised governments have never lasted long in India. Even the British tried to recognise the territorial principle by ruling through Governors.

Today, the case for a strong Union Government rests on the need to protect the interests of small States against the bigger ones, to protect human rights all over the country, to safeguard the interests and rights of minorities, to ensure that democratic rule and the will of the people prevail against any arbitrary power assumption by an unscrupulous oligarchy or the like, and to ensure the needed transfer of resources and removal of economic growth imbalances and regional disparities.

Ideally, there is no dichotomy between a strong Union and strong States. Both are needed. But the way the Union Governments – irrespective of the colour of the party in power – have operated during the last over half-a-century particularly under articles 352 and 356—Proclamation of Emergency and imposition of President's rule in the States has weakened the case of the Union.

Imposition of President's Rule

Under article 356, if the President is satisfied that Government of a State cannot be carried on in accordance with the Constitution, he may issue a Proclamation taking over any of the functions and powers of the State Government. The powers of the State Legislatures may under the Proclamation become exercisable by or on the authority of Parliament. The State Assembly may be dissolved or kept under suspended animation. The President may take all other steps that may be necessary including suspension of the operation of any constitutional provision relating to anybody or authority in the State except the High Courts. Every Proclamation must cease to operate at the expiry of two months unless approved by resolution of the two Houses. After Parliament's approval also, a Proclamation may continue for not more than six months at a time and not for more than a total of three years. But, extension beyond one year is not possible even by a resolution of the two Houses of Parliament except during the operation of a Proclamation of Emergency and when elections to the Assembly cannot be held (article 356(5)).

Article 356 has been one of the must criticised and controversial provisions of the Constitution. Under this provision, State Governments have been taken over on more than 100 occasions during the last 56 years *i.e.* on an average involving more than two States each year. Opposition members and critics have said that the article has been misused, more often than not, for political and partisan purposes by the party in power at the Union level, usually to dismiss State Governments of parties in opposition. In the Constituent Assembly, while replying to the critics of this provision, Dr. Ambedkar had expressed the hope that it might remain a dead letter and might never be used except as a last resort, after everything else failed. In *State of Rajasthan v. Union of India* (AIR 1977 SC 1361) the Supreme Court held that a Proclamation under

356 depended on the subjective satisfaction of the President and the Court could not substitute its own satisfaction for that of the President nor could it, in view of article 74(2), enquire into the advice given to the President by the Council of Ministers. The Court, however, significantly added that if the satisfaction of the President was *mala fide*, based on extraneous or irrelevant considerations or no satisfaction at all, it could interfere. Thus, exercise of President's power under article 356 was brought under judicial review to that extent.

In the *Bommai case*, the Supreme Court stressed the desirability of the question of majority support of the government being settled on the floor of the House. This had also been emphasised by the Sarkaria Commission. An interesting case in this matter to go before the Courts was that of the "fresh" proclamation of 17 October 1996 "reimposing" President's rule over U.P. The Division bench of the Allahabad High Court in their judgement of 19 December 1996 even after taking note of the fact that proclamation had been approved by the two Houses of the Parliament quashed it as *ultra vires* the Constitution.

In this connection, the National Commission to Review the Working of the Constitution has made the following significant recommendation:

> In the considered view of the Commission, it should be possible without any constitutional amendment to provide for the election of the Leader of the House (Lok Sabha/State Assembly) along with the election of the Speaker and in like manner under the Rules of Procedure. The person so elected may be appointed the Prime Minister/Chief Minister. [See Chapter 4. 'The Executive']

So far as article 356 is concerned, there is another matter to which enough attention does not seem to have been paid either by the Government or by the Judiciary and that concerns its reading with other relevant articles of the Constitution. As stated by the present writer elsewhere:

> It is important that article 356 is read with articles 355, 256, 257, 353 and 365. This is usually not done. Insofar as article 355 speaks

of the duty of the Union to ensure that government of every State is carried on in accordance with the provisions of the Constitution, it is obvious that article 356 is not the only one to take care of a situation of failure of constitutional machinery. The Union can also act under article 355 *i.e.* without imposing President's rule in a matter of 'external aggression' or 'internal disturbance'. Article 355 can stand on its own. Also, Union Government can issue certain directions under articles 256, 257 and 353.

It is true that article 356 clearly authorises the President to issue a proclamation imposing President's rule over a State if he is satisfied that a situation has arisen in which the Government of the State cannot be carried on in accordance with the provisions of this Constitution" but a question may be asked when can the President lawfully hold that such a situation has actually arisen. A very specific and categorical answer is contained in article 365 when it says that where a State fails to comply with Union directions (under articles 256, 257 and others) "it shall be lawful for the President to hold that a situation has arisen in which the Government of the State cannot be carried on in accordance with the provisions of this Constitution". It is unfortunate that before rushing to issue proclamations under article 356, no efforts appeared to have been made to ensure that (i) the Union had done all that it could in discharge of its duty under article 355 and (ii) that the State had "failed to comply with, or give effect to" those directions. It seems in many cases recourse to 356 has been taken without keeping other provisions in view.

The National Commission to Review the Working of the Constitution has also fully endored this position (para 8.15.2).

The recent judgement of the Supreme Court (24 January 2006) in the Bihar Assembly dissolution case (*Rameshwar Pd. v. Union of India)* has thrown up several important questions. The facts of the case were simple: Following the announcement of results to the Bihar Legislative Assembly held in 2005 but before the Assembly could meet, President's rule under article 356 was imposed on the recommendation of the Governor *vide* notification dated 7.03.05 on the ground that no political party was in a position to form a government. The Assembly, however was kept under suspended animation. The Governor sent to the President two reports on 27.04.05 and 21.05.05 stating that according to various reports, MLAs were being lured by money, posts etc., that political instability may give rise to further horse trading by various parties and that, therefore, it would be desirable to dissolve the Assembly. The second report of the Governor also specifically made the point that a "particular party may be close to getting majority" and "claim may be staked to form the government". This report was received by the Union Government on 22.5.2005 and on the same day, Union Cabinet met at about 11 p.m. and decided to accept the report and sent fax to the President who was in Moscow recommending dissolution of the Bihar Assembly. President faxed his approval and notification was issued on 23.05.2005.

The Court held that dissolution to be unconstitutional but did not direct return to *status quo ante.* What was held to be unconstitutional by the Supreme Court was the Presidential notification of 23 May 2005 dissolving the Bihar Assembly with the President exercising powers under article 174(2) read with article 356.

The Governor only made a recommendation, gave his own assessment of the situation. He took no decisions and no action. He had, in fact, no power to do either. Bihar being under President's rule, the powers of the Governor to dissolve the Assembly under article 174(2) stood transferred to the President.

The second and the most important player in the Bihar drama was the Union Cabinet headed by the Prime Minister. The Cabinet armed with all the relevant information from all available sources, after careful consideration, took the decision to recommend to the President issuance of the notification dissolving the Assembly.

The third player was the President who was unfortunately misled and hurried into signing a blatantly "unconstitutional" notification.

Fourth and the last but not the least responsible player has been the Supreme Court itself. The judgement concentrated on the Governor's role and reiterated earlier recommendations about the type of persons who should not be appointed as Governors. It appeared to be too soft on the role of other players particularly the Union Cabinet when it merely said:

> The Governor may be the main player, but Council of Ministers should have verified facts stated in the report of the Governor before hurriedly accepting it as a gospel truth as to what Governor stated. Clearly, the Governor has misled the Council of Ministers....

Democratic Decentralisation

The federal structure in India has come to stay and needs to be strengthened. The central problem is not of Union-State relations now but of greater decentralisation of economic and political powers to lower and lower levels, with several tiers of functioning and people at the grassroots having real power, with the system growing up from there rather than coming down from above. The only way to strengthen the Union is to make it lose its extra weight, to shed its monopoly of power in all areas and concentrate on essentials. With economic liberalisation must come decentralisation of political power and management. [See Chapter 8. 'Decentralisation and Local Government']

Conclusion

India's needs of stability, security and development demand a new marriage between unitary and federal polity so that both stability of the system and responsibility to the people are ensured. The new federalism should build a united nation of a large number of autonomies – not subordinates or subsidiaries – as federal partners at various levels. It would be a 'federal union' with multiple tiers of governance and sharing of powers from the grassroots of Panchayats to Parliament.

i. We should de-link the ethnic aspirations from political demands for separate states. On principle, smaller States may be better for good governance due to growing populations. A larger number of States may strengthen the Union. In some cases, instead of creating new States, sub-State structures may be created. Combined with strong zonal councils, this would lead to greater stability, more accountability, stronger Union and better administered and more developed or fast-developing States.

ii. Norms for Governor's appointments need revamping. Sarkaria Commission recommendations should be examined and implemented.

iii. Problems regarding article 356 are only due to improper operation and interpretation of articles 256,257,355, 356 and 365. These need to be read together. Under article 355, *i.e.* without imposing President's rule under article 356, *sou motu* deployment of central para-military forces would be entirely in order.

iv. With liberalising economy, central control may get irrelevant. Income tax, corporation tax and indirect taxes can be moved to the concurrent list to facilitate harmonisation of taxes and a full vat.

v. There is every case for a wholesale review of Union-State relations and decentralisation of political power in a four-tier system of governance down to the grassroots levels. With a larger number of States and a four-tier system of governance, it may be possible to involve various groups in governance more closely and this may make the Union stronger and the nation more integrated, emotionally and culturally.

8

DECENTRALISATION AND LOCAL GOVERNMENT

PANCHAYATI RAJ INSTITUTIONS

The ethos of democracy can find real nourishment only when power reaches the grass-roots level. For the ordinary citizen, it is local democracy which can have real meaning and significance. In a vast country where large masses are still unlettered, village panchayats and participative democracy can do wonders. If the aim is to establish a democratic society, where change is brought about by voluntary consent and willing cooperation and not by the force of arms, there may be no alternative to Panchayati Raj or Local Self Government institutions.

Panchayat as an institution of local self-government at the village level had its origin in ancient India. A sort of village council or an association of the residents of the village often consisting of the village elders, *Panchayat* or *Gram Sangha* performed administrative and judicial functions. Sometimes, the *Gram Sanghas* or *Panchayats* were elected from among the villagers who regulated their own lives through these bodies. We find references to *Gram Sanghas* in the *Manusmriti* (code of Manu), Kautilya's *Arthashastra* (400 B.C.) and the *Mahabharata*. The *Shanti Parva* of *Mahabharata* refers to a *Sabha* named *Sansad* also. This consisted of the common people and was, therefore, called the *Jan Sansad*. Valmiki's *Ramayana* speaks of the *Ganapada* which was a sort of federation of village republics. Only those persons could become its members who had the general welfare of the people at their hearts; the membership was denied to *durjana* or impious persons. Later, village commonwealths are mentioned in *Sukra Niti* (Sukracharya's *Nitisara*). In fact, the institution of village *Panchayats* in one form or the other, has had an unbroken continuity almost all over India and throughout her long history.

With the beginning of British rule in India came centralization of administration and gradual erosion of surviving local self-governing institutions. This was resented by the people at large. And, from the earliest stages of India's national struggle for representative institutions and freedom from foreign rule, the nostalgia in the Indian psyche for Panchayati Raj was the result of this resentment against administrative centralisation. The mere mention of Panchayats brought back fond memories of the distant past immortalised in folklore going back to five thousand years and to the era when there flourished a network of village republics and Panchayats in the country. Jawaharlal Nehru also referred to the existence of democratic institutions at the village level in ancient India and said that India's strength really lay in 'her widespread system of village republics or self-governing Panchayats'. These Panchayats, he noted, were 'elected by the village folk and thus there was a basis of democracy in this system'.

On a philosophical plane, the value of a decentralised system of government and village self-sufficiency was upheld and propagated by thinkers like Annie Besant and Rabindra Nath Tagore. The *Gandhian Constitution for free India* drafted by S.N. Agarwal envisaged self-sufficient, self-governing village communities. Gandhiji was an ardent exponent and devotee of village swaraj (self-rule). Under the Gandhian concepts of a constitutional scheme for India, the village Panchayat was visualised as the primary political unit enjoying maximum autonomy in internal village administration including full control over the village watchman, patwari, the police and the schools, assessing and collecting land revenue, supervising cooperative farming, irrigation, interest rates, khadi and other village industries. Members of the village Panchayat were to be elected by all the adults in the village. The village was to be the primary unit and the foundation of development planning. A hierarchical pattern linking the taluka, district, provincial and Central governments was envisaged which provided for indirect election of various office bearers at all levels except that of the village Panchayat. The judicial system was also to be reorganised so as to be in line with the decentralised form of polity which allowed the largest measure of local autonomy at every level and the minimum necessary functions for national government. It was a concept of grass-roots democracy in the remotest villages linked to higher units at the regional and national levels. Later on, the Sarvodaya movement had also drawn on this philosophy of diffused democracy and decentralisation.

While Panchayati Raj was always close to the hearts of Indians, the British rulers for the first time thought of reversing the trend of centralisation only in 1882 when the Government of Lord Rippon issued a resolution proposing steps in the direction of local self-government. It was deemed desirable not for providing better government but as "an instrument of political and popular education." The resolution called upon the provincial governments to establish a network of Local Boards charged with definite duties and entrusted with definite funds throughout the country. These Boards were to have preponderance of non-official members chosen by election wherever possible. The control exercised by provincial governments was to be only from outside and only supervisory. The Collector was no longer to be the *ex officio* chairman of the Board. But, despite the very progressive and comprehensive nature of these Rippon reform proposals, precious little was done in the matter of implementation. The Local Boards continued to be wholly nominated. The collectors continued to be *ex officio* Presidents. The Boards practically became sort of departments of Government administration subject to excessive outside control.

The Decentralisation Commission which reported in 1909 made some far reaching suggestions to remove some of the defects in the working of Local Boards. In 1915 a Government resolution endorsed the Commission proposals. But, again no concerte steps in the matter were taken by the provincial governments and in practice the *status quo ante* continued.

Following the Montagu declaration of 1917 regarding introduction of responsible government in gradual stages beginning with the local bodies, a resolution was issued by the Government of India in 1918 and, under the scheme of provincial dyarchy, by 1919, rural self-government was put under the charge of the Indian ministers. Some progress was made. Besides Municipal and Local Boards Acts, laws were also passed in almost all the provinces to introduce Panchayats in villages. There was, however, no uniform pattern of local self-government in the country.

Under the Government of India Act, 1935 Provincial Autonomy started functioning in the provinces from April 1937. Congress Gvoernments took office in eight of the eleven provinces. Considerable progress in the direction of Panchayati Raj was made during the period of the Congress rule. Specially because of the Gandhian influence and direction, constitution of village Panchayats had become an important item in the programme of the Congress. Congress Ministries in the Provinces, however, did not last long and resigned following the declaration of war.

It was only natural that, after Independence, demands would be made in the Constituent Assembly for the revival of the Panchayat system of government at local level. The ideal of a revived village life with the Panchayats bringing democracy to the grass-roots had a special appeal for the Congress members of the Constituent Assembly. According to the January 1948 Plan of Gandhiji, each village Panchayat would constitute a working party with an elected leader; fifty such leaders would elect a second-grade leader who would coordinate their efforts and who would also be available for national service. Above the village Panchayat came the hierarchy of indirectly elected bodies – taluka and district panchayats – each of which comprised of the sarpanches of the next lower panchayats. Members from the district and municipal panchayats would make up the provincial panchayat. Presidents of provincial panchayats would comprise the All India Panchayat whose President will also be the Head of the State and of the Government. Among the responsibilities of the provincial panchayats would be transport, irrigation, natural resources and cooperative banks. The national panchayat would be responsible for defence, currency, customs, running of key industries of national inportance and the coordination of provincial economic development plans.

When it came to putting it down in the Constitution, it seems, the constitution makers felt that in the context of the needs of a welfare state of the modern age, it would be difficult and improper to take India back to the era of village republics. They opted for a system of parliamentary Government both at the Union and State levels with the popular Houses of the Union Parliament and the State legislatures being directly elected on the basis of universal adult franchise. In the Objectives Resolution drafted and moved by Nehru there was no reference to Panchayats. The Constituent Assembly also did not deal with the subject in any detail. When the reports of the Union and Provincial Constitution Committees were debated in the Assembly, there were only a few references to Panchayats and a lone member voiced sentiments favouring the village being accepted as the primary unit of political organisation with the Government rising from the grass-roots to the province and then to the Centre. Later, in a letter to B.N. Rau, the President of the Assembly, Dr. Rajendra Prasad expressed himself strongly in favour of the idea of "making the Constitution begin with the village and go up to the Centre" with the adult franchise being utilised only for the village panchayats which could in turn act as the electoral college for electing representatives to the provinces and the Centre.

Panchayati Raj in India after Independence

The need for popular participation in development tasks under the Five Year Plans prompted the Congress leaders now in government to look in the direction of strengthening the panchayat system. Accordingly, Balwant Rai Mehta Committee was appointed to enquire into, among other things, the lack of initiative, apathy and indifference on the part of the rural population. The Committee, officially designated as the "team for the study of Community Projects and National Extension Service", visited all the States and held extensive discussions with all those concerned. It examined whether the existing local bodies could be entrusted with the job of undertaking the administrative and development work. In its opinion, there was need for an intermediary agency between the district board and the village panchayat, as the former covered a vast area and possibly could not do justice to the role assigned to it. According to the Committee, there was to be a Panchayat Samiti at the Block level which was to be indirectly elected by the Village Panchayats, some representation being given also to municipalities and cooperative organisations in the Block area. The Samiti was to be assigned specific functions and specific items of revenue. At the district level there was to be a coordinating body called the Zilla Parishad consisting of the Presidents of the Panchayats Samities, Members of State Legislatures and Parliament and all district level officers of the development departments as members and, with the Collector as the Chairman.

The village panchayat was to be constituted by direct election on the basis of adult franchise with a special provision to co-opt two women members and one member each from scheduled castes and scheduled tribes. The Panchayat was to have specific items of revenue like a share in land revenue and certain obligatory duties like acting as the agents of the Panchayats Samiti for executing schemes. Thus the plan envisaged a three-tier system of decentralisation, namely the Village Panchayat, the Panchayat Samiti and the Zilla Parishad. The above scheme recommended by the Committee was endorsed by the National Development Council on 12 January 1958. It was also decided at the national level that while the broad pattern and the fundamentals of the new system may be uniform throughout the country, there should not be any rigidity. What was important was the genuine transfer of power to the people, not the details of the pattern adopted.

According to Nehru, Panchayats were the "foundations of democracy" in India. It was only by providing opportunity to the people that they can be trained to shoulder responsibilities. It became imperative that a bold step be taken whereby more and more responsibility could be transferred to the people. People were not merely to be consulted but effective power was to be entrusted to them. Nehru was of the opinion that India would make real progress only when people living in villages became politically conscious. If they made progress, the nation ultimately was bound to be prosperous, strong and united. Except for Kerala and Jammu & Kashmir all the States had then adopted the three-tier Panchayati Raj system. In these two States the lowest level organisation of Panchayat was established while the other two levels of Panchayat Samiti and Zilla Parishad remained to be formed. A village or a group of villages, formed a Panchayat of elected representatives, a few Panchayats formed a Panchayat Samiti and the various Panchayat Samities of a district were governed by a Zilla Parishad and these three institutions had a threefold purpose:

(i) to be autonomous and self-governing to some extent;
(ii) to play an effective role in drawing up the 5 year plans; and
(iii) to have scope for initiative and readjustment in implementing the plans to suit local needs

It would be of interest to note that throughout the period 1950 to 1964, the government headed by Nehru was all along keenly interested in the decentralisation of governmental authority and in the establishment of village Panchayats. The Congress Working Committee had in a resolution, stated:

> The Working committee have noted with appreciation the progressive introduction of the Panchayat system in various parts of India. This is not only in keeping with the ancient tradition of India but is suited to present day conditions. A modern state tends inevitably to become more and more centralised. This tendency should be balanced by the growth of

> self-governing institutions, so that the mass of the people should themselves participate in this business of adminsitration and in other aspects of community life, social, economic and judicial. This can best be done by the development of Panchayats in the villages of India. These Panchayats should have an administrative function as well as a judicial function. The CWC particularly welcome the establishment of *Nyaya* or judicial Panchayats which should reduce the burden on the regular courts and make justice available on the spot in a considerable number of relatively petty matters and thus make it both speedy and inexpensive. Such Panchayats should be developed throughout the country in accordance with local conditions and traditions and represent the entire community in the area concerned, irrespective of caste or creed.

After the Balwant Rai Mehta Committee report was presented and implementation of its various recommendations had begun in right earnest, the 1961 Bhavnagar session of the Indian National Congress again took up the subject of Panchayati Raj for consideration. The Resolution on "Panchayati Raj" was moved by Balwantrai Mehta himself who said that a welfare state would never be achieved in reality so long as local self-government did not function at the District, Taluka and village levels with elective elements. According to him, Panchayats and the cooperatives were the two institutions through which the people could be trained for leadership. He called upon the Congressmen to take direct interest in the working of Panchayats and to see that the new venture really achieved its object. S.K. Dey, the Minister of Community Development and Cooperation, Raghubir Sahay who was the leader of the Study Team of Congress MPs on Panchayati Raj and Smt. Ram Dulari Sinha also spoke strongly in support of the Panchayati Raj. Jawaharlal Nehru, participating in the discussion said that Panchayati Raj had immense possibilities. He allayed the fear that if at one stroke a lot of power was given to the Sarpanches or Panches it would be harmful. On the other hand, he felt, they would learn from mistakes and improve their performance. The real meaning of democracy lay in enabling the people to go forward. Panchayats could form the strong foundations of democracy and only on strong foundations could solid structure be built. The general opinion on the issue of participation of political parties in the elections on Panchayati Raj bodies was that preferably the elections should be on non-political basis. The Resolution which was adopted at the session, *inter alia*, welcomed the Panchayati Raj movement and congratulated the States which had already adopted it and expressed the hope that other States and Union Territories would also establish Panchayati Raj bodies in the course of the year and transfer responsibility to them in as large a measure as possible.

By the year 1962 Panchayati Raj had come to be accepted as a national programme. It was felt necessary that Panchayati Raj got the widest support of the people and therefore the need for avoiding party-politics in the election to village Panchayats was emphasised. It was hoped that the political parties would also avoid setting up candidates on party-lines for Panchayat elections. Speaking on the occasion of Third Annual General Body Meeting of the IIPA, on 6 April 1957, Nehru said:

> There are hundreds and thousands of panchayats in this country. They form the real base of our democracy. If that base is unsound, then we are not cent percent stable democratically, even with the second base of our Parliament. We are told that panchayats have not succeeded because there are squabbles, there are parties, there is corruption and all that. It is true, I think, that our experience of Panchayats has been distressing. But real democracy cannot be at the top, it can be only at the base; and in India, this is not something alien; it is something natural to this soil. The fact remains that the panchayat is the primary base of our democracy and we have to improve it.

Introduction of Panchayati Raj was hailed as one of the most important political innovations in independent India. It was also considered as a revolutionary step. Panchayati Raj is a system of local self government where in the people take upon themselves the responsibility for development. It is also a system of institutional arrangement for achieving rural Development through people's initiative and participation. Panchayati Raj involves a three-tier structure of democratic institutions at district, block and village levels namely, Zila Prishad, Panchayat Samiti and Village Panchayats respectively. These institutions are considered as training ground for democracy and give political education to the massess. These institutions were established in 1959 based on the philosophy of decentralization and *gram swaraj*. Rural development plans and programmes are implemented at this level so that fruits of development can accrue to the community directly.

Both the Central and State Governments have appointed several Committees and Commissions for reviewing and recommending reforms to strengthen Panchayati Raj during the last three decades. Panchayati Raj that emerged in the States is substantially in tune with Balwant Rai Mehta team recommendations though there are distinguishing differences from State to State. Another Committee on Panchayati Raj appointed by the Central Government under the Chairmanship of Shri Ashok Mehta in 1978 reviewed the system of Panchayati Raj in different States in the country and recommended a different structure of Panchayati Raj. Starting with Rajasthan several States introduced Panchayati Raj in quick succession.

However, all these steps proved unsatisfactory and despite the constitutional directive of article 40 and the five year plans, it was disappointing and discouraging that no major steps were taken in reorganising village Panchayats in such a way as to make them instruments of transforming society with popular participation. Of course, there were new enactments or amendments to existing Acts passed by various State legislatures increasing the number of Panchayats and their elected members. The range of powers and functions were also widened. But the power of taxation given to the Panchayats was subject to specific conditions imposed by the Government concerned. Often, rather than meeting the stringent conditions, the panchayats preferred to raise no additional revenue by new taxation resulting in lack of funds for meeting even the essential and obligatory expenses. In short, the village panchayats continued to be more or less in the same condition as in the pre-independence era.

Decline of Panchayati Raj Institutions

After the mid sixties, the process of decline started. In many States, a tendency to postpone the Panchayati Raj elections indefinitely was noticeable. In some states, parallel bodies came to be set up at the district level, thus reducing the role of Panchayati Raj in development planning and implementation.

Some of the major problems and short comings in the working Panchayati Raj institutions can be identified as:

(i) Election not being held on a regular basis.

(ii) Lack of adequate transfer of powers and resources to Panchayati institutions.

(iii) Lack of Panchayati Raj bodies to generate their own resources such as tax on sale of land.

(iv) Non-Representation of women and weaker sections on the elected bodies.

The G.V.K. Rao committee appointed by the Planning Commission in 1985 to review the existing administrative arrangements for rural development strongly recommended the revival of Panchayati Raj institutitons all over the country and highlighting the need to transfer power of state to democratic bodies at the local level. The government of India then set up another committee in June 1986 headed by L.M. Singhvi.

To prepare a concept paper on the revitalisation of the Panchayati Raj institutions, the Committee recommended that the Panchayati Raj should be constitutionally recognised, protected and preserved by the inclusion of a new chapter in the Constitution. It also suggested a constitutional provision to ensure regular, free and fair elections for Panchayati Raj institutions. Accepting these recommendations of the Committee the central government headed by late Rajiv Gandhi brought in the Constitution 64th amendment Bill which was passed by the Lok Sabha on the 16th August 1989. This was a comprehensive Bill covering all vital aspects of PRI's. Unfortunately, this Bill could not be enacted as it was not approved by the Rajya Sabha. In the year 1990, the issues relating to strengthening of Panchayati Raj institutitions were considered afresh based on detailed discussions in the Cabinet committee set up for this purpose. It was considered that a new Constitution Amendment Bill may be drawn up. The matter was brought up before a Conference of Chief Ministers held in June, 1990 presided over by the then Prime Minister. The Conference endorsed the proposals for the introduction of Constitution Amendment Bill and also the model guidelines with the modification that the number of tiers in the Panchayati Raj structure, may be left to be decided by the State governments and the arrangement for conduct of elections for PRI's may also be left to be made by the States themselves. The Constitutiton Amendment Bill and model guidelines were approved by the Cabinet in July 1990 and it was decided that there should be Constitutiton Amendment both for PRI's and Urban Local bodies Further modifications were made on the basis of the discussions with the leaders of various political parties.

Seventy-third and Seventy-fourth Amendments

Narasimha Rao as Prime Minister succeeded in seeing through Parliament the two Bills in a somewhat diluted form. The seventy-third and seventy-fourth Amendments laid down the framework and guidelines in regard to the obligation to holding regular elections, restricting the period of supercession, providing for reservation for SC/ST and women, etc. It was perhaps very unfortunate that instead of relying on the Election Commission, a parallel and separate State election machinery was provided. It should be possible to somehow integrate the two and avoid duplication and frittering away of national resources-both financial and man-power.

The 73rd and 74th Amendment to the Constitution of India constituted a milestone in the process of establishing decentralised democratic administration through local bodies and taking administration to the doorsteps of the people to ensure economic and social justice. The important thing is that now Panchayats are to be directly elected by the people like the Lok Sabha and State Assemblies.

The peculiarities of the administrative system that came into being as a result of the 73rd and 74th Amendments were as follows:

- The local self governments got structural uniformity throughout the state;
- Quinquinnial election became compulsory at the level of local administration (*i.e.*, at the Panchayats);
- The responsibility to conduct the election to the three tiers of panchayats was entrusted to the State Election Commission;
- 33% of the seats of the Panchayats were reserved for women;
- Gramsabhas were constituted to ensure people's participation in the developmental process;
- The responsibility of the local bodies in developmental planning activities was emphasised.

24 April 1993 is a red-letter day in the history of Panchayati Raj in India as on this day the Constitution (73rd Amendment) Act,1992 came into force to provide constitutional status to the Panchayati Raj institutions. The Constitution guarantees the institutional existence of Panchayats through the 73rd Amendment Act (1992). The Eleventh Schedule added to the Amendment Act (1992) distributes the powers between the State legislature and the panchayat paving the way for an innovative three-tier federalism. Also, the Constitution empowers the State legislatures to confer on the Panchayats such powers and authority as may be necessary to enable them to function as institutions of Self-Government.

The salient features of the 73rd Amendment Act, 1992 were:

- To provide 3-tier system of Panchayati Raj for all States having population of over 20 lakh.
- To hold Panchayat elections regularly every 5 years.
- To provide reservation of seats for Scheduled Castes, Scheduled Tribes and women (not less than 33%)
- To appoint State Finance Commission to make recommendations as regards the financial powers of the Panchayats.
- To constitute District Planning Committee to prepare draft development plan for the district as a whole.

Panchayats were given powers and authority to function as institutions of self-government. The following powers and responsibilities were to be delegated to Panchayats at the appropriate level:

- Preparation of plan for economic development and social justice.
- Implementation of schemes for economic development and social justice in relation to 29 subjects given in the Eleventh Schedule of the Constitution.
- To levy, collect and appropriate taxes, duties, tolls and fees.

Gram Sabha

In the Panchayati Raj set up, the Gram Sabha, the general assembly of villagers, has a key role for effective functioning of Panchayats. In the Gram Sabha meeting, the rural poor, the women and the marginalised people get an opportunity to join in decision making on matters affecting their lives. Active functioning of the Gram Sabha would ensure participatory democracy with transparency, accountability and achievement.

- Gram Sabha should meet at least once in each quarter preferably on Republic Day, Labour Day, Independence Day and Gandhi Jayanti.
- Decide developmental work to be undertaken by Panchayats based on needs assessment.
- Suggest remedial measures for economy and efficiency in the functioning of the Panchayats.
- Question and scrutinise the decisions of Panchayats in the meeting of Gram Sabha.
- Discuss the Annual Financial Statement of Gram Panchayats.

The Panchayats (Extension to the Scheduled Areas) Act, 1996: This Act extends Panchayats to the tribal areas of eight States, namely Andhra Pradesh, Bihar, Gujarat, Himachal Pradesh, Maharashtra, Madhya Pradesh, Orissa and Rajasthan. This came into force on 24 December, 1996. Except Rajasthan and Bihar all States passed laws to give effect to the provisions contained in the Act (40 of 1996).

Under the Act, Gram Sabha has been vested with powers of -

- Ownership of Minor Forest Produce
- Development plans approval
- Selection of beneficiaries under various programmes
- Consultation on land acquisition
- Management minor water bodies
- Control over mineral leases
- Regulate/Prohibit sale of intoxicants
- Prevent alienation of land and restore unlawfully alienated land of STs
- Manage village markets
- Control money lending to STs
- Control institutions and functionaries in all social sectors.

Training and awareness generation programme: The Ministry of Rural Development extends limited financial assistance to the States in their effort to train and create awareness among the elected members of Panchayats and functionaries. The State Governments are being asked to conduct such training courses. The Ministry has also been providing financial assistance through the Council for Advancement of People's Action & Rural Technology (CAPART) to the non-governmental organisations for conducting training and awareness generation programmes on Panchayati Raj. This Ministry also commissions research and evaluation studies related to Panchayati Raj from voluntary organisations/institutions.

Eleventh Schedule

(Article 243G)

1. Agriculture, including agricultural extension.
2. Land improvement, implementation of land reforms, land consolidation and soil conservation.
3. Minor irrigation, water management and watershed development.
4. Animal husbandry, dairying and poultry.
5. Fisheries.
6. Social forestry and farm forestry.
7. Minor forest produce.
8. Small scale industries, including food processing industries.

9. Khadi, village and cottage industries.
10. Rural housing.
11. Drinking water.
12. Fuel and fodder.
13. Roads, culverts, bridges, ferries, waterways and other means of communication.
14. Rural electrification, including distribution of electricity.
15. Non-conventional energy sources.
16. Poverty alleviation programme.
17. Education, including primary and secondary schools.
18. Technical training and vocational education.
19. Adult and non-formal education.
20. Libraries.
21. Cultural activities.
22. Markets and fairs.
23. Health and sanitation, including hospitals, primary health centres and dispensaries.
24. Family welfare.
25. Women and child development.
26. Social welfare, including welfare of the handicapped and mentally retarded.
27. Welfare of the weaker sections, and in particular, of the Scheduled Castes and the Scheduled Tribes.
28. Public distribution system.
29. Maintenance of community assets.

74th Constitution Amendment Act (urban local bodies): The Constitution (74th Amendment) Act has set up a new trend in the process of decentralisation and urban governance in India. With its enactment, urban local bodies have acquired a statutory status. Municipalities have become the principal representative platforms for urban population in the country. They have a right to live: the specter of supercession that loomed large for 5 decades since independence has been removed. The 74th Constitution Amendment Act, 1992 came into force on 1 June, 1993. All the State Governments passed the conformity legislation and brought into force within the constitutionally stipulated deadline of 1 June, 1994. The amending laws of the existing municipal legislations have provided for regularity of elections, representation and reservations. The new laws under the Constitution have made municipal elections mandatory every five years. Some of the important features of the Act are as follows:

1. devolution of more functions and taxation powers.
2. revenue sharing with State Government funds.
3. regular conduct of elections.
4. reservation of seats for SCs, STs and for women.
5. uniform composition of the urban bodies throughout the country.
6. prescription of criteria for categorising urban local bodies like Town Panchayat, Municipalities, City Municipal Corporations.
7. restriction on the formation of Townships only to industrial areas where the entire municipal services are provided or proposed to be provided by the industry.
8. formation of District Planning and Metropolitan Planning Committee.

The 74th Constitution Amendment Act provides for constitution of Ward Committees, consisting of one or more wards, within the territorial area of a Municipality having a population of three lakhs or more. The essence of this provision is to bring about proximity between the people and local governments so that these Committees could play an effective role at the Mohalla level in the delivery of municipal services. West Bengal and Kerala have provided for a Ward Committee for each municipal ward for all municipalities. Some other States have provided for Ward Committees only in corporation areas for groups of wards with members to be nominated by the ward councillor or by the corporation as a whole or by the State government or a combination of these.

Unlike the functional jurisdiction of the States which follow a constitutional delimitation, the functional domain of local bodies in India, including municipal governments, is derived from the responsibilities which are delegated by the States to the Municipalities, through legislation. Article 243W of the Indian Constitution read with the Twelfth Schedule provides the basis for the State Legislatures in India to assign functions to the Municipalities in the respective States. It is, however, known that provisions of Article 243W are not mandatory. It is for the Legislature of a State to decide as to which powers and authority it may devolve on a Municipality.

In India, traditionally, the Municipal Acts listed the functions under two categories, namely, "Obligatory Functions" and "Discretionary Functions". The 74th Constitution Amendment Act, however, has listed 18 functions and proposed that the State Legislatures may, by law, specify those which they choose to include in their respective municipal enactments.

The Twelfth Schedule of 74th Constitution Amendment provides the basis for State Legislatures to assign functions to the municipalities in their respective States. It Includes 18 items and provides an illustrative list of functions. At the time of implementing the 74th Constitution Amendment Act the State governments were expected to review the functions entrusted to municipalities and formulate a new set of municipal functions while amending conformity legislations.

Twelfth Schedule

(Article 243W)

1. Urban Planning including town planning
2. Regulation of land-use and constructionof buildings
3. Planning for economic and social development
4. Roads and bridges
5. Water supply for domestic, industrial and commercial purposes
6. Public health, sanitation, conservancy and solid waste management
7. Fire services
8. Urban forestry, protection of environment and promotion of ecological aspects
9. Safeguarding the interests of the weaker sections of society, including the handicapped and mentally retarded
10. Slum improvement and upgradation
11. Urban poverty alleviation
12. Provision for urban amenities and facilities such as parks, gardens and playgrounds
13. Promotion of cultural, educational and aesthetic aspects
14. Burials and burial grounds; cremations, cremation grounds and electric crematoriums

15. Cattle pounds; prevention of cruelty to animals
16. Vital statistics including registration of births and deaths
17. Public amenities including street lighting, parking lots, bus stops and public conveniences
18. Regulation of slaughter houses and tanneries

Since 1994 there have been two rounds of elections in Andhra Pradesh, Gujarat, Haryana, Kerala, Madhya Pradesh, Maharashtra, Orissa, Rajasthan, Uttar Pradesh and West Bengal. With the exception of Bihar and Pondicherry, other States had one round of elections. Jammu and Kashmir has also adopted the 74th Amendment. It has not yet been applied to Mizoram, Nagaland and Meghalaya. There are no Urban Local Bodies in Arunahcal Pradesh, Nagaland, Dadra and Nagar Haveli and Lakshadweep.

Role of Panchayati Raj Institutions in the Rural Developmnent Programmes:

Sampoorna Grameen Rozgar Yojana (SGRY): The objectives of the Sampoorna Grameen Rozgar Yojana are to provide additional employment in the rural areas as also food security, alongside the creation of durable community, social and economic intrastrucutre in the rural areas. The programme is self-targeting in nature with special emphasis to provide Wage Employment to women, SCs, STs and parents of children withdrawn from hazardous occupations. This Programme is being implemented by the three tiers of Panchayats in two streams :-

- The First Stream of the Programme will be implemented at the District and Intermediate level Panchayats. 50% of the funds are earmarked out of the total funds available under the SGRY and distributed between the District Panchayat and the Intermediate Panchayats in the ratio of 40:60.
- The Second Stream of the Programme will be implemented at the Village Panchayat level. 50% of the SGRY funds are earmarked for this Stream. The entire funds are released to the Village Panchayats through the DRDAs/District Panchayats.

Swarnjayanit Gram Swarozgar Yojana (SGSY): The objective of SGSY is to bring the assisted poor families above the poverty line by providing them income generating assets through a mix of bank credit and government subsidy. The families of below poverty line (BPL) including artisans, identified through the BPL Census are eligible for assistance under the Scheme. While selecting the new activities priority may be given to those having inherent skill which is primarily constituted by the rural artisans. The role of PRIs in the implementation of this Scheme are as under:

- The Gram Sabha will approve the list of BPL families.
- The list of key activities and the list of villages identified under the scheme in the Block should be approved by the Intermediate Panchayat.
- The list of swarozgaris finally selected should be made available to the Gram Panchayat for placing it before the next Gram Sabha.
- The Gram Panchayat would actively monitor the performance of the Swarozgaris particularly repayment of loan.
- The District Panchayat will review the performance under this scheme in its General Body Meetings.

Pradhan Mantri Gram Sadak Yojana (PMGSY): This is a 100% Centrally Sponsored Scheme. This Scheme seeks to provide connectivity to all unconnected habitations in the rural areas with a population of more than 500 persons through good All-weather roads by the end of the Tenth Plan. In Hill States and Desert Areas, the objective would be to connect habitations with a population of 250 persons and above.

The role of PRIs in implementation of this scheme are as under:

- The District Panchayats (or DRDAs where the District Panchayats do not exist) shall be the competent authority to select the variable best suited for the District, categories them and accord relative weightage to them and shall communicate it to all concerned.
- The Plan should be finalised by the Intermediate Panchayat. Any changes made by the Intermediate Panchayat should

be separately mentioned and reasons, thereof, should be indicated.

- The Draft District Rural Roads Plan would be presented to the District Panchayat by the Chief Executive of the District Planning Committee. It should be discussed and adopted by the District Panchayat, with such changes, as may be considered appropriate, but strictly within the framework of the Manual.
- The Rural Raods constructed/upgraded under this Programe will be maintained by the concerned District/ Intermediate Panchayat. Efforts will be made to involve local peoples' participation in the maintenance of Rural Roads.
- All the Road Works will be subjected to Social Audit by way of discussion in the Gram Sabha and the relevant information in this regard will be made available to the Gram Sabha.

Indira Awaas Yojana (IAY): This scheme provides assistance to the BPL rural households belonging primarily to SCs/STs and freed bonded labour categories. Benefits of the scheme have also been extended to families of servicemen of the armed and paramilitary forces killed in action. 3% of the houses are also reserved for BPL physically and mentally challenged persons living in rural areas.

The role of PRIs in implementation of this scheme are :-

- The Zilla Parishads or DRDAs on the basis of allocations made and targets fixed shall decide the number of houses to be constructed/upgraded Panchayat wise under IAY, during a particular financial year.
- The Zila Parishads/ DRDAs shall intimate the same to the Gram Panchayat. Thereafter, the Gram Sabha will select the beneficiaries from the list of eligible households, according to IAY Guidelines as per priorities fixed, restricting this number to the target allotted.
- Panchayat Samiti's approval is not required. The Panchayat Samiti should however, be sent a list of selected beneficiaries for their information.

Pradhan Mantri Gramodaya Yojana (PMGY): This scheme envisages allocation of Additional Central Assistance to the

States/UTs for providing /improving the outlay of Basic Minimum Services including "Rural Shelter" in the rural areas. The funds under this Scheme are released by the Ministry of Finance/Ministry of Home Affairs on the basis of recommendations made by the Ministry of Rural Development, being the nodal Ministry for implementation and monitoring of the scheme.

The role of PRIs in implementation of this scheme

- The Zilla Parishads/DRDAs will decide the number of houses to be constructed, Panchayat-wise, and the same will immediately be intimated to the Gram Panchayat.
- The Gram Sabha will select the beneficiaries from the list of eligible households, restricting this number to the target allotted.
- The Intermediate-level Panchayat (Panchayat Samiti) will invariably be sent a list of selected beneficiaries.

Credit-Cum-Subsidy Scheme: This Scheme targets rural families having annual income upto Rs.32,000/-. While subsidy is restricted to Rs.10,000/-, the maximum loan amount can be availed upto Rs.40,000/- under this scheme.

The role of PRIs in implementation of this scheme are :-

- One of the Agencies for implementing the scheme is Zilla Panchayat. The identification of the most appropriate implementing agency under the Credit-cum Subsidy Scheme shall be left to the State Government.

Samagra Awaas Yojana: This is a comprehensive Housing Scheme with a view to ensuring integrated provision of shelter, sanitation and drinking water. This is being implemented in one block each of 25 districts of 24 States and one UT.

The role of PRIs in implementation of this scheme:

- The Zila Parishad, the Block Samiti and the Gram Panchayat will be fully involved in the implementation of this Scheme.
- The special IEC funds of Rs. 5 lakh per district and habitat development funds of Rs. 20 lakh will be routed through DRDAs. DRDAs/ZPs and Public Health Department will be the main implementing agencies.

Innovative Scheme For Housing And Habitat Development And Rural Building Centres: The innovative scheme for housing and habitat development has been designed for standardising and popularising/ replicating/propagating cost-effective, environment-friendly housing construction technologies, designs and materials and evolving ideal types of sustainable rural human settlements consistent with agro-climatic variations and natural disaster proneness. The Rural Building Centres Scheme is *inter alia* designed with the purpose of technology transfer and information dissemination, skill up gradation through training and production of cost effective and environment friendly material components.

- Panchayati Raj Institutions are one of the Implementing Agencies under these schemes.

Annapurna: The Annapurna Scheme aims at providing food security to meet the requirement of those senior citizens who though eligible have remained uncovered under the National Old Age Pension Scheme.

The role of PRIs in implementation of this scheme:

- The Panchayat identifies the Beneficiaries and communicates the same to Collector/CEO.
- The Gram Sabhas are required to select the Beneficiaries for the Scheme and the lists of beneficiaries so selected by Gram Sabha will be displayed by the Gram Panchayats.
- The Gram Panchayats distribute the Entitlement Cards to the Beneficiaries in Gram Sabha Meetings.
- The Gram Panchayats will give wide publicity to the Scheme and will also be responsible for dissemination of information in regard to the procedure for securing benefits under the Scheme.

Watershed Development Programmes Under DPAP and DDP: The Drought Prone Areas Programme (DPAP), Desert Development Programme (DDP) and Integrated Wasteland Development Programme (IWDP) are being implemented on watershed basis and aim at drought proofing and controlling desertification by regeneration of depleted natural resource base.

All these three programmes were brought under the Guidelines for Watershed Development with effect from 1.4.1995.

The role of PRIs in implementation of this scheme:

- The District Panchayats and other Panchayati Raj Institutions shall have very important role to play in Watershed Development Programmes.
- The PRIs shall have the right to monitor and review the implementation of the programme and provide guidance for improvements in the administrative arrangements and procedures with a view to ensure convergence of other programmes of Ministry of Rural Development such as SGRY, SGSY, IAY, Central Rural Sanitation Programme (CRSP), Rural Drinking Water Supply, etc.
- At the Village level, the Gram Panchayat shall be fully involved in the implementation of the programme, specially community organisation, formation of SHGs and training programmes.
- Gram Panchayat will be responsible for operation and maintenance of assets created during the project.
- The Watershed Action Plan should have the approval of Gram Sabha and it should be a part of annual action plan of Gram Sabha.
- The District Panchayat/DRDA in whose favour the project has been sanctioned will be entitled to affect recovery of funds from any institutions/ organisation/ individuals and take appropriate action under law if the project is not properly implemented or funds are misutilised or not spent as per Guidelines.
- The Panchayats at any level are also entitled to take on the responsibility of implementing a cluster of watershed projects in the capacity of Project Implementation Agencies(PIAs), if they so desire.
- PIAs will motivate the Gram Panchayats to pass necessary resolutions to make public contribution, conduct Participatory Rural Appraisal (PRA) exercises, prepare the development plans for the watershed, undertake community organisation and training for the village communities, provide technical guidance and supervision of watershed Development activities, inspect and authenticate project accounts, undertake action research to adapt low-cost technologies and /or validate and build upon indigenous technical knowledge, monitor and review

the overall project maintenance and further development of the assets created during the project period.

- Under the new initiative 'Haryali', the watershed programmes are to be executed by the Gram Panchayats by facilitating project funds to them. The District and Intermediate Panchayars are to act as PIAs

Computerisation of Land Records (CLR) and Strengthening of Revenue Administration & Updating Of Land Records: Under these Schemes funds are released to Revenue Department of the States/UTs for implementation in various districts of the State and not to Panchayati Raj Institutions of State Governments.

The Panchayati Raj Institutions are not being involved in the implementation of these two Schemes.

Accelerated Rural Water Supply Programme (ARWSP): Under ARWSP, the Central Government is to supplement the efforts of the State Governments in providing access to safe drinking water to all rural habitations of the country.

The role of PRIs in implementation of this scheme:

- Panchayati Raj Institutions should be involved in the implementation of schemes particularly in selecting the location of standpost, spot sources, operation and maintenance, fixing of cess/water tariff, etc.
- The implementation of the Sector Reform Projects in the identified pilot districts, are also to be carried out either by the District Panchayats or through the District Water and Sanitation Missions (DWSM), which are to be registered societies under the supervision, control and guidance of District Panchayat.
- Wherever PRIs are themselves firmly in place and willing to take up the responsibility and are strong enough to do so, they implement the projects themselves instead of DWSM.
- At the village level, the individual Rural Water Supply Schemes are to be implemented through Village Water and Sanitation Committees which should be committees of Gram Panchayats.
- Drinking water supply assets are transferred to the appropriate level of Panchayats and such Panchayats are

to be empowered to undertake operation and maintenance of drinking water systems.

Central Rural Sanitation Programme (CRSP): This programme aims at improving the general quality of life in rural areas; accelerating coverage in rural areas; generating demand through awareness creation and health education; and controlling incidence of water sanitation related diseases.

The role of PRIs in implementation if this scheme:

- Total Sanitation Campaign (TSC) is a community based programme where Panchayati Raj Institutons are in the forefront.
- As per TSC Guidelines, the implementation at the district level is to be done by the District Panchayats. Panchayats at block and village level are to be fully involved for implementation of the programme.
- Where District Panchayat is not in a position to implement the programme, it is being implemented by District Water & Sanitation Mission which is chaired by Chairperson of District Panchayat and the Village Committees are chaired by the Chairpersons of Gram Panchayats. In the later case, the Village Water & Sanitation Mission are part of the Gram Panchayat.

Swajaldhara: This programme aims at providing Community-based Rural Drinking Water Supply. The key elements of this programmes are namely, (i) demand-driven and community participation approach, (ii) panchayats / communities to plan, implement, operate, maintain and manage all drinking water schemes, (iii) partial capital cost sharing by the communities upfront in cash, (iv) full ownership of drinking water assets with Gram Panchayats and (v) full Operation and Maintenance by the users/ Panchayats.

The role of PRIs in implementation of this scheme:

- Gram Panchayat shall convene a Gram Sabha Meeting where the Drinking Water Supply Scheme of People's choice including design and cost etc. must be finalised. Gram Panchayats are to undertake procurement of materials/ services for execution of schemes and supervise the scheme execution.

- A resolution must be passed in the Gram Panchayat meeting calling for users/beneficiaries to contribute 10% of the capital expenditure. However, Gram Panchayat can remit towards community contribution from its tax revinue (Not from Government Grants) with the approval of Gram Sabha.
- Gram Panchayat will decide whether the Panchayat wants to execute Scheme on its own or wants the State Government Agency to undertake the execution.
- After completion of such schemes, the Gram Panchayat will take over the Schemes for Operation & Maintenance(O&M).
- Panchayat must decide on the user charges from the community so that adequate funds available with Panchayat to undertake O&M.

Conclusion

The seventy-third and seventy-fourth amendments left a great deal for implementation by State governments through State laws to be passed by their legislatures. Whether as institutions or as individuals, no one ever surrenders power voluntarily. The result has been that most grudgingly and reluctantly and at the last minute, different States have passed laws which are at considerable variance with each other and in varying degrees try to deny the substance of functional and more particularly financial powers to the directly elected representatives in the PRIs. The local MPs and MLAs consider the new emerging leadership in the Panchayats and Nagar Palikas as their rivals in the power structure who threaten to take away a share of the cake.

The 73rd and 74th Amendments have considerably increased the number of elected representatives at different levels. Panchayats and municipalities are electoral building blocks for the Assembly and the Parliament.

Despite all the imperfections and loopholes which need to be plugged it must be agreed that the seventy-third and seventy-fourth amendments have the potential of bringing about revolutionary changes in the political power structure and system of governance. But, if we are really serious about providing multi level governance and taking power to the doorsteps of the people at the grassroots, the Constitution should clearly provide for distribution of powers between the Union, the States and the local governments of Panchayats and Nagarpalikas by suitably amending articles 245, 246 and other relevant articles and the Seventh Schedule. It would certainly do no violence to the basic structure or features of the Constitution or to the parliamentary system. It has the potential to powerfully contribute to the needs of good governance and development.

The seventy-third and seventy-fourth Amendments left the question of association of MPs and MLAs to be tackled at the level of States. Accepted at that time as a political compromise, this needs to be looked at afresh from the angle of constitutional propriety and clean and people friendly governance. If the aim of PRIs was to reduce the unhealthy role of MPs and MLAs, the decision of some of the States to include them in PRIs with or without votes does not seem to be justified. MPs and MLAs must appreciate that their role is that of law makers and policy setters at the Union level for the whole of India and at the State level for the State as a whole. Local matters must be left to be handled at local levels by the representatives of the people elected to the local bodies. Also, executive functions have to be left to executive agencies at concerned levels. Schemes like the MP and MLA LADS —Local Area Development Schemes with some 3000 crores of public money involved each year—are an affront to the constitutional principles of distribution of powers between the Union and the States and separation of executive and legislative functions. Also, these schemes make the financially bankrupt PRIs look insignificant and powerless with each MP and MLA having large funds at his disposal for spending on local area schemes which are most legitimately the concern of PRIs under the seventy-third and seventy-fourth Amendments. Even if largely suggestive and illustrative, the 11th and 12th Schedules to the Constitution become irrelevant if members of the Union Parliament and of State legislatures exercise executive powers in matters of local development otherwise supposedly reserved for Panchayats and Nagarpalikas.

All the shortcomings notwithstanding, grassroots democracy unleashed by the seventy third and seventy-fourth amendments has come to stay and as time passes, its financial and functional domains will get extended. It can only get more assertive and strengthened till sovereign power really comes to belong to the people and the Gandhian dream of building from below, of the bottom up rather than the top down approach can be fulfilled.

Distribution of powers should be so designed that only the most essential or minimum necessary powers are assigned to each higher level. For example, whatever can be done by the local grassroots institutions like the Village Panchayats or Municipalities, should be left entirely in their hands. Government at a higher tier should have no power to remove or supercede a duly elected Government at a lower tier. Efficient bureaucracy cannot be a substitute for democratic decentralised government. Also, Eleventh and Twelfth schedules should be made mandatory and merged into a common list. Decentralisation of law and order functions to the local elected bodies would be most desirable. Powers of *Gram Sabha* and *Gram Panchayats* need to be classified. Local staffing is most desirable for local bodies.

In the North-East States, local traditional institutions of Government need to be modernised with gender justice for women and used as institutions of governance. Overlapping jurisdiction of State Government, Autonomous District Councils (ADCs) and traditional system of governance and the problems thereof must be removed and jurisdictions of each clearly defined. Greater autonomy should be provided to ADCs by amending the Sixth Schedule. Problems with regard to participation of non-tribals in ADCs. need to be addressed. Problems in judicial administration are due to multiple overlapping jurisdictions of the traditional institutions, ADCs and the subordinate judiciary should be resolved and the emerging conflict between human rights and tribal rights and between conservation laws and tribal rights to be analysed and resolved.

To preserve "India, that is Bharat" as a "Union of States" it is necessary to work for building it as a "federal union" of what Aurobindo referred to as a union of "autonomies" with multiple tiers of government and sharing of powers from the lowest grassroots level of Panchayats to the Parliament and the Government of the Union. This would also be close to Gandhiji's model polity of concentric circles instead of the present pyramidical structure. Distribution of powers should be so designed that only the most essential or minimum necessary powers are assigned to each higher level. This would be in keeping with what is now called the subsidiarity principal. Incidentally, this would be the most rational and practical way of operationalising the Gandhian vision of a Constitution for India which recognises the sovereign power vesting in the people at the grassroots and building from below, in a bottom-up rather than top-down approach.

9

ELECTIONS AND POLITICAL PARTIES
PROBLEMS AND PROCESSES

Democracy and Universal Adult Franchise

At the root of all variants of democratic polity is the concept of sovereignty vesting in the hands of the people. "We, the people" of India exercise our sovereign powers while casting votes to elect representatives to Lok Sabha and State Assemblies. Sustainable parliamentary democracy depends on a healthy electoral system and clean, free and fair elections. The founding fathers expected that through universal adult franchise, people would be able to elect such representatives who would represent them, tend to their needs and aspirations and provide them a responsive and responsible government geared to ensuring security and good governance to all without any discrimination.

The biggest revolution since the Independence of the country was the adoption of universal adult franchise for elections to the Lok Sabha and the Legislative Assemblies of the States. In a newly independent country with appalling backwardness, dismal poverty and rampant illiteracy, it was an act of faith for the founding fathers to give a vote to every citizen who was not less than 21 years of age (since reduced to 18) and not otherwise disqualified under any law on grounds of non residence, unsoundness of mind, crime or corrupt or illegal practice (Article 326). It was also a bold and ambitious political experiment and a symbol of the abiding confidence in the great masses of the country and their innate wisdom.

With more than 671 million registered voters in 2004, India

is legitimately regarded as "the world's largest democracy". What is not often mentioned is that India today also has the largest number – 3.2 million from Panchayats to Parliament – of elected representatives as law makers and rulers. At the heart of our democratic polity lies a commitment to hold regular, free and fair elections. Elections determine the composition of Government, both at the Union and in the States, the membership of the Houses of Parliament and of the Legislatures in the States and Union Territories.

The Election Commission

With a view to ensuring free and fair elections, the Constitution *vide* article 324 vests "the superintendence, direction and control" of the preparation of electoral rolls and conduct of elections to the Houses of Parliament and State Legislatures and the offices of the President and Vice-President in an independent Election Commission. Article 327 vests legislative power in Parliament to make laws relating to all matters concerning elections to either House of Parliament or to the House or either House of a State Legislature, including the preparation of electoral rolls, the delimitation of constituencies and all other matters "necessary for securing the due constitution of such House or Houses". Article 328 confers powers on State Legislatures to make laws relating to elections to the House or either House of a Legislature of the State. [See Chapter 10. 'Independent Offices']

Election Schedule

The Commission normally announces the schedule of elections in a major Press Conference a few weeks before the formal process is set in motion. The Model Code of Conduct for guidance of candidates and Political Parties immediately comes into effect after such announcement. The formal process for the elections starts with the Notification or Notifications calling upon the electorate to elect Members of a House. As soon as Notifications are issued, Candidates can start filing their nominations in the constituencies from where they wish to contest. These are scrutinised by the Returning Officer of the constituency concerned after the last date for the same is over after about a week. The validly nominated candidates can withdraw from the contest within two days from the date of scrutiny.

Contesting candidates get at least two weeks for political campaign before the actual date of poll. On account of the vast magnitude of operations and the massive size of the electorate, polling is held at least on three days for the national elections. A separate date for counting is fixed and the results declared for each constituency by the concerned Returning Officer. The Commission compiles the complete list of Members elected and issues an appropriate Notification for the due constitution of the House. With this, the process of elections is complete and the President, in case of the Lok Sabha, and the Governors of the concerned States, in case of Vidhan Sabhas, can then convene their respective Houses to hold their sessions. The entire process takes between 5 to 8 weeks for the national elections, 4 to 5 weeks for separate elections only for Legislative Assemblies.

The Gigantic Task

A general election to Lok Sabha is a gigantic exercise. It has been said that holding general elections in India is equal to holding them for Europe, United States, Canada and Australia all put together. Statistically, of the 671 million electorate, some 390 million actually turned up to vote in 2004, the number of polling booths all over the country adds up to about 900,000 (9 lakhs). To manage these polling booths about four million election personnel and an additional two million security personnel have to be mobilised. In the 2004 general elections, over 1 million EVMs were deployed, direct expenditure alone amounted to some 13,000 million rupees. Taking States elections into account, the figures become more staggering. During the last half a-century, there have been fourteen general elections to Lok Sabha and a much larger number to various State Legislative Assemblies.

Polling in the 2004 election was held in four phases during

April-May 2004. For the first time, the election processes were fully electronic with EVMs used throughout the country. There were more than 1200 counting centres in 850 towns. There were 5,435 candidates for 543 seats. Women candidates were 354. Following a Supreme Court judgement and Election Commission directives, all the candidates were required to file affidavits declaring their assets and liabilities, educational qualifications, government dues and criminal cases etc., if any, pending.

Table 9.1 gives a State-wise allocation of seats in the two Houses of Parliament.

Constituencies and Reservation of Seats

The country has been divided into 543 Parliamentary Constituencies, each of which returns one MP to the Lok Sabha. In keeping with the 'one man, one vote' principle with value of each vote being the same, the size and shape of the Parliamentary constituencies was required to be determined by an independent Delimitation Commission, which was expected to create constituencies which had roughly the same population, subject to geographical considerations and the boundaries of the States and administrative areas.

Boundaries were meant to be examined after every ten-yearly census to reflect changes in population, for which Parliament by law established an independent Delimitation Commission. However, under constitutional amendment, delimitation was suspended until after the census of 2001, ostensibly so that states' family-planning programmes would not affect their political representation in the Lok Sabha and Vidhan Sabhas. This led to wide discrepancies in the size of constituencies, with the largest having over 25,00,000 electors, and the smallest less than 50,000.

The position is now frozen for another 25 years by substituting the figures "2026" for the figure "2000" in articles 55, 81, 81, 82, 330 and 332 by the Constitution 84th Amendment Act 2001. In article 82, third proviso (ii) which provided for readjustment of territorial constituencies in each State on the

Table 9.1

State-wise Allocation of Seats in the Two Houses of Parliament

State/ Uts	No. of seats in Rajya Sabha	No. of seats in Lok Sabha
STATES		
Andhra Pradesh	18	42
Arunachal Pradesh	1	2
Assam	7	14
Bihar	16	40
Chhattisgarh	5	11
Goa	1	2
Gujarat	11	26
Haryana	5	10
Himachal Pradesh	3	4
J & K	4	6
Jharkhand	6	14
Karnataka	12	28
Kerala	9	20
Madhya Pradesh	11	29
Maharashtra	19	48
Manipur	1	2
Meghalaya	1	2
Mizoram	1	1
Nagaland	1	1
Orissa	10	21
Punjab	7	13
Rajasthan	10	25
Sikkim	1	1
Tamilnadu	18	39
Tripura	1	2
Uttaranchal	3	5
Uttar Pradesh	31	80
West Bengal	16	42
Nominated	12	2
UNION TERRITORIES		
Andaman & Nicobar Islands		1
Chandigarh		1
Dadra & Nagar Haveli		1
Daman & Diu		1
The NCT of Delhi	3	7
Lakshadweep		1
Pondicherry	1	1
Total	**245**	**545**

basis of 1991 census remaining valid the Constitution (87th Amendment) Act 2003 substituted the figure '2001' for the figure '1991'.

The Constitution puts a limit on the size of the Lok Sabha of 550 elected members, apart from a maximum of two members who can be nominated by the President to represent the Anglo-Indian community. There are also provisions to ensure the representation of Scheduled Castes and Scheduled Tribes, with reserved constituencies where only candidates from these communities can stand for election. Seats are reserved for the Scheduled Castes and Scheduled Tribes in Lok Sabha Statewise on the basis of population ratios. Originally, the reservation was for ten years but it is being extended every time for the next ten years (articles 330 and 334). The Seventy-ninth Amendment has extended it to 2010.

The total number of Lok Sabha seats for which elections were held in 2004 was 543. Of these 423 were general seats, 79 were reserved for the Scheduled Castes and 41 for the Scheduled Tribes.

SYSTEM OF ELECTION

Electoral Laws and System

Elections are conducted according to the constitutional provisions, supplemented by laws made by Parliament. The major laws are Representation of the People Act, 1950, which mainly deals with the preparation and revision of electoral rolls, the Representation of the People Act, 1951 which deals, in detail, with all aspects of conduct of elections and post election disputes. The Supreme Court of India has held that where the enacted laws are silent or make insufficient provision to deal with a given situation in the conduct of elections, the Election Commission has the residuary powers under the Constitution to act in an appropriate manner.

First-past-the-post

Elections to the Lok Sabha are carried out using a first-past-the-post electoral system. The country is split up into separate geographical areas, known as constituencies, and the electors can cast one vote each for a candidate, the winner being the candidate who gets the maximum votes. It is not necessary that in order to win, a candidate must get majority of votes or any minimum percentage of votes cast. One who gets more votes than others wins (see Table 9.2)

Electoral Rolls

The electoral roll consisting of a list of all people in the constituency who are registered to vote is prepared. Only those people with their names on the electoral roll are allowed to vote. Every citizen over the age of 18 can vote in an election (before 1989 the age limit was 21). The right to vote is irrespective of caste, creed, religion or gender. Only those who are deemed to be of unsound of mind, convicted of certain criminal offences or of corrupt or illegal practice, non-residence etc. may be disqualified by law for being registered as voters. The electoral roll is normally revised every year to add the names of those who are to turn 18 on the 1st January of that year or have moved into a constituency and to remove the names of those who have died or moved out of a constituency. If one is eligible to vote and is not on the electoral roll, he can apply to the Electoral Registration Officer of the constituency, who will update the register. The updating of the Electoral Roll only stops during an election campaign, after the nominations for candidates have closed.

In 1998 the Commission took an important decision to computerise the entire electoral rolls of all (now 670 million plus) voters. This work has been completed and now well printed electoral rolls are available. The photo identity card number of the voter has also been printed in the electoral rolls, for cross linking. The printed electoral rolls as well as CDs containing these rolls are available for sale to general public. National and State parties are provided these free of cost after every revision of electoral rolls. Entire country's rolls are also available on the Election Commission's website.

Table 9.2

Percentage of Votes Polled by Winning Candidates during some recent Lok Sabha Elections

State	*Total No. of Seats*	*11th General Election 1996*		*12th General Election 1998*		*13th General Election 1999*	
		Above 50%	Below 50%	Above 50%	Below 50%	Above 50%	Below 50%
Andhra Pradesh	42	9.52%	90.48%	11.90%	88.10%	59.52%	40.48%
Arunachal Pradesh	2	50.00%	50.00%	100.00%	0.00%	100.00%	0.00%
Assam	14M	14.29%	85.71%	30.77%	69.23%	7.14%	92.86%
Bihar	54	33.33%	66.67%	12.96%	87.04%	37.04%	62.96%
Goa	2	0.00%	100.00%	0.00%	100.00%	50.00%	50.00%
Gujarat	26	65.38%	34.62%	53.85%	46.15%	80.77%	19.23%
Haryana	10	10.00%	90.00%	0.00%	100.00%	90.00%	10.00%
Himachal Pradesh	4	50.00%	50.00%	75.00%	25.00%	100.00%	0.00%
J & K	6	16.67%	83.33%	50.00%	50.00%	16.67%	83.33%
Karnataka	28	3.57%	96.43%	25.00%	75.00%	35.71%	64.29%
Kerala	20	20.00%	80.00%	25.00%	75.00%	25.00%	75.00%
Madhya Pradesh	40	25.00%	75.00%	32.50%	67.50%	57.50%	42.50%
Maharashtra	48	16.67%	83.33%	64.58%	35.42%	18.75%	81.25%
Manipur	2	0.00%	100.00%	0.00%	100.00%	0.00%	100.00%
Meghalaya	2	100.00%	0.00%	50.00%	50.00%	50.00%	50.00%
Mizoram	1	0.00%	100.00%	0.00%	100.00%	100.00%	0.00%
Nagaland	1	100.00%	0.00%	100.00%	0.00%	100.00%	0.00%

State	*Total No. of Seats*	*11th General Election 1996*		*12th General Election 1998*		*13th General Election 1999*	
		Above 50%	Below 50%	Above 50%	Below 50%	Above 50%	Below 50%
Orissa	21	33.33%	66.67%	61.90%	38.10%	95.24%	4.76%
Punjab	13	0.00%	100.00%	84.62%	15.38%	30.77%	69.23%
Rajasthan	25	28.00%	72.00%	48.00%	52.00%	72.00%	28.00%
Sikkim	1	100.00%	0.00%	100.00%	0.00%	100.00%	0.00%
Tamilnadu	39	76.92%	23.08%	46.15%	53.85%	30.77%	69.23%
Tripura	2	100.00%	0.00%	50.00%	50.00%	100.00%	0.00%
Uttar Pradesh	85	7.06%	92.94%	8.24%	91.76%	4.71%	95.29%
West Bengal	42	38.10%	61.90%	30.95%	69.05%	35.71%	64.29%
Andaman & Nicobar	1	100.00%	0.00%	0.00%	100.00%	100.00%	0.00%
Chandigarh	1	0.00%	100.00%	0.00%	100.00%	0.00%	100.00%
Dadra & Nagar Haveli	1	100.00%	0.00%	100.00%	0.00%	0.00%	100.00%
Daman & Diu	1	100.00%	0.00%	0.00%	100.00%	0.00%	100.00%
Delhi	7	57.14%	42.86%	57.14%	42.86%	71.43%	28.57%
Lakshadweep	1	100.00%	0.00%	100.00%	0.00%	100.00%	0.00%
Pondicherry	1	0.00%	100.00%	0.00%	100.00%	0.00%	100.00%
Total	**543**	**27.44%**	**72.56%**	**32.84%**	**67.16%**	**39.96%**	**60.04%**

* Result for 13 seats only in case of the 12th General Election

[*Source*: *NCRWC Report*]

Electors' Photo Identity Cards (EPIC)

In an attempt to improve the accuracy of the electoral rolls and prevent electoral fraud, the Election Commission ordered the making of photo identity cards for all voters in the country in August 1993. To take advantage of latest technological innovations, the Commission issued revised guidelines for EPIC Program in May 2000. More than 450 million Identity cards have been distributed till now.

Timing of Elections

Elections for the Lok Sabha and every State Legislative Assembly have to take place every five years, unless called earlier. The President can dissolve Lok Sabha and call a general election before five years, if the government can no longer command the confidence of the Lok Sabha, and if there is no alternative government available to take over. It is recognised that interruptions of regular elections are acceptable only in extraordinary circumstances.

When the five-year limit is up, or the legislature has been dissolved and new elections have been called, the Election Commission puts into effect the machinery for holding an election. Article 85(1) of the Constitution states that there can be no longer than 6 months' gap between two sessions of each House.

In a country as huge and diverse as India, finding a period when elections can be held throughout the country is not simple. The Election Commission, which decides the schedule for elections, has to take into account (i) the weather – during winter some constituencies may be snow-bound, and during the monsoon access to some remote areas restricted, (ii) the agricultural cycle so that the planting or harvesting of crops is not disrupted, (iii) examination schedules as schools are used as polling stations and teachers employed as election officials, and (iv) religious festivals and public holidays. Added to this there are the logistical difficulties that go with holding an election – sending out ballot boxes or EVMs, setting up polling booths, recruiting officials to oversee the elections, making necessary security arrangements, etc.

Eligibility for Contesting Elections

Any Indian citizen who is registered as a voter and is over 25 years of age is allowed to contest elections to the Lok Sabha or State Legislative Assemblies. For the Rajya Sabha the minimum age limit is 30 years. Every candidate has to make a deposit of Rs. 10,000/- for Lok Sabha election and 5,000/- for Rajya Sabha or Vidhan Sabha elections, except for candidates from the Scheduled Castes and Scheduled Tribes who pay half of these amounts. The deposit is returned if the candidate wins or receives more than one-sixth of the total number of valid votes polled in the constituency. Nominations must be supported at least by one registered elector of the constituency, in the case of a candidate sponsored by a registered Party and by ten registered electors from the constituency in the case of other candidates. Returning Officers, appointed by the Election Commission, are put in charge to receive nominations of candidates in each constituency, and oversee the formalities of the election.

The number of candidates contesting in each election has steadily increased. In the general election of 1952 the average number of candidates in each constituency was 3.8; by 1991 it had risen to 16.3, and in 1996 stood at 25.6. As it was far too easy for 'frivolous' candidates to stand for election, certain remedial measures were taken in August 1996, which included increasing the size of the deposit and making the number of people who have to nominate a candidate larger. The impact of such measures was quite considerable at the elections which were subsequently held. As a result, in 1998 Lok Sabha elections, the number of candidates came down to an average of 8.74 per constituency. In 1999 Lok Sabha elections, it was 8.6, and in 2004 it was 10.

Election Campaign

The campaign is the period when the political parties put forward their candidates and arguments with which they hope to persuade people to vote for their candidates and parties. Candidates are given a week to put forward their nominations.

These are scrutinised by the Returning Officers and if not found to be in order can be rejected after a summary hearing. Validly nominated candidates can withdraw within two days after nominations have been scrutinised. The official campaign lasts two weeks from the drawing up of the list of nominated candidates, and officially ends 48 hours before polling closes.

During the election campaign, the political parties and contesting candidates are expected to abide by a Model Code of Conduct evolved by the Election Commission on the basis of a consensus among political parties. The Model Code lays down broad guidelines as to how the political parties and candidates should conduct themselves during the election campaign. It is intended to maintain the election campaign on healthy lines, avoid clashes and conflicts between political parties or their supporters and to ensure peace and order during the campaign period and thereafter, until the results are declared. The model code also prescribes guidelines for the ruling party either at the Centre or in the State to ensure that a level playing field is maintained and that no cause is given for any complaint that the ruling party has used its official position for the purposes of its election campaign.

Once an election has been called, parties issue manifestos detailing the programmes they wish to implement if elected to government, the strengths of their leaders, and the failures of opposing parties and their leaders. Slogans are used to popularise and identify parties and issues, and pamphlets and posters distributed to the electorate. Rallies and meetings where the candidates try to persuade, cajole and enthuse supporters, and denigrate opponents, are held throughout the constituencies. Personal appeals and promises of reform are made, with candidates travelling the length and breadth of the constituency to try to influence as many potential supporters as possible. Party symbols abound, printed on posters and placards.

All the recognised National and State parties have been allowed by the Election Commission free access to the State owned electronic media – AIR and Doordarshan – on an extensive scale for their campaigns during elections. The total free time allocated extends over 122 hours on the State owned Television and Radio channels. This is allocated equitably by combining a base limit and additional time linked to poll performance of the party in recent election.

The Election Commission appoints a large number of Observers to ensure that the campaign is conducted fairly, and that people are free to vote as they choose. Election expenditure Observers keeps a check on the amount that each candidate and party spends on the election.

After nomination of candidates is complete, a list of competing candidates is prepared by the Returning Officer, and ballot papers are printed. Ballot papers are printed with the names of the candidates (in languages set by the Election Commission) and the symbols allotted to each of the candidates. Candidates of recognised Parties are allotted their Party symbols.

Voting Procedure

Polling is normally held on a number of different days in different constituencies, to enable the security forces and those monitoring the election to keep law and order and ensure that voting during the election is fair.

Voting is by secret ballot. Polling stations are usually set up in public institutions, such as schools and community halls. To enable as many electors as possible to vote, the officials of the Election Commission try to ensure that there is a polling station within 2km of every voter, and that no polling stations should have to deal with more than 1500 voters. Each polling station is open for at least 8 hours on the day of the election.

On entering the polling station, the elector is checked against the Electoral Roll, and allocated a ballot paper. The elector votes by marking the ballot paper with a rubber stamp on or near the symbol of the candidate of his choice, inside a screened compartment in the polling station. The voter then folds the ballot paper and inserts it in a common ballot box which is kept in full view of the Presiding Officer and polling agents of the candidates. This marking system eliminates the possibility of ballot papers being surreptitiously taken out of the polling station or not being put in the ballot box.

Since 1998, the Commission has increasingly used Electronic Voting Machines instead of ballot boxes. In 2003, all state elections and bye elections were held using EVMs. Encouraged by this the Commission took a historic decision to use only EVMs for the Lok Sabha election in 2004. More than 1 million EVMs were used in this election.

After the polling has finished, the votes are counted under the supervision of Returning Officers and Observers appointed by the Election Commission. After the counting of votes is over, the Returning Officer declares the name of the candidate to whom the largest number of votes have been given as the winner, and as having been returned by the constituency to the concerned house. In order to bring as much transparency as possible to the electoral process, the media are encouraged and provided with facilities to cover the election, although subject to maintaining the secrecy of the vote. Media persons are given special passes to enter polling stations to cover the poll process and the counting halls during the actual counting of votes.

Any elector or candidate can file an election petition if he or she thinks there has been malpractice during the election. An election petition is not an ordinary civil suit, but treated as a contest in which the whole constituency is involved. Election petitions are tried by the High Court of the State, and if upheld can even lead to the restaging of the election in that constituency.

Limit on Poll Expenses

There are tight legal limits on the amount of money a candidate can spend during the election campaign. Since December 1997, in most Lok Sabha constituencies the limit was Rs 15,00,000/-, although in some States the limit was Rs 6,00,000/- (for Vidhan Sabha elections the highest limit was Rs 6,00,000/-, the lowest Rs 3,00,000/-). Amendment in October 2003 increased these limits. For Lok Sabha seats in bigger States, it is now Rs 25,00,000. In other States and Union Territories, it varies between Rs 10,00,000 to Rs 25,00,000. Similarly, for Assembly seats, in bigger

States, it is now Rs 10,00,000, while in other States and Union Territories, it varies between Rs 5,00,000 to Rs 10,00,000. Although supporters of a candidate can spend as much as they like to help out with a campaign, they have to get written permission of the candidate, and whilst parties are allowed to spend as much money on campaigns as they want, recent Supreme Court judgments have said that, unless a political party can specifically account for money spent during the campaign, it will consider any activities as being funded by the candidates and counting towards their election expenses. The accountability imposed on the candidates and parties is expected to curtail some of the more extravagant campaigning that was previously a part of Indian elections.

Political Parties

Although political parties were not mentioned in the Constitution until the fifty-second constitutional amendment enacted in 1985, the fact remains that representative democratic polity under the Constitution presumed a well-organised system of political parties. Political parties are an important institution in any democratic polity. Both the party or parties in power and those in opposition are essential to the functioning of a democratic government.

Political parties are an inseparable part of modern democracy and in the conduct of elections, the role of political parties is crucial. Although a good number of candidates in Indian elections are independent, the winning candidates for Lok Sabha and Vidhan Sabha elections usually are party candidates, and election results show that people tend to vote for parties or party candidates and very rarely for independents.

Parties offer candidates organisational support. During the election campaign, they project their policies, programmes and achievements, put forward alternative proposals and help voters make a choice about how the government is run.

Political parties have to be registered with the Election Commission. The Commission determines whether the party is structured and committed to principles of democracy, secularism and socialism in accordance with the Indian Constitution and would uphold the sovereignty, unity and integrity of India. Parties are expected to hold organisational elections and have a written constitution.

Allocation of Symbols

Integral to the electoral system in India is the use of pictorial symbols to identify a political party and its candidates at the time of elections. As the Supreme Court noted in one of its landmark judgements (*Kanhaiya Lal Omar vs. R.K. Trivedi and Ors.*, AIR 1986 SC III), "...There is need for using symbols to denote the candidates who contest elections so that illiterate voter may cast his vote in secrecy in favour of the candidate of his choice by identifying him with the help of symbol printed on the ballot paper against his name."

Election symbols have been associated with political parties since the first general elections held in 1952 but these were determined on the basis of confabulations that the Election Commission had with political parties and were, in the absence of data, *ad hoc* recognition of parties. In 1968, after gaining experience over four general elections, the Election Commission considered it desirable to codify the provisions relating to recognition of political parties as National party, State party and Registered but unrecognised party. These were set out in the Election Symbols (Reservation and Allotment) Order, 1968 issued under the plenary powers of the Commission vested under article 324 of the Constitution. These provisions with minor amendments continue to be operative in deciding the category of the political parties in the electoral fray.

Recognition of Parties

The founding fathers while adopting parliamentary polity and the first-past-the-post system of elections had hoped that a healthy two party system of the British type based on ideological or programmatic considerations or on some political or economic agenda would grow in India. That did not happen. Today, India has a multi-party system with a predominance of small regional parties. National parties are those that are recognised in four or more States. They are accorded this status by the Election Commission of India, which periodically reviews the election results in various States. This recognition helps the political parties to claim a party symbol, until the next review of their status.

A political party shall be treated as a recognised political party in a State, if and only if the conditions specified in Clause (A), or Clause (B) are, fulfilled by that party and not otherwise, that is to say-

(A) that such party –

- has been engaged in political activity for a continuous period of five years; and
- has, at the last general election in that State to the House of the People, or, as the case may be, to the Legislative Assembly of the State, returned-

  either (i) at least one member to the House of the People for every twenty-five members of that House or any fraction of that number from that State;

  or (ii) at least one member to the Legislative Assembly of that State for every thirty members of that Assembly or any fraction of that number;

(B) that the total number of valid votes polled by all the contesting candidates set up by such party at the last general election in the State to the House of the People, or as the case may be, to the Legislative Assembly of the State, is not less than six per cent of the total number of valid votes polled by all the contesting candidates at such general election in the State.

The conditions in Clause (A) or Clause (B) above shall not be deemed to have been fulfilled by a political party, if a member of the House of the People or the Legislative Assembly of the State becomes a member of that political party after his election to that House or, as the case may be, that Assembly.

State, for the above purpose, includes the National Capital Territory of Delhi and the Union Territory of Pondicherry.

If a political party is treated as a recognised political party in four or more States, it shall be known as a 'National Party' throughout the whole of India, but only so long as that political party continues to fulfill thereafter the conditions for recognition in four or more States on the results of any subsequent general election either to the House of the People or to the Legislative Assembly of any State.

If a political party is treated as a recognised political party in less than four States, it should be known as a 'State Party' in the State or States in which it is so recognised, but only so long as that political party continues to fulfill thereafter the conditions for recognition on the results of any subsequent general election to the House of the People or, as the case may be, to the Legislative Assembly of the State, in the said State or States.

All parties contesting elections have to choose a symbol from a list of available symbols offered by the Election Commission. All 28 States along with the Union Territory of Pondicherry and the National Capital Territory of Delhi usually have an elected government unless President's rule is imposed under certain conditions.

Parties recognised by the Election Commission as 'National Parties' for purposes of allocation of symbols at present are six, *viz.*, Bharatiya Janata Party, Bahujan Samaj Party, Communist Party of India, Communist Party cf India (Marxist), Indian National Congress and Nationalist Congress Party.

Parties recognised as State Parties are 45, *viz.* (i) *Andhra Pradesh*: Telugu Desam; (ii) *Arunachal Pradesh*: Arunachal Congress; (iii) *Assam*: (a) Asom Gana Parishad, (b) Communist Party of India (Marxist-Leninist) (Liberation); (iv)*Bihar*: (a) Jharkhand Mukti Morcha, (b) Rashtriya Janata Dal, (c) Janata Dal (United); (v) *Goa*: (a) Maharashtrawadi Gomantak, (b) United Goans Democratic Party; (vi) *Haryana*: Indian National Lok Dal; (vii) *Himachal Pradesh*: Himachal Vikas Congress; (viii) *Jammu and Kashmir*: (a) Jammu and Kashmir National Conference, (b) Jammu and Kashmir National Panthers Party, (c) Jammu and Kashmir Peoples Democratic Party; (ix) *Jharkhand*: (a) Jharkhand Mukti Morcha, (b) Rashtriya Janata Dal, (c) Janata Dal (United); (x) *Karnataka*: (a) Janata Dal (Secular), (b) Janata Dal (United); (xi) *Kerala*: (a) Kerala Congress, (b) Kerala Congress (M), (c) Muslim League Kerala State

Committee, (d) Janadhipathya Samrakshana Samithi; (xii) *Madhya Pradesh*: Samajwadi Party; (xiii) *Maharashtra*: Shiv Sena; (xiv) *Manipur*: (a) Federal Party of Manipur, (b) Manipur People's Party; (xv) *Meghalaya*: (a) Hill State People's Democratic Party, (b) *Meghalaya* Democratic Party, (c) United Democratic Party; (xvi) *Mizoram*: (a) Mizo National Front, (b) Zoram Nationalist Party, (c) Mizoram People's Conference; (xvii) *Nagaland*: (a) Janata Dal (United), (b) Nationalist Democratic Movement, (c) Nagaland Peoples Front; (xviii) *Orissa*: Biju Janata Dal; (xix) *Pondicherry*: (a) All India Anna Dravida Munnetra Kazhagam, (b) Dravida Munnetra Kazhagam, (c) Pattali Makkal Katchi; (xx) *Punjab*: (a) Shiromani Akali Dal, (b) Shiromani Akali Dal (Simranjit Singh Mann); (xxi) *Sikkim*: Sikkim Democratic Front; (xxii) *Tamil Nadu*: (a) All India Anna Dravida Munnetra Kazhagam, (b) Dravida Munnetra Kazhagam, (c) Marumalarchi Dravida Munnetra Kazhagam, (d) Pattali Makkal Katchi (xxiii) *Tripura*: (a) Indigenous Nationalist Party of Tripura, (b) All India Trinamool Congress*; (xxiv) *Uttar Pradesh*: (a) Rashtriya Lok Dal, (b) Samajwadi Party; (xxv) *Uttaranchal*: (a) Samajwadi Party, (b) Uttarakhand Kranti Dal; (xxvi) *West Bengal*: (a) All India Forward Bloc, (b) Revolutionary Socialist Party, (c) All India Trinamool Congress*

Apart from the 6 Recognised National Parties and 45 Recognised State Parties there are now 703 Registered but unrecognised parties. In the 2004 election to Lok Sabha there were 1351 candidates from 6 National parties, 801 candidates from 36 State parties, 898 candidates from officially registered parties and 2385 Independent candidates.

Major Parties

Indian National Congress (also known as the Congress Party, abbreviated INC) is a major political party and also the oldest in India. Founded in 1885, the Indian National Congress became

---

* All India Trinamool Congress of Mamata Banerjee merged with a faction of the Nationalist Congress Party in 2004 and formed Nationalist Trinamool Congress

the nation's leader in the Independence Movement, with over 15 million Indians involved in its organisations and over 70 million participants in its struggle against the British Empire. After Independence in 1947, it became the nation's dominant political party.

After the assassination of Mahatma Gandhi in 1948 and the death of Sardar Patel in 1950, the INC under the leadership of Jawaharlal Nehru, embraced secularism, socialist economic policies and a non-aligned foreign policy, which became its hallmark. Nehru's policies challenged the landed class, the business class and improved the position of religious minorities and lower castes. Nehru led the INC to consecutive majorities in the elections of 1952, 1957 and 1962.

After Nehru's death in 1964, Lal Bahadur Shastri was chosen for the Prime Minister's office. Shastri remained Prime Minister till his death in 1966 when the Congress Party opted for Indira Gandhi, Nehru's daughter, over the right-wing, conservative Morarji Desai.

The first serious challenge to the dominance of the Congress came in 1967 when a united opposition, under the banner of Samyukt Vidhayak Dal, won control over several States in the Hindi belt. Indira Gandhi, Congress President, was challenged by the majority of the party leadership. The conflict led to a split, and Indira launched a separate INC. Initially this party was known as Congress (R), but it soon came to be generally known as the *New Congress*. The official party became known as Indian National Congress (Organisation) led by Kamaraj. It was informally called the *Old Congress*. As Indira Priyadarshini had control over the state machinery, her faction was recognised as the "real" INC by the Election Commission of India, although her organisation was the break-away group.

Indira Gandhi used a populist agenda in order to mobilise popular support for the party. She raised slogans such as *Garibi Hatao* (Remove Poverty), and wanted to develop closer ties with the Soviet Union. The regional party elites, who formed the INC(O), stood for a more right-wing agenda, and distrusted Soviet help. INC(O) later merged into the Janata Party.

Indira Gandhi proclaimed a state of emergency in 1975. After she lifted the emergency in 1977, more Congress factions were formed, the one remaining loyal to Indira Gandhi being popularly known as Congress (I) with an 'I' for Indira. The Congress (I) was routed in the general elections by the Janata Party. The Congress (I) was, however able to return to power in the 1980 elections. In 1984 Indira Gandhi was assassinated by two of her bodyguards.

After Indira Gandhi, her son Rajiv Gandhi, took over as Congress leader and led the party to a large majority in the 1984 Lok Sabha elections. Congress was defeated in the 1989 general election. Rajiv Gandhi was also assassinated in 1991. Following Rajiv Gandhi's assassination, P.V. Narasimha Rao suceeded him as Congress leader.

The 1990s was a period of prolonged crisis for the Congress. After gradually losing political influence, the party asked the widow of Rajiv Gandhi, the Italian-born Sonia Gandhi, to accept the position as Congress President. With her refusal in 1991, the Congress stuck with Narasimha Rao and after him, Sitaram Kesri. Although Rao was Prime Minister of a coalition Congress government from 1991-1996, Kesri led the Congress to a historic low in the 1998 elections. It appeared that the Congress politically had no real future. In 1998, Sonia Gandhi was finally said to have saved the Congress by accepting the presidency of the party.

After the election of Sonia Gandhi as party leader, a section broke away and formed the Nationalist Congress Party.

In the 2004 general elections, the Congress alliance won the largest number of seats and got an assurance of support from the Left Front upsetting the Atal Bihari Vajpayee-led National Democratic Alliance. Dr. Manmohan Singh was sworn-in as Prime Minister on 22 May 2004. In the 14th Lok Sabha (2004-2009), 145 INC members, the largest contingent amongst all parties, served the house. The party is currently the leading member of the ruling United Progressive Alliance coalition government supported by the Left Front from outside.

The organisation developed by Gandhi's Congress in the years of 1918 to 1920 has largely been retained till today. In every Indian State and Union Territory, there is a *Pradesh Congress Committee,* which is the State unit of the party, responsible for directing political campaigns at local and State levels and assisting the campaigns for Parliamentary constituencies. Each PCC has a Working Committee of 10-15 key members, and the State president is the leader of the State unit. The Congressmen elected as members of the States legislative assemblies form the Congress Legislature Parties in the various State assemblies, and their chairperson is usually the party's nominee for Chief Ministership.

The All India Congress Committee is formed of delegates sent from the PCCs around the country. The delegates elect various Congress committees, including the Congress Working Committee, which consists of senior party leaders and office bearers, and takes all important executive and political decisions.

The President of the Indian National Congress is in effect the party's national leader, head of the organisation, head of the Working Committee and all chief Congress committees, chief spokesman and the Congress choice to become the Prime Minister of India. Constitutionally, the President is to be elected by the vote of the PCCs and members of the AICC. However, this procedure has often been by-passed by the Working Committee, choosing to elect its own candidate as an emergency measure.

The Congress Parliamentary Party is the group of elected MPs in the Lok Sabha and Rajya Sabha. Their elected chair-person is the leader of the majority, and supposed to be the Prime Minister. However, there have been notable exceptions.

Bharatiya Janata Party (BJP), founded in 1980, is today one of the largest national political parties in India. It claims to be a champion of socio-religious cultural values of the country's Hindu majority, conservative social policies and strong national defence. It finds its primary base of support in the urban and semi-urban middle class, business and merchant classes and religious and social conservatives. Its constituency is strengthened by the broad umbrella of Hindu nationalist organisations, informally known as the Sangh Parivar, where the Rashtriya Swayamsevak Sangh plays a leading role.

Throughout its existence, the main opponent of BJP has been the Indian National Congress. The BJP has allied with regional political forces to counter its main rival, the Congress Party, which dominated central government for four decades. The ideological rallying cry of the BJP is Hindutva, which is interpreted by the Party as "Hinduness," or cultural Hindu nationalism, an interpretation which is contested by many other intellectuals and leaders belonging to the Hindu community.

BJP led the Government of India between 1998 and 2004, under Prime Minister Atal Bihari Vajpayee and Deputy Prime Minister Lal Krishna Advani, its senior most leaders. However, it has done so as the leading party within the National Democratic Alliance, of which it remains a part even today, and leads the opposition.

In the 1991 Lok Sabha elections, the BJP became the premier Opposition party, while the Congress managed to form coalition government. In 1996, the BJP became the single-largest political party in Parliament, with the Congress at its lowest ever. The President of India, Dr. Shankar Dayal Sharma, appointed A.B. Vajpayee as Prime Minister and the BJP worked to foster a coalition that could command a majority in the Lok Sabha, but the opponents of BJP were able to rally a majority and Vajpayee had to resign after only 13 days in power. A broad centre-left coalition government was formed.

Lok Sabha elections were again held in 1998, and the BJP again won the largest bloc of seats. This time, the BJP formed the National Democratic Alliance (NDA) with allied political parties. NDA had a slim majority, and A.B. Vajpayee returned as Prime Minister. But the coalition ruptured in May 1999, and fresh elections were again called.

On October 13, 1999, the BJP-led NDA won as many as 303 seats. The BJP won an all-time high of 183 seats. Vajpayee won his third-term as Prime Minister, and L.K. Advani became the Deputy Prime Minister and held the Home Ministry.

Under Prime Minister Atal Bihari Vajpayee, the new Government undertook 5 nuclear tests at Pokhran in Rajasthan in 1998, making India a new-age nuclear power with a considerable weapons arsenal and technology. The Vajpayee administration also oversaw the country's defences during the Kargil conflict, where thousands of soldiers, with artillery, aircraft and extremely dangerous assaults and operations, recovered strategic hills from Pakistani militants who had occupied and intruded into the Indian side of the Line of Control.

The BJP-led National Democratic Alliance passed the Prevention of Terrorism Act in 2002, a stringent law increasing the powers of police authorities and intelligence agencies in an effort to destroy subversive political activities and terrorism. The POTA was promulgated chiefly in response to the December 13, 2001 terrorist attacks on the Union Parliament.

Vajpayee and his economic team also pushed through major privatizations of big government corporations, the Freedom of Information Bill, the liberalization of trade rules, free trade, opening the skies to commercial airlines, foreign investment and ownership and developed "Special Economic Zones" where industries could enjoy special infrastructure. The Government specially catered to the rising Information Technology industry, and lowered taxes for middle-class Indians and businesses.

Vajpayee's Golden Quadrilateral road system was developed to link the four corners of the nation with heavy, industrial roads, and improve surface transport in the country as such. His education programs boosted the enrollment of children into primary schools, expanded aid for schools and pushed new-age technologies to improve schooling.

The BJP believes that the Vajpayee administration presided over the biggest and longest-sustained economic boom in the country's history, starting in late 2002. High increases in agricultural and industrial production matched by increasing foreign trade and investment are cited by the party as its major achievements. In 2004, the Government signed the South Asia Free Trade Agreement with Pakistan, Nepal, Bangladesh, Bhutan, Sri Lanka and the Maldives, a decision bound to benefit over 1.6 billion people.

Vajpayee Government was also responsible for sustained efforts to build peaceful relations with Pakistan. In 1999, Vajpayee rode on the Delhi-Lahore bus inaugural, and signed the Lahore Declaration with the Pakistani PM, committing India to peace. Despite the betrayal that came 3 months later in Kargil, Vajpayee in 2001 invited the military ruler, Pervez Musharaff to Delhi. Though the summit failed, and despite the terrorist attacks that froze relations for two and a half years, Vajpayee, in a speech to Parliament in August 2004, spoke of the "absolute last attempt of my life" to foster peace with Pakistan, de-freezing relations and invoking praise from world leaders.

The BJP and the NDA suffered a defeat in the general elections in 2004, and failed to muster a Parliamentary majority. A.B. Vajpayee passed on the premiership to Dr. Manmohan Singh of the Congress Party, and its United Progressive Alliance.

The rank-and-file leadership of BJP largely derives from the cadre of the RSS, which has millions of affiliates. It also maintains close links to other Sangh Parivar organisations, such as Vishwa Hindu Parishad and Swadeshi Jagran Manch (an organisation promoting consumption of domestic goods).

Nationalist Congress Party (NCP) was formed on May 25, 1999, by Sharad Pawar, P.A. Sangma, and Tariq Anwar after they were thrown out of the Congress Party due to their stating their belief that a person of foreign origin should not become the Prime Minister of India.

In January 2004, Sangma quit the NCP because he felt Sharad Pawar was getting closer to the Congress Party in spite of no change of leadership in the Congress. For a brief period Sangma's faction tried to claim the right to the name and symbol of NCP. The Election Commission acknowledged Pawar's group as the genuine NCP. Following the decision of the Election Commission, Sangma's group merged with All India Trinmool Congress to form the Nationalist Trinamool Congress. But Sangma has since returned to the NCP.

The NCP advertises itself as a progressive, secular party that stands for "democracy, Gandhian secularism, equity, social justice, and federalism." It positions itself as a moderate, left-leaning alternative to the Bharatiya Janata Party (BJP) and the Congress. The party's election symbol is an analog clock that reads 10:10. The party is in power in the state of Maharashtra in alliance with Congress(I). Since 2004 NCP is a member of the United Progressive Alliance.

Communist Party of India (CPI) is a political party supposed to have been set up on 26 December 1925 which is celebrated as its foundation day.

During the 1920s and beginning of 1930s, British colonial authorities had banned all communist activity, which made the task of building a united party very difficult. Only in 1935 was the party ready to be accepted as the Indian section of the Communist Third International. In connection with the change of policy of the Comintern toward Popular Front politics, the Indian communists changed their relation to the Indian National Congress. The communists joined the Congress Socialist Party (CSP), the left wing of Congress. In Kerala communists won control over CSP, and for a brief period controlled Congress there.

During the Second World War, there were drastic changes for the Indian communists. After the USSR sided with Britain in the war, the Communist Party of India was legalised. Communists strengthened their control over the All India Trade Union Congress. At the same time, communists were politically cornered for their apparent opposition to the Quit India Movement.

In 1957, the CPI won the state elections in Kerala. This was the first time that a opposition party won control over an Indian state. E. M. S. Namboodiripad became Chief Minister. A serious rift within the party surfaced in 1962. One reason was the Sino-Indian War, where the Soviet faction of the Indian communists backed the position of the Indian government, while other sections of the party claimed that it was a conflict between a socialist and a capitalist state, and thus took a pro-Chinese position. Hundreds of CPI leaders, such as E. M. S. Namboodiripad and B.T. Ranadive, accused of being pro-Chinese were imprisoned. The internal split was sealed in 1964 when two different party conferences were held, one of CPI and one of the Communist Party of India (Marxist).

During the period 1970-77, CPI was allied with Congress. In Kerala, they formed government together with Congress, with the CPI-leader Achutha Menon as Chief Minister. After the fall of the regime of Indira Gandhi, CPI reoriented itself towards cooperation with CPI(M). To date, CPI happens to be the only national political party from India to have contested all the general elections on the same electoral symbol.

On the national level they support the new Indian National Congress-led United Progressive Alliance government, but without taking part in it.

In West Bengal and Tripura it participates in Left Front-governments. It is also taking part in the State government in Manipur. In Kerala the party is part of Left Democratic Front. In Tamil Nadu it is part of the Progressive Democratic Alliance.

The current general secretary of CPI is A.B. Bardhan. The principal mass organisations of the CPI are:

- All India Trade Union Congress
- All India Youth Federation
- All India Students Federation
- National Federation of Indian Women
- All India Kisan Sabha (peasants organisation)
- Bharatiya Khet Mazdoor Union (agricultural workers)

Communist Party of India (Marxist), or CPI(M), is strongest in the States of Kerala, West Bengal and Tripura. In West Bengal and Tripura States, it constitutes the government. It split from the Communist Party of India in 1964 because of what it describes as the latter's revisionism and sectarianism. The Party pledges to work for the establishment of a socialist society in India, free from class exploitation and social oppression.

CPI(M) got 5.66% of votes polled in last Parliamentary election (May 2004) and it has 43 MPs. It won 42.31% on an average in the 69 seats it contested. Like the CPI, it also supports the new Indian National Congress-led United Progressive Alliance government, but without becoming a part of it.

In West Bengal and Tripura it participates in the Left Front. In Kerala the party is part of the Left Democratic Front. In Tamil Nadu it is part of the Progressive Democratic Alliance.

The principal mass organisations of CPI(M) are:

- Democratic Youth Federation of India
- Students Federation of India
- Centre of Indian Trade Unions class organisation
- All India Kisan Sabha peasants' organisation
- All India Agricultural Workers Union
- All India Democratic Women's Association
- Bank Employees Federation of India
- All India Lawyers Union

In Tripura, the Ganamukti Parishad is a major mass organisation.

In Kerala the Adivasi Kshema Samithi, a tribal organisation is controlled by CPI(M).

Bahujan Samaj Party (BSP) is a party formed to represent both low caste and Dalit (depressed) persons, those at the bottom of India's caste system. The BSP had two high-profile, charismatic leaders, Kanshi Ram and Mayawati. With Kanshi Ram's demise, Mayavati is practically the sole and supreme leader of the BSP. In the 13th Lok Sabha (1999-2004) it had 14 (out of 545) members. Though avowedly a national party, the BSP has yet to exert much influence outside of the large State of Uttar Pradesh, whose government the party has led several times. The deep and mutual hostility between the BSP and the Samajwadi Party – the other leading State party in Uttar Pradesh, whose support is mainly OBC or kshatriya – has led the BSP into government with its erstwhile ideological enemies, the Bharatiya Janata Party. The party's political symbol is an Elephant.

The Bahujan Samaj Party is a relatively new entrant in the field of politics. It was formed with the avowed aim of espousing the rights of the oppressed sections of society—the Dalits. Since its inception, the party has travelled a long way.

The BSP first entered the election fray in 1984 but fared badly, losing 207 seats. The 1991 elections saw it bidding for power on its own, after which began the era of alliances-with Mulayam Singh Yadav in 1993 and with the BJP in 1995. However, these did not suit its restive leaders Kanshi Ram and Mayawati, and in the 1996 elections, it again went alone.

While in power in 1995, the BSP was embroiled in several controversies in land deals, formation of new districts, regularisation of dalit houses etc. With its emergence as a frontline party dedicated solely to the betterment of the dalits, the Congress was the main loser whose traditional vote bank they had been. The biggest achievement of the BSP, according to Mayawati, was the rightful restoration of a Dalit's individual dignity. As a party, its weakness was said to be its casteist credentials, and its strict adherence to only dalit causes, which limited its scope of growth. But, the recently (May 2007) concluded elections in U.P.—the most populous State in India—have shown that all this has changed. The BSP has cast its old image and slogans, entered into a strategic alliance (particularly with the Brahmins) and won an absolute majority of seats in the U.P. Legislative Assembly on its own with Mayavati forming a government that promises to be stable.

Coalitions and Alliances

Coalition is the *ad hoc* coming together or entering into an alliance of two or more separate parties, persons or interests, for a temporary period and with a specific objective of taking combined action like formation of government and carrying on the activities of the State. Coalition arrangements presume that the parties coming together retain their distinct identities but they usually agree on a common minimum programme or a national agenda to be followed by their government.

Advocates of proportional representation system suggest that a coalition government leads to more consensual politics, in that a government comprised of differing parties (often based on different ideologies) would have to concur in regard to governmental policy. Another advantage is that a coalition government better reflects the popular opinion of the electorate within a country. People who disapprove of coalition governments believe that such governments have a tendency to be fractious and prone to disharmony. This is because coalitions would be comprised of different parties with differing beliefs, who may not always agree on the correct path for governmental policy. Sometimes the results of an election are of such nature that the coalitions that are mathematically most probable are ideologically unfeasible.

In 1998, the BJP formed the National Democratic Alliance (NDA) along with smaller parties and became the first non-Congress government to sustain the full five year term after it returned to power in 1999.

The decade prior to 1999 was marked by short-lasting governments, with seven separate governments formed within a ten-year period. However, a Congress government formed in 1991, lasted the full five years and initiated significant economic reforms.

In the 2004 Indian elections the Congress party returned to power after winning the largest number of seats, by a narrow margin. Congress formed the government in alliance with several smaller parties and the leftist parties supporting the alliance from outside. The alliance is called the United Progressive Alliance (UPA). The NDA, led by the BJP, currently forms the main opposition. All governments formed since 1996 have been coalitions, with no single majority party, due to the steady rise of regional parties at the national level.

Formation of coalition governments reflects the transition in Indian politics away from the national parties toward smaller, narrower-based regional parties. This process has been underway throughout much of the past decade and is likely to continue in the future.

United Progressive Alliance (UPA) is the present 15-party ruling coalition of political parties in India. Its constituents include:

- Indian National Congress (INC)
- Rashtriya Janata Dal (RJD)
- Dravida Munnetra Kazhagam (DMK)
- Nationalist Congress Party (NCP)
- Pattali Makkal Katchi (PMK)
- Telangana Rashtra Samithi (TRS)
- Jharkhand Mukti Morcha (JMM)
- Marumalarchi Dravida Munnetra Kazhagam (MDMK)
- Lok Jan Shakti Party (LJNSP)
- Indian Union Muslim League (IUML)
- Jammu and Kashmir Peoples Democratic Party (JKPDP)
- Republican Party of India (Athvale) (RPI(A))
- Republican Party of India (Gavai) (RPI(G))
- All India Majlis-e-Ittehadul Muslimen (AIMIM)
- Kerala Congress (KC)

This alliance is externally supported (supporters are not part of the government) by the four left parties; Communist Party of India (Marxist), Communist Party of India, Revolutionary Socialist Party and All India Forward Bloc. In order to coordinate the cooperation, a UPA-Left Coordination Committee has been formed.

The National Democratic Alliance (NDA) is led by the Bharatiya Janata Party and had 13 constituent parties at the time of its formation in 1998. The convenor of NDA was George Fernandes, and its honorary Chairman the former Prime Minister Atal Bihari Vajpayee.

The NDA formed the Government in 1998, which collapsed within a year due to the AIADMK pulling out, but it won the

1999 elections and formed a stronger majority. The NDA of some 23 parties under Prime Minister Vajpayee governed for almost the full term of five years, and was widely expected to win the 2004 elections. But the BJP lost too many key seats along with the major allies. The Alliance could not bid for power. Former Deputy Prime Minister and BJP chief Lal Krishna Advani is now the Leader of the Opposition in Lok Sabha.

Currently, the other parties in the NDA are: Shiv Sena, Janata Dal (United), Biju Janata Dal, Trinamool Congress, Indian National Lok Dal, Shiromani Akali Dal and Himachal Vikas Congress. Several of the smaller parties have pulled out of the NDA in the course of its five year term, the latest being the DMK, the PMK and the MDMK which, along with the Indian National Congress have formed the "Democratic Progressive Alliance" in Tamil Nadu, and are part of the ruling United Progressive Alliance at the centre.

There are four types of interest-cum-pressure-groups working in India. These are:

1) Associational pressure-groups based on traditional social structures like religion, caste, tribe, language, or culture. Examples: The Parsee Anjumans, DAV educational institutions, Jamat-I-Islami, Rashtriya Swayamsewak Sangh, Nadar Caste Association, Hindi Sahitya Sammelan and the like.
2) Associational pressure-groups based on business, labour and peasants. Examples: (a) Business such as Federation of Indian Chambers of Commerce and Industry; All-India Manufacturers' Organisation; (b) Labour such as All-India Trade Union Congress (AITUC), Indian National Trade Union Congress (INTUC), Centre of Indian Trade Union (CITU), Hind Mazdoor Parishad (HMP); (c) Kisan Sabhas such as All-India Kisan Sabha, United Kisan Sabha, All-India Kisan Kamgar Sammelan.
3) Other associations and institutional interest/pressure groups such as based on modern professions (Editors' Guild, etc.), on important segments of society (Akhil Bhartiya Vidyarathi Parishad, Students' Federation of India, National Students Union of India, Janwadi Mahila Samiti) and on significant economic interests (Civil Services Association, Police Welfare Organisation, Defence Personnel Association, Delhi University Teachers' Association, etc.)

4) The business interest groups such as FICCI seek to promote the interests of business and industry. These work through strategies by keeping close contact with those who matter in decision-making. The labour organisations such as trade unions seek to promote the interests of the working classes and usually adopt strategies ranging from talks with the government/management to strike work and launch bandhs and marches. The Kisan Sabhas seek to promote and protect peasants' interests by arranging Kisan rallies and say, marches to the Parliament.

The distinction between political parties and pressure groups can be made as under:

(1) Political parties are political in the sense that they are part of the political system; pressure groups are non-political in the sense that they are part of the social system.
(2) Political parties stay in the midst of political arena; pressure groups stay out of the political arena.
(3) Political parties participate in the working of the political system: they contest the elections and form either the government or the opposition; pressure groups do not contest elections, nor do they participate in the working of the government.
(4) Political parties seek political power and as such their object is general; pressure groups seek specific objects. In fact, pressure groups act as attributes of political parties.
(5) Political parties are too formal, and too open; pressure groups are too secretive.
(6) Political parties are outward-oriented; pressure groups are inward-oriented.

Conclusion

To conclude we can say that political parties are the main organisations which allow participation in the political system. Though, originally not mentioned in the Constitution, they are crucial to understanding the realities of Indian political system. Political parties are the transmission belts to power. Elections are fought and governments formed by political parties. In another sense, political parties are the communication links between the people and the government.

Unfortunately, at present, there is a tremendous disconnect between the people and political parties. All political parties are suspect for indulging in vote bank politics, for dividing society to serve their vested interests, for placing the highest value on somehow getting to power and staying there by whatever means and for giving the lowest priority to the interests and needs of the people. There is every need for cleansing the electoral system and processes and for reforming the working of our political parties. [See Chapter 12. 'Blueprint for Good Governance']

10

INDEPENDENT OFFICES
CONSTITUTIONAL AND STATUTORY BODIES

Comptroller and Auditor General of India

Article 148 of the Constitution of India provides for a Comptroller and Auditor-General of India who shall be appointed by the President by warrant under his hand and seal. His term of office is six years or upto the age of 65 years.

Public audit ensures parliamentary control over expenditures voted by the legislature and renders public authorities accountable for the public moneys raised and spent by them to implement policies and programmes approved by the legislature. Accountability and transparency, the two cardinal principles of good governance in a democratic set-up, depend for their observance, to a large extent, on how well the public audit function is discharged. It is for this reason that the C&AG has been given special status by the Constitution in articles 148 to 152. It is his responsibility to ensure that money is spent and revenue raised not only in accordance with the law, but also with due regard to economy, efficiency and effectiveness. The C&AG is the constitutional authority entrusted with the high responsibility of maintaining probity in the use of public funds (NCRWC Report, para 5.16.1).

To ensure the independence of this office from the executive government of the day, it has been provided that the Comptroller and Auditor General shall not be removed from his office except on grounds of proved misbehaviour or incapacity, on an address passed by each of the two Houses of

Parliament by two thirds majority of those present and voting and a majority of the total membership of each House being presented to the President in the same manner as applicable to the judges of the Supreme Court under article 124(4). Also, the Comptroller and Auditor General has been made ineligible for any other office under the Government of India or any State Government. His salary etc. is left to be determined by Parliament by law. The Comptroller and Auditor General (Duties, Powers and Conditions of Service) Act, 1971 as amended regulates the position. The salary, etc. of Comptroller and Auditor General have been equated with the judges of the Supreme Court. The service conditions of those serving in the Audit and Accounts Department and the administrative powers of the Comptroller and Auditor General are to be laid down by the President by rules framed after consultation with the Comptroller and Auditor General. The administrative expenses of the office of the Comptroller and Auditor General are to be charged upon the Consolidated Fund of India (article 148).

The Comptroller and Auditor General of India, as the head of the Indian Audit and Accounts Department, is neither a part of the Legislature nor the Executive but is an officer created by the Constitution to see that diverse authorities act in regard to all financial matters in accordance with the Constitution and the laws and rules framed thereunder.

As the most important instrument of accountability, the Comptroller and Auditor General has a dual role to perform as an agency to function on behalf of the Legislature to ensure that the executive complies with the various laws passed by the Legislature in letter and spirit, and secondly, on behalf of the Executive to ensure compliance by subordinate authorities with the rules and orders issued by it.

Powers: *Under the Comptroller and Auditor General's (Duties, Powers and Conditions of Service) Act 1971, he is empowered to :*

- make rules for carrying out the provisions relating to the maintenance of accounts.
- make regulations for carrying out the provisions relating to the scope and extent of audit, including laying down for

the guidance of the Government departments the general principles of Government accounting and the broad principles in regard to audit of receipts and expenditure.

- requisitioning of all records of the auditee departments/ organisations.
- access the computer systems of the auditees and to download and use electronic data either in site or off site.
- review the development of computer systems of auditees and suggest/enforce controls
- the appointment of external auditors engaged by the auditees for meeting any statutory requirements but only with reference to Government companies.
- to supervise and regulate external auditors' work under the Indian Companies Act.
- dispense with, when circumstances so warrant, any part of detailed audit of any accounts or class of transactions and to apply such limited check in relation to such accounts or transactions as he may determine.

Jurisdiction

The organisations subject to audit of the Comptroller and Auditor General of India are:

- All the Union and State Government departments, including departmental commercial undertakings such as the Indian Railways, Posts and Telecommunications.
- Public commercial enterprises controlled by the Union and the State Governments- i.e. Government companies and corporations.
- Non-commercial autonomous bodies and authorities owned or controlled by the Union or the States.
- Authorities and bodies substantially financed from Union or State Revenues.
- Companies where the equity participation by Government is 51 per cent or more.
- Any authority or body, not being a foreign state or international organisation, which get any grant or loan for any specific purpose from the Consolidated Fund of India or of any State or any Union territory having a Legislative Assembly.
- Audit of all receipts which are payable into the Consolidated Fund of India and each of State and each of Union territory having a Legislative Assembly.

- Audit of the Regulatory bodies such as Telecom Regulatory Authority of India (TRAI), Central Electricity Regulatory Commission (CERC), State Electricity Regulatory Commissions (SERCs) and Insurance Regulatory Authority and Development Authority. However, role of audit of the Regulatory Authorities are at present confined only to the extent of certifications of their accounts as audit scrutiny over regulatory functions is still somewhat nebulous.

Audit Procedures and Functions

While fulfilling his constitutional obligations, the Comptroller and Auditor General of India conducts the following types of audit:

- Financial Audit
- Compliance Audit
- Performance Audit
- EDP Audit

Further, the Comptroller and Auditor General of India undertakes Special Audit at the request of the Government.

The Comptroller and Auditor is required to follow specific standards, practices and guidelines in conducting auditing and reporting. He can engage consultants and/or obtain professional services in conducting audit. He can also consult and collaborate with other countries/ Supreme Audit Institutions (SAIs) and International Organisations on matters relating to audit.

Apart from the certificates of the Appropriation and Finance accounts of the Union and of various States and submission of separate Audit reports on Statutory Corporations and other autonomous bodies for which he is the sole auditor, the Comptroller and Auditor General of India brings out a large number of reports relating to the Union Government and the State Governments. These reports incorporate important audit findings and performance reviews of systems, projects and programmes and comprehensive appraisals of public enterprises and other bodies and authorities. He also reports on acts that infringe upon State economic interest like mass embezzlement of State assets, serious losses and wastes. These reports are laid before the Parliament and State Legislatures concerned, every year. He can share his audit reports with public and media only after laying them in the Parliament and the State Legislatures. Some of these reports are selected by the Public Accounts Committees of Parliament and State Legislatures for detailed discussions and recommendations. The Comptroller and Auditor General of India assists the Public Accounts Committee by vetting the Action Taken Notes on selected Reports.

Administrative Functions

The basic level of audit and accounts personnel are given rigorous induction training and equipped with the expertise for their work on passing a departmental examination. For their up-gradation, the department also organises higher level professional training and qualifying examinations in various branches of accounts and audit. Further, eight Regional Training Institutes located in various regions of the country conduct a large number of refresher and specialisation courses.

The officers directly recruited through the Union Public service Commission or on promotion from within the department are exposed to a foundational course at the National Academy of Administration and imparted professional training at the National Academy of Audit and Accounts and at the National Institute of Financial Management in the areas of accounting and auditing, financial management, personnel regulations, cost and management accounting, management concepts, quantitative techniques and electronic data processing.

In order to share the experience with other sister institutions, the Comptroller and Auditor General of India has established an International Training Centre which organises a. number of training programmes for the Supreme Audit Institutions of the African, Asian, and Pacific regions on a variety of audit themes.

The basic objective of the office of the CAG is to promote excellence in public sector Audit and Accounting Services towards improving the quality of governance. It seeks to enhance accountability of the executive to the Parliament and State Legislatures by carrying out audits in the public sector and providing accounting services in the states in accordance with the Constitution of India and laws as well as best international practices.

There is a strong realisation that the quality of governance in a democratic country like India is dependent, above all, on the extent that constitutional institutions like the CandAG can manage effectively the task that they are enjoined to perform without fear or favour. In this regard, public audit in India has risen to the challenge of change in India's dynamic democracy and it has evolved and continues to evolve to provide the assurance required by the Parliament and the State Legislatures.

Election Commission

Election Commission of India is a permanent constitutional body. The Election Commission was established in accordance with the Constitution on 25 January 1950. Since its inception in 1950 and till October 1989, the Commission functioned as a single member body consisting of the Chief Election Commissioner. For the first time two additional Commissioners were appointed on 16 October 1989 but they had a very short tenure till 1 January 1990. Later, on 1 October 1993 two additional Election Commissioners were appointed. The Chief Election Commissioner and other Election Commissioners (Conditions of Service) Act, 1991 was amended to provide that the chief Election Commissioner and other Election Commissioners will enjoy equal powers and will receive equal salary, allowances and other prerequisites as payable to a judge of the Supreme Court of India. The Act further provided that in case of difference of opinion amongst the Chief Election Commissioners and/or two other Election Commissioners, the matter will be decided by the Commission by majority. The validity of that Act (renamed in 1993 as the Election Commission) (Conditions of Service of Election Commissioners and Transaction of Business) Act, 1991 was challenged before the Supreme Court. The Constitution Bench dismissed the petitions and upheld the provisions of the above law by a unanimous judgement on 14 July 1995. The concept of multi-member Commission has been in operation since then, with decision making power by majority vote.

The Commision presently consists of a Chief Election Commissioner and two Election Commissioners. The Constitution of India has vested in the Election Commission of India the superintendence, direction and control of the entire process for conduct of elections to Parliament and Legislature of every State and to the offices of President and Vice-President of India.

The Election Commission prepares, maintains and periodically updates the Electoral Roll, which shows who is entitled to vote, supervises the nomination of candidates, registers political parties, monitors the election campaign, including candidates' expenditure. It also facilitates the coverage of the election process by the media, organises the polling booths where voting takes place, and looks after the counting of votes and the declaration of results. All this is done to ensure that elections can take place in an orderly and fair manner.

Appointment and Tenure of Commissioners

The President appoints the Chief Election Commissioner and Election Commissioners. They have tenure of six years, or up to the age of 65 years, whichever is earlier. They enjoy the same status and receive salary and perks as available to Judges of the Supreme Court of India. To ensure the independence of Chief Election Commissioner, it is provided that he shall not be removed from his office except in like manner and on like grounds as a Judge of the Supreme Court and conditions of his service shall not be varied to his disadvantage after his appointment. The other Election Commissioners cannot be removed from office except on recommendation of the Chief Election Commissioner.

Election Machinery

The Commission has a separate Secretariat at New Delhi,

consisting of about 300 officials, in a hierarchical set up. Two Deputy Election Commissioners who are the senior most officers in the Secretariat assist the Commission. They are generally appointed from the national civil service of the country and are selected and appointed by the Commission on tenure basis. Directors, Principal Secretaries, and Secretaries, Under Secretaries and Deputy Directors support the Deputy Election Commissioners in turn. There is functional and territorial distribution of work in the Commission. The work is organised in Divisions, Branches and sections; each of the last mentioned units is in charge of a Section Officer. The main functional divisions are Planning, Judicial, Administration, Information Systems, Media and Secretariat Co-ordination.

The territorial work is distributed among separate units responsible for different Zones into which the 35 constituent States and Union Territories of the country are grouped for convenience of management. At the state level, the election work is supervised, subject to overall superintendence, direction and control of the Commission, by the Chief Electoral Officer of the State, who is appointed by the Commission from amongst senior civil servants proposed by the concerned State government. He is, in most of the States, a full time officer and has a team of supporting staff.

At the district and constituency levels, the District Election Officers, Electoral Registration Officers and Returning Officers, who are assisted by a large number of junior functionaries, perform election work. They all perform their functions relating to elections in addition to their other responsibilities. During election time, however, they are available to the Commission, more or less, on a full time basis.

Budget and Expenditure

The Secretariat of the Commission has an independent budget, which is finalised directly in consultation between the Commission and the Finance Ministry of the Union Government. The latter generally accepts the recommendations of the Commission for its budget.

The major expenditure on actual conduct of elections is, however, reflected in the budgets of the concerned constituent unit of the Union-State and Union Territory. If elections are being held only for the Parliament, the expenditure is borne entirely by the Union Government while for the elections being held only for the State Legislature, the expenditure is borne entirely by the concerned State. In case of simultaneous elections to the Parliament and State Legislatures, the expenditure is shared equally between the Union and the State Governments. For Capital Equipment, expenditure related to preparation for electoral rolls and the scheme for Electors' Identity Cards too, the expenditure is shared equally.

Executive Interference Barred

In the performance of its functions, Election Commission is insulated from executive interference. It is the Commission which decides the election schedules for the conduct of elections, whether general elections or bye-elections. Again, it is the Commission, which decides on the location of polling stations, assignment of voters to the polling stations, location of counting centres, arrangements to be made in and around polling stations and counting centres and all allied matters.

Political Parties and the Commission

Political parties are registered with the Election Commission under the law. The Commission ensures inner party democracy in their functioning by insisting upon them to hold their organisational elections at periodic intervals. Political Parties registered with it are granted recognition at the State and National levels by the Election Commission on the basis of their poll performance at general elections according to criteria prescribed by it.

The Commission, under its quasi-judicial jurisdiction, also settles disputes between the splinter groups of recognised parties. Election Commission ensures a level playing field for the political parties in election fray, through strict observance by them of a Model Code of Conduct evolved with the consensus of political parties. The Commission holds periodical consultations with the political parties on matters connected with the conduct of elections; compliance of Model Code of Conduct and new measures proposed to be introduced by the Commission on election related matters. [Also see Chapter 9. 'Election and Political Parties]

Advisory Jurisdiction and Quasi-Judicial Functions

Under article 103 of the Constitution, the Commission also has advisory jurisdiction in the matter of post election disqualification of sitting members of Parliament and State Legislatures. Further, the cases of persons found guilty of corrupt practices at elections which come before the Supreme Court and High Courts are also referred to the Commission for its opinion on the question as to whether such person shall be disqualified and, if so, for what period. The opinion of the Commission in all such matters is the President or, as the case may be, the Governor to whom such opinion is tendered. The Commission has the power to disqualify a candidate who has failed to lodge an account of his election expenses within the time and in the manner prescribed by law. The Commission has also the power for removing or reducing the period of such disqualification as also other disqualification under the law.

The decisions of the Commission can be challenged in the High Court and the Supreme Court of India by appropriate petitions. By long standing convention and several judicial pronouncements, once the actual process of elections has started, the judiciary does not intervene in the actual conduct of the polls. Once the polls are completed and result declared, the Commission cannot review any result on its own. This can only be reviewed through the process of an election petition, which can be filed before the High Court, in respect of elections to the Parliament and State Legislatures. In respect of elections for the offices of the President and Vice President, such petitions can be filed only before the Supreme Court.

Media Policy

The Commission has a comprehensive policy for the media. It holds regular briefings for the mass media – print and electronic – on a regular basis, at close intervals during the election period and on specific occasions as necessary on other occasions. The representatives of the media are also provided facilities to report on actual conduct of poll and counting. They are allowed entry into polling stations and counting centres on the basis of authority letters issued by the Commission. They include members of both international and national media. The Commission also publishes statistical reports and other documents which are available in the public domain. The library of the Commission is available for research and study to members of the academic fraternity; media representatives and anybody else interested. The Commission has, in co-operation with the state owned media-Doordarshan and All India Radio – taken up a major campaign for awareness of voters.

International Co-operation

India is a founding member of the International Institute for Democracy and Electoral Assistance (IDEA), Stockholm, Sweden. Its Board of Directors includes an expert from India. In the recent past, the Commission has expanded international contacts by way of sharing of experience and expertise in the areas of Electoral Management and Administration, Electoral Laws and Reforms. Delegates of the Commission have visited Sweden, U.K, Russia, Bangladesh, and the Philippines in recent years. Election Officials from the national electoral bodies and other delegates from the several countries-Russia, Sri Lanka, Nepal, Indonesia, South Africa, Bangladesh, Thailand, Nigeria, Australia, the United States and Afganistan have visited the Commission for a better understanding of the Indian Electoral Process. The Commission has also provided experts and observers for elections to other countries in co-operation with the United Nations and the Commonwealth Secretariat.

New Initiatives by the Election Commission

The Commission has taken several new initiatives in the recent past. Notable among these are, a scheme for use of State owned Electronic Media for broadcast/telecast by Political parties, checking criminalisation of politics, computerisation of electoral rolls, providing electors with Identity Cards, simplifying the procedure for maintenance of accounts and filling of the same by candidates and a variety of measures for strict compliance of Model Code of Conduct, for providing a level playing field to contestants during the elections.

Planning Commission

The Planning Commission was set up by a Resolution of the Government of India in March 1950 in pursuance of declared objectives of the Government to promote a rapid rise in the standard of living of the people by efficient exploitation of the resources of the country, increasing production and offering opportunities to all for employment in the service of the community. The Planning Commission was charged with the responsibility of making assessment of all resources of the country, augmenting deficient resources, formulating plans for the most effective and balanced utilisation of resources and determining priorities. Jawaharlal Nehru was the first Chairman of the Planning Commission.

The first Five-year Plan was launched in 1951 and two subsequent five-year plans were formulated till 1965, when there was a break because of the Indo-Pakistan Conflict. Two successive years of drought, devaluation of the currency, a general rise in prices and erosion of resources disrupted the planning process and after three Annual Plans between 1966 and 1969, the fourth Five-year plan was started in 1969.

The Eighth Plan could not take off in 1990 due to the fast changing political situation at the Centre and the years 1990-91 and 1991-92 were treated as Annual Plans. The Eighth Plan was finally launched in 1992 after the initiation of structural adjustment policies.

For the first eight Plans the emphasis was on a growing public sector with massive investments in basic and heavy industries, but since the launch of the Ninth Plan in 1997, the emphasis on the public sector has become less pronounced and the current thinking on planning in the country, in general, is that it should increasingly be of an indicative nature.

Organisation

The Prime Minister is the Chairman of the Planning Commission, which works under the overall guidance of the National Development Council. The Deputy Chairman and the full time Members of the Commission, as a composite body, provide advice and guidance to the subject Divisions for the formulation of Five Year Plans, Annual Plans, State Plans, Monitoring Plan Programmes, Projects and Schemes.

Functions

The 1950 resolution setting up the Planning Commission outlined its functions as to:

a. Make an assessment of the material, capital and human resources of the country, including technical personnel, and investigate the possibilities of augmenting such of these resources as are found to be deficient in relation to the nation's requirement;
b. Formulate a Plan for the most effective and balanced utilisation of country's resources;
c. On a determination of priorities, define the stages in which the Plan should be carried out and propose the allocation of resources for the due completion of each stage;
d. Indicate the factors which are tending to retard economic development, and determine the conditions which, in view of the current social and political situation, should be established for the successful execution of the Plan;
e. Determine the nature of the machinery which will be necessary for securing the successful implementation of each stage of the Plan in all its aspects;
f. Appraise from time to time the progress achieved in the execution of each stage of the Plan and recommend the adjustments of policy and measures that such appraisal may show to be necessary; and

g. Make such interim or ancillary recommendations as appear to it to be appropriate either for facilitating the discharge of the duties assigned to it, or on a consideration of prevailing economic conditions, current policies, measures and development programmes or on an examination of such specific problems as may be referred to it for advice by Central or State Governments.

Evolving Functions

From a highly centralised planning system, the Indian economy is gradually moving towards indicative planning where Planning Commission concerns itself with the building of a long term strategic vision of the future and decides on national priorities. It works out sectoral targets and provides promotional stimulus to the economy to grow in the desired direction.

Planning Commission plays an integrative role in the development of a holistic approach to policy formulation in critical areas of human and economic development. In the social sector, schemes which require coordination and synthesis like rural health, drinking water, rural energy needs, literacy and environment protection have yet to be subjected to coordinated policy formulation. It has led to multiplicity of agencies. An integrated approach can lead to better results at much lower costs.

The emphasis of the Commission is on maximising the output by using our limited resources optimally. Instead of looking for mere increase in the plan outlays, the effort is to look for increases in the efficiency of utilisation of the allocations being made.

With the emergence of severe constraints on available budgetary resources, the resource allocation system between the States and Ministries of the Central Government is under strain. This requires the Planning Commission to play a mediatory and facilitating role, keeping in view the best interests of all concerned. It has to ensure smooth management of the change and help in creating a culture of high productivity and efficiency in the Government.

The key to efficient utilisation of resources lies in the

creation of appropriate self-managed organisations at all levels. In this area, Planning Commission attempts to play a systems change role and provide consultancy within the Government for developing better systems. In order to spread the gains of experience more widely, Planning Commission also plays an information dissemination role.

Table 10.1

Growth Performance in the Five-Year Plans

S. No.	Plan	Target	Actual
1.	First Plan (1951-56)	2.1	3.60
2.	Second Plan (1956-61)	4.5	4.21
3.	Third Plan (1961-66)	5.6	2.72
4.	Fourth Plan (1969-74)	5.7	2.05
5.	Fifth Plan (1974-79)	4.4	4.83
6.	Sixth Plan (1980-85)	5.2	5.54
7.	Seventh Plan (1985-90)	5.0	6.02
8.	Eight Plan (1992-97)	5.6	6.68
9.	Ninth Plan (1997-2002)	6.5	5.5
10.	Tenth Plan (2002-2007)	8.1	-

Central Vigilance Commission

The Central Vigilance Commission was set up by the Government in February,1964 on the recommendations of the Committee on Prevention of Corruption, headed by Shri K. Santhanam, to advise and guide Central Government agencies in the field of vigilance.

CVC is conceived to be the apex vigilance institution, free of control from any executive authority, monitoring all vigilance activity under the Central Government and advising various authorities in Central Government organisations in planning, executing, reviewing and reforming their vigilance work.

Consequent upon promulgation of an Ordinance by the President, the Central Vigilance Commission has been made a multi member Commission with "statutory status" with effect from 25 August,1998.

The CVC Bill was passed by both the houses of Parliament in 2003 and the President gave his assent on 11 September 2003. Thus the Central Vigilance Commission Act 2003 (No45 Of 2003) came into effect from that date.

The Commission shall consist of:

- a Central Vigilance Commissioner-Chairperson;
- not more than two Vigilance Commissioners-Members.

Vide GOI Resolution on "Public Interest Disclosure and Protection of Informer" dated April 2004, the Government of India has authorised the Central Vigilance Commission as the "Designated Agency" to receive written complaints for disclosure on any allegation of corruption or misuse of office and recommend appropriate action.

The Central Vigilance Commission has its own Secretariat. The Secretariat consists of a Secretary of the rank of Additional Secretary to the GOI, one officer of the rank of Joint Secretary to the GOI, ten officers of the rank of Director/Deputy Secretary, four Under Secretaries and office staff.

Chief Technical Examiners' Wing (CTE)

The Chief Technical Examiner's Organisation constitutes the technical wing of the Central Vigilance Commission (India) and is manned by two Engineers of the rank of Chief Engineers(designated as Chief Technical Examiners) with supporting engineering staff. The main functions assigned to this organisation are:

- Technical audit of construction works of Governmental organisations from a vigilance angle;
- Investigation of specific cases of complaints relating to construction works;
- Extension of assistance to CBI in their investigations involving technical matters and for evaluation of properties in Delhi; and

Tendering of advice/assistance to the Commission and Chief Vigilance Officers in vigilance cases involving technical matters.

Commissioners for Departmental Inquiries (CDIs)

There are fifteen posts of Commissioners for Departmental Inquiries (CDI) in the Commission, 14 in the rank of Deputy Secretaries/Directors and one in the rank of Joint Secretary to Government of India. The CDIs function as Inquiry Officers to conduct Oral inquiries in departmental proceedings initiated against public servants.

Powers and Functions of CVC

To exercise superintendence over the functioning of the Delhi Special Police Establishment (DSPE) with respect to investigation under the Prevention of Corruption Act, 1988; or offence under CRPC for certain categories of public servants and to give directions to the DSPE for purpose of discharging this responsibility;

a) to review the progress of investigations conducted by the DSPE into offences alleged to have been committed under the Prevention of Corruption Act;

b) to undertake an inquiry or cause an inquiry or investigation to be made into any transaction in which a public servant working in any organisation, to which the executive control of the Government of India extends, is suspected or alleged to have acted for an improper purpose or in a corrupt manner;

c) to tender independent and impartial advice to the disciplinary and other authorities in disciplinary cases, involving vigilance angle at different stages i.e. investigation, inquiry, appeal, review etc.;

d) to exercise a general check and supervision over vigilance and anti-corruption work in Ministries or Departments of the Govt. of India and other organisations to which the executive power of the Union extends; and

e) to chair the Committee for selection of Director (CBI), Director (Enforcement Directorate) and officers of the level of SP and above in DSPE.

f) to undertake or cause an inquiry into complaints received under the Public Interest Disclosure and Protection of Informer and recommend appropriate action.

Commission's Jurisdiction under CVC Act:

- Members of All India Services serving in connection with the affairs of the Union and Group A officers of the Central Government.
- Board level appointees and other senior officers upto two grades below the Board level, in the Public Sector Undertakings of the Central Government;
- Officers of the rank of Scale V and above in the Public Sector Banks;
- Officers of the rank of Assistant Manager and above in the Insurance Sector (covered by LIC and GIC and four non-life insurance companies in the Public sector); and
- Officers drawing basic pay of Rs. 8700/- per month and above in autonomous bodies/local authorities or societies owned or controlled by the Central Government.

Chief Vigilance Officers

The Chief Vigilance Officers are extended hands of the CVC. The Chief Vigilance Officers are considerably higher level officers who are appointed in each and every Department/Organisation to assist the Head of the Department/Organisation in all vigilance matters.

The Chief Vigilance Officers constitute an important link between the organisations concerned and the Central Vigilance Commission (as also the CBI). The following procedures have been laid down/evolved in the matter of appointment of CVOs:

a. Prior approval of the Commission for appointment of an officer as CVO;

b. As far as possible, the Chief Vigilance Officers should be from outside the Organisation in which he is to be appointed. The initial tenure of full-time CVO in PSUs is for three years extendable by two years in the same organisation with the approval of the Commission or upto a further period of three years on transfer to another PSU on completion of initial tenure of three years in the previous PSU.

c. In cases where the scale of operation of a particular organisation does not justify creation of a full-time post, an officer within the organisation sufficiently senior in rank to be able to report directly to the Chief Executive on vigilance matters may be considered for such appointments;

d. The officer to be given additional charge of the post of CVO should not be one whose normal duties involve dealing with matters sensitive from vigilance point of view (like recruitment, purchase, etc.);

e. Once an officer has worked as CVO in an organisation, he should not go back as CVO to the same organisation again;

f. An officer who is appointed from outside as CVO in Central Public Undertaking shall not be permanently absorbed in the same organisation on expiry or in continuation of his tenure as CVO in that organisation; and

g. The "Vigilance" and "Security" function in an organisation should be separated as both the activities are equally demanding and the discharge of "security" functions by a Chief Vigilance Officer only leads to dilution of supervision on vigilance matters. However, an exception has been made in respect of the hotel industry.

Role and functions of Chief Vigilance Officers

Even though detection and punishment of corruption and other malpractices are certainly important, what is more important is taking preventive measures instead of hunting for the guilty in the post corruption stage. Therefore, the role and functions of CVOs have been broadly divided in to two parts, which are (I) Preventive and (II) Punitive.

On the preventive side: The CVOs undertake various measures, which include:

(a) To examine in detail the existing Rules and procedures of the Organisation with a view to eliminate or minimise the scope for corruption or malpractices;

(b) To identify the sensitive/corruption prone spots in the Organisation and keep an eye on personnel posted in such areas;

(c) To plan and enforce surprise inspections and regular inspections to detect the system failures and existence of corruption or malpractices;

(d) To maintain proper surveillance on officers of doubtful integrity; and

(e) To ensure prompt observance of Conduct Rules relating to integrity of the Officers, like

   (i) The Annual Property Returns;

(ii) Gifts accepted by the officials
(iii) Benami transactions
(iv) Regarding relatives employed in private firms or doing private business etc.

On the punitive side, the CVOs try

(i) To ensure speedy processing of vigilance cases at all stages. In regard to cases requiring consultation with the Central Vigilance Commission, a decision as to whether the case had a vigilance angle shall in every case be taken by the CVO who, when in doubt, may refer the matter to his administrative head, i.e. Secretary in the case of Ministries/Departments and Chief Executive in the case of public sector organisations;

(ii) To ensure that charge-sheet, statement of imputations, lists of witness and documents etc. are carefully prepared and copies of all the documents relied upon and the statements of witnesses cited on behalf of the disciplinary authority are supplied wherever possible to the accused officer alongwith the charge-sheet;

(iii) To ensure that all documents required to be forwarded to the Inquiring Officer are carefully sorted out and sent promptly;

(iv) To ensure that there is no delay in the appointment of the Inquiring Officer, and that no dilatory tactics are adopted by the accused officer or the Presenting Officer;

(v) To ensure that the processing of the Inquiry Officer's Reports for final orders of the Disciplinary Authority is done properly and quickly;

(vi) To scrutinise final orders passed by the Disciplinary Authorities subordinate to the Ministry/Department, with a view to see whether a case for review is made out or not;

(vii) To see that proper assistance is given to the C.B.I. in the investigation of cases entrusted to them or started by them on their own source of information;

(viii) To take proper and adequate action with regard to writ petitions filed by accused officers;

(ix) To ensure that the Central Vigilance Commission is consulted at all stages where it is to be consulted and that as far as possible, the time limits prescribed in the Vigilance Manual for various stages are adhered to;

(x) To ensure prompt submission of returns to the Commission;

(xi) To review from time to time the existing arrangements for vigilance work in the Ministry/Department for vigilance work subordinate officers to see if they are adequate to ensure expeditious and effective disposal of vigilance work;

(xii) To ensure that the competent disciplinary authorities do not adopt a dilatory or law attitude in processing vigilance cases, thus knowingly otherwise helping the subject public servants, particularly in cases of officers due to retire;

(xiii) To ensure that cases against the public servants on the verge of retirement do not lapse due to time-limit for reasons such as misplacement of files etc. and that the orders passed in the cases of retiring officers are implemented in time; and

(xiv) To ensure that the period from the date of serving a charge-sheet in a disciplinary case to the submission of the report of the Inquiry Officer, should, ordinarily, not exceed six months.

Central Bureau of Investigation (CBI)

The Central Bureau of Investigation traces its origin to the Special Police Establishment (SPE) which was set up in 1941 by the Government of India. The functions of the SPE then were to investigate cases of bribery and corruption in transactions with the War and Supply Deptt. Of India during World War II. Superintendence of the S.P.E. was vested with the War Department.

Even after the end of the War, the need for a Central Government agency to investigate cases of bribery and corruption by Central Government employees was felt. The Delhi Special Police Establishment Act was passed in 1963. Initially the offences that were notified by the Central Government related only to corruption by Central Govt. servants. In due course, with the setting up of a large number of public sector undertakings, the employees of these undertakings were also brought under CBI purview. Similarly, with the nationalisation of the banks in 1969, the Public Sector Banks and their employees also came within the ambit of the CBI.

From 1965 onwards, the CBI has also been entrusted with the investigation of Economic Offences and important conventional crimes such as murders, kidnapping, terrorist crimes, etc., on a selective basis.

The SPE initially had two Wings. They were the General Offences Wing (GOW) and the Economic Offences Wing (EOW). The GOW dealt with cases of bribery and corruption involving the employees of Central Government and Public Sector Undertakings. The EOW dealt with cases of violation of various economic/fiscal laws. Under this set-up, the GOW had at least one Branch in each State and the EOW in the four metropolitan cities, *i.e,* Delhi, Madras, Bombay and Calcutta. These EOW Branches dealt with offences reported from the Regions, *i.e,* each Branch had jurisdiction over several States.

As the CBI, over the years, established a reputation for impartiality and competence, demands were made on it to take up investigation of more cases of conventional crime such as murder, kidnapping, terrorist crime, etc. Apart from this, even the Supreme court and the various High Courts of the country also started entrusting such cases for investigation to the CBI on petitions filed by aggrieved parties. Taking into account the fact that several cases falling under this category were being taken up for investigation by the CBI, it was found expedient to entrust such cases to the Branches having local jurisdiction.

It was decided in 1987 to constitute two investigation divisions in the CBI, namely, Anti-Corruption Division and Special Crimes Division, the latter dealing with cases of conventional crime, besides economic offences.

Role and Functions

The Central Bureau of Investigation (CBI), functioning under Deptt. of Personnel,Ministry of Personnel, Pension and Public Grievances, Government of India, is the premier investigating police agency in India. It is an elite force playing a major role in preservation of values in public life and in ensuring the health of the national economy. It is also the nodal police agency in India which coordinates investigation on behalf of Interpol Member countries.

Over the years CBI has built up an image for professionalism and integrity. The services of its investigating officers are sought for all major investigations in the country.

CBI as an organisation is held in high esteem by the Supreme Court, the High Courts, the Parliament and the public. The CBI has to investigate major crimes in the country having interstate and international ramifications. It is also involved in collection of criminal intelligence pertaining to three of its main areas of operation, *viz.*, Anti-Corruption, Economic Crimes and Special Crimes.

The Anti-Corruption Division of the CBI has handled cases against Chief Ministers, Ministers, Secretaries to Government, Officers of the All India Services, CMDs of Banks, Financial Institutions, Public Sector Undertakings, etc.

CBI investigations have a major impact on the political and economic life of the nation. The following broad categories of criminal cases are handled by the CBI:

1. Cases of corruption and fraud committed by public servants of all Central Govt. Departments, Central Public Sector Undertakings and Central Financial Institutions.
2. Economic crimes, including bank frauds, financial frauds, Import Export and Foreign Exchange violations, large-scale smuggling of narcotics, antiques, cultural property and smuggling of other contraband items etc.
3. Special Crimes, such as cases of terrorism, bomb blasts, sensational homicides, kidnapping for ransom and crimes committed by the mafia/the underworld.

Anti-Corruption Division

The Anti-Corruption Division is responsible for collection of intelligence with regard to corruption, maintaining liaison with various Departments through their Vigilance Officers, enquiries into complaints about bribery and corruption, investigation and prosecution of offences pertaining to bribery and corruption and tasks relating to preventive aspects of corruption. The Anti-Corruption Division investigates cases against public servants under the control of the Central Government, public servants in Public Sector Undertakings under the control of Central Government and cases against the public servants working under State Govt. entrusted to the CBI by the State Governments and serious departmental irregularities committed by the above mentioned public servants.

Special Crimes Division

The Special Crimes Division handles all cases of economic offences and all cases of conventional nature such as offences relating to internal security, espionage, sabotage, narcotics and psychotropic substances, antiquities, murders, dacoities/robberies, cheating, criminal breach of trust, forgeries, dowry deaths, suspicious deaths and other IPC offences as well as offences under other laws notified under the DSPE Act. It is also responsible for investigation of interstate and international rackets, large-scale frauds affecting the property or revenue of the Government and crimes of national importance.

Economic Offences Division

The Economic Offences Division investigates financial crimes, bank frauds, money laundering, illegal money market operations, graft in Public Sector Undertakings and Banks.

Technical Advisory Units

The Technical Advisory Units provide expert guidance and assistance in banking, taxation, engineering and foreign trading/foreign exchange matters during enquiries and investigations taken up by the CBI. The technical advisory units are:

1. Banking Company Law/Insurance Advisory Unit.
2. Engineering Advisory Unit (Civil/Electrical matters)
3. Taxation Advisory Unit (Direct/Indirect Tax matters)
4. Foreign trading/Foreign Exchange Advisory Unit.

Directorate of Prosecution

The Directorate of Prosecution was established in pursuance of the orders of Supreme Court in Vineet Narain case. The Directorate tenders legal advice in CBI cases, besides conducting prosecution in CBI cases. The Directorate also attends to matters relating to legal matters raised in the IGPs/

DGPs conference, matters relating to interpretation of laws, appointment of special counsels, statutory rules and regulations and amendments thereof, preparation of notes on Legal matters for publication in CBI Gazette etc.

Policy Division

The Policy Division deals with all matters relating to policy, procedure, organisation, vigilance and security in the CBI, correspondence and liaison with Ministries and implementation of Special Programmes for vigilance and anti-corruption, etc.

Administration Division

The Administration Division of the CBI looks after all matters relating to personnel, establishment and accounts of all the Divisions of the CBI and is headed by an officer of the rank of Joint Director/IG.

Systems Division

The Systems Division looks after the information technology needs of the CBI. It generates data required for answering parliament questions, CBI clearances for appointments/awards of medals etc. This division also monitors the current ongoing comprehensive computerisation plan of the CBI. The CBI Command Centre consisting of Strategic Communication Centre and Network Monitoring Centre functions under the Systems Division.

Co-Ordination Division

The Co-ordination Division comprises of Co-ordination Unit, and Interpol Unit. The Co-ordination Unit takes part in the organisation of Directors General of Police, CID and other Conferences and is also incharge of the publication of the CBI Bulletin. The INTERPOL Unit is the Secretariat of the National Central Bureau and assists the Director CBI in his capacity as the Head of the National Central Bureau. The INTERPOL Unit, in its capacity as the Secretariat of the National Central Bureau, liaises with the International Criminal Police Organisation-

INTERPOL and is required to maintain liaison with the member countries of the INTERPOL. It handles and follows up the correspondence relating to requests for investigation to be carried out abroad in cases under investigation with the CBI or the State Police. Similarly, requests received from foreign countries for investigation in India are forwarded by the Interpol Unit to the State Police and then followed up.

Central Forensic Science Laboratory

The Central Forensic Science Laboratory (CFSL) provides Expert Opinion on various aspects of forensic science concerning crime investigation. Apart from Delhi Police and the CBI, it assists Central Govt. Departments, States, State Forensic Science Laboratories, Defence Forces, Govt. Undertakings, Universities, Banks, etc. in criminal cases. The laboratory has a research and development set-up to tackle special problems. The expertise available at the CFSL is also utilised in teaching and training activities conducted by the CBI, ICFS, Police Training Institutions, Universities and Government Departments conducting Law Enforcement Courses.

The Cyber Forensic Laboratory and Digital Imaging Centre functioning under CFSL assists enforcement agencies in the collection and forensic analysis of electronic evidence. CFSL experts are summoned for appearing before courts. Their services are also utilised by investigating agencies for the inspection of scenes of crime.

Training Division

The CBI Academy at Ghaziabad is a modern police training centre and imparts the specialised knowledge and skills that make a modern crime investigator. Residential foundation courses are conducted for freshly selected Dy.Supdts., Sub-Inspectors and Constables. Refresher courses and courses on specialised subjects are also offered to officers of CBI and State Police, as well as to Vigilance Officers of various departments.

Jurisdictions

Powers, privileges and liabilities: The legal powers of investigation of CBI are derived from the DSPE Act 1946. This Act confers concurrent and coextensive powers, duties, privileges and liabilities on the members of Delhi Special Police Establishment (CBI) with Police Officers of the Union Territories. The Central Government may extend to any area, besides Union Territories, the powers and jurisdiction of members of the CBI for investigation subject to the consent of the Government of the concerned State Govt. While exercising such powers, members of the CBI of or above the rank of Sub Inspector shall be deemed to be officers incharge of Police Stations of respective jurisdictions. The CBI can investigate only such of the offences as are notified by the Central Government under the DSPE Act.

Jurisdiction of CBI vis-a-vis State Police: Law and Order is a State subject and the basic jurisdiction to investigate crime lies with State Police. Besides, due to limited resources, CBI cannot investigate crimes of all kind. CBI may investigate:

- Cases which are essentially against Central Govt. employees or concerning affairs of the Central Govt.
- Cases in which the financial interests of the Central Government are involved.
- Cases relating to the breaches of Central Laws with the enforcement of which the Government of India is mainly concerned.
- Big cases of fraud, cheating, embezzlement and the like relating to companies in which large funds are involved and similar other cases when committed by organised gangs or professional criminals having ramifications in several States.
- Cases having interstate and international ramifications and involving several official agencies where, from all angles, it is considered necessary that a single investigating agency should be incharge of the investigation.

Union Public Service Commission

Indianisation of the superior Civil Services became one of the major demands of the political movement compelling the British

Indian Government to consider setting up of a Public Service Commission for recruitment to its services in the territory. The first Public Service Commission was set up on 1 October 1926. However, its limited advisory functions failed to satisfy the people's aspirations and the continued stress on this aspect by the leaders of our freedom movement resulted in the setting up of the Federal Public Service Commission under the Government of India Act 1935. Under this Act, for the first time, provision was also made for the formation of Public Service Commissions at the provincial level.

The Constituent Assembly, after independence, saw the need for giving a secure and autonomous status to Public Service Commissions both at Federal and Provincial levels for ensuring unbiased recruitment to Civil Services as also for protection of service interests. With the promulgation of the new Constitution for independent India on 26 January 1950, the Federal Public Service Commission was accorded a constitutional status as an autonomous entity and given the title – Union Public Service Commission

Under article 315 of the Constitution of India, the Union Public Service Commission consists of a Chairman and ten Members. The terms and conditions of service of Chairman and Members of the Commission are governed by the Union Public Service Commission (Members) Regulations, 1969.

The Commission is serviced by a Secretariat headed by a Secretary with two Additional Secretaries, a number of Joint Secretaries, Deputy Secretaries and other supporting staff.

The Union Public Service Commission has been entrusted with the following duties and role under the Constitution:

1. Recruitment to services and posts under the Union through conduct of competitive examinations;
2. Recruitment to services and posts under the Central Government by Selection through Interviews;
3. Advising on the suitability of officers for appointment on promotion as well as transfer-on-deputation;
4. Advising the Government on all matters relating to methods of Recruitment to various services and posts;
5. Disciplinary cases relating to different civil services; and

6. Miscellaneous matters relating to grant of extra ordinary pensions, reimbursement of legal expenses etc.

The most important job of the Commission is to select persons to man the various Central Civil Services and Posts and the Services common to the Union and States (*viz.* All-India Services).

Under article 320 of the Constitution of India, the Commission is, *inter-alia,* required to be consulted on all matters relating to recruitment to civil services and posts.

Recruitment is made by one of the following three methods:

1. Direct Recruitment;
2. Promotion; and
3. Transfer

Direct Recruitment is conducted broadly under the following two methods:

1. Recruitment by Competitive Examination: Under the Constitution one of the functions of the Commission is to conduct examinations for appointment to Civil Services/Posts of the Union. In addition, competitive examinations are also held by the Commission under arrangements with the Ministry of Defence for entry to certain Defence Services, through the National Defence Academy, Indian Military Academy, Naval Academy, Air Force Academy and the Officers Training Academy. The Commission usually conducts over a dozen examinations every year on an all India basis. These include Examinations for recruitment to services/posts in various fields, such as Civil Services, Engineering, Medical and Forest Service, etc. At present the Union Public Service Commission conduct their examinations at numerous venues spread over 42 regular centers throughout the country.

2. Recruitment by Selection Through Interview: Recruitment by Selection is made by the following methods:

1. By Interview Only
2. By Recruitment Test Followed By Interview

By Interview Only: Where the number of applicants is very large, it is not practicable to call for interview all the applicants who fulfill the minimum eligibility conditions prescribed. The Commission, therefore, shortlists the candidates to be called for the interview on the basis of certain pre-determined criteria related to the job. A large number of recruitment cases are handled by the Commission by method (1) above.

By Written Test Followed by Interview: In this category, there are two types of procedure followed:

a. An objective-type written and/or practical test to test the skill of the candidates followed by Interview, the final selection being decided by interview, aided by the performance of the candidates in the written test and/or practical test.

b. An objective-type written and/or practical test to screen candidates to be called for interview, the final selection being decided by interview only.

Appointment by Promotion and Transfer on Deputation/ Transfer

In accordance with the procedure decided by the Government, in consultation with the Commission, Chairman or a Member of the Commission presides over the Departmental Promotion Committee Meetings to consider promotions from Group B to Group A and from one grade to another within group A, where promotion is to be made by Selection.

Deputation

The Recruitment Rules for a number of posts provide for appointment by Transfer on Deputation (including short term contract) and Transfer. When the field of consideration consists of Central Government as well as State Government officers, prior consultation with the Commission is necessary for selection of an officer. When the file for consideration is made more broad-based and consists of not only Central/State Government officers but also officers from Non-Government Institutions, the selection has to be made in consultation with the Union Public Service Commission.

All India Services

The All India Services Act, 1951 and Rules and Regulations framed thereunder regulate the recruitment and conditions of service in respect of the All India Services viz. Indian Administrative Service, Indian Police Service and Indian Forest Service.

As far as direct recruitment to the Indian Administrative Service and Indian Police Service Examination are concerned, it is done through the Civil Services Examination and for the Indian Forest Service through the Indian Forest Service Examination held by the Commission.

The relevant Rules and Regulations provide that 33% of the vacancies in the IAS/IPS/IFS should be filled by promotion from amongst the officers of the State Service in consultation with the Commission. The Selection Committee presided over by Chairman/Member of the Commission consists of senior Government representatives of the Central Government and the State.

Mechanisation-Project Sampera

The Commission have recently undertaken a project called "SAMPERA" (Screening and Mechanised Processing of Examination and Recruitment Applications). A simplified single sheet common application form for all the examinations has been devised which will be scanned by using OMR/ICR technology. The implementation of this project will mainly help in high speed scanning of data from forms eliminating manual entry. Other benefits will be accurate and faster generation of Admit Cards, Attendance lists with photo replica and signature facsimile of each candidate, and Error-free list of doubtful cases. The main aim of this project is to cope with the increasing volume of applications through innovations and mechanised handling so as to reduce the processing time and send communications faster to minimised errors. The cases of impersonation/malpractices will also be eliminated and wasteful expenditure will be reduced.

Binding Nature of the Advice of the Commission

A convention has been established by the Government of India, that in the following classes of the cases referred to the Commission, the recommendations made by them shall be accepted, save in exceptional circumstances.

a. Quasi-judicial cases.
b. Selection for appointments of candidates.
c. Appointment of a candidate on a higher initial pay than that of a minimum pay of the posts.
d. Claims of expenditure incurred by the Government servants in defending legal proceedings instituted against him in respect of acts done or purporting to be done in the execution of his duty.

National Human Rights Commission (NHRC)

The National Human Rights Commission is an expression of India's concern for the protection and promotion of human rights. It came into being in October,1993. In terms of Section 2 of the Protection of Human Rights Act, 1993 (hereafter referred to as 'the Act'), "human rights" means the rights relating to life, liberty, equality and dignity of the individual guaranteed under the Constitution or embodied in the International Covenants and enforceable by courts in India. "International Covenants" means the International Covenant on Civil and Political Rights and the International Covenant on Economic, Social and Cultural Rights adopted by the General Assembly of the United Nations on the 16th December, 1966.

The Commission performs all or any of the following functions, namely:-

a) Inquire, on its own initiative or on a petition presented to it by a victim or any person on his behalf,into complaint of-
    i) violation of human rights or abetment or
    ii) negligence in the prevention of such violation, by a public servant;
b) intervene in any proceeding involving any allegation of violation of human rights pending before a court with the approval of such court;
c) visit, under intimation to the State Government, any jail or any other institution under the control of the State Government,

where persons are detained or lodged for purposes of treatment, reformation or protection to study the living condition of the inmates and make recommendations thereon ;

d) review the safeguards by or under the Constitution or any law for the time being in force for the protection of human rights and recommend measures for their effective implementation;

e) review the factors, including acts of terrorism that inhibit the enjoyment of human rights and recommend appropriate remedial measures;

f) study treaties and other international instruments on human rights and make recommendations for their effective implementation;

g) undertake and promote research in the field of human rights;

h) spread human rights literacy among various sections of society and promote awareness of the safeguards available for the protection of these rights through publications, the media, seminars and other available means;

i) encourage the efforts of non-Governmental organisations and institutions working in the field of human rights;

j) such other functions as it may consider necessary for the promotion of human rights.

While inquiring into complaints under the Act, the Commission shall have all the powers of a civil court trying a suit under the Code of Civil Procedure, 1908, and in particular the following, namely;

a) Summoning and enforcing the attendance of witnesses and examining them on oath;

b) discovery and production of any document;

c) receiving evidence on affidavits;

d) requisitioning any public record or copy thereof from any court or office;

e) issuing commissions for the examination of witnesses or documents;

f) any other matter which may be prescribed.

The autonomy of the Commission derives, *inter-alia*, from the method of appointing its Chairperson and Members, their fixity of tenure, and statutory guarantees thereto, the status they have been accorded and the manner in which the staff responsible to the Commission – including its investigative agency – are appointed and conduct themselves. The financial autonomy of the Commission is spelt out in Section 32 of the Act.

The Chairperson and Members of the Commission are appointed by the President on the basis of recommendations of a Committee comprising the Prime Minister as the Chairperson, the Speaker of Lok Sabha, the Home Minister, the leaders of the opposition in the Lok Sabha and Rajya Sabha and the Deputy Chairman of the Rajya Sabha as Members.

Inquiring into complaints is one of the major activities of the Commission. In several instances individual complaints have led the Commission to the generic issues involved in violation of rights, and enabled it to move the concerned authorities for systemic improvements. However, the Commission also actively seeks out issues in human rights which are of significance, either *suo motu*, or when brought to its notice by the civil society, the media, concerned citizens, or expert advisers. Its focus is to strengthen the extension of human rights to all sections of society, in particular,the vulnerable groups.

The Commission's purview covers the entire range of civil and political, as well as economic, social and cultural rights. Areas facing terrorism and insurgency, custodial death, rape and torture, reform of the police, prisons, and other institutions such as juvenile homes, mental hospitals and shelters for women have been given special attention. The Commission has urged the provision of primary health facilities to ensure maternal and child welfare essential to a life with dignity, basic needs such as potable drinking water, food and nutrition, and highlighted fundamental questions of equity and justice to the less privileged, namely the Scheduled Castes and Scheduled Tribes and the prevention of atrocities perpetrated against them. Rights of the disabled,access to public services, displacement of populations and especially of tribals by mega projects, food scarcity and allegation of death by starvation, rights of the child, rights of women subjected to violence, sexual harassment and discrimination, and rights of minorities, have been the focus of the Commission's action on numerous occasions.

Ever since its constitution in 1993, the National Human Rights Commission has been discharging a role complementary to that of the Supreme Court of India by performing those tasks which by their very nature the NHRC can perform better *e.g.* monitoring any situation or functioning of an institution. The complementarity between these institutions has considerably improved the mechanism for the protection of human rights in the country, which is primarily a state responsibility.

National Commission for Women

The National Commission for Women was set up as a statutory body in January 1992 under the National Commission for Women Act, 1990 (Act No. 20 of 1990) of Government of India, to review the constitutional and legal safeguards for women; recommend remedial legislative measures, facilitate redressal of grievances and advise the Government on all policy matters affecting women. The Mandate of the Commission is as follows:

a. Investigate and examine all matters relating to the safeguards provided for women under the Constitution and other laws;
b. present to the Central Government, annually and at such other items as the Commission may deem fit, reports upon the working of those safeguards;
c. make in such reports recommendations for the effective implementation of those safeguards for improving the conditions of women by the Union of any State;
d. review, from time to time, the existing provisions of the Constitution and other laws affecting women and recommend amendments thereto so as to suggest remedial legislative measures to meet any lacunae, inadequacies or shortcomings in such legislations;
e. take up cases of violation of the provisions of the Constitution and of other laws relating to women with the appropriate authorities;
f. look into complaints and take suo moto notice of matters relating to :
    i. deprivation of women's rights;
    ii. non-implementation of laws enacted to provide protection to women and also to achieve the objective of equality and development;

iii. non-compliance of policy decisions, guidelines or instructions aimed at mitigating hardships and ensuring welfare and providing relief to women, and take up the issues arising out of such matters with appropriate authorities;

g. call for special studies or investigations into specific problems or situations arising out of discrimination and atrocities against women and identify the constraints so as to recommend strategies for their removal;

h. undertake promotional and educational research so as to suggest ways of ensuring due representation of women in all spheres and identify factors responsible for impending their advancement, such as, lack of access to housing and basic services, inadequate support services and technologies for reducing drudgery and occupational health hazards and for increasing their productivity;

i. participate and advise on the planning process of socio-economic development of women;

j. evaluate the progress of the development of women under the Union and any State;

k. inspect or cause to be inspected a jail, remand home women's institution or other place of custody where women are kept as prisoners or otherwise, and take up with the concerned authorities for remedial action, if found necessary;

l. fund legislation involving issues affecting a large body of women;

m. make periodical reports to the Government on any matter pertaining to women and in particular various difficulties under which women toil;

n. any other matter which may be referred to it by Central Government;

The Central Government shall cause all the reports referred to in clause (b) of sub-section (1) to be laid before each House of Parliament along with a memorandum explaining the action taken or proposed to be taken on the recommendations relating to the Union and the reasons for the non-acceptance, if any, of any of such recommendations.

Where any such report or any part thereof relates to any matter with which any State Government is concerned, the Commission shall forward a copy of such report or part to such

State Government who shall cause it to be laid before the Legislature of the State along with a memorandum explaining the action taken or proposed to be taken on the recommendations relating to the State and the reasons for the non-acceptance, if any, of any of such recommendations.

The Commission shall, while investigating any matter referred to in clause (a) or sub-clause(I) of clause(f) of sub-section (1), have all the powers of a civil court trying a suit and, in particular in respect of the following matters, namely:

a. summoning and enforcing the attendance of any person room any part of India and examining him on oath;
b. requiring the discovery and production of any document;
c. receiving evidence on affidavits;
d. requisitioning any public record or copy thereof from any court or office;
e. issuing commissions for the examination of witnesses and documents; and
f. any other matter which may be prescribed.

Complaints and Counselling Unit

This cell is the "Core" unit of the commission and processes the complaints received oral, written or *suo motu* under Section 10 of the NCW Act.

The complaints received relate to domestic violence, harassment, dowry, torture, desertion, bigamy, rape, refusal to register FIR, cruelty by husband, derivation, gender discrimination and sexual harassment at work place.

The complaints are tackled as below:-

- Investigations by the police are expedited and monitored.
- Disaggregated data are made available to various state authorities to facilitate action.
- Family disputes are resolved or compromised through counselling.

As per the 1997 Supreme Court Judgement on Sexual Harassment at Workplace, (*Vishakha vs. State of Rajasthan*) every employer is required to provide for effective complaints procedures and remedies including awarding of compensation to women victims. In sexual harassment complaints, the concerned organisations are urged to expedite cases and the disposal is monitored.

For serious crimes, the Commission constitutes an Inquiry Committee which makes spot enquiries, examines various witnesses, collects evidence and submits the report with recommendations. The implementation of the report is monitored by the NCW. The State Commission, the NGOs and other experts are involved in these efforts.

The complaints are analysed to understand the gaps in routine functioning of government in tackling violence against women and to suggest correctional measures.

The complaints are also used as case studies for sensitization programmes for the police, judiciary, prosecutors, forensic scientists, defence lawyers and other administrative functionaries.

The Commission constitutes Expert Committees for dealing with such special issues as may be taken up by the Commission from time to time. The Expert Committees established so far are for :-

> Law and legislation, Political empowerment, Custodial justice for women, Social security, Panchayati Raj, Women and media, Development of Scheduled Tribe Women, Development of women of weaker sections, Development of women of minority communities, Transfer of technology in agriculture for development of women.

The Commission interacts and networks with the NGOs and the State Commissions for ensuring gender equality and empowerment of women. The Commission also interacts with the media, social activists and academicians to suggest ways of ensuring due representation of women in all spheres.

The Commission undertakes state visits to evaluate the progress of development of women in various States. It has covered the States of Tamil Nadu, Andhra Pradesh, Rajasthan, Uttar Pradesh, Orissa, Sikkim, Madhya Pradesh, Assam, Tripura and Manipur.

During the visits, discussions are held with the Chief Minister, the Women and Child Development Minister, the Chief Secretary, the Home Secretary and the Secretaries of other departments.

The Commission conducts seminars, workshops and conferences and sponsors such events by providing financial assistance to research organisations and NGOs. The important areas so far covered include violence against women, sexual exploitation of women at work place, educational health and employment aspects, women in agriculture sector, women in Panchayati Raj, custodial justice, mental health institutions etc.

The NCW holds public hearings on issues affecting large sections of women such as crime against women, women in unorganised labour sector, women in agriculture and women of minority groups. The deposition at these enquiries helps in appreciating and initiating remedial action.

Important Court Interventions

The National Commission for Women can and has intervened in some important court matters.

- *Bhateri gang rape case (Rajasthan):* The Commission suo-motu took up the case of M. Bhanwari Devi and extended its full support in going for appeal and also providing security to the victim and appointment of a special public prosecutor to argue her case.
- *Capital Punishment / Death Penalty (Ramshree's case)*: Due to the timely intervention of the National Commission for Women in the Supreme Court, the order of the death sentence was temporarily stayed and the Hon'ble Court, later on commuted the death sentence into life imprisonment.
- *Obscenity cases*:
  1. The Hon'ble High Court of Delhi put an injection on the launching of +21 adult channel by the Ministry of Information and Broadcasting, Govt. of India.
  2. The NCW had moved the Hon'ble High Court of Delhi against Star TV, Zee TV, etc. for showing obscene pictures on television and other media.
- *Against out dated customs and traditions:* Maimon Baskari's Nuh (Haryana) case: The NCW took up the case of Ms. Maimon

Baskari who was allegedly a victim of torture and rape for marrying a person of her choice. The Supreme Court has united the couple.

- *Divorced Muslim Women's Entitlement to Maintenance beyond the lddat period:* In the matter of *Fakhruddin Mubarak Shaik vs. Jaitunbi Mubarak Shaik,* the NCW has intervened in the Supreme Court of India to support the stand of Jaitunbi. The case is pending.

Parivarik Mahila Lok Adalat (PMLA)

An Alternative Justice Delivery System: The National Commission for women has evolved an innovative concept of PMLA for redressal and speedy disposal of cases under Legal Service Authority Act, 1987, which has its roots in the traditional Nyaya Panchayats. The essential features of PMLA are amicable mutual settlement and flexibility in functioning. The NGOs in association with District Legal Aid and Advisory Boards, activists, advocates and others, organise Parivarik Mahila Lok Adalats with the Commission's financial assistance. So far, 130 PLMAs have been held in which about 7500 cases were taken up.

National Commission for Backward Classes

Pursuant to the direction of the Supreme Court in the Mandal case judgement, the Government of India enacted the National Commission for Backward Classes Act, 1993 (Act No. 27 of 1993) for setting up a National Commission for Backward Classes as a permanent body.

The Act came into effect on the 2 April, 1993. Section 3 of the Act provides that the Commission shall consist of five Members, comprising of a Chairperson who is or has been a judge of the Supreme Court or of a High Court; a social scientist; two persons, who have special knowledge in matters relating to backward classes; and a Member-Secretary, who is or has been an officer of the Central Government in the rank of Secretary to the Government of India.

The Government of India constituted the Commission on 14 August 1993 with a term of three years. The Commission was subsequently re-constituted on 28.2.1997 and 28.7.2000.

Article 340 of the Constitution provides for the appointment of a Commission to investigate the conditions of and the difficulties faced by the socially and educationally backward classes and to make appropriate recommendations. The article reads as under :-

340. *Appointment of a Commission to investigate the conditions of backward classes-*

(1) The President may by order appoint a Commission consisting of such persons as he thinks fit to investigate the conditions of the socially and educationally backward classes within the territory of India and the difficulties under which they labour and to make recommendations as to the steps that should be taken by the Union or any State to remove such difficulties and to improve their condition and as to the grants that should be made for the purpose by the Union or any State and the conditions subject to which such grants should be made, and the order appointing such Commission shall define the procedure to be followed by the Commission.

(2) A Commission so appointed shall investigate the matters referred to them and present to the President a report setting out the facts as found by them and make such recommendations as they think proper.

(3) The President shall cause a copy of the report so presented together with a memorandum explaining the action taken thereon to be laid before each house of Parliament. "

Functions of the Commission under the Act

Under Section 9(1) of the National Commission for Backward Classes Act, 1993 the Commission shall examine requests for inclusion of any class of citizens as a backward class in the Central List of Backward Classes and hear complaints of over-inclusion or under-inclusion of any backward class in the lists and tender such advice to the Union Government as it deems appropriate.

Under Section 9(2) of the Act, "The advice of the Commission shall ordinarily be binding upon the Central Government".

Under Section 11(1) of the Act, the Central Government

may at any time, and shall, at the expiration of ten years from the coming into force of this Act and every succeeding period of ten years thereafter, undertake revision of the lists with a view to excluding from such lists those classes who have ceased to be backward classes or for including in such lists new backward classes.

Under Section 11(2) of the Act, the Central Government shall, while undertaking any revision referred to in sub-section (1) consult the Commission.

The Government of India has also evolved the criteria for exclusion of certain socially advanced persons/sections – called the "creamy layer" – from the benefits of reservation available to OBCs in civil posts and services under the Government of India.

National Commission for Minorities

The setting up of Minorities Commission was envisaged in the Ministry of Home Affairs Resolution dated 12.01.1978 which specifically mentioned that, "despite the safeguards provided in the Constitution and the laws in force, there persists among the Minorities a feeling of inequality and discrimination. In order to preserve secular traditions and to promote National Integration the Government of India attaches the highest importance to the enforcement of the safeguards provided for the Minorities and is of the firm view that effective institutional arrangements are urgently required for the enforcement and implementation of all the safeguards provided for the Minorities in the Constitution, in the Central and State Laws and in the government policies and administrative schemes enunciated from time to time." The Minorities Commission was accordingly set up to safeguard the interests of minorities whether based on religion or language. The Commission was renamed as National Commission for Minorities and the first statutory Commission was constituted on 17.05.1993.

Constitutional Provisions

Minorities in Indian Legal Culture: The National Constitution does not define the word 'Minority'. It only refers to Minorities and speaks of those "based on religion or language".

The Preamble (as amended in 1976) declares the State to be "Secular", and this is of special relevance for the religious minorities. Equally relevant, especially, is the prefatory declaration of the Constitution in its Preamble that all citizens of India are to be secured "liberty of thought, expression, belief, faith and worship and "equality of status and of opportunity."

Part III of the Constitution of India, on Fundamental Rights contains the following principles relating to, or having a bearing on the rights of the minorities:

- people's right to "equality before the law" and "equal protection of the laws";
- prohibition of discrimination against citizens on grounds of religion, race, caste, sex or place of birth;
- authority of State to make "any special provision for the advancement of any socially and educationally backward classes of citizens" (besides the Scheduled Castes and Scheduled Tribes);
- citizens' right to "equality of opportunity" in matters relating to employment or appointment to any office under the State – and prohibition in this regard of discrimination on grounds of religion, race, caste, sex or place of birth.
- authority of State to make "any provision for the reservation of appointments or posts in favour of any backward class of citizens which, in the opinion of the State, is not adequately represented in the services under the State;
- people's freedom of conscience and right to freely profess, practise and propagate religion – subject to public order, morality and other Fundamental Rights;
- authority of State to make laws for "regulating or restricting any economic financial, political or other secular activity which may be associated with religious practice", and for "providing for social welfare and reform";
- authority of State to make laws for "throwing open" of Hindu, Sikh, Jain or Buddhist "religious institutions of a public character to "all classes and sections of the respective communities;

- Sikh community's right of "wearing and carrying of *kirpans*";
- right of "every religious denomination or any section thereof – subject to public order, morality and health – to establish and maintain institutions for religious and charitable proposes, "manage its own affairs of religion", and own and acquire movable or immovable property and administer it "in accordance with law";
- people's "freedom as to payment of taxes for promotion of any particular religion";
- people's "freedom as to attendance at religious instruction or religious worship in educational institutions" wholly maintained, recognised, or aided by the State;
- right of "any section of the citizens" to conserve its "distinct language, script or culture"
- restriction on denial of admission to any citizen, to any educational institution maintained or aided by the State, "on grounds only of religion, race, caste, language or any of them";
- right of all Religious and Linguistic Minorities to establish and administer educational institutions of their choice; and
- freedom of minority-managed educational institutions from discrimination in the matter of receiving aid from the State.

Part IV of the Constitution of India, containing non-justiciable Directive Principles of State Policy, includes the following provisions having significant implications for the minorities:

i. obligation of the State "to endeavour to eliminate inequalities in status, facilities and opportunities" amongst individuals and groups of people residing in different areas or engaged in different vocations;
ii. obligation of State to "endeavour to secure for the citizens a uniform civil code throughout the territory of India";
iii. obligation of State "to promote with special care" the educational and economic interests of "the weaker sections of the people" (besides Scheduled Castes and Scheduled Tribes; and
iv. obligation of State to "take steps" for "prohibiting the slaughter of cows and calves and other milch and draught cattle".

Part IV-A of the Constitution, relating to Fundamental Duties, applies in full to all citizens, including those belonging to minorities and of special relevance for the minorities are the following provisions in this Part:

i. citizens' duty to promote harmony and the spirit of common brotherhood amongst all the people of India "transcending religious, linguistic and regional or sectional diversities; and
ii. citizens' duty to "value and preserve the rich heritage of our *composite* culture".

Some other provisions of the Constitution having special relevance and implications for the minorities are:

i. official obligation to pay out of the Consolidated Funds of the States of Kerala and Tamilnadu 46.5 and 13.5 lakh rupees respectively to the local "Dewasom Funds" for the maintenance of Hindu temples and shrines in the territories of the erstwhile State of Travancore-Cochin;
ii. special provision relating to the language spoken by a section of the population of any State;
iii. provision for facilities for instruction in mother-tongue at primary stage;
iv. provision for a Special Officer for Linguistic Minorities and his duties;
v. special provision with respect to Naga religious or social practices, customary law and procedure, and "administration of civil and criminal justice involving decisions according to Naga customary law.";
vi. identical special provision for the Mizos; and
vii. provision relating to continuation in force of pre-Constitution laws "until altered or repealed or amended by a competent legislature or other competent authority"

Part III of the Constitution gives certain fundamental rights. Some of these rights are common to all the citizens of India including minorities. These rights are enshrined in –

Article 14: which ensures equality before law and equal protection of law;

Article 15: which prohibits discrimination on any ground *i.e.* religion, race, caste, sex, place of birth;

Article 21: which lays down that no person shall be deprived of his life or personal liberty except according to procedure established by law;

Article 25: which ensures freedom of conscience and the right freely to profess, practise and propogate religion;

Article 26: which ensures a right to manage religious institutions, religious affairs, subject to public order, morality and health;

Article 29: which gives minorities a right to conserve their language, script or culture;

Article 30: which provides for the protection of the interests of minorities by giving them a right to establish and administer educational institutions of their choice with the State directed not to discriminate against minority institutions in granting aid; and

Article 350A: which directs the State to provide facilities for instruction in the mother tongue at the primary stage of education.

National Commission for Scheduled Castes

As per the Eighty-ninth Amendment Act, 2003, the erstwhile National Commission for Scheduled Castes and Tribes was bifurcated into two independent Commissions—National Commission for Scheduled Castes and National Commission for Scheduled Tribes.

Article 338 of the Constitution provides for a National Commission for Scheduled Castes—

(1) There shall be a Commission for the Scheduled Castes to be known as the National Commission for the Scheduled Castes.

(2) Subject to the provisions of any law made in this behalf by Parliament, the Commission shall consist of a Chairperson, Vice-Chairperson and three other Members and the conditions of service and tenure of office of the Chairperson, Vice-Chairperson and other Members so appointed shall be such as the President may by rule determine.

(3) The Chairperson, Vice-Chairperson and other Members of the Commission shall be appointed by the President by warrant under his hand and seal.

force or under any order of the Government and to evaluate the working of such safeguards;

(*b*) to inquire into specific complaints with respect to the deprivation of rights and safeguards of the Scheduled Tribes;

(*c*) to participate and advise on the planning process of socio-economic development of the Scheduled Tribes and to evaluate the progress of their development under the Union and any State;

(*d*) to present to the President, annually and at such other times as the Commission may deem fit, reports upon the working of those safeguards;

(*e*) to make in such reports recommendations as to the measures that should be taken by the Union or any State for the effective implementation of those safeguards and other measures for the protection, welfare and socioeconomic development of the Scheduled Tribes; and

(*f*) to discharge such other functions in relation to the protection, welfare and development and advancement of the Scheduled Tribes as the President may, subject to the provisions of any law made by Parliament, by rule specify.

(*6*) The President shall cause all such reports to be laid before each House of Parliament along with a memorandum explaining the action taken or proposed to be taken on the recommendations relating to the Union and the reasons for the non-acceptance, if any, of any such recommendations.

(*7*) Where any such report, or any part thereof, relates to any matter with which any State Government is concerned, a copy of such report shall be forwarded to the Governor of the State who shall cause it to be laid before the Legislature of the State along with a memorandum explaining the action taken or proposed to be taken on the recommendations relating to the State and the reasons for the non-acceptance, if any, of any of such recommendations.

(*8*) The Commission shall, while investigating any matter referred to in sub-clause (*a*) or inquiring into any complaint referred to in sub-clause (*b*) of clause (5), have all the powers of a civil court trying a suit and in particular in respect of the following matters, namely: —

(*a*) summoning and enforcing the attendance of any person from any part of India and examining him on oath;

(*b*) requiring the discovery and production of any document;

(*c*) receiving evidence on affidavits;
(*d*) requisitioning any public record or copy thereof from any court or office;
(*e*) issuing commissions for the examination of witnesses and documents;
(*f*) any other matter which the President may, by rule, determine.

(9) The Union and every State Government shall consult the Commission on all major policy matters affecting Scheduled Tribes.

Finance Commission

[See under Chapter 7. 'Indian Federalism']

11

WORKING OF THE POLITICAL SYSTEM
AN APPRAISAL

The founding fathers of our Republic sought to build a united India and an integrated nation from a highly heterogeneous, widely segmented and fragmented society with many linguistic, regional, religious and other pulls of various sorts. Framing and adoption of an acceptable Constitution and a political system for a country of India's past, size and nature was no easy task. To have worked it without any major breakdown for more than five decades full of many crises and tribulations was even more creditable. In fact, our political system has been the greatest force for national integration. For half-a-century plus, we have remained a vibrant, functioning, democratic polity.

The present political system was the result of great many efforts at mutual accommodation, compromise and wide ranging consensus. Though we adopted the parliamentary system, we gave to ourselves a written Constitution which means that the position, powers and jurisdictions of the Executive, Legislature and Judiciary are only as defined and delimited by the Constitution. The Executive or the Government is part of Parliament, comes out of it and remains responsible to it. On the other hand, independence of the judiciary is guaranteed in several ways.

The structure at the State level is also broadly parliamentary and similar to the Union. Relationship between the Union and the States is determined by distribution of legislative powers. It is said that Indian polity is unitary in spirit but federal in structure. India is described as a Union of States but the Union is indestructible and indissoluble. We are thus in the unique position of being at once a parliamentary polity and a Republic with a President at the head. All executive powers vest in the President but are to be exercised only with the advice of the Council of Ministers responsible to Lok Sabha.

In an age where events move at a hurricane speed and the fast emerging newer and newer technologies keep changing the face of the universe and the ferment of our lives almost every day, half-a-century plus is not too short a period to take stock of the situation and attempt a self-appraisal of the working of our polity and the democratic institutions established thereunder.

Achievements and Failures

We began well. The five decades and more gone by were some of the most eventful in history. Centuries were compressed into years. Despite a succession of crises, the Constitution and the polity established thereunder stood the test of times. We were fortunate in having a galaxy of patriotic leaders of great calibre, competence and commitment during the early years of independence and the operation of the Constitution. The system withstood the Chinese aggression in 1962, Prime Minister Nehru's demise in 1964, four wars with Pakistan in 1947-48, 1965, 1971 and 1999, Prime Minister Lal Bahadur Shastri's sudden death in Tashkent in 1965, another Prime Minister Indira Gandhi's assassination in 1984, several severe floods and droughts, external and internal emergencies, Naxalite and terrorist onslaughts and a few secessionist threats. Parliament and State Legislatures functioned all through even during the periods of emergency. There were scores of achievements:

- integration of some 600 odd states,
- resettlement of refugees,
- abolition of zamindari and other land reforms,
- liberation of Portuguese and French possessions in India,
- accession of the States of Hyderabad and Jammu and Kashmir,

- development of a meaningful foreign policy with the cardinal principles of non alignment and peaceful co existence (with over a hundred nations at one time accepting India's philosophy and leadership),
- conducting of fourteen general elections to the popular house of Parliament – Lok Sabha – with the base of democracy in India getting widened with every election and nation building continuing through constitutionalism and democratic mobilisation,
- peaceful transfer of power more than once from one party to another party or alliance,
- surviving many pressures, stresses and strains inflicted on our body politic by malevolent forces, both internal and external, and finally
- the revolutionary 73rd and 74th amendments promising transfer of power to the people at the grassroots with 3.2 million elected rulers – one million women among them – at different tiers of governance.

It was under the present democratic polity that many conflicts were satisfactorily resolved. During the colonial period, the British Indian provinces were multi-ethnic. But, after the commencement of the Constitution, the Union Government while it was strong and stable showed tremendous capacity to accommodate ethnic demands and cultural diversities. A separate State of Andhra Pradesh on linguistic basis was conceded as early as in 1953. In 1955 five Zonal Councils were set up. This was followed by the States Reorganisation Commission and the redrawal of the map of India on largely linguistic lines. Still later, in 1973 a North-Eastern Council was created. To respect the tribal and other regional or cultural aspirations, separate States of Nagaland, Meghalaya, Mizoram, Arunachal Pradesh, Goa, etc., were established. Necessary constitutional amendments were also made allowing different degrees of autonomy and making some special provisions. Some of the secessionist insurgency movements were controlled, occasionally through the use of the stick and repression but usually through political processes, constitutional devices, compromises, power sharing and accommodative management of crisis within the system. With the transfer of power from the Congress to the DMK/AIADMK at the State level in Tamil Nadu, and revival of political processes, the separatist urges of Tamils lost their sharp edges. The same happened with the Sikh movement for Khalistan. True, not all ethnicity related issues have died down and not all groups and regions are satisfied. The problems and processes of conflict-resolution continue. The latest additions to the list of States are Uttaranchal, Chhatisgarh and Jharkhand. There are other pending demands for separate statehood and/or autonomy. These include among others: Maithlis of Bihar, Vidarbha in Maharashtra, Saurashtra in Gujarat, Telangana in Andhra and others.

There were many significant successes which would do pride to any new nation anywhere in the world. After Pokhran II, India was an indisputable nuclear power with a considerable mastery over the state of the art technology in the field of ballistic missiles, remote sensing satellites and generally in the field of space research. The latest negotiations and agreements with the United States are a recognition of India's new status. During the last few years, inflation has been reported to have been one of the lowest ever (hovering between 3 to 7 to 10%). Foodgrain production has touched all-time high figures. India was today the second largest producer in the world both of wheat and rice. It is already first in milk production. Foreign reserves are comfortable. FDI inflows in 2005-06 are already up by 60.5 per cent to $ 4.34 billion. There has been an upsurge of patriotism and a sense of pride in being Indians. The whole country is united against terrorism and we are facing its ugly onslaughts with equanimity and courage. The country is poised to achieve an economic growth rate of eight to ten percent.

As the Constitution Commission (NCRWC) appropriately put it, an assessment of half-a-century of the Constitution at work involves an appraisal of the performance of all the three organs of the State, *viz.* the Executive, the Legislature and the Judiciary. The accomplishments include:

Political Accomplishments

- India's democratic base has stabilised as a working federal polity. With the Constitution 73rd and 74th amendments, the base of democratic debate has widened. There is greater push towards non-centralisation. General Elections have been held with regularity; and transfers of power consequent upon the results of elections have been orderly, peaceful and democratic.
- The educational qualifications of the Members of Parliament and Legislatures have shown marked improvements. The Parliament and Legislatures are increasingly more representative of the composition of society. More and more members of the hitherto backward classes are moving up on the political ladder.

Economic or Physical Infrastructure

- There has been marked expansion and diversification of production. New technologies and modern management techniques are increasingly employed. There are marked advances in Science, Technology, Medicine, Engineering and Information Technology.
- Between 1950-2000, the index of agricultural production increased from 46.2 to 176.8.
- Between 1960-2000, wheat production went up from 11 m. tons to 75.6 million tons.
- Between 1960-2000, rice production went up from 35 m. tons to 89.5 million tons.
- Impressive expansion of industrial and service sectors has taken place.
- Index of industrial production went up from 7.9 in 1950-51 to 154.7 in1999-2000.
- Electricity generation increased from 5.1 billion KWH in 1950-51 to 480.7 billion KWH in 1999-2000.
- 6 to 8% annual growth of GNP between 1994-2000 (except in 1997-98) was achieved.
- Revenues from Information Technology industry grew from $150 million in 1990 to $ 4 billion in 1999.
- India's *per capita* Net National Product (NNP) in 1999-2000 was more than 2.75 times than what it was in 1951.

Social Infrastructure

- Between 1950 to 1998 infant mortality rate halved to 72 births per 1000 down from 146.
- Life expectancy at birth has grown up from 32 years in 1950-51 to 63 years in 2000.
- A child born in Kerala today can expect to live longer than a child born in Washington. Life expectancy of women in Kerala is now 75 years.
- India has put in place an extensive system of Public Health Services and medical network. In 1951, the country had only 725 primary health centers. By 1995, this had increased to more than 1,50,000.
- The number of primary schools increased significantly between 1951 and 1995 from 2,10,000 to 5,90,000.
- Close to 95% of the villages have a primary school within a walking distance of one kilometer.

The balance sheet contains a long list of equally – if not more – significant failures on various fronts. These *inter alia* include:

Political

- The electoral process has not been able to keep out criminal, anti-social and undesirable elements from participating in and even dominating the political scene and polluting the electoral and parliamentary processes.
- The enormity of the costs of elections and electoral corruption have been having grievous deleterious effect on national progress and have led to the degradation of political processes to the detriment of common good.
- Political parties, which have a fair share of the criminal elements, handle enormous funds collected ostensibly for meeting party and electoral expenditure. Money-power and criminal elements have contributed to pervasive degeneration of standards in public life and have criminalised politics. This is reflected in the quality of governments and of the governing processes.
- There are no legal instrumentalities or set of laws regulating the conduct of the political parties, legitimacy of fund-raising, audit and account requirements and inner-party democracy.

- National political parties are more divided on the definition of 'common national purpose' than ever before; the noble purposes of public life have degenerated more than ever before into opportunistic and self-seeking politics of competitive personal gain.
- 'Fraternity', the noble ideal of brotherhood of man enshrined in the Preamble of the Constitution has remained unrealised. The people of India today are more divided amongst themselves than at the time of the country's independence.
- There is increasing criminalisation and exploitation of the political climate and processes and an increasing criminals-politicians-bureaucrats nexus.
- There is crisis of confidence. There is crisis of leadership. Political leaders, owing to narrow partisan and sectarian interests and desire for short-time political gains, are unable even to agree upon broad common national purposes.

Economic

- The richest top quintile of population has 85% of the income. In India, the poorest quintile has only 1.5% of the country's income. The second, the third and the fourth quintile from top have respectively 8%, 3.5% and 2% of the income.
- 260 million people live below the poverty line.
- The state of the Indian economy is disturbing. Fiscal deficits are getting alarming. The economy is gradually sinking into a debt-trap. Economic, fiscal and monetary policies, coupled with administrative inefficiency, corruption and wasteful expenditure are increasingly pushing the society into extra-legal systems, crime-syndicates, mob-rule and hoodlum out-fits. Black-money, parallel economy and even parallel governments are the overarching economic and social realities. Legitimate governments will, in due course, find it increasingly difficult to confront them. In course of time these illegal criminal out-fits will dictate terms to the legitimate governments.

Social

- India's maternal mortality rate in 1998 was 407 per 100,000 live births. These levels are more than 100 times the levels found in the West.

- Some 53% children (almost 60 million) under five remain malnourished – nearly twice the levels reported in many parts of sub-Saharan Africa.
- The proportion of low birth weight babies born in India is 33%. It is only 9% in China and South Korea, 6% in Thailand and 8% in Indonesia.
- India was a signatory to the Alma Ata Declaration in 1978 that assured 'health for all' by the year 2000. Only 42% of the children between 12-23 months are fully immunised – 37% in rural areas and 61% in urban areas. The coverage is shockingly low in Bihar – 11% and in Rajasthan – 17%.
- Population control measures in the northern States have not succeeded. Fertility rates in Uttar Pradesh indicate that State is almost a century behind Kerala.

Civil and Judicial

In the matter of civil and judicial administration, NCRWC made the following observations:

- Corruption, insensitivity and inefficiency of administration have resulted in extra-legal systems and parallel economies and even parallel governments. Bureaucratic corruption and pettifoggeries, which cause frustration in people in their daily lives has more serious fallout of pushing more and more people into extra-legal systems. The pervasive cynicism that mal-administration generates results in a lack of faith in and disenchantment with institutions of democracy.
- There is an increasing non-accountability. Corruption has been pervasive. Public interest has suffered.
- Constitutional protection for the Services under article 311 has largely been exploited by dishonest officials to protect themselves from the consequences of their wrong-doings.
- Judicial system has not been able to meet even the modest expectations of the society. Its delays and costs are frustrating, its processes slow and uncertain. People are pushed to seek recourse to extra-legal methods for relief. Trial system both on the civil and criminal side has utterly broken down.

Nevertheless, India's achievements during the first five

decades and more in the larger historical perspective have been far reaching.

It is in the area of economic, technological and social development that India, during the last fifty years and more, has had to face formidable challenges. Though we registered significant successes, the fact of the matter is that we have not been able to abolish poverty, ignorance and disease from among our people. The massive programmes that we have launched in these fields have not yielded the desired fruits. At the same time, we ought not to underestimate our achievements. India is today a considerable industrial and technological world power, and promises to be an economic giant of the twenty first century. The economic reforms launched six years ago with the liberalization and opening up of our economy have reached a decisive stage. Gross Domestic Product (GDP) in nominal terms of US$692 billion in 2004, has made the country the world's tenth largest economy. Real GDP grew by 6.9 percent in 2004/05 compared to 8.5 percent a year earlier. Prospects for real GDP growth for 2005-06 is 6.5 to 7 percent. External position of the economy is becoming significantly stronger. Exports have grown, especially exports of services, which grew by 105 percent in 2004-05. Growth in services has largely been fueled by the information technology boom in which India is emerging as a world leader.

The country has moved to a high trajectory of growth with a growth rate of 8 to 10 percent of GNP envisaged for the next five years. This is a record-breaking achievement. We have accomplished this by standing on the shoulders of our basic policies. In this context we have made the two broad parameters of progress. One is the revolution in the production of foodgrains making the country self-sufficient in food, and the other, is the rise in the average expectation of life of an Indian, which has more than doubled since Independence. Notwithstanding all these we have yet to provide for our people safe drinking water, basic health facilities, electricity supply and other basic necessities of daily life.

India's educational development is a mixed bag of

remarkable successes and glaring gaps. In the post-Independence period, the pace of educational development was unprecedented by any standard. Today 108 million children attend primary schools in India by making the country's education system the second largest in the world after China. However, even after more than 50 years of planned effort in the sector, nearly one-third of the population or close to 300 million persons of age seven and above, are illiterate. The Census of India defines the literacy rate as the proportion of literates to the total population of age seven and above. From a mere 18.3 per cent (for the age five years and above) in 1951 to 43.6 per cent in 1981, this percentage rose to 65.2 per cent in the Census of 2001.

In the post-Independence period, higher education has expanded fast with more than 345 universities as on May 31, 2005, and as many as 15,437 colleges in January, 2002.

Without going into the details, it can be safely asserted that on the political plane, by far our greatest achievements have been to (i) bring about and maintain the unity and integrity of the nation and the secular character of the polity, and (ii) preserve the system of representative parliamentary democracy, ensuring the freedom and dignity of the individual. Since the polity functions through its three main organs – the Legislature, the Executive and the Judiciary – it would be necessary to study the working of the system through them and to suggest reforms in regard to the three institutions. In view of the federal structure of our polity and the stresses and strains in its working noticed during the last 56 years, it would be essential also to analyse Union-State Relations. Inasmuch as we are a representative parliamentary democracy, at the source of many of the maladies of corruption, criminalisation, casteism and communalism or money, muscle and mafia power afflicting the present political system are the electoral processes and the system of political parties. Reform options in all these areas need to be examined on a priority basis.

Areas of Concern

Several areas have emerged as the most crisis-prone in our polity during the last half-a-century and more. Union-State relations, misuse of powers under article 356 by Governors and the Union Government, reorganisation of States, the relationship between Fundamental Rights and Directive Principles-from non enforceability to some primacy and respect for Directive Principles-the property clause leading to several laws being invalidated by courts, Parliament going in for animated debates and finally ending with right to property being abolished from the category of Fundamental Rights, the legislature-executive-judiciary interface, privileges of Parliament versus rights of individuals and freedom of the press, appointment of judges-transfer of a decisive voice from the government to the judiciary, President-Prime Minister relationship, the long-drawn debate on decentralisation of powers and setting up the Panchayats, Nagarpalikas etc., Election Law and Election Commission-leading to three-member Commission, official language-formula for the continuance of English, reservations for OBCs etc. While some of these matters were sought to be regulated by ordinary legislation or judicial intervention and some remained unresolved, there were others that led to constitutional amendments.

Parliament in India: It is natural that in a system of parliamentary democracy, Parliament should occupy a place of primacy in the governance of the country. At the level of States, their legislatures occupy similar position. It is important to remember that in a parliamentary polity, just as government is responsible to the legislature, the legislature is also responsible to the people who are the ultimate sovereign.

An overview of developments in parliamentary institutions since the first Lok Sabha reveals some very interesting and some disturbing facts. The number of days on which the Houses of Parliament sit each year to transact business has come down in recent years. Even when they do meet, often little gets done. In the face of disturbances and shouting, the Houses have to be adjourned frequently.

Parliament was conceived as the Legislature or the law making body but of late law making has ceased to be even the most important of its functions either qualitatively or quantitatively. From about 48 per cent, it has come down to occupy less than 14 per cent of its time.

The character of Parliament has changed as a result of changes in membership composition. Attention needs to be drawn towards a distinct change in the content, canvas and culture of debates right from the first Lok Sabha days. In the earlier Lok Sabhas, there was much greater emphasis on discussion of national and international issues. Regional issues and local problems were left to be taken up in the State Legislatures. It seems that gradually but increasingly more regional and even local problems are coming to acquire greater relevance and importance for our members. What perhaps may cause the greatest concern is not only the shift in emphasis but the fundamental change in approach and outlook. Sometimes it appears as if we are more and more looking at national problems from regional, communal, linguistic or otherwise parochial angles rather than the other way round.

That representative democracy and parliamentary institutions have endured in India for five decades is a great tribute to their strength and resilience. There, has however been in recent years quite some thinking and debate about decline of Parliament, devaluation of parliamentary authority, deterioration in the quality of Members, poor levels of participation and the like. Today, one notices a certain cynicism towards parliamentary institutions and an erosion in the respect for normal parliamentary processes and the parliamentarians. Nothing can be sadder for Democracy. Something has got to be done to restore to Parliament and parliamentarians their legitimate place of honour and esteem in our democratic polity. Case for some parliamentary reforms is unassailable.

Executive: While the Council of Ministers is the political executive and constitutes the Government, real execution of the policies and programmes of the Government is in the hands of the permanent services. In a modern democratic state, no

government can function without the help of officers. It is, in fact, the non political and non elected functionaries who are responsible for carrying on the administration under the direction and control of the elected representatives of the people. Bureaucracy signifies a body of full-time professional administrators organised on a constitutional basis with a view to discharging their functions in accordance with rules and principles. In a more popular sense and by usage, however, bureaucracy has also become synonymous with 'civil service'- a more polite expression for the same people.

At the time of independence, we inherited a well organised framework of All India Services. In addition, there was a network of central, provincial and subordinate services. There were nearly 1000 officers in the ICS, roughly half of them were Indians. Owing to the state of affairs prevailing in the country as well as to avoid creation of any void in the Services, the Interim Government under Nehru promised those who were inclined to continue in the service "the same terms as to scales of pay, leave, pension rights and safeguard in matters of discipline as hitherto".

The attainment of independence and the introduction of the system of parliamentary democracy made the civil services fully accountable to the political executive and the Parliament. The Constitution also provided for the setting up of an independent Public Service Commission for the Union and a Public Service Commission for each State. The provisions for the Union and State Services applied to the whole of India except the State of Jammu & Kashmir (article 308).

A civil servant must possess the traditional service virtues of integrity and efficiency. His honesty should be above reproach and his loyalty unquestioned and his competence must conform to the recognised statndards. His loyalty or his commitment is not to the government in power but to the Constitution and to the service of the citizens at large. During the colonial regime, the higher services of the State had arrogated to themselves a special status and position of superiority and aloofness from the general public. But, under the new democratic value system, the services were expected to give evidence of the passion for social service and willingness to identify themselves with the people and the efforts at eliminating poverty, disease and ignorance.

With the new free market economy and policy of liberalisation etc., the role of the public services is again in the process of undergoing some fundamental change and re-orientation inasmuch as the State now would be increasingly expected to play the role only of the infrastructure provider and facilitator in economic development unlike the erstwhile role as an active agent of social engineering and economic change.

Whatever the system or policy changes, public servants are the backbone of the structure of the state and provide continuity to the system even in the event of change of government at the Union or State level or breakdown of the constitutional machinery in a State. It is therefore, of utmost importance that they are afforded speedy justice in service matters. A disgruntled public servant who is unable to get justice in his own case can hardly ensure justice to his fellow citizens.

Since, the Constitution has made every endeavour to protect the interests of the public servants, they are also expected to function fairly, fearlessly and honestly so that the administration of the State runs smoothly and socio-economic growth and justice and the welfare of the citizens at large are ensured.

So far as the administrative services at all levels are concerned, it is most essential that they move out of the colonial mind set of being the masters and rulers and assume the role of servants of the people to provide clean, transparent, citizen-friendly governance to all without any discrimination. This would require decentralisation and delegation of power, full use of new technologies, downsizing of the bureaucracy, inculcating a work culture and ensuring greater efficiency and accountability, grievance redressal and open government.

The Second Administrative Reforms Commission is currently examining the need and proposals for necessary reforms in the system of administration.

Judiciary

Of late, like the legislature and the executive, judiciary also seems to be failing in many parts. Things are getting increasingly disturbing and one is no more in a position to say that all is well with the judiciary. There is every need to review the working of the judiciary during the last half-a-century and more, to assess how far our justice delivery system has been able to provide equal justice to all the people as ordained by the basic scheme of the Constitution. And, if we have failed or there are shortcomings in the system, what can be done to remedy the situation. How far the judiciary has been able to fulfil the role expectations and how can we prevent the fault lines from bringing down the entire edifice can best be examined by focusing on the problems that have arisen in the course of interplay of the judiciary with the executive, the legislature and the people at large. An alternative or supplementary approach may be to look at systemic problems of the judiciary and its constraints in relating to the other organs of the State, becoming more citizen-friendly and providing speedy justice at affordable costs. Possibly, a distortion in the mechanism of checks and balances or overstepping the jurisdictional limits could have resulted in aberrations.

A matter causing the greatest concern is that of judicial delays. In addition to long holidays that cause delays in dispensation of quick and smooth justice, frivolous litigation and the frequent strikes by the lawyers also disrupt the work of courts and cause harassment to the law-abiding citizens. Expeditious, efficient and inexpensive justice rarely, if ever, reaches the ordinary citizens. Besides cases of custodial deaths and other instances of human rights violations of undertrial prisoners, it was appalling to find many accused persons having spent in jails longer years than the maximum jail sentence prescribed for the offence they were alleged to have committed.

Costs of seeking justice are high and ordinary citizens can hardly afford. The lawyers are also guilty of charging unreasonably high fees – many partly in cash – and having little interest in early disposal of cases. Not all lawyers conform to any professional ethics. On one pretext or the other, the advocates representing the parties keep asking for repeated adjournments and judges gladly oblige. Also, on the slightest pretext, the lawyers proceed on strike thereby paralysing the judicial process, causing delays and adding to the cost of litigation.

Urgent judicial reforms are a high priority categorical imperative. These are at least as necessary as reforms in any other sector. While it is of the utmost importance that people's faith in the Judiciary remains inviolate, it is also true that problems in the Judiciary are part of the larger national malaise and that judicial reforms cannot be viewed in isolation nor can these be the panacea for all the maladies that afflict Indian polity today. An integrated approach to reforms agenda is called for. Judicial reforms themselves can succeed only when accompanied by other essential reforms. It would be necessary, for example, that the Legislature and the Executive are made to discharge their responsibilities, that the quality of legislation and administration improves, that there is greater probity in public life and administration and that the citizens themselves realise their democratic obligations and build the necessary pressure to ensure that the Judiciary, the Executive and the Legislature all function in the interests of the people and remain fully accountable to them under the Constitution and rule of law.

Constitutional Amendments

That the political system had some serious defects or too many fault-lines developed later, is obvious *inter alia* from the fact that the Constitution had to be amended as many as 93 times in 57 years, making our Constitution the most amended Constitution of the world.

Of the 93 formal constitutional amendments effected so far under the constituent power of Parliament in article 368, not all can be considered equally important or of substantial consequence. The more wide-ranging and covering a vast number of provisions were the seventh, the forty-second and

the forty-fourth. Some of the amendments can be divided under four broad heads:

(1) *Minor, clarificatory or consequential amendments:* For instance, the second amendment removed the upper population limit for a parliamentary constituency from article 81(1)(b); the fifth amendment enabled the President to prescribe a period for the State concerned to convey its views in respect of a Bill referred to it under article 34; the eleventh amendment omitted the unnecessary requirement of a joint sitting for electing the Vice-President and clarified that the election could not be questioned on the ground of there being any vacancy in the electoral college (articles 66 and 71); and the thirteenth amendment inserted a new article 371A to implement the agreement on the creation of the new State of Nagaland.

(2) *Amendments to the property clause and restricting other Fundamental Rights or giving primacy to Directive Principles:* The first amendment sought to place restrictions on the right to freedom of speech in the interests of friendly relations with foreign states, public order etc. and to protect agrarian reform measures from being struck down by the courts on grounds of violating the Fundamental Rights of the landlords. It also clarified the right of the state to implement its scheme of nationalisation in public interest (articles 15, 19 & 31). Articles 85, 87, 174 and 176 were amended to simplify and rationalise convening and proroguing of sessions of Parliament and State legislatures and addresses by the President and Governors. Also, a few minor amendments were made in articles 341, 342, 372 and 376.

In the face of the Supreme Court decisions in regard to acquisition of property and the need for compensation, the fourth amendment sought to restate more precisely the state's power of compulsory acquisition or requisitioning of private property for public purpose and distinguish it from 'deprivation of property'. Also, it was clarified that state monopoly in a particular trade or business did not conflict with the fundamental freedom of trade and commerce (articles 31, 31A, and 305 and the Ninth Schedule). The seventeenth amendment modified the definition of the term `estate' in article 31 A and included some more State Acts in the Ninth Schedule. The fortieth amendment added 64 new entries to the Ninth Schedule and substituted article 297 by a new article vesting in the Union all lands, minerals and other things of value underlying the ocean. The forty-second amendment enacted during the

Emergency was thus far the most controversial, comprehensive and far-reaching amendment. It sought *inter alia* to spell out expressly the ideas of socialism, secularism and integrity of the nation in the Preamble, to add a chapter on fundamental duties of the citizens and to make the directive principles more comprehensive and give them precedence over fundamental rights.

The forty-fourth amendment sought to remove or correct the distortions brought about during the period of internal emergency. Also, it strengthened safeguards against the Emergency provisions and made it impermissible for the executive to continue the Emergency beyond one month without parliamentary approval. Right to property had been the subject-matter of many of the constitutional amendments. The forty-fourth amendment took it away from the category of fundamental rights.

(3) *Safeguarding the interests of the Scheduled Castes, Schedules Tribes and Minorities:* The first, seventh, eighth, twenty-first, twenty-second, thirty-third, fifty-first, fifty-third, fifty-seventh, sixty-second, sixty-fifth, seventy-sixth, seventy-seventh, seventy-ninth, eighty-first, eighty-second, eighty-third and eighty-fourth amendments all sought to provide better safeguards for the rights and interests of the Scheduled Castes, Scheduled Tribes and Minorities. Some of these amendments were only to provide for reservations or extend the ten-year period thereof again and again.

(4) *Admission of new territories into the Union:* The tenth, twelfth and the fourteenth amendments were necessitated in order to admit into the Indian Union the erstwhile Portuguese and French possessions in India.

Several amendments also became necessary to implement the schemes of States reorganisation, to put all the States on the same footing and then on linguistic lines (*e.g.*, the Seventh Amendment) etc. and to honour the agreements with the people in the North-East-the Mizos, the Nagas and others. Two amendments pertained to the admission of the State of Sikkim into the Indian Union.

The fifty-second amendment passed in 1985 outlawed defections by members of Parliament and State legislatures. The sixty-first amendment reduced the voting age from 21 to 18 years by amending article 326. The most revolutionary and significant constitutional amendments in recent years, however, have been the seventy-third and seventy-fourth amendments which have sought to bring power to the people at the grass- roots in a more meaningful way by giving some continuity, stability and constitutional status to local self-government institutions-Panchayats and Nagar Palikas.

Of the amendments enacted during 2000-2002, the eightieth amendment amends article 269-272 regarding taxes levied and collected by the Union and assigned to or shared with the States. The eighty-first amendment adds a new clause to article 16 to provide for considering unfilled reserved vacancies as a separate class of vacancies not to be included under the present ceiling of 50 per cent reservation of vacancies of the year. The eighty-second amendment adds a proviso to article 335 to clarify that it would be in order to provide for reducing the standards of evaluation and requirement of minimum marks for filling by promotion vacancies reserved for Scheduled Castes and Scheduled Tribes in the services of the Union and the States. The eighty-third amendment provides in clause 3A added to article 243M that the reservation of seats for Scheduled Castes provided under article 243D shall not apply to Arunachal Pradesh. The eighty-fourth amendment amends article 16 to allow provision for reservation in matters of promotion *with consequential seniority* in services under the State for SC/ST employees.

The eighty-fifth amendment amends articles 16, 55, 81, 82, 330 and 332 to provide (a) that reference to 'population of the State' in articles concerning elections to the office of the President and to Lok Sabha shall continue to mean population as ascertained by the 1971 census until the census after 2026, (b) that until 2026 the allocation of seats in Lok Sabha to the States shall continue to be on the basis of 1971 census but the constituencies within each State may be readjusted on the basis of 1991 census, and (c) that reservation of seats in the Lok Sabha and State Assemblies for SC/ST shall be on the basis of the 1991 census until after 2026.

Some of the latest amendments include the Eighty-sixth Amendment Act of 2002, which has inserted a new article 21A in the list of Fundamental Rights i.e. right to education. It has also added a new fundamental duty, which reads "who is a parent or guardian to provide opportunities for education to his child or ward between the age of six and fourteen years." The 87th Amendment sought to provide for readjustment of electoral constituencies including those reserved for Scheduled Castes and Scheduled Tribes based on the 2001 population census, without affecting the number of seats allocated to States in the Legislative bodies.

The 88th Amendment provided for tax on services as a specific entry in the Union List and for a law to determine the moralities for levying and collecting the service tax.

The 89th Amendment establishes the National Commission for Scheduled Tribes and the National Commission for Scheduled Castes as separate bodies by bifurcating the erstwhile Commission for S.C. and S.T.

The 90th Amendment sought to protect the rights of the non-tribals by keeping in tact the existing representation of S.T. and non S.T. in the Legislative Assembly of Assam from the Bodoland Territorial Council Areas District.

According to the 91st Amendment, the following clauses have been inserted in article 75 of the Constitution. (i) the total number of Ministers, including the Prime Minister, in the Council of Ministers shall not exceed fifteen per cent of the total number of members of the House of People. (ii) the total number of Ministers, in the Council of Ministers in the State shall not exceed fifteen percent of the total number of members of the legislative Assembly of that State.

The 92nd Amendment added to the Eighth Schedule four more languages *viz.* Bodo, Dogri, Maithali and Santhali.

The 93rd Amendment (20 January 2006) amends article 15 to provide for special provisions by law for the admission of S.C., S.T. and OBC to aided or unaided educational institutions including private ones but excluding minority educational institutions.

An important reason for the frequency of amendments has been the unusually large size of our Constitution. Many matters which are usually regulated by ordinary legislation were included in the text of the Constitution itself under historical constraints or on other grounds. Any modifications therein could, therefore, be done only by constitutional amendments. While some of the amendments have definitely improved the content and quality of the constitutional document in the context of the changed and changing societal, economic or political needs and some others were either inevitable or consequential for implementation of policy decisions, there were quite a few which were avoidable, unnecessary or motivated by merely political and partisan interest considerations of the ruling party. On principle, the Constitution must never be subject to easy amendments by temporary party majorities in legislatures.

Conclusion

On balance, our political system has stood the test of times. It has survived with many remarkable achievements to its credit and with all the flexibility potential and dynamism to get over its difficulties and failures.

12

BLUEPRINT FOR GOOD GOVERNANCE

A CITIZEN-FRIENDLY POLITY

India is on the march. We can look forward to the future as proud Indians. However, there is also a cause for concern. Faith of the people in the quality, integrity and efficiency of governmental institutions stands seriously eroded. Case for a review of the working of the institutions – Executive, Legislature and Judiciary – and for wide ranging political reforms is unassailable. Some rethinking is called for on our failure to work the political system we gave to ourselves. The time is ripe for a fresh look and for considering necessary systemic amends.

There is nothing wrong with the fundamentals of our political system of representative parliamentary democracy. But for the health and vigour of this system itself, it is of the utmost importance constantly to review and refurbish its structural-functional requirements and from time to time to consider renewing and reinventing the entire gamut of its operational mechanisms to guard against putrefaction and decay.

Concept of Governance

In recent years, considerable attention in academia has been focussed on problems of realising good governance. Both in the developed and developing parts of the world, there has been a welcome shift of focus from traditional concepts of government and politics to the concept of good governance and its attributes.

In a sense, there is nothing new in stressing the principles and paradigms of good governance. The concept in ancient Indian polity of the rulers being bound by *Dharma* was precisely that of ensuring good governance to the people. Kautilya's *Arthashastra* and many other classics are replete with descriptions of tenets of good governance. Ancient Indian polity recognised the rights of the people to good governance.

The end of all economy and polity was social good and improvement in the quality of human life. Human beings were not to be considered a a mere resource for administration or development but they were the ultimate end and all administration, development etc. were the resource for their good. The watchword for Ashoka was *Yogakshema* or public welfare. And, this could be achieved only through good governance.

Kautilya says, if the ruler is strong and full of energy, the people will be equally so. It is necessary that the ruler is always wide awake and alert. With the help of the Prime Minister, he is expected to keep an examining watch over the character and conduct of his ministers incharge of different departments of Government (Chapters X and XIX, Book I). Kautilya is emphatic that before decisions of the State are made or any important administrative measures taken, these should be discussed in well-constituted Council of Ministers. In the most categorical pronouncement of the principles of good governance, Kautilya says:

> In the happiness of his people lies his happiness;
> in their welfare his welfare;
> whatever pleases himself he shall not consider as good, but
> whatever pleases his people he shall consider as good.

Thus, Kautilya is for a welfare state where the welfare and prosperity of the people are the supreme concerns of the ruler. The ruler is for the service of the people. He can have no likes or interests of his own. This is the fundamental good governance principle of accountability and of justice being the basis of lawful rule.

Governance refers to the manner in which power is exercised by governments in managing a country's social and economic resources. "Good" governance is the exercise of power by various levels of government that is effective, honest, equitable, transparent and accountable.

Besides the World Bank indicators of good governance encompassing democracy, transparency and accountability, it may be said that the whole idea of good governance is that of a participative system in which those who are called upon to govern on behalf of the people are motivated with a will to giving their best, serving and doing good to the people, solving their problems and making their lives more liveable, satisfying and enjoyable. The essential prerequisites for quality governance are that the system should be good and suited to the needs, aspirations, background and ethos of the people concerned and those selected for operating the system should be endowed with character and competence and motivated by the spirit of public service.

Since governance is the process of decision-making and the process by which decisions are implemented, an analysis of governance focuses on the formal and informal actors involved in decision-making and implementing the decisions made and the formal and informal structures that have been set in place to arrive at and implement the decisions. Government is one of the actors in governance. In urban areas the major actors constitute political parties, voluntary organisations, research institutes, religious leaders, finance institutions, the military etc. At the national level, in addition to the above actors, media, lobbyists, international donors, multi-national corporations, etc. may play a role in decision-making or in influencing the decision-making processes. In rural areas, for example, other actors may include influential landlords, associations of peasant farmers, cooperatives, NGOs etc. All actors other than government and the military are grouped together as part of the "civil society." In some countries, in addition to the civil society, organised crime syndicates also influence decision-making, particularly in urban areas and at the national level.

Some of the major characteristics of "good" governance are—participation, consensus orientation, accountability, transparency, responsiveness, effectiveness and efficiency, equitability and inclusiveness and the rule of law. It ensures that corruption is minimised, the views of minorities are taken into account and that the voices of the most vulnerable in society are heard in decision-making. It is also responsive to the present and future needs of society.

The foundational norm of any democratic polity is that sovereignty vest in the hands of the people. Today, sovereignty of 'We, the people' stands grievously eroded. During the last few years, it has come to be widely believed that the administration has failed to meet fully the hopes, aspirations and requirements of the people. In this background what has become imperative is clean and quality governance as it affects the lives of the people.

Besides, people-centred development, the balance among the legislature, executive and judiciary has to be maintained in any constitutional democracy for good governance. Parliament and State assemblies legislate or amend existing laws; the executive in the form of ministers and bureaucracy administer laws and draft policy; and courts interpret the laws. The media, as the fourth pillar of democracy, is meant to serve as a watchdog and commentator. Good governance requires that all three organs of government stick to their basic duty or *dharma* and refrain from stepping on the other's turf. Whenever there is lack of harmony, smooth functioning of the government is affected.

Governance is viewed as the exercise of economic, political, and administrative authority to manage a country's affairs at all levels and as the means by which states promote social cohesion, integration, and ensure the well-being of their populations. It embraces all methods used to distribute power and manage public resources, and the organisations that shape government and the execution of policy. It encompasses the mechanisms, processes, and institutions through which citizens and groups articulate their interests, exercise their legal rights, meet their obligations, and resolve their differences. In terms of

UNDP's Policy Document (1997), Good governance therefore depends on public participation to ensure that political, social and economic priorities are based on a broad societal consensus and that the poorest and most vulnerable populations can directly influence political decision-making, particularly with respect to the allocation of development resources. Good governance is also effective and equitable, and promotes the rule of law and the transparency of institutions, officials, and transactions. Governance encompasses the state, but it clearly transcends it by including roles for both the private sector and civil society organisations. The private sector has a crucial role to play in sustainable human development since it is the primary source of opportunities for productivity, employment, income-generation, public investment, enterprise development, and economic growth. Civil society organisations facilitate public participation through social mobilisation. The capacity of governments to engage civil society is critical to a nation's capability to sustain political and economic opportunities and social cohesion. Sustainable human development is impossible without the participation of a number of actors and institutions.

Sustainable Human Development

Sustainable human development is defined as the process by which the range of opportunities and choices for people can increase and be expanded, while protecting those same opportunities and choices for future generations as well as the natural systems upon which all life depend. The expansion of peoples' choices is empowering when it increases their abilities to participate in the political, social, and economic forces of the society to free it from hunger, want and deprivation. This view of participation also means that there is mutual cooperation and people work, interact and collaborate for development. That same expansion of choices and opportunities can also promote equity, including equity of access to services, goods, employment, income and technology. The needs of this generation must be met without compromising the right of future generations to realise their potential and enhance their capabilities free from poverty and deprivation.

Governance and sustainable human development can be seen to be indivisible. Governance in the *economic* setting has major implications for equity, poverty, and quality of life. Governance in the *political* setting is the process of decision-making to formulate policy and laws, which in turn has ramifications for security, equity, participation and co-operation.

Citizen-Friendly Governance

Shorn of all jargon, for our model polity, good governance is citizen-friendly governance. The founding fathers of India's Republic built the entire edifice of her Constitution and democratic polity on the quintessential principle of sovereignty vesting in the people. Once freed from colonial rule, the people were expected to have ceased to be subjects of the foreign masters and become citizens of independent India. With the adoption of a democratic polity, the citizens were to function both as the rulers and the ruled. But, the transfer of power on the midnight of 14-15 August 1947 and our becoming a Republic on 26 January 1950 did not mean transfer of power to the people of India. Notwithstanding the significant progress and remarkable achievements of the nation on various fronts, the fact remains that the ordinary citizen of India is only very gradually beginning to feel the glow of freedom and the transfer of power to his/her hands. We need good governance, citizen-friendly administration, economic growth and nation building.

The founding fathers of our Republic who gave us our Constitution were not oblivious of the imperatives of good governance for the success of Indian polity. Perhaps, the best blueprint for reforms needed to be urgently enforced is already contained in the "principles" that article 37 of the Constitution ordained to be "fundamental in the governance of the country." Adherence to some of these fundamental principles of governance would require the State to secure:

- a social order for the promotion of the welfare of the people with social, economic and political justice for all (article 38(1));

- minimisation of inequalities in income and elimination of inequalities in status, facilities and opportunities among individuals and groups of people (article 38 (2));
- right to adequate means of livelihood for all citizens – men and women equally (article 39 (a));
- opportunities and facilities for children to develop in a healthy manner and in conditions of freedom and dignity (article 39 (f));
- right to work, to education and to public assistance in cases of unemployment, old age, sickness, disablement etc. (article 41);
- just and humane conditions of work and maternity relief (article 42);
- a living wage for workers with conditions of work ensuring a decent standard of life and full enjoyment of leisure (article 43);
- childhood care and education to children (article 45);
- raising the level of nutrition and the standard of living and to improve public health (article 47);
- protection and improvement of environment and safeguarding of forests and wild life (article 48A).

The source of many of our maladies is in the disregard of the interests of the citizen and in the absence of good governance. Civic sovereignty has got to be asserted and the citizen put at the centre of the political system and citizen-friendly governance brought about on a high priority basis. Above all, the citizens themselves have to realise their citizenship obligations and come forward to be active participants. Every citizen, in whatever position has certain responsibilities towards fellow citizens. Good Governance, is citizen-friendly governance.

In this connection, one also remembers the Blueprint of an "Action Plan for Effective and Responsive Government" that came out of the Conference of the Chief Ministers of States in 1997. Only if it was taken more seriously for implementation, things would have been very different today.

Citizenship Responsibilities

In a modern democracy the role and responsibilities of the citizen are enormous. As the state in a democratic polity is the creation of citizens, it must afford them maximum opportunity of participating in the political system and of exercising not only rights but also their special responsibilities. Without them a democratic polity will cease to function. In addition to such requirements as obedience to law and payment of taxes, which characterise all societies, democracy necessitates the citizens' active political participation and obligates the citizens to accept responsibilities. In a democratic polity, almost by definition, people are participants in the processes of governance. We, the citizens of India must understand both the rights and the responsibilities that flow from our position as citizens. Unfortunately, we don't. The tasks of nation-building and economic development cannot succeed unless the citizens at large feel intimately involved, responsible and committed to contribute their mite in every way. To give votes and leave everything else to look after itself can be most suicidal for ourselves. Responsibility is cast upon citizens to also exercise constant and organised vigilance over the conduct and activities of those elected to public offices.

Unfortunately, of late, there has been some rather disproportionate emphasis on the rights of citizens as against their duties even though the traditions and temper of Indian thought through the ages laid greater emphasis on duties.

The hope for building a united and integrated nation with dignity of the individual lies in the growth of institutions of civil society and we, the citizens of India, rising above petty self-interests, identifying the hard core of citizenship values enjoined by the Constitution and making a determined bid to work together to protect and promote them by contributing all our mite.

Every citizen must accept the position that as citizens all are equal, have the same rights and responsibilities and are entitled to equality before law without any discrimination.

Everyone of us must treat all our fellow citizens as equals and must not discriminate between them on any grounds such as sex, religion, caste etc. Every citizen must enjoy the same fundamental rights of freedom of thought and expression, freedom of religion, freedom from exploitation etc. It follows that we must respect the freedom of all our fellow citizens and must do nothing which may result in exploitation of anyone.

The privilege of being citizens of the Republic of India makes adherence to citizenship values a matter of sacred obligation for all of us in whatever position. These values are rooted not merely in our legal status as citizens but in some foundational norms which permeate the provisions of the Constitution. Citizens must respect citizenship values as these bring valuable rights and at the same time ordain required duties. As proud citizens we must realise that democratic way of life is the most civilised way because it is based on the dignity of every individual citizen. This also means that every citizen has to respect and protect the individual dignity of every other citizen.

Citizens voted to be in positions of power and governance must never forget that they are citizens first and always accountable, answerable and responsible to their fellow citizens at large. They must respect dissent, listen to complaints and never try to gag opposition. Certain standards of behaviour and discipline and of responsibility are essential to democratic ethos. Each citizen must therefore imbibe a spirit of self-discipline and a sense of his or her responsibilities to his fellow citizens and society.

Right to vote under universal adult franchise gives to every citizen an opportunity to participate in the democratic process and to select the government. This right must be used not only to operate and defend democracy but also to make it more effective and meaningful. This is a tremendous responsibility. This right has to be exercised with meticulous care and careful thought, without fear or favour. Also, the more competent ones willing and in a position to be able to rise above petty self-interests and with a desire to serve must come forward to more actively participate in the process as candidates and political activists. A full recognition of our democratic rights and responsibilities as citizens will automatically rid the system of corruption, criminalisation, money, muscle power and the like ills.

Universal adult franchise presumes an educated and wide awake citizenry. As Jawaharlal Nehru put it while speaking at a reception on 16 January 1955: "democracy only flourishes, as freedom only flourishes, when the responsibilities of freedom are understood and carried out. If the responsibilities are not understood and carried out, then freedom itself tends to slip away." It is unfortunate that "no systematic effort is being made to prepare the citizen for the discharge of this great responsibility".

Citizen and the State: The citizen needs to be restored to a position of pre-eminence at the centre of all state objectives and activities. Ways and means have to be found for reasserting the will of "We, the People" over the organs of the state – Legislature, Executive and Judiciary – and restoring power to the citizen where it belongs. This would call for respect for citizenship values and emergence and strengthening of a civil society with an aware, awake, responsible and participant citizenry.

Constitutional democratic government has got to be limited government with state jurisdiction and role restricted to essentials. The state must function as a facilitator and infrastructure provider not only to business and industry but to the citizens at large and to the goal of improving their quality of life.

The citizen's role would have no meaning in a society where the citizens are not prepared to make sacrifices for protecting and promoting them or where they view them only in terms of their own interests and rights. The role of a citizen in the polity would imply all the rights, responsibilities and duties of citizens *vis-a-vis* fellow citizens, society at large and the state.

Exercise of the rights and responsibilities of freedom also involves a certain degree of tolerance of others and their opinions even when they strongly differ from ours. It requires acceptance of even unpalatable decisions taken democratically. The democratic method inevitably implies trying to understand each other's opinion, a certain give and take and a certain mutual adjustment.

In a democratic polity, the administration must be run by the citizens for the citizens. Corruption, delays and harassment at levels of public dealing need to be attended to and remedied on a high priority basis. No one should forget that sovereignty vests in the people and that the highest functionaries of the state – Legislature, Executive and Judiciary – are all appointed or voted to positions of power and governance as the creatures of the people. They are citizens first and always accountable, answerable and responsible to their fellow citizens at large.

It is only when we fulfill the basic duty of politics of restoring the power of the Constitution and its institutions back to their legitimate owners – the people – that things will begin to change. Really, no reforms shall succeed and nothing can change unless the sovereign power is excercised by the people and they use it to discharge their citizenship responsibilities.

The most essential prerequisites for the success of any democratic polity are the willing interest, cooperation and participation of the politically aware, conscientious and intelligent citizenry in the affairs of the State, total respect for citizenship values, spirit of public service and dedication to the cause of democracy and freedom, protection of the civil and economic rights of fellow citizens and the full discharge of their duties and responsibilities by all citizens in whatever position.

Electoral and Political Party Reforms

The electoral and political party reforms considered necessary may be grouped uner two major heads, *viz.* (1) practice and procedure related and (2) system related. Most of these do not call for any constitutional amendments. They are matters for political reforms which can be brought about through ordinary legislation or through rules, regulations and executive orders provided that the political will gets crystallised with an agreement between political parties. The entire matter is in the legislative domain.

Election Commission

The Election Commission's powers and jurisdiction are limited to holding elections and are specifically for the duration of the election process. While it is for the Commission to suggest the precise dates of election, he cannot defer elections indefinitely on grounds of law and order situation not being conducive to holding free and fair polls or such other things. The Commission's job is to hold elections and not to withhold them. In case of premature dissolution of Lok Sabha or a State Assembly, elections must be held as soon as possible and in any case, within six months of the date of dissolution of the House.

Representational Legitimacy

The most fundamental problem that presents itself in the present scheme of things is that of the representational legitimacy of the elected representatives of the people. As it is, the representative character of the representatives itself has become doubtful. Majority of them are elected by minority of votes cast. In the three general elections nearly 70% of them were elected by minority of votes cast. More votes were cast against each one of them than for them. There have been legislators elected who received less than 15 per cent of the votes cast.

The first-past-the-post system was adopted by us in the hope that it would help in building a more united Indian nation, that politics would grow on ideological basis and that a healthy two party system would develop. What happened was the reverse. The system proved to be terribly divisive. The society got more and more fragmented on caste, communal, linguistic and such other narrower identity lines. It was naked vote bank politics that ruled the roost.

Clearly, if a candidate could win on less than one-third share of the votes polled, he did not need to generate a wider appeal. By making caste and community a factor in political power play, we made the divide even wider and deeper in the Indian society and rendered it nearly impossible for Babasaheb Dr. Ambedkar's vision of a casteless and classless society ever coming true.

To ensure representational legitimacy to legislators within the existing system, it could be laid down that in order to be declared a winner, a candidate must secure a minimum of 50 per cent plus votes so that it becomes necessary for every winning candidate to woo more than his caste, community or narrow group vote bank and seek a wider consensus. If, in the first round, nobody gets over 50% then there should be a run-off contest the very next day or soon thereafter between the top two candidates.

Compulsory Voting

Voting should be made compulsory as a fundamental citizenship obligation. The advantage of compulsory voting is that the voter realises that he is not conferring a favour on the candidate but exercising his duty as a citizen. If in our present situation making voting compulsory is not found to be a feasible or enforceable proposition, a scheme of incentives/disincentives linked to certificate of voting could be considered.

Independent Candidates

Something has got to be done to discourage independents and bring down their number by increasing the security deposit in their case, disqualifying them for future elections if they get less than say, 5% of the votes polled and providing for their proposers and seconders being Panchayat or Nagar Palika members.

Electoral Malpractices

In the area procedural malapractices during election processes, the following need attention:

i. Foolproof method of preparing electoral rolls at the village and

Nagar Palika or ward level and keeping them constantly updated.

ii. Display of electoral rolls at post offices in each Constituency Headquarters for public scrutiny.

iii. Authorising the Election Commission to take more stringent action in cases of booth capturing, as recommended by the Goswami Committee, and to take a decision in regard to countermanding the election or ordering repoll etc., and

iv. security deposits of candidates securing less than 25% votes to be forfeited,

v. CEC and ECs to be appointed on the recommendations of a body consisting of PM, Leaders of the Opposition in L.S. and R.S., Speaker of Lok Sabha and Dy. Chairman of Rajya Sabha.

Role of Money Power: Cost of Elections – Need of Funding

If the electoral process has to steer clear of tainted and motivated sources of funds, some of the following suggestions may need to be considered:

(i) The cost of elections must be reduced. This can be done by changing the ground rules for electoral campaigns – partly by encouraging the use of electronic and digital technology to campaign at state cost and simultaneously by totally and effectively banning other overt and wasteful tamashaas of campaigning including the use of auto-traffic to ferry people to election rallies of any kind. Wall writings, display of cut-outs, hoardings and banners, hoisting of flags (except at party offices, public meetings and other specified places), use of more than a specified number of vehicles for election campaign and for processions, announcements of publicity by more than a specified number of moving vehicles, holding of public meetings beyond the specified hours, display of posters at places, other than those specified by the district/electoral authorities, should be banned.

(ii) To the extent possible, State and parliamentary elections should be held simultaneously.

(iii) No one should be allowed to contest from more than one constituency.

(iv) Code of conduct should be made into a law and its violation should attract penal action.

(v) Candidate must be required to clear all government dues and vacate unauthorised government accommodation etc. before being allowed to go to polls.

(vi) A suitable law should be enacted providing penalties against damaging or desecrating public or private property by candidates, political parties or the agents, through painting of slogans or erecting cut-outs and hoarding or putting banners and buntings.

(vii) Legitimate sources for the essentially needed funds would have to be identified. For one, company and individual donations should be encouraged with higher limits placed on the maximum permissible amounts and liberal tax rebates allowed.

(viii) In case the present ceilings are to be continued, they should be linked to the cost of living index so that they remain realistic. But, the expenditure incurred on a candidate's election by his friends, by the political party or by others should also be included while examining adherence to the ceiling. Full disclosure of the sources of election funds and audit of receipt and expenditure should be made compulsory.

Criminalisation

In the area of criminalisation of electoral processes and politicisation of crime, following suggestions deserve consideration:

i. *Disqualification for those charged with serious offences and derecognisiton of parties:* Once charges relating to certain crimes have been framed by a court against a person, he should not be permitted to contest elections unless cleared.

ii. *Speedy trial by special courts of cases involving candidates:* A potential candidate against whom charges have been framed by the police may take the matter to a special electoral court. This court would be obliged to enquire and take a decision in a strictly time bound manner. Basically, this court may decide whether there is indeed a *prima facie* case justifying the framing of charges. If yes, the person should not be allowed to contest.

iii. The law should provide that whoever is convicted of any offence by a Court of law and sentenced to imprisonment for six months or more should be debarred from contesting elections, for a period totalling the sentence imposed plus an additional six years.

iv. *Disqualification on conviction to apply to sitting legislators:*If an elected representative gets convicted on charges related to specific crimes, he should be required to withdraw from the legislature for six months and if within that period he fails to get an acquittal, he should be disqualified.

v. *Heinous Crimes*: Permanent disqualification for life of those convicted of heinous crimes.

vi. *Caste and Communcal Violence:* Statutory provision should be made prescribing imprisonment and disqualification for spreading caste or communal hatred during election campaigns.

vii. A question closely related to the criminalisation of politics is the issue of financing politics. For last many years, a question that remains unanswered is regarding the financing of politics. For running a political party, for any political activity or for contesting any election to State Legislature or Parliament, tons of money is required. Almost everyone in politics needs it. Where is it to come from? Where does it come from? No body pays his hard earned, tax paid white money to parties or to politicians. Also, even black or tainted money can be expected only when one is part of the establishment as a Minister or a member or the like in a position to harm or help. And, elections are a tricky business. One has to prepare for the worst case scenario, for the rainy day, particularly if one is a whole time professional politician or publicman with no other known means of comfortable living to fall back upon.

While there are some excellent men and women of high calibre and great integrity in Indian political life today, the general, even though most unfortunate, perception seems to be that politics has ceased to be a vocation for sacrifice and service and has descended into being the most lucrative business with the highest ROI for getting rich quick. And, the problem is not peculiar to India. Even in the more advanced western democracies there have been cases similar to ours. In UK., for example, payment of £1000 for a question, resulted in the Nolan Committee Report and the introduction of the Register of Members' interests.

Almost all those elected to legislatures have to begin their legislative career with giving incorrect statements of election expenses. One may ask, if there is a general crisis of character in the nation as a whole, in all walks of life and all professions, all-pervading devaluation of all values, if money, success and power, at whatever cost, become supreme concerns, can we blame only the legislators for all the ills? Is the problem not more fundamental calling for systemic rethinking and holistic reforms.

Political Parties

In the ultimate analysis, electoral reforms cannot be considered in isolation from other areas, in particular that of political parties. Although political parties were not mentioned in the Constitution until the fifty-second constitutional amendment enacted in 1985, the fact remains that representative democratic polity under the Constitution presumed a well-organised system of political parties.

Political parties are an important institution in any democratic polity. Both the party or parties in power and those in opposition are essential to the functioning of a democratic government. It is for that very reason necessary that the parties themselves must be wedded to democratic principles and run democratically.

It is a common spectacle after every election that all the politics degenerates into purely personal struggles for Chief Ministership, Ministership or other lucrative offices with influence, status and power. No wonder, people are beginning to lose faith in the system and in their representatives who are seen as not devoted to public service but engaged in seeking narrow personal ends of wielding power and amassing wealth with service to the people not being any part of their priorities. Representatives of the people losing the respect of the people should cause us the greatest worry if we are for preserving our hard earned freedom and democracy.

Concept of Opposition

The concept of official opposition in the parliamentary model is that of a part of the government in the wider sense. But in India, opposition has a tendency not to want to be a participant in the process and assume a share of responsibility. Every party when in power behaves in a particular way and in quite a different way when in opposition. It would be most desirable that when in government, the party remembers that one day it may again be in opposition and when in opposition, it should be aware that it may have to assume the responsibilities of the ruling party tomorrow and therefore should behave today in the same way as it expects its opposition to behave. Thus, it is necessary for safeguarding freedom and democracy and their political institutions that the parties in power and those in opposition understand the delicate situation, accept each other's legitimacy and realise that they are not adversaries but partners in a common cause of serving the people.

In parliamentary polity, the main opposition has to be accepted and respected as a legitimate alternative and not to be shunned as an untouchable. It is in the mutual interest of major parties or national alliances to ensure that they remain the only viable alternative to each other. If we really believe in democracy and have faith in the people, no party which gets the largest or the second largest number of elective seats and popular votes can be regarded with any legitimacy as pariah. It is dangerous for parliamentary polity to paint either of them as a villain. Also, it must be understood that the so-called regional parties are also national and equally patriotic in their perspective and that as partners in national alliances they can be as effective as any All India party.

Law for Political Parties

Political parties should be institutionalised through a comprehensive legislation to govern and regulate their number and activities, lay down criteria for their registration and recognition as national or State level parties and their deregistration and/or derecognition in case of violation of norms laid down. The law should make it compulsory for the parties to maintain accounts of the receipt of funds and expenditure in a systematic and regular way. The accounts should also be compulsorily audited and made available to public for study and inspection. The proposed law should also provide for certain other matters like funding and democratic and clean internal functioning of parties. It should be laid down in law that no political party should sponsor or provide ticket to a candidate for contesting elections if he was convicted by any court for any criminal offence or if the courts had framed criminal charges against him. The law should specifically provide that if any party violated this provision, the candidate involved should be liable to be disqualified and the party deregistered and derecognised forthwith. If implemented, this would be obviously an effective check on criminals' increasing clout and control in political parties.

Regulating the Number of Parties

Unless the number of political parties and/or alliances at the national and State levels is regulated by law, representational legitimacy of our legislators with a first-pass-the-post system cannot be assured. Also, no scheme of state funding can succeed. Only recognised national parties and pre-poll alliances (*i.e.* those that secure at least 10% of the votes cast) should be allotted common symbols to contest elections to Lok Sabha. State Parties may be allowed common symbols to contest elections for State Legislatures and the Council of States (Rajya Sabha). This would, by prompting pre-poll alliances, automatically consolidate the vote and help in evolving some sort of federal parties or alliances providing more stable governments. There could be no difficulty in passing such a law in both houses of Parliament because it was in the best interests of major parties.

Funding of Parties

Reform proposals in regard to political funding should revolve round (1) reducing costs, (2) better utilisation of funds, (3) curtailing influence peddling and political corruption, (4) strengthening public disclosure and transparency mechanisms with respect to the sources and the use of funds, (5) permitting higher corporate donations with higher limits and tax exemptions, and (6) submission of false or incorrect returns bringing immediate derecognition of the party.

Seats for Women

Reservation by law should be made for atleast 30 per cent of organisational positions at various levels in every political party and the same percentage of party tickets for parliamentary and State legislature seats to women with failure to do so inviting penalty of the party losing recognition.

Training to Party Cadres

It is important that political parties in India realise the importance of imparting to their members necessary professional training in the modern techniques, tools and methods of political management, legislative functioning, leadership roles etc.

Parliamentary Reforms

As a first step, processes, control mechanisms, debating and decision making procedures would have to be revamped and made faster. Floor management techniques would have to be professionalised at the level of whips, parliamentary officials and the Presiding Officers.

Building a better image of Parliament

Parliament connects the people and the government. It is necessary to establish a new rapport between the people and the Parliament. The two must be brought closer to each other. Parliament belongs to the people. It is ordinary people who have to be enabled to feel that they are participants in the decision-making and legislative processes and that through Parliament their voice can reach the Government and that it counts. Parliament must have access to public opinion and public must have access to Parliament.

The people should know what their representatives are doing or not doing for them. Media – electronic and print – must be used effectively to highlight important issues for legislatures and legislators and to pursue and enforce their accountability to the people at large.

It is necessary that the press and public relations in Parliament are suitably reoriented and developed as a highly specialised and dynamic service charged with the responsibility *inter alia* of educating public opinion in regard to Parliament and its activities. Arrangements should be made for attending to enquiries from the public, publicising the telephone numbers and addresses from which information about Parliament and its activities may be sought and providing some public computer terminals and a more meaningful and communicative internet website from which any citizen can hope to get any information he may need regarding the Parliament and its activities including for example the status of pending legislation.

Improving the Conduct of Members

The already existing Code of Conduct and Guidelines first circulated as early as in 1952 deserve to be observed. There is a strong need for M.P.s to invigilate themselves to uphold norms of parliamentary behaviour within and outside the Houses of Parliament.

Improving information supply

Parliament must build its own independent national information reservoir with a network of feeding and retrieval points. Developing an independent and transparent infra-structure of information support system in Parliament would have a profound effect on revitalising and transforming the institution of Parliament.

Nodal Standing Committee on Economy

Immediate steps should be taken to set up a nodal Standing Committee on national economy with specific subject-oriented study groups aided by experts and concerned with economic policy formulation and implementation.

Planning Legislation and improving its Quality

Our legislation has often been criticised for hasty drafting and for its being rushed through Parliament in an *ad hoc* and haphazard manner. There is need for a dynamic-not mechanical-approach to legislative engineering and systematic programming of laws which may be proposed for enactment over a period of time. This can be done by (i) streamlining the functions of the Parliamentary and Legal Affairs Committee of the Cabinet; (ii) making greater use of the Law Commission; (iii) setting up a new Legislation Committee of Parliament to oversee and coordinate legislative planning; and (iv) referring all Bills to the Departmental Standing Committees for consideration and scrutiny, consulting concerned interest groups and finalisation of the second reading stage in the relaxed atmosphere of Committees aided by experts thereby reducing the burden of the House without impinging on any of its rights and improving the quality of drafting and content of legislation.

Setting up a Constitution Committee

Instead of the Constitution Amendments being presented to Parliament like ordinary pieces of legislation in the form of Bills for introduction, sometimes at very short notice, it would be desirable if Parliament is associated right from the initial stages of formulation of proposals for constitutional reform, *i.e.* the actual drafting of a Constitution Amendment Bill may be taken up only after the principles involved have been thrashed out in a parliamentary forum and subjected to appropriate a *priori* scrutiny by the constituent power. The proposed involvement of Parliament and a *priori* scrutiny can be achieved through the device of a Constitution Committee of Parliament. As an alternative, after a Constitution Amendment Bill has been formulated but before it has been introduced, it may be subjected to a *priori* scrutiny of the 'Constitution Committee'. If this is done, even the Government would be saved many an embarrassment.

Departmental Committees and Improving Accountability

If the Subject/Ministry based Standing Committees have to have real meaning and fulfill the purposes for which they were conceived and not to become merely part of a spoils system and distribution of perks and benefits, they should embrace the entire spectrum of administration for an in-depth and continuous study.

Codifying Parliamentary Privileges

As a great institution, Parliament should be able to take in its stride, a great deal of the criticism and adverse comments against it. Privileges of Parliament are intended to be privileges enjoyed by Parliament on behalf of the people, to enable members to function freely and fearlessly, in the interest of the people. These privileges should not be allowed to become rights against the people. Time is now ripe for removing the existing uncertainty and anxiety of the press and the people through early codification.

Procedural Reforms

Rules of Procedure and Conduct of Business are intended to be for guidance, for regulating the business of the House and for facilitating the orderly expression of members' views. Procedures must keep pace with the changing needs of the national economy, composition of Membership and the prevailing mood of the Members.

No single reform can provide a miracle cure. Also, parliamentary reforms cannot be effected in a hurry. We must proceed with care and caution and make a beginning by setting up a Parliamentary Reforms Commission or a 'Study of Parliament Group' outside Parliament as was done in the U.K. before the comprehensive procedural reforms in the 70s of the last century. Finally, of course the Rules Committee or a Special Procedure Committee of the concerned House should examine all the reform proposals and report to the House on the matter.

Government

Electing the Leader of the House (PM/CM)

If no party or pre-election alliance of parties secures a clear majority of seats in Lok Sabha or in any of the State Assemblies and the largest single party is unable to promise a stable government, the President or Governor as the case may be, should ask the House to elect its leader just as it elects its Speaker. The person so elected may be appointed the Prime Minister/ Chief Minister. This can be done by the President/Governor sending a message to the House under the existing article 86(2)/ 175(2).

When the simple question is that of determining the majority, the safest and the simplest course would be to hold an election on the floor of the House. It would also not be necessary then to seek a vote of confidence as, in effect, it would have been obtained in advance of appointment through the process of election by the House itself. This would require neither an amendment of the Constitution nor of any law.

Vote of No-Confidence

To ensure that Government so constituted would last for a reasonable period Once the Prime Minister/ Chief Minister is appointed and the Government (Council of Ministers) duly constituted, it should be removable only by a constructive vote of no-confidence passed by a special majority. Under this scheme, the same motion which expresses lack of confidence in the Council of Ministers headed by 'A'. would also contain, the name of the proposed successor, 'B'. This would mean that there would be continuity in Government and if the motion is passed, another leader would immediately take over. This would greatly reduce, if not completely eliminate, chances of getting into a situation where some forces join to bring down a government but are unable to provide an alternative thereby necessitating frequent elections.

Public Administration

To make the administration citizen-friendly, mechanisms have to be developed for citizens' grievance ventilation and redressal. Politicisation of bureaucracy and interference of administration in the lives of citizens will need to be ended. Questions of appointment, promotion, transfer of civil servants and their interface with Ministers, etc. have to be looked into; and healthy norms of accountability to the people established through necessary administrative reforms. Also, questions that deserve to be carefully considered include:

i. First and foremost, there has to be a behavioural and attitudinal change in the civil services. The civil servant must be trained to serve the people, inculcate a work culture and a spirit of efficiency and excellence. Also, we must rid the services of casteism, corruption and politicisation. Above a certain level—say the Joint Secretary level-all posts should be open for recruitment from a wide variety of sources including the open market. Officials, before starting their career, in addition to the taking of an oath of loyalty to the Constitution, should swear to abide by the basic principles of good governance. The administrative structure and systems have to be consciously redesigned. The specialist should not be required to play second fiddle to the generalist at the top.

ii. Denial of timely service to the public must be specifically made a serious conduct offence and subjected to summary and exemplary punishment. We must ensure better accountability procedures by curbing the tendency of having multiplicity of hierarchical levels, diffusion of responsibility and passing the buck. Where public servants cause loss to the State by their *mala fide* actions or omissions, they should be made liable to make good the loss caused and, in addition, pay damages. A law should be enacted to provide for forfeiture of benami property of corrupt public servants as well as non-public servants. The Prevention of Corruption Act, 1988 should be amended to provide for confiscation of the property of a public servant who is found to be in possession of property disproportionate to his/her known sources of income and is convicted for the said offence.

iii. There is need to review the prescribed procedures for inquiries, punishments, appeals, etc., to shorten their duration and to reduce the possibility of interlocutory delays or, more than one appeal. Constitutional safeguards to services under article 311 may need reconsideration to ensure greater accountability.

iv. Supervision and inspection must be prescribed as primary duties of the higher echelons and negligence in this matter made a black mark for the purpose of performance evaluation and promotion. The reformed system should provide effective ways of prompt decision making, quick disposal and avoidance of delays, misuse of discretion and attendant corruption.

v. A prominently displayed and widely published Citizens' Charter may be the principal declaratory mission statement on behalf of each department and office having dealings with the public. Such a declaration should list the services lawfully available, the charges to be paid if any, the time usually taken (same day in most cases), and it should further specify the point at which delays or harassment can be reported, or queries as to status of an application made.

[Some departments/offices in the States as also at the Union Government level have come up with such charters but generally the progress has been slow. Out of about 400 expected only 68 have been issued at the Union Government level. Also, adherence remains weak and red tape is still strong. Also, all others particularly those with direct public dealings need to issue and publicise their charters for the citizens.]

vi. At the points at which reports of crime, or of fear for safety of person or property are to be made, there must be a very clear enunciation of the rights of the complainant and, as a corollary, the rights of an accused person.

vii. The basic requirements for the success of the above prescriptions are:

a. A true and effective decentralisation of powers and decision making, clear assignment of responsibility, decentralised decision-making and delegation of authority, transparency in administration and right to information, bringing almost all rule-based non-discretionary powers for granting citizen services, down to the very cutting edge. In other words the citizen should go to only one point where he would hand in his request and get the service he requires. Right to information can usher in many benefits, such as speedy disposal of cases, minimising manipulative and dilatory tactics of the babudom, and, last but most importantly, putting a considerable check on graft and corruption.

b. Full use of all the new and emerging technologies for more efficient governance. For every office having a large number of public dealings, schemes for total computerisation should be set in motion. Every citizen request (and report), should be entered into the system on receipt, and automatically go into a central data bank, as should the date of issue of sanction, permit, etc. Once the computerised system is established, there should be a central point of enquiry where, on giving particulars about a request or case, the reception desk should itself access the data bank on its computer, get a response about the status of the citizen's request, and give the citizen a printout with an indication about the time that would be required for fulfilling his request.

viii. The elimination of out-of-date and unnecessary laws is said to be already in process. This should be completed as quickly as possible. The same applies to redundant, or unnecessarily complex rules, regulations and forms so as to simplify matters for the citizen.

ix. Publication and printing of Acts, rules and regulations and guidelines for the citizen must be kept up-to-date and their availability singly should be an obligatory service of government.

x. There is every need for rationalisation and drastic downsizing of the bureaucracy, cutting down the non-governmental functions of government and reducing the overall costs of administration at every level,

xi. It should obligatory for bureaucrats at all levels to make a declaration of all assets and liabilities of self, spouse and dependents – declaration to be available to citizens on demand,

xii. It may be advisable to consider establishment of a Civil Service Board entrusted with transfers and promotions and of disciplinary matters affecting a person serving under the government.

xiii. The 1861 Police Act and old Police Manuals should be replaced. The Police Commission and Vohra Committee reports should be considered for early implementation. Police should be provided modern training and equipment, insulated from political interference and its senior officers held accountable for the lapses of the force. Those in sensitive posts should be assured a fixed tenure and law and order cadre, investigation branch, armed police and traffic police should all be separate structures. To strengthen the criminal justice system, Criminal. Procedure Code and Evidence Act should be amended. Public grievance cells should supplement the vigilance cells within the Police Department.

So far as the administrative services at all levels are

concerned, it is most essential that they move out of the colonial mind set of being the masters and rulers and assume the role of servants of the people to provide clean, transparent, citizen-friendly governance to all without any discrimination.

Union State Relations

The federal structure in India has come to stay and needs to be strengthened. The central problem is not of Union-State relations now but of greater decentralisation of economic and political powers to lower and lower levels, with several tiers of functioning and people at the grassroots having real power, with the system growing up from there rather than coming down from above.

Decentralisation

The only way to strengthen the Union is to make it lose its extra weight, to shed its monopoly of power in all areas and concentrate on essentials. With economic liberalisation must come decentralisation of political power and management. To preserve "India, that is Bharat" as a "Union of States" it is necessary to work for building it as a "federal union" or what Aurobindo referred to as a union of "autonomies" with multiple tiers of government and sharing of powers from the lowest grassroots level of Panchayats to the Parliament and the Government of the Union. This would also be close to Gandhiji's model polity of concentric circles instead of the present pyramidical structure. Distribution of powers should be so designed that only the most essential or minimum necessary powers are assigned to each higher level. For example, whatever can be done by the local grassroots institutions like the village panchayats or municipalities, should be left entirely in their hands. This would be in keeping with what is now called the subsidiarity principle. Government at a higher tier should have no power to remove or supersede a duly elected government at a lower tier.

If we are really serious about providing multi level governance and taking power to the doorsteps of the people at the grassroots, the Constitution should clearly provide for distribution of powers between the Union, the States and the local governments of Panchayats and Nagarpalikas by suitably amending articles 245, 246 and other relevant articles and the Seventh Schedule. It would certainly do no violence to the basic structure or features of the Constitution or to the parliamentary system. It has the potential to powerfully contribute to the needs of good governance and development.

Time has come for a comprehensive review of Union State relations and Local Governance institutions. There can be no single universally applicable model. India's needs of stability, security and development demand a new marriage between unitary and federal polity so that both stability of the system and responsibility to the people are ensured. The new federalism should build a united nation of a large number of autonomies – not subordinates or subsidiaries – as federal partners at various levels. It would be a 'federal union' with multiple tiers of governance and sharing of powers from the grassroots of Panchayats to Parliament.

i. We should de-link the ethnic aspirations from political demands for separate states. On principle, smaller States may be better for good governance due to growing populations. A larger number of States may strengthen the Union. In some cases, instead of creating new States, sub-State structures may be created. Combined with strong zonal councils, this would lead to greater stability, more accountability, stronger Union and better administered and more developed or fast-developing States.

ii. Norms for Governor's appointments need revamping. Sarkaria Commission recommendations should be examined and implemented.

iii. Problems regarding article 356 are only due to improper operation and interpretation of articles 256,257,355, 356 and 365. These need to be read together. Under article 355, *i.e.* without imposing President's rule under article 356, *sou motu* deployment of central para-military forces would be entirely in order.

iv. With liberalising economy, central control may get irrelevant. Income tax, corporation tax and indirect taxes can be moved to the concurrent list to facilitate harmonisation of taxes and a full vat.

v. With a large number of smaller States and a four-tier system of governance, it may be possible to involve various groups in governance more closely and this may make the Union stronger and the nation more integrated, emotionally and culturally. Distribution of powers should be so designed that only the most essential or minimum necessary powers are assigned to each higher level. For example, whatever can be done by the local grassroots institutions like the Village Panchayats or Municipalities, should be left entirely in their hands. Government at a higher tier should have no power to remove or supersede a duly elected Government at a lower tier. Efficient bureaucracy cannot be a substitute for democratic decentralised government.

vi. Eleventh and Twelfth schedule should be made mandatory and merged into a common list.

vii. In the North-East States, illegal migration must be checked. Local traditional institutions of Government need to be modernised with gender justice for women and used as institutions of governance. Overlapping jurisdiction of State Government, Autonomous District Councils (ADCs) and traditional system of governance and the problems thereof must be removed and jurisdictions of each clearly defined. Greater autonomy should be provided to ADCs by amending the Sixth Schedule. Problems with regard to participation of non-tribals in ADCs. need to be addressed. Problems in judicial administration due to multiple overlapping jurisdictions of the traditional institutions, ADCs and the subordinate judiciary should be resolved and the emerging conflict between human rights and tribal rights and between conservation laws and tribal rights to be analysed and resolved.

Corruption

Corruption poses a serious development challenge. In the political realm, it undermines democracy and good governance by flouting or even subverting formal processes. Corruption in elections and in legislative bodies reduces accountability and distorts representation in policymaking; corruption in the judiciary compromises the rule of law; and corruption in public administration results in the unfair provision of services. More generally, corruption erodes the institutional capacity of government as procedures are disregarded, resources are siphoned off, and public offices are bought and sold. At the same time, corruption undermines the legitimacy of government and such democratic values as trust and tolerance.

There is nothing entirely new in corrupt conduct of public servants. Kautilya mentions forty ways of embezzlement of public funds. What is currently talked about as corruption may be defined simply as lack of public and private morality and probity and of a sense of honesty and integrity. It is the abuse of public resources or position for private gain. Corruption may involve receiving illegitimate personal gratification for extending to another person illegitimate private benefit.

In a democracy, nothing can be more tragic, and cause greater worry than a situation where all politicians, representatives of people, are regarded as corrupt. But, then politicians alone were not to be blamed nor was corruption confined to their ranks. Corruption and other forms of unethical conduct are rampant. This is so in administration and no more only in departments like the police and public works. This is so in the public sector and in the private sector, in labour unions, in professional bodies, in the functioning of NGOs, in business and in industry. Howsoever reluctantly one has to say, not even the judiciary [Bench and Bar] or the defence sectors today can be regarded as entirely free from corruption. A Chief Justice of India was constrained to admit that 20 per cent of the judges could be corrupt. Also, who can say with any honesty that educational institutions, the academia or the media function with greater transparency, that the intellectuals do not sell themselves for project grants, foreign trips and the like or that any class can boast of better integrity or is inflicted with less corruption. Corruption has literally entered every walk of life, every profession and every area of activity. We all are guilty.

Corruption, delays, and harassment at lower levels of public dealing need to be attended to and remedied. Potent mechanisms have to be developed for citizens' grievance ventilation and redressal. Healthy norms of accountability of administrators directly to the people would have to be established through necessary administrative reforms. At present, the system is not even accessible to the ordinary citizen. As somebody said, the administrators – the officers and petty *babus* – treat the citizens as dirt.

Today, clean and quality governance has become a categorical imperative for our very survival as a democracy and a free nation. The most important task is that of cleansing the system and making the Government and the administration really ordinary citizen-friendly. In the ultimate analysis, this can happen only if power is accepted, as Gandhi said, as a trust and an opportunity of service and politics and public administration themselves are viewed as a mission for sacrifice and service.

Nations that forget their roots and lose their vision perish. Societies that fail to transmit to their children their heritage, the quintessence of the accumulated wisdom of centuries and their system of values are relegated to debris. The rubble and the shambles of history and the stories of dead civilisations are a mute testimony to many such fallen stars.

Society runs on reward-punishment principles. If corruption ceases to pay or yield rich dividends and if punishment becomes certain, swift, deterrent and really hurtful, corruption would certainly come down.

Citizen and the Administration: If there is one area which affects the daily life of the citizen most vitally, it is where he or she has to come in direct contact with the administration at the ground level. Unfortunately, public administration in India in its tenor and approach has largely continued to be colonial, one that suited the ethos and needs of the imperial masters and centralised authority. Far from being treated as the masters, the citizens are still treated as subjects and worse. The administrators or bureaucrats instead of being at the service of the people, continue the colonial *mai-baap* model.

In a democratic polity, the administration must be run by the citizens for the citizens. Corruption, delays and harassment at levels of public dealing need to be attended to and remedied on a high priority basis. No one should forget the highest functionaries of the state – in the Executive, Legislature and Judiciary – are all appointed or voted to positions of power and governance as the creatures of the people. They are citizens first and always accountable, answerable and responsible to their fellow citizens at large.

The elected rulers *viz.* the Ministers and the legislators and the administrators, have to be conscious not only of the fundamental duties of citizens at large but also of their own duties as citizens. It is one of their most fundamental constitutional obligations to be all the time aware of the fundamental rights of the citizens under the Constitution. For, wherever an obligation is cast on the 'state' it is for the citizens in positions of authority to implement it. Ultimately, the people would have to wake up and rise and armed with a full realization of their responsibilities, they would have to assert their inherent sovereign powers to put the citizen at the centre of the political system and to bring about on a high priority basis citizen-friendly governance.

Conclusion

In a democracy, the real and the ultimate masters are the people, the citizens. Not enough has been done to educate or orient them to their responsibilities as voters and participants in the democratic process. There is no reason, why citizens' vigilance groups and committees should not come up at every level and on a wide scale. The citizens need to be educated in and for democracy and constitutionalism and in the matter of their own citizenship obligations in a representative, participatory democratic polity. For, ultimately the responsibility to save freedom and democracy is that of 'We, the People of India'.

Nations are made only when people rise above their narrow self interests and are prepared to make sacrifices for their fellow citizens. Unless we, the citizen of India at large, are vigilant and conscious of our obligations as citizens, there is no reason why freedom and democracy should continue for ever.

Annexure 1

GOVERNMENT OF INDIA
ORGANISATIONAL STRUCTURE

President of India

Prime Minister's Office

Cabinet Secretariat

Ministries of the Government
[The Ministries/Departments are created, bifurcated, merged or suitably reorganised from time to time as deemed necessary by the President on the advice of the Prime Minister under the Allocation of Business Rules 1961]

- **Ministry of Agriculture**
  - Department of Agricultural Research and Education DARE)
  - Department of Agriculture and Co-operation
  - Department of Animal Husbandry and Dairying
- **Ministry of Agro and Rural Industries**
- **Ministry of Chemicals and Fertilizers**
  - Department of Chemicals and Petrochemicals
  - Department of Fertilizers
- **Ministry of Civil Aviation**
- **Ministry of Coal**
- **Ministry of Commerce and Industry**
  - Department of Commerce
  - Department of Industrial Policy and Promotion

- **Ministry of Communications and Information Technology**
  - Department of Informhation Technology (DIT)
  - Department of Post
  - Department of Telecommunications (DOT)

- **Ministry of Company Affairs**

- **Ministry of Consumer Affairs, Food and Public Distribution**
  - Department of Consumer Affairs
  - Department of Food and Public Distribution

- **Ministry of Culture**

- **Ministry of Defence**
  - Department of Defence
  - Department of Defence Production and Supplies
  - Department of Defence Research and Development

- **Ministry of Environment and Forests**

- **Ministry of External Affairs**

- **Ministry of Finance**
  - Department of Economic Affairs
  - Department of Expenditure
  - Department of Disinvestment
  - Department of Revenue

- **Ministry of Food Processing Industries**

- **Ministry of Health and Family Welfare**
  - Department of Ayurveda, Yoga and Naturopathy, Unani, Siddha and Homoeopathy (AYUSH)
  - Department of Family Welfare
  - Department of Health

- **Ministry of Heavy Industries and Public Enterprises**
  - Department of Heavy Industries
  - Department of Public Enterprises

- **Ministry of Home Affairs**
  - Department of Internal Security
  - Department of Official Language
  - Department of States
  - Department of Home
  - Department of J&K Affairs

- **Ministry of Human Resource Development**
  - Department of Elementary Education and Literacy
  - Department of Secondary and Higher Education
  - Department of Women and Child Development
- **Ministry of Information and Broadcasting**
- **Ministry of Labour and Employment**
- **Ministry of Law and Justice**
  - Department of Justice
  - Department of Legal Affairs
  - Legislative Department
- **Ministry of Mines**
- **Ministry of Non-Conventional Energy Sources**
- **Ministry of Non-Resident Indians Affairs**
- **Ministry of Panchayati Raj**
- **Ministry of Parliamentary Affairs**
- **Ministry of Personnel, Public Grievances and Pensions**
  - Department of Administrative Reforms and Public Grievances (DARPG)
  - Department of Personnel and Training
  - Department of Pensions and Pensioners' Welfare
- **Ministry of Petroleum and Natural Gas**
- **Ministry of Planning**
- **Ministry of Power**
- **Ministry of Railways**
- **Ministry of Rural Development**
  - Department of Drinking Water Supply (DDWS)
  - Department of Land Resources (DLR)
  - Department of Rural Development (DRD)
- **Ministry of Science and Technology**
  - Department of Bio-Technology (DBT)
  - Department of Science and Technology (DST)
  - Department of Scientific and Industrial Research (DSIR)

- **Ministry of Shipping, Road Transport and Highways**
- **Ministry of Small Scale Industries**
- **Ministry of Social Justice and Empowerment**
- **Ministry of Statistics and Programme Implementation**
- **Ministry of Steel**
- **Ministry of Textiles**
- **Ministry of Tourism**
- **Ministry of Tribal Affairs**
- **Ministry of Urban Development**
- **Ministry of Urban Employment and Poverty Alleviation**
- **Ministry of Water Resources**
- **Ministry of Youth Affairs and Sports**
- **Central Government (Independent Departments)**
  - Department of Atomic Energy
  - Department of Ocean Development
  - Department of Space
  - Department of Development of North-Eastern Region
  - Prime Minister's Office
  - Cabinet Secretariat
  - President's Secretariat
  - Planning Commission

Select Bibliography and References

Almond, Gabriel A. et. al., *Comparative Politics Today: A World View* (7th Ed.), 2000.

Altekar, A.S., *State and Government in Ancient India*, Delhi, 1949.

Heywood, Andrew, *Political Theory*, Palgrave, 2004.

Ashokvardhan, C., *Political Legacy of the Rigveda*, 1987.

Asirwatham, Eddy, *Political Theory*. S Chand. 2002.

Aurobindo, Sri, *The Foundations of Indian Culture*, (on Ancient Indian Polity), Pondicherry, 1975 (6th ed.).

Austin Granville. *Working of a democratic Constitution: The Indian Experience*. OUP. 1999.

_________, *Indian Constitution: Cornerstone of the Nation*, OUP, 1966.

Barry, Norman P., Modern *Political Theory*, Macmillan, 1989.

Bhattacharya, Harihar, *Making Local Democracy Work in India*, Vedams Books, 2002.

Brass, Paul, *Politics of India Since Independence*. Cambridge. 1994.

Chakrabarty, Bidyut and Bhattacharya, Mohit, *Public Administration-A Reader*. Oxford University Press, 2006.

Chatterjee, Partha, *State & Politics in India*, Oxford University Press, 1995

Chhibber, Pradeep K., *Democracy without Associations: Transformation of the Party System and Social Cleavages in India*, University of Michigan Press, 1999.

Chibber, Pradeep and Kollman, Ken *Party Aggregation and Number of Parties in India and the United States*, American Political Science Review, Vol.92. No.2. June 1998.

Chopra, S.K. (ed.), *Towards Good Governance*, Konark, Delhi, 1997.

Choudhury, M.L. Roy, *The State and Religion in Mughal India*, 1951.

Conquest, Robert, Downloading Democracy, *The National Interest*, Winter 2004-5.

Cowell, Herbert, *History and Constitution of the Courts and Legislative Authorities in India*, Calcutta, 1936.

Dahl, Robert A., *On Democracy*, New Haven, Yale University Press, 1999.

Derbyshire, J. Denis and Ian, *Political Systems of the World*, Helicon, Oxford, 1999 Ed., 2 Vols.

Desai, Meghnad and Ahsan Aitzaz. *Divided By Democracy*, Roli Books 2005.

Desikachar, S.V., *Centralised Legislation – A History of Legislative System of British India from 1834 to 1861*, Delhi, 1963.

Dicey A.V. *Introduction to the study of the law of the constitution*. Oxford, 1914.

Frankel, Francine R., *India's Political Economy: 1947 – 2004*, Oxford Univ. Press 2005

Ghosh, Soma, *An Independent and Accountable Judiciary : Pillar of Democracy*, Kolkata, Pragatishil Prokashak, 2005.

Gopal,S., *The Viceroyalty of Lord Rippon, 1880-84*, London, 1953.

HMSO, *Report on Indian Constitutional Reforms* (Montagu-Chelmsford Report), London, 1918.

Holmes, Stephen, Theories of Constitutionalism, in *Encyclopedia of Democracy*, pp. 299-306.

Ilbert, C., *The Government of India*, Oxford, 1922.

Inter-parliamentary Union, *Parliaments of the World*, Oxford, 1986, 2 Vols.

International Encyclopaedia of Social Sciences, Corwell Collier and Macmillan, 1968.

Jain, U. C. and Jeevan Nair, *Judiciary in India*, Jaipur, Pointer, 2000

Jain, R.B., *Contemporary Issues in Indian Administration*, Vishal, 1976.

Janjua, Sansar Singh, *Panchayati Raj: Problems and Prospects*, Punjabi University, Patiala, http://www.punjabiheritage.com/panchayat.htm

Jayaswal, K.P., *Hindu Polity*, Bangalore, 1936 (1955)

Jha, Manoranjan, *Role of Central Legislature in Freedom Struggle*, Delhi.

Kapur, Devesh and Mehta, Pratap Bhanu, *Public Institutions in India-Performance and Design*, Oxford University Press 2005

Kashyap, Subhash C.,*Our Constitution*, N.B.T., New Delhi, 2005 ed.

_____, *Our Parliament*, N.B.T., New Delhi, 2004 ed.

_____, *Framing of India's Constitution – A Study* (2nd Ed), Universal, New Delhi, 2004.

_____, *Constitution Making Since 1950 – An Overview* (1950-2004), Universal, New Delhi, 2004.

_____, *History of the Parliament of India* – 6 Volumes, (1994-2004), Shipra, New Delhi, (Vol.1).

_____, *Blueprint of Political Reforms*, Shipra, New Delhi, 2003.

_____, *Concept of Good Governance & Kautilya's Arthashastra*, ICSSR, New Delhi, 2003.

_____, *Anti-Defection Law and Parliamentary Privileges*, Universal, New Delhi, 2nd ed., 2003.

_____, (ed.), *The Citizen and Judicial Reforms under Indian Polity*, Universal, New Delhi, 2003.

_____, (ed), *National Resurgence through Electoral Reforms*, Shipra, Delhi, 2002.

_____, *The Citizens and the Constitution*, Pub. Div., Ministry of I. & B., Govt. of India, 2002.

_____, *Parliamentary Procedure, Law, Privileges, Practice and Precedents* – 2 volumes, Universal, New Delhi, 2000, 2 Vols.

_____, *The Political System and Institution Building Under Jawaharlal Nehru*, National, Delhi, 1990

_____, (ed.), *Indian Polity – Retrospect and Prospect*, National, Delhi, 1989.

_____, *The Politics of Power*, National, Delhi, 1974.

_____, Parliament, reform thyself, *The Tribune* (125 years Special Supplement), 24 September 2005.

_____, Human Rights Provisions in the UN Documents and in the Constitution and Laws of India, *India and International Law* ed. by B.N.Patel, Martinum, Leiden/Boston, 2005.

_____, Executive-Legislature Interface in the Indian Polity, *The Journal of Legislative Studies*, Vol.10, Nos. 2 &3, Spl. Issue, 2004, pp. 278-294.

_____, Coalitions in Indian Politics, *Making a Success of Coalitions*, ed. by L. Krishnamurthi & Others, East West Books, Chennai.

_____, Structural, Institutional and Functional Aspects (of Federalism) – Need for Review of the Indian Constitution, *Indian Journal of Federal Studies*, vol.1, No, 2000.

_____, Indian Democracy at Work, *50 years of Indian Republic*, Publications Division, Ministry of I&B, GOI, 2000.

_____, Coalition Governments in India, *Law and Justice*, Supreme Court Golden Jubilee Issue, Vol. 4-7 (1997-2000).

_____, Accountability in Indian Polity, *Public Accountability in Indian Polity*, ed. by Raj K. Nigam, ADC Publication, New Delhi, 1998.

_____, Ethnicity and Constitutional Reforms in India in Iftekharuzzaman (ed.) *Ethnicity and Constitutional Reform in South Asia*, RCSS, Colombo, Manohar, New Delhi, 1998.

_____, Parliament-a mixed balance sheet in Hiranmay Karlekar (ed), *Independent India-The First Fifty Years*, Oxford, New Delhi, 1998.

_____, Democratic Model for India *in* DD Khanna and others (ed.), *Democracy, Diversity, Stability*, Macmillan, New Delhi, 1998, pp.23-36.

_____, Five Decades of Parliament, *India: 50 Years*, ICCR, Oxford.

_____, Towards Good Governance: Need for Political Reforms, *Indian Journal of Public Administration*, Vol.XLIV, No.3, IIPA, New Delhi, 1998, pp.318-327.

_____, Recipe for Stability and More, *Nation and Polity Under Strain*, ed. by Kashyap, Uppal, New Delhi, 1996.

_____, Reviewing Parliamentary Polity *in* Ajit M Banerjee & KA Chandrasekaran (Ed.), *Renewing Governance*, Tata McGraw, New Delhi, 1996, pp.227-304.

_____, Indian Polity and the Constitution: Retrospect and Prospect, *Perspectives on the Constitution*, ed. by Kashyap, Shipra, Delhi, 1993.

_____, A New Parliamentary Initiative-Subject-based Standing Committees of Parliament, *Economic and Political Weekly*, 6 October 1990.

_____, On a Presidential System for India, *Journal of Political Studies*, Sept. 1968.

Keith, A.B., *A Constitutional History of India: 1600-1935*, London, 1936.

Kothari, Rajani, *Rethinking Democracy*, Orient Longman, 2005

_____, *Politics in India*, Orient Longman. 1995

Maddick, Henry, *Panchayati Raj – A Study of Rural Local Government in India*, London, 1970.

Maheshwari S.R. *Indian Administration*. Orient Longman. 2005.

_____, *Administration in India*, Mcmillan, New Delhi, 2003.

Metcalfe, Thomas R., *The Aftermath of Revolt: India 1857-70*, Princeton, 1965.

Mishra, S.N., *Ancient Indian Republic*, Lucknow, 1976.

Mookerjee, Radha Kumud, *Glimpses of Ancient India*, Bombay, 1970.

_____, *Local Government in Ancient India*, Oxford, 1920.

Mukarji, Nirmal and Arora, Balveer, *Federalism in India: Origins and Development*, Vikas,1992.

Mukherji, P., *Indian Constitutional Documents* (1600-1918), Calcutta, 1918.

Nehru, Jawaharlal, *Discovery of India*, New Delhi, 1981 ed.

_____, *Glimpses of World History*, Oxford, New Delhi, 1982 ed.

Prasad, B.B., *Political Organisation of North India (A.D. 950-1184)*, 1979.
Pub. Div., Min. of I&B, Govt. of India, *India 2006*, New Delhi, 2006.

Pylee M. V, *Constitutional History of India*. Asia Publishing House. 1967.

Rajkumar, N.V., *Development of the Congress Constitution*, Delhi, 1948.

Rao, G.V.K. Committee, *Panchayati Raj: Past, Present and Future*, 1985.

Rashiduzzaman, M., *The Central Legislature in India, 1921-47*, Dacca, 1965.

Rao, M. Govinda and Nirvikar Singh, *Political Economy of Federalism in India*, Oxford University Press, 2005.

Report of the National Commission to Review the Working of the Constitution (NCRWC Report), New Delhi, 2002.

Revitalisation of Panchayati Raj Institutions for Democracy and Development, L.M. Singhvi Committee,1986.

Eatwell, Roger and Wright, Anthony, *Contemporary Political Ideologies*, London, Pointer Publication, 1993.

Samaddar, Ranabir (ed.), *The Politics of Autonomy: Indian Experiences*, Sage Publications India Pvt. Ltd. 2005.

Saran, P., *The Provincial Government of the Mughals (1526-1658)*, 1973.

Sarkar, J.N., *Mughal Polity*, 1984.

Shakdher, S.L., *Glimpses of the Working of Parliament*, Metropolitan, New Delhi, 1977.

Sharma, Baijnath, *Harsa and his times*, 1970.

Sharma, J.P., *Republics in Ancient India*, London, 1965.

Sharma, S.R., *Mughal Government and Administration*, 1951.

Thompson, E. and Garrat, G.T., *Rise and Fulfilment of British Rule in India*, London, 1935.

Udgaonkar, *The Political Institutions and Administration of Northern India during Medieval Times (from 750 to 1200 AD)*, 1969.

Vaidya, C.V., *Downfall of Hindu India*, 1986.

Varshney, Ashutosh, *India and the Politics of Developing Countries*, Sage Pub., 2004.

Venkataramaih, E.S., *The Working of Indian Democratic Polity – An Appraisal*, IIPA, New Delhi.

Verma, J.S., 'Judiciary and Judicial Reforms', in Subhash C. Kashyap (ed.), *The Citizen and Judicial Reforms*, Universal, New Delhi, 2003.

Zavos, John, Hansen, Thomas Blom, Jaffrelot, Christophe (ed). *Hindu Nationalism and Indian Politics* Oxford University Press. 2004

http://presidentofindia.nic.in/
http://pmindia.nic.in/
http://parliamentofindia.nic.in/
www.supremecourtofindia.nic.in

Index

Printed at : Salasar Imaging Systems, Noida